"In this delightfully simple yet deeply resourced volume Dr. David Rabin addresses what is most essential in health and least appreciated in medical training: our vulnerable humanity. The many gems of wisdom he offers act, each, as an antidote to what he aptly calls the "ambient terror" of our lives in a supercharged culture. Suffused with acumen based on decades of clinical practice and research and written with wit and vivacity, this book calls you to life in your body and soul."

- Dr. Gabor Mate, MD | Physician & *New York Times* Bestselling Author of *The Myth of Normal*

"*A Simple Guide to Being Alive* is a compassionate wake-up call. With remarkable clarity, Dr. Rabin bridges neuroscience and ancient wisdom, offering a clear path back to what it truly means to feel safe, present, and alive."

- Dr. David Perlmutter, MD | Physician & #1 New York Times Bestselling Author of *Grain Brain* and *Brain Defenders*

"There is a generosity to this book that stands out. It seeks not merely to inform, but to help readers recover something easily lost: the ability to be present in their own lives. Drawing on neuroscience without being constrained by it, the author provides a thoughtful and engaging guide to a more attentive and meaningful way of living."

-Dr. Ken Ford, PhD | Author, Scientist, Former Scientific Advisor to the President, Former Director of NASA, CEO emeritus IHMC

"*A Simple Guide to Being Alive* is a high-performance manual for upgrading your biology without losing your humanity. Dr. Dave distills neuroscience, spirituality, and state-shifting practices into tools that measurably improve energy, sleep, and resilience. If you want to run a cleaner nervous system, think sharper, live longer, and feel better doing it, this book is a must have in your stack!"

- **Dave Asprey** | 4X *New York Times* Bestselling Author & Founder of Bulletproof

"*A Simple Guide to Being Alive* is a landmark contribution to the emerging field of psychedelic medicine and integrative mental health care. Dr. Rabin accomplishes something remarkably important and long overdue: he clearly explains, in scientifically grounded and deeply human terms, how psychedelics actually work to catalyze healing, not as magical substances, but as tools that enhance safety, connection, neuroplasticity, emotional learning, and meaning-making within the nervous system.

At a moment when Western medicine is urgently searching for more effective treatments for trauma, depression, addiction, and existential distress, this book provides an essential bridge between neuroscience, psychotherapy, contemplative practice, and the wisdom of indigenous traditions. Dr. Rabin's voice is compassionate, rigorous, and visionary. This book will help clinicians, researchers, and the public better understand not only psychedelic therapies, but what it truly means to heal when we stop ignoring the role of trauma and start paying attention."

- **Dr. Rick Doblin, PhD** | Founder & President of The Multidisciplinary Association for Psychedelic Studies (MAPS)

"*A Simple Guide to Being Alive* is a rare gem that bridges science, spirituality, and practical wisdom in a way that's both deeply grounding and immediately actionable. Dr. Rabin masterfully translates the language of the nervous system into something you can actually feel, helping readers reclaim sleep, safety, and a sense of playful presence in their daily lives. This is the kind of book I recommend not just to patients, but to anyone who wants to truly rest, recover, and remember what it feels like to be human again."

- Dr. Michael Breus, PhD | The Sleep Doctor & Bestselling Author of *The Power of When*

"*A Simple Guide to Being Alive* is an extraordinary, heart opening masterpiece. Dr. Rabin has created something truly rare: a book that beautifully weaves rigorous neuroscience with the timeless wisdom of mindfulness, compassion, and healing.

This is far more than a book. It is a transformative invitation to come home to yourself. With remarkable clarity, depth, and warmth, Dr. Rabin illuminates how awareness, kindness, and nervous system safety form the essential foundations of true healing and lasting well being. His words do not merely inform; they awaken, soothe, and gently reshape the way we relate to our minds, our bodies, and one another.

This book has the power to change lives. It is wise, deeply compassionate, and profoundly needed, a guiding light for anyone longing to live with greater presence, wholeness, and aliveness."

- Dr. Shauna Shapiro, PhD | Professor, Santa Clara University & Bestselling Author of *Good Morning I Love You*

"*A Simple Guide to Being Alive* is a powerful blueprint for extending not just lifespan, but healthspan. Dr. Rabin translates cutting-edge neuroscience into practical, daily strategies that support nervous system balance, recovery, and long-term vitality. This is a smart, actionable guide for anyone serious about living longer, better, and with intention."

- Dr. Darshan Shah MD | Surgeon, Author, & Founder of Next Health

"*A Simple Guide to Being Alive* is a rare and timely contribution that bridges rigorous neuroscience with practical strategies for optimizing human performance, well-being, and preventing burnout. Drawing on his extensive clinical and research experience, Dr. Rabin presents a clear, evidence-based framework for enhancing resilience, improving autonomic balance, and restoring a sense of purpose and vitality in daily life. This book offers both clinicians and the general public an accessible roadmap to better health by integrating mind, body, and behavior in a way that is both scientifically grounded and immediately applicable."

- Dr. Joseph Maroon MD | Clinical Professor, Vice Chairman of Neurosurgery, University of Pittsburgh Medical Center; Heindl Scholar in Neuroscience; Team Neurosurgeon for the Pittsburgh Steelers

"Dr. Rabin bridges a gap that brings psychology, neuroscience and nutrition (and just enough spirituality) to create a well rounded picture on recovery and performance. Not to mention, it's actionable and simple to apply; mainly because it just makes sense"

- Thomas DeLauer | Leading Nutrition Coach to NFL & MLB Athletes

A SIMPLE GUIDE TO BEING ALIVE

Cover Design and Illustrations by Philip E. Pascuzzo

Published and distributed by Merack Publishing
San Diego, USA
www.merackpublishing.com

Produced By Future Medicine Media, Inc.
www.FutureMedicineMedia.com

A Simple Guide to Being Alive™

ISBN Hardcover 978-1-964421-23-0
eBook 978-1-964421-24-7

A SIMPLE GUIDE TO BEING ALIVE

Dr. David M. L. Rabin, MD, PhD

To my parents, Arnold and Sandy,
for teaching me to see, think, write, and read.

To my wife, Kathryn, for teaching me to believe.

To my son, Sammy, for teaching me to be.

To Bob Dylan for Blowin' in the Wind.

In loving memory of Dr. Joseph Skowronek, MD (1985–2025).

Simplicity is the ultimate sophistication.

—Leonardo da Vinci (1452–1519 CE)

Contents

Foreword

Finding our way through life these days forces a crucial choice on all of us:

You can trust the science and everything they taught you in grade school and Sunday school.

And it works.

Sort of.

Until all the error messages and warning codes fill the screen. And you end up stressed out, freaked out, sick, and miserable.

Or you can, as the bumper sticker encourages, "question the dominant paradigm."

But where does that usually lead?

Onto TherapyTok, or "doing your own research" on YouTube.

Which really means getting hijacked by the algorithm and sucked down whatever rabbit hole is optimized to monetize your darkest fears and wildest delusions.

Neither of these options works all that well.

Submitting to the Norm.

Or

Choosing Your Own Reality.

One's too tight.

The other's too loose.

So where's the middle path when we really need it?

One grounded in science and the best the Western tradition has to offer.

But inspired by the spirit of Eastern and Indigenous wisdom.

That's what Dr. Dave Rabin is serving up in this book.

A synthesis to overcome these irreconcilable opposites.

Blending his own medical career with his life as a curious seeker, Dave has woven a story that is both rare and timely.

A bridge over our increasingly troubled waters.

Between science and mysticism.

Between knowing and feeling.

Between testing and trusting.

And these aren't just blueprints rolled up in the corner of an architect's office. Designed, but never delivered.

Dave has built this bridge himself, sawing and hammering, jumping up and down to make sure it's solid.

The Indian mystic Nisagardatta once wrote, "Love tells me I am everything, wisdom tells me I am nothing. And between these two banks flows the river of my life!"

A Simple Guide to Being Alive bridges that love and wisdom, and gives us the permission and the inspiration to dive into our lives.

—**Jamie Wheal** | Author of the global bestseller *Stealing Fire*

Introduction

As young as five years old, I was running nightly simulations of the multiverse. The dreams weren't fuzzy cartoons. These were IMAX, surround sound, full-sensory immersion. I flew over neighborhoods like a small ecstatic god, celebrated victories that didn't exist yet, and laughed with my little brother in worlds as vibrant as daylight. When I woke up, I sometimes had to check the room like a juror returning from deliberation: which one was real?

Then school happened. Somewhere between the alphabet and organized recess, I learned what it feels like to be slightly out of phase with the herd. Nothing dramatic. Just enough sideways glances, enough social misfires, enough exile to make a mammal nervous. And my dreamscape followed suit, as if my subconscious was taking meeting minutes.

Now I was falling. Now I was being chased. Now I was trapped in elaborate psychological escape rooms designed by a five-year-old Salvador Dalí with separation anxiety. I tried to steer the plot, attempted dream-heroics, flapped my arms mid-fall, bargained with the monsters, reasoned with the darkness like I was arguing a case in the Supreme Court of Nighttime. No dice.

The dreams felt so real that bedtime became a negotiation. Sleep was no longer a soft landing; it was Russian roulette with my subconscious. So I did what any small, confused primate would do: I went to my parents and asked, "What are dreams?" as if they might hand me the operating manual I suspected was hidden somewhere between the encyclopedias and the good china.

"Dreams aren't real," my mom said gently. "They can feel very real, but they can't hurt you." This was useful information because, for a brief period, I had concluded I might be murdered by a concept. Knowing dreams couldn't physically harm me reduced the terror, but it didn't solve the bigger question blooming in my tiny would-be neuroscientist brain: if dreams aren't real...why do they feel real? And if "real" is defined by experience...then who exactly is confused here?

That was the first time I remember trusting sensation over instruction, feeling over authority, the body over the rulebook. It would not be the last.

Around that same time, school started to get more interesting. Mrs. Elizabeth Terwilliger (1909–2006) educated us on the history and natural beauty of our local habitat in the San Francisco Bay Area, while Mrs. Dee Uyeda (1933–2006) taught us the basics of intentional breathing and origami. I was also introduced to Indigenous cultures of North America. Two cultures in particular lodged themselves in my imagination: the Miwok people of Northern California, where I grew up, and the Chippewa of the Midwest, who crafted dream catchers. A dream catcher, in case you've forgotten, is a hoop of red willow threaded with a web of fibers, adorned with beads and feathers, and hung above a child's bed to filter out bad dreams.

My ten-year-old brain lit up like a lab rat spotting cheese. So you're telling me there is a device that modulates dream content? I had to get my hands on one. At our local flea market, an anthropological wonderland of incense, bootleg VHS tapes, and questionable jewelry, I found it: a perfect little dream catcher. My heart pounded like I had discovered a new incredible flavor of ice cream.

I showed it to my dad, a physician, a man of science, a champion of empiricism, and told him, with utter seriousness, "I'd like to run an experiment!" He bought it. I suspect he found me adorable. I found myself unstoppable.

Back home, I strung it up with surgical precision: one end tied to the blinds, the other to a dresser handle, suspended over my bed like a sacred satellite dish.

And then…

It worked.

The nightmares evaporated. Gone. In their place came luminous dreams: peaceful landscapes, joy, flying, laughter. "Correlation is not causation," the adult scientist in me whispers. The ten-year-old scientist replies: "I don't care. Data set of one. Result: dramatic."

Something shifted. Whether placebo, belief, ritual, subconscious reorganization, or ancestral internet, I experienced relief. And that was the real breakthrough, because what that experiment taught me wasn't that dream catchers are magical objects. It taught me that belief interacts with biology, that meaning modulates physiology, and that ritual changes experience.

Welcome to the nervous system, kid.

Years later, I would learn that dreams are generated from subconscious and unconscious material, memory fragments, emotional imprints, unresolved narratives stored far outside daily awareness. They are as "real" as waking life in the sense that they are lived experiences of consciousness.

At ten, I didn't have that vocabulary, but I knew three things that turned out to be foundational:

The mind is powerful.

The body responds to story.

And reality is more flexible than adults are willing to admit.

Meanwhile, the waking world was not exactly a utopia. The more history I studied, the clearer the pattern came into view: suffering stretches back like a geological layer: war, exile, famine, cruelty. Hurt people hurting people in an unbroken chain, often unintentionally. And I wasn't exempt; I was a sensitive kid trying to navigate the brutal social laboratory known as elementary school, where emotional assault masquerades as teasing and children bleed their own unprocessed pain onto whoever stands nearby.

I started to notice something uncomfortable. On days I was picked on more in school, I picked on my little brother more at home in an attempt to make myself feel better. Short story. It didn't work, and I apologized to him profusely for it as a teenager.

Not only did it not work, but it felt awful all around. So I decided to run another experiment. All the religions I had learned about at the time emphasized the importance of kindness, so I decided to give it a shot. When I did, I noticed something curious: kindness really helped. Not in a naïve Care Bear way, but in a practical nervous-system way. When I stayed kind, even when it wasn't reciprocated, my internal world stabilized. So I followed that thread, and it led me on a twenty-year journey from chronic stress, aging, and neuroplasticity to medicine, and then to psychiatry, where I treated addiction and trauma disorders on the daily; a headfirst dive into the epicenter of human suffering.

After college and the subsequent twelve years of neuroscience research and psychiatry training, a startling theme became impossible to ignore: Trauma. Everywhere. Shame, neglect, violence, resentment, anxiety, and the like. Severity aside, every single patient I treated had one or more moments in their lives when they felt so unsafe and unsupported that it changed how they saw themselves as human beings. It transformed self-trust into self-doubt, agency into victimhood. If self-trust were a bone, traumatic experiences appeared to break it little by little.

Another pattern was undeniable across patients I treated for everything from schizophrenia and personality disorders to ADHD, addiction, depression, and performance anxiety: stress reliably made symptoms worse. Non-clinical signs such as poor sleep, irritability, perfectionism, self-loathing, and restlessness all predicted clinical symptoms over time.

The medications we had were powerful stabilizers in crisis, but with continued use over time, they began to increasingly resemble Band-Aids over festering emotional wounds. Talk therapy held real answers, but often required years of effort and enough stamina to run a psychological marathon barefoot.

What both frustrated and electrified me was this: much of the suffering was preventable, addressable, and often curable. Indigenous and Eastern traditions have been tending to trauma for millennia using community, ritual, breath, song, touch, movement, story, and nature. Western medicine is brilliant at acute care, but often allergic to invisible wounds.

An emotional injury is like a physical wound you can't see, and because we can't see it, we pretend it's not bleeding.

If someone comes into the ER with a broken leg, we don't toss them Tylenol with Codeine, send them home, and say, "Good luck!" We stop the bleeding, clean the wound, align the bones, stabilize the fracture, and send them home with a cast, antibiotics, and an aftercare routine to heal properly with minimal scarring. Emotional wounds, by contrast, are treated with numbing, distraction, productivity hacks, and the cultural religion of "suck it up." We avoid the center of the injury because it's messy and uncomfortable, and it asks us to feel things we've spent a lifetime learning not to feel.

I became fascinated by Eastern, Indigenous, and contemplative traditions, and I studied them for fun in what little spare time I had during my Western medical training. I quickly discovered that, while Western medicine has an unparalleled ability to save our lives in an urgent crisis, these much older approaches possess enormous practical wisdom about healing, particularly when it comes to chronic illness and disease prevention. At the core, they spoke different dialects of the same truth:

The source of our healing comes from within us. Everything else is a tool.

Realizing that there was a translation problem, I decided to become bilingual: translational neuroscientist and bridge-builder between temple and laboratory.

In 2012, psychedelic research began resurfacing in peer-reviewed journals with results so compelling that it piqued my interest. Treatment-resistant depression dramatically improved from just one dose of psilocybin, with benefits lasting over six months. Post-Traumatic Stress Disorder (PTSD) recovery rates leaps and bounds better with MDMA-Assisted Therapy compared to our current gold-standard treatment approaches. Enduring improvements after just a few doses of medicine that continued after the treatment was stopped, in patients like mine who, Western medicine had already admitted it had failed by labeling them "treatment-resistant." The effect was similar to condensing ten years of therapy into twelve weeks. Many of the subjects described it as the most meaningful experience of their entire lives.

Something different was happening, and I needed to understand it. I read everything I could find, and the more I learned about how psychedelics accelerate trauma healing, the more I noticed the uncanny similarities in the brain between psychedelic states, dreams, and soothing touch. In the context of healing, they can all profoundly activate neural networks involved in the feeling of safety.

We must feel safe to heal. Not intellectually safe, physiologically safe. Safe in the belly. Safe in the chest. Safe in the reptilian brain that decides, in milliseconds, whether we are in danger or relaxing at home. This pulled me full circle back to childhood, back to wondering how much of the dream catcher's effect on my dreams was because I felt safer falling asleep. Back to the question of what "real" really means when consciousness is the thing doing the experiencing behind billions of eyes, each believing that their perspective is the truth.

These insights fueled the next decade of my work studying trauma and safety learning in the brain and body, and treating everyone from our society's most high-performing artists, athletes, and doctors to our sickest patients—translating ancient practices into measurable nervous system interventions and teachings accessible to anyone.

And yet, even with all the knowledge I had accumulated and was regularly imparting to my patients to facilitate their successful healing experiences, I still had a quiet confession: I could not confidently say that I felt safe enough to just be a *human being*. I knew how to achieve, diagnose, treat, publish, and perform.

Human doing? Gold medal.

Human being? Questionable.

It shouldn't be that surprising. Elementary school never covered grief or how to sit quietly and observe your thoughts. Medical school skipped "how to feel at home in your own body." No one handed us instructions for heartbreak, ecological anxiety, or the existential dread of missing the one email that will change everything. Instead, we got juice boxes, shame, and standardized tests, and then we were released into society like sugar-high raccoons with jobs and responsibilities.

So I started investigating the basics. Turns out being human isn't that complicated. It's just ignored.

We are essentially emotionally complex houseplants: we need frequent light, water, attention, nutrients from the Earth, and preferably someone whispering nice things to us in the morning. We do not thrive on constant cortisol, shame spirals, or gluten-free nihilism. We need connection, play, safety, and, let's be honest, healthy snacks a little more often.

Most of us are just grown-up children wearing blazers, trying not to cry in the Whole Foods parking lot.

The first clue came in the form of a beautiful children's book my mother read to me as a child, *The Forgotten Secret*, written by Robert Pack in 1959, that left its mark on the top of my mind to this day. In the story, an old man walks to town each day, carrying a large sack on his back. The children flock to him, peer into his sack, and squeal with delight. Despite the lack of evidence of wrongdoing, some of the adults, including the mayor, become suspicious. One night, the mayor sneaks into the old man's home while he's asleep. He looks into the sack and is astonished by what he sees; it is his own face as it was when he was a boy staring back at him, innocent, and full of wonder and joy. Shaken, the mayor realizes that the sack holds childhood happiness. He quietly closes the sack, sneaks away, and promises never to forget what he saw that night.

The second clue came from Genesis, the first book of the Old Testament. We read this in middle school, with a strong focus on the creation story and the exile of Adam and Eve from their garden paradise. Adam and Eve are described as innocent and childlike in their joyful experience of their peaceful world until they disobey the Almighty by eating the fruit from the Tree of Knowledge. Something about this story made me think that there had to be a lot more to it than just "don't disobey God," the key takeaway that was passed down to us at the time.

Our inner child and all the playful joy that comes with childhood still live inside each of us. That part isn't gone; it's just been intimidated into hiding. This part of us isn't irresponsible. It balances us when it feels safe enough to explore. When safety is restored, play becomes possible, discovery is unlocked, and healing accelerates. As it turns out, play is one of the most impactful, and certainly the most fun, science-backed activities for healing, well-being, and longevity. Understanding this means that reminding your inner child that it is safe enough to come out and play, and be curious, becomes one of the most important strategies for winning as a human being.

Feeding this curiosity led me to study trauma, addiction, play, meaning-making, and learning from the perspective of a wounded child that wasn't given the proper support to heal at the time of the injury.

Then it led me to coordinate a clinical research expedition to the jungles of Peru in 2017 to study the Indigenous uses of Amazonian plants as medicines for healing trauma with the Shipibo tribespeople, who have been at it for over 10,000 years. Right away, I noticed that psychedelic medicines accelerated trauma healing, in both the modern Western and the ancient Shipibo approaches, by safely granting access to the most wounded, vulnerable parts of ourselves so that they could come to the surface to be healed.

The similarities were uncanny. I knew I was onto something. When I returned home from Peru, I brought together an incredible team of physicians and scientists to launch a clinical trial to study how psychedelic medicines facilitate rapid, long-lasting healing responses in our sickest mental health patients by helping them to safely remake meaning around past traumatic events.

A common thread ties successful healing practices together—safety in the environment and felt safety in the body allow the nervous system to return to balance, and the mind to relax long enough to permit change and allocate resources to it.

Consider it this way: when stressed for whatever reason, taking a deep breath is physiologically hard. In that state, you're clenched, braced for impact, scanning for threat. It's justifiably hard to sleep and without recovery, you can't learn new healthy habits or unlearn old useless ones because you're in survival mode.

When those in my field work with patients, it's our goal to create a safe therapeutic environment where someone can let their guard down, feel their emotions, remember what it feels like to trust, recontextualize their experiences, and ultimately heal. When I say it is hard work, I mean it—the person doing the healing is doing the work, we're the facilitators holding the safe space in which the healing work can be done. Our job is to make the process as easy and smooth as possible.

Understanding just how hard it is to meditate, breathe, or talk your way to calm when your nervous system is oh-so-overstimulated led to the creation of Apollo Neuro®. Apollo is a new category of technology that augments *emotional intelligence* (EQ). I originally discovered it with my research team in our lab at the Department of Psychiatry at the University of Pittsburgh Medical Center. Apollo sends low-frequency (bass) sound waves to the skin that restore balance to the nervous system, helping the body relax into sleep, calm, and presence more easily.

Apollo's vibrations, which we colloquially call Vibes®, can be thought of as soundtracks for your body. Silent vibrational music composed from neuroscience, for your body instead of your ears. When your body feels these vibrations, it recognizes them as safe in the same way as receiving a warm hug or snuggling a pet, and vagus nerve activity improves instantly. Heart rate slows, heart rate variability increases, your mind clears, and calm is restored, like noise-canceling for your brain.

Apollo's AI listens to your body, knowing, for instance, when you're about to wake up in the night and responding in real time, with soothing vibrations that help you sleep peacefully and more deeply. AI with the single purpose of relieving tension, not creating it. In releasing this seemingly simple solution, my purpose is to offer a tool for the modern person to combat the anxiety drip of modernity, helping the body feel safe again. When the body knows it's safe, learning turns on.

Before we begin, it is important that you understand something that unfortunately took me decades to figure out for myself. Human beings have two ways of learning: bottom-up and top-down. If we want the things that we've spent time learning to really stick, we must learn them in both ways. Notably, bottom-up learning is also more sticky than top-down learning.

Apollo Neuro, like a hug from a friend on a tough day or learning to ride a bike, is a bottom-up, body-to-brain, experiential learning tool. It immediately reminds the body what safety feels like without the use of words, like training wheels for nervous system regulation. When the brain stops arguing with the body long enough to feel, new learning can stick. Apollo exists because the body often needs to *feel* the lesson before the mind can receive it.

This book (like all books) is a top-down, brain-to-body, cognitive learning tool. Through understanding and practice, it boosts your IQ (*intelligence quotient*) by teaching you the concepts, the maps, the mental models, and the daily rituals that train your nervous system how to automatically access safety; the key that unlocks the door to your full human potential to live a long, happy, healthy life.

This is your long-lost user manual to being a human being, written for the part of you that remembers how to play, how to imagine, and how to believe the world is still full of magic, even when it's been buried under bills, trauma, and that time you accidentally sent a text meant for your ex to your boss.

We're bringing the child part of you safely back online: the you that sees beauty in puddles, the you that's awestruck by clouds and sunsets, the you that intuitively knows time and love and safety are things we can curate with a shift in attention. We're going to use neuroscience, ancient wisdom, breath, touch, movement, and yes, humor, quite possibly the most advanced skill of all, to help you remember what it means to feel terrific being alive.

To kick off, I'm giving you a gift. It's called The Human Toolbox (Figure 1). In your new toolbox, you will find three sets of tools. Cognitive tools, such as the scientific understanding of the world described in this book, can improve your thinking. Emotional tools, such as Apollo and gratitude practices, can improve your ability to feel and interpret feelings. Behavioral tools, like taking more walks in nature and getting more hugs, make it easier to do all the things you do. These tools are arranged in a triangle because our thoughts, feelings, and behaviors are deeply interconnected. By the end of this book, you will not only have a full Human Toolbox, but a complete understanding of how to use each tool to achieve your goals.

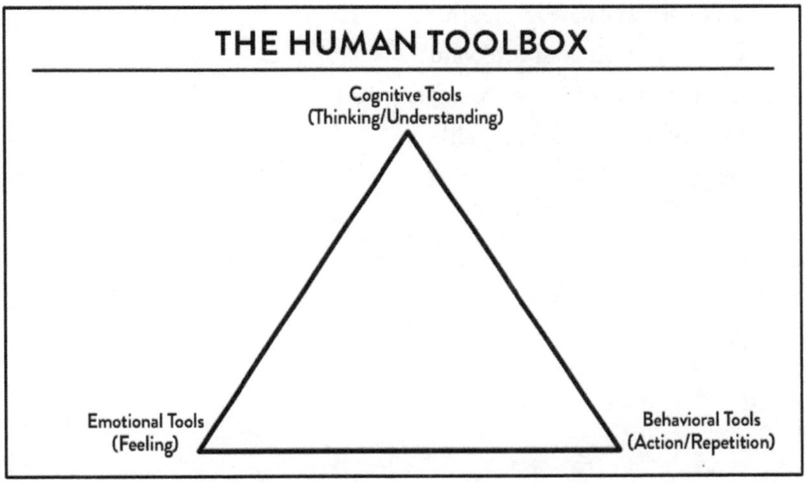

Figure 1. The Human Toolbox

George Santayana, the Spanish philosopher, famously wrote in 1905: *Those who cannot remember the past are condemned to repeat it.* One of the greatest contributions from Western medicine to humanity is its diagnostic approach, deeply rooted in the scientific method. To unlock long-lasting growth and healing, we must first learn to use this approach to understand how we drifted so far from simplicity, so we don't repeat the mistakes of the past.

How did we forget that we are mammals?

How did we forget that we depend on the Earth for survival?

How did we replace awe with anxiety?

How did we trade play for performance?

We'll get there.

The point of all this is not to change who we are. The point is to remember who we really are by remembering that breath regulates, play heals, kindness stabilizes, connection restores, and we are not separate from the systems that sustain us.

So, let's start here. Now. The moment in which the real you lives. The only moment that actually exists.

Take one slow, deep breath.

Inhale and fill your lungs full.

Exhale as much air as you can until they're empty.

Welcome back to being alive.

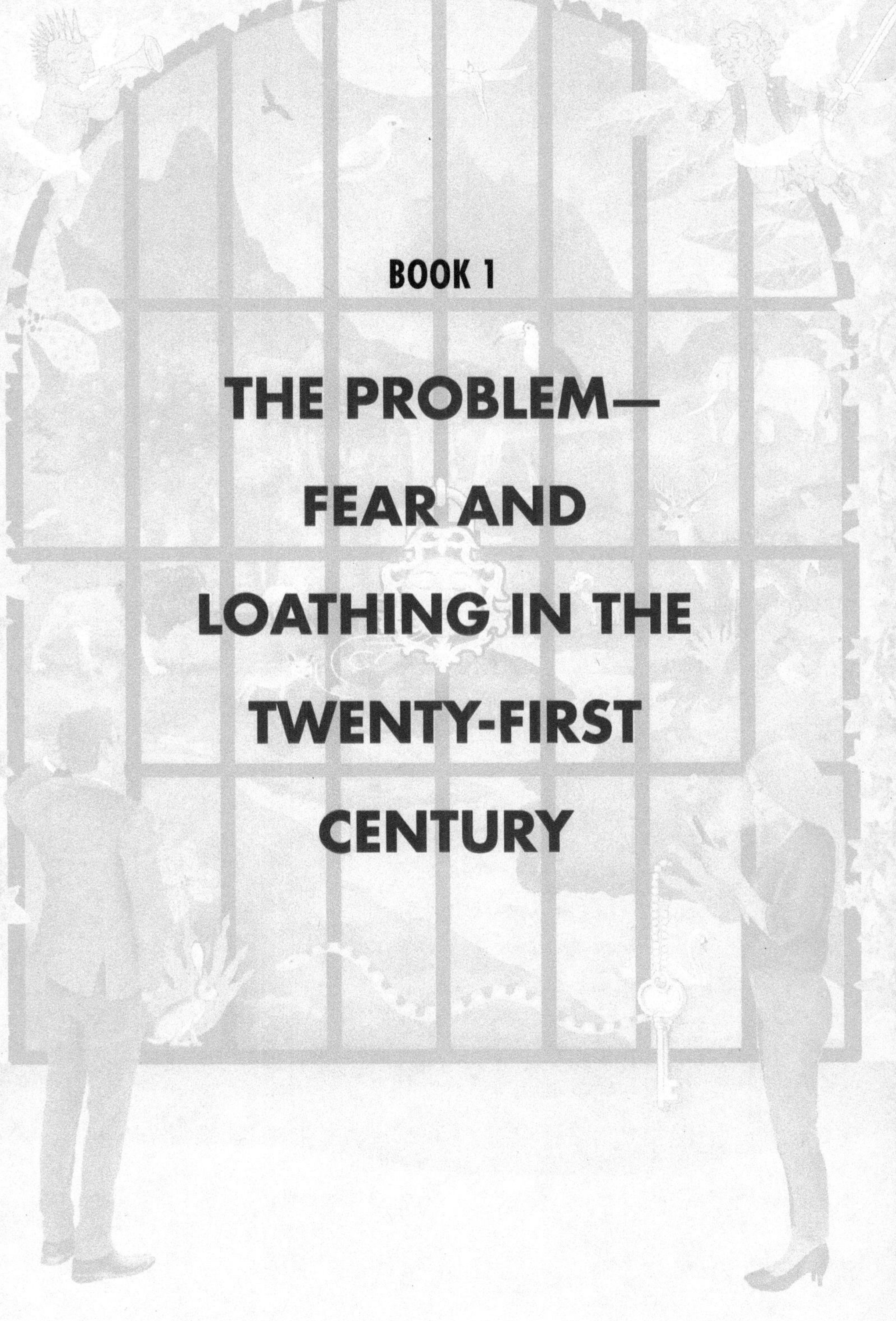

BOOK 1

THE PROBLEM—FEAR AND LOATHING IN THE TWENTY-FIRST CENTURY

CHAPTER 1
Welcome to the Human Zoo

Human nature is no more than one particular kind of animal nature.
—Desmond Morris

There's a moment every morning, sometime between the first coffee and the third notification, when the world feels like it's wobbling on the edge of a collective panic attack. You can see it in people's eyes: that haunted, caffeinated glaze of the chronically over-stimulated. Their pupils are dilated not from LSD or adrenaline, but from the slow intravenous drip of modern life; a thousand invisible hits of fear per minute, straight through the retina, mainlined by blue light.

I call this phenomenon ambient terror. The low hum of existential dread that passes for normal in the twenty-first century. The baseline pulse of a civilization that's forgotten how to breathe without Wi-Fi. It's everywhere. The woman in yoga pants, checking her Instagram every six seconds. The man in the airport bathroom, talking to his smartwatch like it's a priest at a confessional. The teenager on the subway, twitching with phantom notifications, scrolling like an addict searching for the next divine hit of dopamine.

These are not pathological cases. These are citizens in good standing. These are the normal people.

And I, God bless us all, am their psychiatrist.

Psychiatry used to be about madness. The wild stuff. Hallucinations, delusions, the human mind tearing through the membrane of consensus reality like a moth through silk, but now, most of my patients aren't "crazy." They're just *terrified.*

Not in the cinematic sense, but in the slow-boil, background-radiation way. The terror of not keeping up, of being left behind, of missing the one email that determines their value as a human being, of not optimizing correctly, of sleeping wrong, of breathing wrong; the terror of becoming the only primate in the troop without a skincare routine and a six-figure side hustle.

"I think something's wrong with me," they say.

And I want to take them by the hand and proclaim:

"Of course, something feels wrong! You're a mammal living inside a slot machine!"

This is not a mental health crisis.

This is a habitat crisis.

I am not the first person to write about this idea. The renowned zoologist Desmond Morris, in his book *The Human Zoo*, published in 1969, characterized the stresses of urban life as so significant that they make the behavior of human beings resemble that of animals in captivity [1].

The good news is that nothing has gone wrong with you. Your nervous system is doing exactly what it evolved to do. It has just been dropped into an environment that looks like Times Square had a baby with a casino and raised it on espresso and Xanax.

DR. DAVE'S MINDBLOWER™ #1

The mind and the body are intimately and irreversibly interconnected. What happens in the body is experienced by the mind, and what happens in the mind is experienced by the body.

Emotional stress, including fear, increases heart rate and creates tension in the body. Slow, deep breathing decreases heart rate and reduces emotional stress and tension in the body.

You can measure this terror in the body. Faster breathing, higher blood pressure, and heart rate variability flatter than a Kansas highway [2-4]. This is why your heart rate spikes when your phone buzzes. This is why your shoulders live somewhere near your ears. This is why lying in bed feels less restful than scrolling.

Stillness now registers as suspicious, like the quiet right before a horror movie jump scare. We've trained ourselves to fear the absence of stimulation the way earlier humans feared the absence of fire.

The first time I truly noticed the scope of the problem was at a Silicon Valley "wellness summit." The kind of event where you have to ask whether the snacks contain supplements, and every participant has the skin tone of someone who bathes in blue light for at least eight hours a day.

The theme was "conscious optimization." I'd been invited to speak about wearable tech and the vagus nerve, an underappreciated cranial nerve that governs all rest-and-recovery systems throughout the body (Figure 2). It was a talk about how the body is a self-regulating feedback system if you just give it the right cues. Backstage, surrounded by CEOs, biohackers, and tech priests all wearing various blinking devices, I realized something alarming: they were *terrified of stillness.*

Stillness, the original operating system of life, had become a bug.

Even sleep, the bare minimum period of stillness we require for survival, has been colonized. We track it, score it, and shame ourselves for not doing it right.

I had a patient with data-driven anxiety who kept telling me, "Doc! I can't sleep, and I'm anxious about it all day. I don't know what to do!"

"How do you know you're not sleeping well?" I replied.

"Because my Apple Watch tells me my sleep scores are terrible every day..."

I inquired further, "How did you feel when you first woke up? Before you looked at your data."

"Actually, I thought I slept fine, but my smartwatch must be right, right?"

The machines are judging us now.

I suggested he take his watch off for a week, not look at the data, and rate his sleep in a notebook (the old school sleep diary way) to compare how he felt with and without it.

He did not schedule a follow-up appointment.

Not only are the machines judging us, but many of us don't realize they're guessing about their conclusions using statistics. Human clinical assessments have always been more accurate than consumer wearables, but some of us prefer to trust machines that didn't go to medical school.

Data as narcotic. Validation by graph. The measurable replacing the meaningful.

DR. DAVE'S MINDBLOWER #2

Your brain's threat detector (the amygdala) does NOT distinguish the difference between *physical danger* and *social or informational threats.*

To your nervous system, an unread text message = possible exile from the tribe.

Take a moment to realize how incredible our lives are right now. Back just thirty years ago, if I wanted to order my dad his favorite Italian almond cookies (that aren't available in the U.S.) for his birthday, I would have to go to every Italian importer I could find to get a private hookup that could take weeks. Today, I can open an app on my smartphone and, in four clicks, my Pops has his almond cookies with his coffee two days later.

And that's not all you can do with your smartphone. You can wake up late to your phone alarm, realize you've slept through your early morning flight because you were out late enjoying yourself the night before, purchase a new plane ticket in a foreign city where you don't speak the language, and order coffee and breakfast to the door of your rental apartment while you request a late checkout from your Airbnb host. Then, you can call a taxi right to your door within minutes, the cab ride being just enough time to ask your AI to proofread your thirty-page proposal for typos so you can submit it to your boss in time for a critical deadline. With the Wi-Fi on the plane, you can upload all your Instagram and TikTok content to pay your bills, reschedule your rental car at your destination, make your dinner reservations, and tuck yourself in for the rest of the flight with sleepy music and soothing vibes to make sure you're well rested in your new time zone.

That's just a few examples, let alone cars and planes and smartphones themselves, and the astounding effort and millions of people it took to discover the centuries of science needed to build them. It's simply stunning how much work and human collaboration across millions of people over the years were required to build a car…and to give us all a hope of having one someday.

Yet, despite the extraordinary level of convenience and comfort for which our forefathers and foremothers fought tooth and nail so that all future generations could have easier lives, we now find ourselves, in this current generation, on the brink of not only losing it all, but of complete self-annihilation of our species (i.e., by creating conditions whereby the Earth is no longer hospitable for human life).

Did we become so comfortable that we forgot certain critically important parts about being human beings? What happened to collaboration itself, play, empathy, and connection? The components of which greatness is built. The very stuff that helped us to finally achieve the tremendous victory of becoming the most comfortable generation in human history. Was too much convenience toxic to the human brain? I had to find out for myself, but one thing I did know for certain: if one of us doesn't figure this out quickly, we're in for a very uncomfortable ride, to say the least.

Hunter S. Thompson once wrote, "Buy the ticket, take the ride." What he didn't say is that the ride is now on subscription, auto-renewing monthly.

The new madness is sanity itself, or at least its imitation. Everyone's so busy *appearing* balanced that they've forgotten what balance feels like. They meditate to perform calmness. They journal to prove self-awareness. They microdose to make their anxiety more productive.

You start to realize that what we call "mental health" and "wellness" have become a social performance, an algorithmic dance between public neurosis and private collapse. Our institutions reward dysregulation. Our technologies monetize attention. And our culture celebrates exhaustion as a kind of sacrament.

I see it clinically every day. Most of the patients who come to me aren't looking for truth. They're looking for relief from the absurdity of pretending to have it all together.

What they really need, though most don't know it, is *permission to stop running*. To feel their bodies again. To remember that peace isn't a prize at the end of the productivity marathon. It's the default state beneath the noise.

We've medicalized discomfort and industrialized distraction. The tobacco companies sell nicotine; the pharmaceutical companies sell serotonin; the tech companies sell dopamine; the spiritual influencers sell oxytocin. In between them all is the human animal, sweating, scrolling, and wondering why life feels like a panic attack in slow motion.

When I look at the data, not the wearable kind, but the deep, biological kind, the problem is clear. We're overstimulated primates with undernourished nervous systems. Our ancestors faced tigers; we face email. Same amygdala, different jungle.

Fear is supposed to keep us alive. In this current version of real life, it's keeping us from living.

This is the Human Zoo.

A place where ancient biology is trying its very best inside a world built by caffeinated apes with broadband. Where we confuse stimulation for aliveness and exhaustion for importance. Where rest feels like failure and presence feels unproductive.

Here's the paradox: nothing about this makes you weak.

It makes us exquisitely human. I say "us" because we're all in this zoo together.

Your nervous system is not broken.

It's over-informed, overstimulated.

It has been asked to track more social signals in a single morning than the average human being encountered in a week in the 1950s.

I'm not here to scold you for struggling.

I'm here to sit beside you on the enclosure floor.

To slide you a banana and say, "*Yeah...this place is loud.*"

To remind you that many of the zoo's cage bars are imaginary.

And to help you remember what safety actually feels like in a body.

Because beneath the buzzing, the striving, the cortisol-marinated ambition and endless self-monitoring, there is a calm, wise animal inside you.

One who knows how to breathe.

One who remembers stillness.

One who values connection more than performance.

One who never asked to become a notification receptacle.

That animal isn't gone.

It's just been waiting for you to notice it again.

CHAPTER 2
The Gods of Optimization

Very little is needed to make a happy life; it is all within yourself.
Marcus Aurelius (121–180 CE)

The gods are back.

They don't live on mountaintops anymore, or demand sacrifices of goats and virgins. They live in your phone, on your wrist, and in your sleep data. They glow softly at night, whispering judgments in percentage points.

You know them well.

Calories burned.

Steps taken.

Sleep efficiency.

Focus score.

Productivity streaks.

They promise salvation through numbers.

These are the *Gods of Optimization.* A polite, spreadsheet-driven religion built on the quiet terror that you are never quite enough as you are.

Like all religions, it started with good intentions.

We wanted to feel better, healthier, calmer, and more alive.

So we measured.

At first, measurement was a mirror. A way to notice patterns, to learn from the body, but somewhere along the line, the mirror became a judge, and the judge never sleeps.

Now, instead of asking *How do I feel?* We ask, *What does the data say I'm supposed to feel?*

I see this every day in my clinic.

"I feel terrible all the time," someone says, eyes dull, shoulders tight.

"How do you know?" I ask.

"My watch told me."

I ask how they felt before they checked the watch.

Brief pause. Blink.

"Actually…fine."

That's when I know what's really happening.

They're outsourcing trust.

DR. DAVE'S MINDBLOWER #3

Your nervous system evolved to trust *felt experience*, not dashboards or data.

When external data consistently overrides internal signals, anxiety rises, not just because the data could be wrong, but because your body is being ignored.

As many of our tests are invasive and/or painful, we have a rule in clinical medicine that goes something like this:

Don't measure something…

1. Without a good reason and
2. When the outcome of the test won't change the decision you're going to make.

Measurement for the sake of measurement can waste a lot of time and money and can cause significant harm.

I met a man in Los Angeles who was tracking his serotonin levels with a gut microbiome app. He told me, very earnestly, that he was "reverse-engineering happiness."

"That's wonderful," I said, "but how do you feel right now?"

He paused. "I'll have to check."

One woman whispered to me that ChatGPT was her therapist.

Another confided that she and her husband stopped having sex because they started playing video games together instead.

A man wearing a linen blazer over a black t-shirt bragged he had invented an AI to train young adults how to talk to each other to start relationships because "they just can't seem to get it right on their own."

These people worshiped their technology with a fervor that would make a televangelist blush. They didn't believe in God; they believed in machines. They prayed to dashboards. They tithed to the cloud.

Everywhere I looked was the same manic gleam. The hungry stare of those who believe transcendence, healing, and longevity are just one software update away.

Here's the thing they don't understand: the nervous system doesn't give a damn about your metrics. It only knows: *Am I safe?*

That's the foundational equation. The only code that matters.

And we, in our infinite brilliance, have managed to make safety feel like failure.

DR. DAVE'S MINDBLOWER #4

Every test, from medical-grade lab tests to wearable trackers, has a false-positive and a false-negative rate. This means that, no matter how reliable a given test seems, there is always a non-zero chance that it will produce a positive or negative result by mistake. You can look up false-positive and false-negative rates of tests in advance and discuss with your doctor which medical tests are indicated to save yourself some hassle.

The irony, of course, is that I build technology too. Seeing so many of my PTSD patients, many of whom were military veterans who all had significant training preparing them to face stressful situations, struggling despite multiple full courses of gold-standard psychiatric treatments, I realized that we couldn't medicate people back to safety. Perhaps safety had to be felt.

When my wife Kathryn and I founded Apollo Neuroscience in 2017, we set out on an audacious mission to create technology that heals humanity. It also had to be proven to work with real science because we weren't seeing enough of that in the health and wellness space. We desperately needed more tools to accelerate the healing process. All we had at that time were medications, psychotherapy, and trackers that tell us what's wrong with us. Most of us already know. We needed more tools in our toolbox that actively improve our quality of life and remind the body how to heal itself.

The vibration technology I invented based on my research in the Department of Psychiatry at the University of Pittsburgh Medical Center has now been proven to accomplish this by improving vagus nerve activity around the clock. This nerve, which is activated by soothing sensations, is the core nerve governing activity in the parasympathetic rest-and-digest nervous system (Figure 2).

Apollo improves the function of the vagus nerve by sending gentle, silent sound-wave vibrations to the body that are recognized by the brain as soothing touch [5-8]. Now with seventeen completed clinical studies involving over 2,000 research subjects, Apollo is the very first technology scientifically proven to boost heart rate variability (HRV), one of our best biomarkers of vagus nerve activity that predicts longevity, recovery, illness, and performance, simply by wearing it. No screens and no data review required!

Apollo Vibes are barely perceptible—quiet, rhythmic pulses felt against the skin, subtle by design so as not to distract from the present moment. Each one is composed like a piece of music, built from waveforms whose frequency, amplitude, and rhythm are drawn directly from the body's own signals of safety: the cadence of calming breath, the steady rhythm of a resting heart. The nervous system doesn't need to be

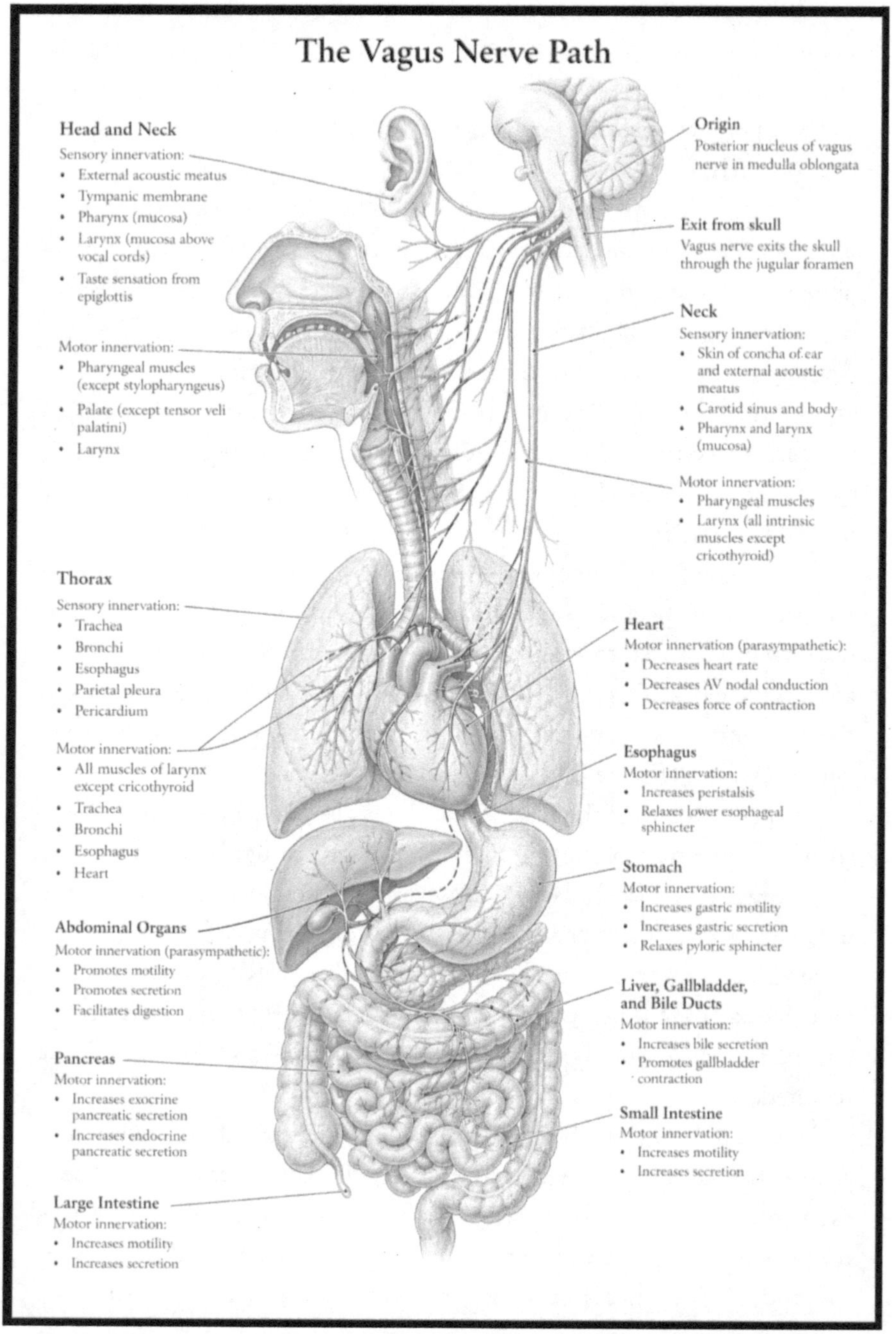

Figure 2. The Vagus Nerve Path

overwhelmed to be reached; it needs to be spoken to in a language it already knows. Vibes are that language. This explains why the effects of Apollo are so similar to those of music, including improved mood, energy, focus, calm, and sleep, on demand.

In 2023, we trained the Apollo wearable to track sleep and released the first closed-loop AI system (SmartVibes®) that observes your sleep patterns, predicts sleep disturbances, and turns Apollo on in real time to rock you back to sleep before you wake up with oodles of racing thoughts. In 2025 alone, Apollo SmartVibes gave the world back over 143 million minutes of sleep [9]. That's 273 years of sleep given back to humanity in just one year. It was not known that mobile technology could have this significant of an impact on public health until now.

As Kathryn and I firmly believe that healing is a right, not a privilege, we spent three years hacking the iPhone to make some of Apollo's most therapeutic Vibes available via the iPhone's built-in haptic engine. Today, anyone in the world with an iPhone can access free, instantaneous science-backed stress relief by downloading the Apollo Neuro app in the Apple App Store.

This is the first demonstration that smartphones can become sources of healing rather than solely sources of stress. The outcome of using a tool depends much more on how we choose to use it than on the tool itself.

Apollo activates a feedback system built on the ancient truth that touch heals, rhythm regulates, and safety must be felt for healing to be possible. When we are safe enough to come back to ourselves, we realize that we are safe enough to feel anything, and feeling is the source of healing.

These optimization cultists, however, don't want to *feel.* They want to *control.*

One of them pulled me aside after my talk, sweating through his smart fabric shirt.

"Doc," he said, "this Apollo thing…does it work on, like, an AI feedback loop?"

"Yes, but that's not the most interesting part," I told him. "It works on a human feedback loop."

He scowled, as if I'd confessed to witchcraft.

You could trace this mania for optimization back to our cultural DNA. The Protestant work ethic, the techno-utopian fantasy, the billion-dollar health and wellness industry selling the same gospel: "You're a machine, and machines can be perfected."

Never mind that perfection is a psychotic delusion.

I've treated patients who track their bowel movements with military precision. Men who are so obsessed with perfect cleanliness that they wash their hands until they bleed and require bandages. Women who tell me the only time in their lives that they're with people they can trust is at the doctor's office.

All terrified of entropy.

All allergic to rest.

It's less narcissism and more *existential terror.* If we stop optimizing and stop producing, we have to face the unbearable question: *Who am I when I'm not improving?*

That silence is what keeps the market alive. The optimization cult sells relief from stillness.

I once met a high priest of this new religion. A CEO who claimed he could extend human life to 150 through "quantum bio-alignment." He invited me to his million-dollar yacht, docked outside Miami for the moment.

It looked like a Bond villain's lair designed by Goop. Cryotherapy chambers next to crystal altars. Incense and candles dripping wax onto vibrating plates.

"Fear," he told me, "is just a software bug."

I nearly applauded the metaphor. "So, what's the patch?" I asked.

"Neural entrainment through proprietary binaural wave harmonics with a sprinkle of ketamine."

In plain English: expensive psychedelic sound baths.

He leaned in close. "We're going to delete suffering."

That's when I realized he wasn't joking. These weren't scientists. They were colonizers of consciousness trying to terraform the human experience into something profitable and predictable. They'd built their temple on the bones of uncertainty, declared war on discomfort, and called it innovation.

What they don't understand is that suffering isn't a bug to be deleted. It's a core part of the code. It's the part of the code designed to trigger when we *resist feeling*.

DR. DAVE'S MINDBLOWER #5

We spend a lot of time trying to ignore our emotions because they're uncomfortable at times. It turns out that feeling emotions when they come up (or shortly thereafter) is required for them to process in the body and move on. Emotions we refuse to feel stick around and try to get our attention, in the form of rumination, anxiety, and suffering, until they are felt fully and released.

Felt emotions, including those we often associate with suffering, typically last only 90–120 seconds. Once acknowledged and felt, they can be processed in the body with some type of physical, mental, or emotional release (e.g., crying, jumping up and down, journaling, talking, etc.) and then go on their merry way, restoring your attention back under your control.

Unfelt emotions can last a lifetime.

Here's the problem: the human nervous system evolved over hundreds of thousands of years to respond to short bursts of danger followed by long stretches of safety, rest, feeling, and connection.

What it got instead was capitalism with Wi-Fi.

Modern stress is not sharp and brief; it's smeared. It's constant. It's the emotional equivalent of someone lightly poking you every six seconds and then acting confused when you snap.

Emails. Deadlines. News cycles. Performance reviews. Parenting. Dating apps. Doomscrolling. Self-optimization podcasts hosted by men who sleep four hours a night and call it "discipline."

Your nervous system does not understand any of this.

It understands:

- Loud = maybe danger
- Fast = maybe danger
- Unpredictable = definitely danger
- Social rejection = exile = death

So, it does what it knows how to do.

It tightens.

It braces.

It prepares.

It never fully stands down.

The nervous system, in all its ancient brilliance, doesn't optimize for happiness. It optimizes for *survival.* And survival doesn't mean endless pleasure or uninterrupted peace. It means rhythm. Chaos and order dancing in time. Fear and safety alternating like the tide.

You can try to hack around it, distract it, suppress it, but the body always wins.

The body remembers what the mind refuses to feel.

This is why so many people feel like they're "on edge" all the time. Like they can't fully relax, even on vacation. Like rest feels suspicious. Like stillness makes their thoughts scream louder.

That's not a personal failure.

That's what happens when a nervous system is denied closure.

In a healthy biological rhythm, stress looks like this:

activation → resolution → rest → connection → play

In modern life, stress looks like this:

activation → activation → activation →
"have you tried meditation?" → activation

Your body is not confused.

It's responding accurately to an environment that never lets it land.

Which brings us to one of the cruelest misunderstandings of modern self-help culture: the idea that your nervous system is *the problem.*

That you need to conquer it.

Fight it.

Override it.

Dominate it with cold plunges and motivational quotes yelled at you by men named Chad.

We can't fight for peace. The system just doesn't work that way. Your nervous system is not the enemy. It's an extremely loyal, slightly traumatized bodyguard who has not had a day off since 2001.

This is where so many people get stuck. They try to *think* their way out of a body-based problem. They reason with panic. They argue with insomnia. They shame themselves for being "too sensitive."

The nervous system does not speak English.

It speaks:

- Breath
- Rhythm
- Touch
- Tone
- Repetition
- Presence
- Feeling

Trying to talk your way out of fear without involving the body is like trying to calm a horse by emailing it.

What your nervous system is asking for, over and over again, is not perfection or optimization.

It's reassurance. Not once. Not intellectually.

Consistently.

Somatically.

Gently.

Unconditionally.

It wants to know:

"Am I safe now?"

"Am I allowed to rest?"

"Is someone looking out for me when my guard is down?"

And if the answer is unclear, it stays activated. Not to punish you, but to protect you.

There's a strange relief in realizing that perfection isn't the goal. That healing isn't a linear graph; it's filled with peaks and valleys. That life isn't meant to be constantly optimized, but *experienced.*

This is where compassion becomes not just nice, but necessary. When you start approaching your nervous system like a trusted ally or a best friend instead of a malfunctioning appliance, something remarkable happens: it softens.

Not all at once. Not magically, but measurably.

The guard dog stops pacing.

The alarms quiet.

The body begins to believe you.

Here's the quiet truth most people never hear:

Your nervous system doesn't need to be fixed.

It needs to be met.

Upon completion of this book, you will know how to meet it where it is with patience, with humor, with respect, and with kindness that borders on stubbornness.

We are not fragile.

We are exquisitely adaptive.

And your nervous system?

It has been waiting a long time for you to stop yelling at it and start listening.

I left that boat compound feeling like I'd just witnessed the digital resurrection of Narcissus; an entire generation drowning in their own reflections, mistaking data for divinity. Driving back toward my hotel, the lights of downtown Miami glittering like a motherboard beneath the dusk, I couldn't shake the thought:

We built the smartest machines in history and programmed them to make us feel inadequate.

Now we kneel before them, begging for permission to be human.

CHAPTER 3
The Dopamine Economy

We are not made for the world our minds created.
Arthur De Vany (1937–2026)

It's 9:37 a.m. in America, and someone somewhere has just sold your attention for thirteen cents.

You didn't notice. You were busy checking the weather, liking a photo, or doomscrolling through the latest planetary collapse, but make no mistake: your eyeballs were traded like pork futures in a silent marketplace that never closes.

Welcome to the *Dopamine Economy*: where every click, swipe, and scroll is a microtransaction of the soul.

You are not the customer here. You're the product. An ambulatory dopamine slot machine dressed in AloYoga, Supreme, and existential dread.

And I am your consciousness concierge.

There was a time when dopamine was simple. A humble neurotransmitter doing its best to help us survive, find food, mate successfully, run from tigers, and celebrate not dying. A biological pat on the back.

Now, it's a global commodity. Entire empires are built on its manipulation.

Tobacco companies really figured it out first, possibly without fully understanding the neuroscience behind what they had discovered. Then, somehow, Silicon Valley realized what they had before the psychiatrists did: If you can hijack dopamine, you can control behavior. Not through fear or violence or drugs. Those are crude tools. Through anticipation. The exquisite itch of *almost.*

Every app, every notification badge, every "see more" button is engineered to whisper: "You're about to feel something good...any second now..."

That's the genius of it. They don't even have to deliver the reward, just the *possibility* of it, because a big dopamine spike comes *before* satisfaction, not just after [10-11]. Desire, not fulfillment, is the product.

It's Skinner Box theory: push button, get pellet [12]. Only now the pellets are likes, views, and imaginary internet clout, and like rats in the lab, we're pressing the lever until our fingers go numb.

DR. DAVE'S MINDBLOWER #6

Fear and safety are highly trainable states in the body. B. F. Skinner conducted experiments on rats in the early twentieth century and trained them to press a button to receive food, as well as to perform many other more complex tasks. Skinner discovered that discomfort resulted in withdrawal behavior, and reward resulted in attraction [13]. He also found that providing a reward unpredictably, not every time the button is pressed, produces the highest habit formation rates. Learning works the same way in humans.

One afternoon in my clinic, I watched a twenty-seven-year-old patient scroll Instagram during her therapy session. She wasn't rude, just compulsively orbiting the feed like a moth around a lantern.

"Why do you think you keep scrolling?" I asked.

She looked up, dazed, as if I'd interrupted a trance. "Because I might miss something important," she said.

"Has that ever happened?"

"Just once," she admitted. "So it could happen again, right?"

There it was. The sacred word of the Dopamine Economy: *could.* The infinite horizon of *maybe.*

When I lecture about this stuff, I try to explain that dopamine is the reward as much as it is the wanting. The gap between where you are and where you think you should be.

The more you chase it, the wider that gap becomes. It's the perfect trap: the hungrier you are, the less you taste. Our ancestors used dopamine to track food across the savanna. We use it to track validation across the algorithm. Same wiring, different predators.

Except now, the lions are invisible and politely ask for permission to send you notifications.

What's even more alarming is that social media companies deny the addictive potential of their products, citing the Diagnostic and Statistical Manual of Mental Disorders (DSM-5), which does not include an "official diagnosis" for social media addiction. So allow me to coin the diagnosis for us all.

Social Media Addiction Disorder (SMAD), characterized by the behaviors we see many times daily, including impulsivity, withdrawal, craving, and impaired self-control, is, in fact, a very real thing and needs to be addressed as such [15-16]. The same could apply to smartphones as well [17-18]. Thinking about this as a clinical diagnosis is critically important because it helps us understand that we must rule out SMAD prior to diagnosing someone with an attention disorder like ADHD, as the symptoms of social media and smartphone addiction can be exacerbated by the amphetamines used to treat ADHD.

Here's the sick poetry of it: dopamine isn't evil. It's neutral, amoral, utterly sincere. It just wants you to survive. It doesn't know the difference between the joy of a ripe mango and a viral meme; between a real kiss and a digital one.

It rewards pursuit, not presence. And in a capitalist system built on endless pursuit, dopamine is the perfect engine.

When the market discovered attention could be harvested like corn, the rest was inevitable. The more anxious, lonely, or uncertain we are, the more predictable our behaviors become.

Predictable behavior is valuable behavior.

The economy runs on our restlessness.

Even psychiatry isn't innocent. We diagnose "attention deficit" as a disorder in a world that's designed to fracture it. We medicalize fatigue while worshipping productivity. We are taught to treat anxiety without questioning the social structure that manufactures it by design.

The truth is, your brain isn't broken. It's *overstimulated.* It's doing exactly what it evolved to do: seek safety through pattern recognition and reward anticipation. It just doesn't realize the patterns are rigged.

You're not actually addicted to your phone. You're addicted to *hope.*

The saddest part is watching what this does to real human connection.

A couple in therapy sits across from me. They came to talk about intimacy issues. "We just haven't been feeling the spark for a while," she says.

"Do you ever look at each other without the phones?" I ask.

A pause. "Not often," he admits. "We're together all the time, though."

Together, but never *with.* Connected, but never *in contact.*

It's a peculiar new form of loneliness: *perpetual partial attention.* The body is present, but the self is outsourced to the cloud.

DR. DAVE'S MINDBLOWER #7

We have infinitely more in common with each other than we have differences. Not only are we 99.9% genetically identical to one another, we share 41% of our DNA with a banana. All humans have the same six core survival needs: air, water, food, shelter (physical safety), sleep, and connection.

When we're stressed or overwhelmed because we are tricked into thinking some of our core survival needs are in jeopardy, "different" and newness become scary by default, and we cling to what's familiar, even if that means being alone.

When we stop to realize how similar we actually are, and that we are all alive and human together before we are anything else, our differences become beautiful and can be cherished, enriching our lives with awe, inspiration, and wonder. Loneliness becomes something of the distant past.

After all, if we were all the same, life would be excruciatingly boring.

When I try to explain this to students, I tell them to imagine attention as a limited resource, similar to glucose. Every notification, every dopamine ping, spends a little of it. The cost adds up.

And what's left, at the end of the day, is a depleted nervous system that doesn't know whether it's in danger or just distracted.

That's the ultimate trick of the Dopamine Economy: it doesn't kill you. It just keeps you *almost alive.*

Sometimes I fantasize about a Great Reset. Not the conspiracy theory kind, but a real human one. Everyone turns off their screens for twenty-four hours. No dopamine IV drips, no algorithmic whispers. Just silence and good old-fashioned in-person connection with each other and nature.

At first, people might panic. Then hallucinate. Then weep. Then, maybe, begin to feel something real.

It's not likely to happen, of course. Not while we're as distracted as we are, and attention is worth more than oil.

So we keep scrolling. Keep refreshing. Keep selling slices of our consciousness to the highest bidder, pretending we're in control of the ride.

Fear and loathing in the twenty-first century isn't about drugs, or madness, or politics. It's about this: the involuntary trip we're all on, wired into an economy that monetizes our very capacity to care.

We're all being treated like lab rats now, chasing the next ping of synthetic purpose.

And somewhere, in a climate-controlled data center, the algorithm smiles.

CHAPTER 4
The Cult of Calm

We suffer so much more in imagination than in reality.
Seneca (4 BCE–65 CE)

There was a time when silence meant peace.

Now it just means your AirPods died.

You can hear it in the collective twitch. The panic that sets in the second the podcast stops playing. We've become allergic to quiet.

And yet, somehow, calm has become the new gold standard. The last frontier for the capitalist soul.

Welcome to *The Cult of Calm*, where serenity is a subscription, enlightenment is a brand, and your nervous system is a growth market.

DR. DAVE'S MINDBLOWER #8

Calm is not the absence of stimulation. It is remembering that *you are not your thoughts. You are the observer of your thoughts.*

You've seen them. The "calmfluencers." Serene smiles stretched taut over the abyss. Everything is beige. The walls, the sweaters, the smoothies. They post mantras like "Just Breathe" over drone footage of Tulum while waiting for their Xanax to kick in.

Their followers, millions deep, study every frame like scripture. They believe calm is something you can buy. A state of mind wrapped in organic hemp packaging and optimized for engagement.

And who can blame them? Stress is out; soft focus is in. Yoga studios look like Apple stores now. Meditation apps have IPOs.

They've made relaxation competitive.

It's a strange thing to watch peace become performance art.

People "meditate" on live streams, complete with ring lights and hashtags. Others wear biometric headbands that gamify Zen, rewarding you with soothing chimes when your EEG reads "calm enough." Some of these, like the Muse headband, are great tools for teaching us how to meditate, but relying on these tools over your intuition is where the trouble lies.

The whole premise defeats itself. Calm isn't something you can track. The moment you measure it, you've lost it. It's like quantum theory.

But we can't help it. We've industrialized everything else, so why not calmness too?

I remember leading a mindfulness workshop for a company in New York. The CEO had invited me after losing 10% of his staff to burnout that quarter. "My therapist says I need to ground myself," he told me.

"Good," I said. "Take a breath."

He inhaled. Exhaled. Checked his smartwatch. "That was 5.3 seconds," he said. "Is that optimal?"

I considered a sedative for a moment.

Here's the neurobiological joke: you can't fake calm.

The body always knows.

Calm isn't the absence of motion. Calm is *coherence*. The synchrony between heart, lungs, and brain when you finally stop fighting yourself. It's the parasympathetic takeover, the vagus nerve whispering: *You're safe.*

You can't get there by force, however. You can't optimize your way to surrender.

The nervous system doesn't speak in goals. It speaks in rhythm.

You can nudge it there temporarily with music, vibration, and psychedelics, but true calm? That's a biological confession. It only happens when you stop lying to your body.

DR. DAVE'S MINDBLOWER #9

You cannot bully a nervous system into safety. Safety, similar to repairing an old house, is not achieved through force. It is learned by repairing our foundation of self-trust. What we build on top of our foundation is unstable if the foundation itself is cracked or damaged. With the techniques described in this book, we repair fractures in self-trust so that what we learn next can be stably rooted to weather the next storm.

That's the real tragedy of The Cult of Calm. It teaches people to *pretend* peace while suppressing the chaos underneath.

It's emotional Botox.

I've treated executives who meditate two hours a day and still grind their teeth to dust at night.

Influencers who preach gratitude, but secretly fear silence more than death.

Yoga teachers with cortisol levels that could power small cities.

You can't post or scroll your way there. You must feel the storm before the stillness.

The market hates that truth. It's not scalable.

So we sell shortcuts: apps, courses, digital ashrams. Serenity on demand. "Press play, feel peace."

I've seen pitch decks for new companies promising "emotional operating systems" for mass tranquility. One even claimed to use machine learning to "detect and delete stress in real time."

Delete stress. Like a pop-up ad.

It's insane and also, somehow, genius.

Because beneath the absurdity lies a fundamental human ache: people are desperate to feel safe again. To stop running. To stop pretending.

The calm industry is just the modern placebo for our collective dysregulation. And what's more is that most of the stuff we're being sold has never even been scientifically proven to work. It's entirely sold and marketed based on theory. A hypothesis that success in this calm experiment is possible with us as the research subjects.

In my more charitable moods, I try to see it as evolution.

We've externalized the nervous system, outsourced attention to devices, to routines, to influencers. Maybe it's a necessary phase before we remember that the original technology—breath, touch, stillness—still works.

The Apollo technology was built on this idea: a bridge between chaos and calm. Not to sell peace, but to remind the body it already knows how to find it when we feel safe enough to look in the right places. To teach us how to get back to those places on our own, any time we want.

That's the paradox. Real calm isn't created. It's *recovered.*

You strip away the noise, the endless optimization, the hollow affirmations, and there it is. Patiently waiting. Unimpressed.

Once, after a lecture, a young woman approached me, tears in her eyes. "I've tried everything," she said. "Yoga, meditation, supplements. Nothing works. How do I stop feeling like this?"

I told her the truth no one wants to sell: "You don't stop feeling. You start listening."

She blinked. "That's it?"

"That's everything."

So here we are. A civilization overdosed on stimulation and addicted to artificial calm. A planet full of nervous systems trying to meditate their way out of evolution.

We chant "I am enough" while refreshing our notifications.

We breathe deeply through curated panic.

We treat serenity as if it were for sale.

And in the background, the body keeps whispering the same thing it's whispered every moment your basic survival needs have been met for the last 200,000 years:

"You don't have to do anything to be safe. You just have to stop pretending you're not."

CHAPTER 5
The Digital Messiah Complex

We shape our tools, and thereafter our tools shape us.
Father John M. Culkin (1928–1993)

Every generation gets the prophets it deserves.

Ours just happen to wear black turtlenecks and talk about consciousness between funding rounds.

They call it "techno-spiritualism." A Frankenstein fusion of neuroscience, market dynamics, and mysticism. It's the new Holy Trinity. God, but monetizable.

These are the *Digital Messiahs*, the gurus of our algorithmic age.

They preach on podcasts rather than from pulpits.

They speak in acronyms instead of parables.

They promise salvation through code, consciousness through crypto, enlightenment through machine learning.

And millions believe them.

DR. DAVE'S MINDBLOWER #10

Humans are most vulnerable to false certainty when they are chronically dysregulated. A calm nervous system can tolerate ambiguity. A stressed one stops listening and seeks rapid relief from ambiguity through numbing, distraction, prophets, and poor decisions.

I met one of these prophets at a conference in Arizona. The air smelled like sage and VC money. Every attendee was either microdosing, fundraising, or both.

One keynote speaker, let's call him Lorenzo, strode onstage in sneakers, wearing a three-piece suit that probably cost more than my car. He opened with a quote from the Bhagavad Gita and closed with a slide showing a $40 million Series A.

His message was simple: *Consumer brainwave technologies are the path to God's nervous system.*

That line got a standing ovation. People wept. Investors scribbled notes. I think someone tried to tithe in Bitcoin.

Lorenzo was selling what he called a "neuro-collective operating system." In practice, it was a glorified EEG brainwave sensor headset paired with an app that harvested emotional data in response to different experiences. It made money by selling that data to advertisers so they could understand what your brainwaves look like when you want to click the "buy" button.

He claimed it could "synchronize human consciousness across networks to end suffering at scale."

"Like Wi-Fi for empathy?" I asked.

He nodded reverently. "Exactly. We're turning compassion into a software platform."

I've seen many things in psychiatry, but never someone so close to achieving enlightenment through buzzwords.

It's easy to laugh, but the psychology behind this is deadly serious. Humans crave meaning, especially in times of uncertainty. When institutions crumble, and the old gods fall silent, we look for new ones, preferably ones that ship with free next-day delivery.

The Digital Messiahs know this. They offer a story we desperately want to believe: that consciousness can be upgraded, that pain is optional, that salvation is just one more update away.

DR. DAVE'S MINDBLOWER #11

Pain is inevitable. Suffering is avoidable. Resisting what is by attaching to what we believe "should" be is the fastest path toward suffering.

When suffering is pathologized rather than contextualized, people seek salvation rather than safety.

It's the same pitch religion has always made, only now the miracles are proprietary.

I met another startup founder who introduced himself as a "spiritual technologist." He told the audience he was building an AI trained on the world's sacred texts. "It will merge science and scripture," he said, "and speak with the unified voice of God."

I took a sip of my coffee and said, "So...Claude with a halo?"

He didn't laugh.

Strangely enough, not six months later, my barber told me he patented the same scripture-savvy AI.

What fascinates me is how these modern prophets borrow the language of neuroscience to baptize their faith in data.

They talk about frequency, vibration, and quantum awareness.

They invoke the limbic system as if it were the Ark of the Covenant.

They quote research they don't understand to justify doubt.

One company claimed to "measure enlightenment" using HRV and pupil dilation.

Another promised "psychedelic-grade transcendence" through virtual reality.

Another offering "AI-assisted shadow work."

Every one of them is selling the same thing: relief from uncertainty, and the pain and discomfort that goes along with it. The same ancient promise, now with better branding.

The irony, of course, is that science and spirituality are both supposed to dismantle illusions, not sell them. But somewhere along the line, we merged them into a single performance art piece called "authenticity."

The scientists want to feel sacred.

The mystics want to sound scientific.

And the rest of us are caught between PowerPoint slides and prayer beads, trying to remember which side of the brain we're supposed to believe.

Here's the thing: transcendence isn't a product. It's a process, and often a messy, terrifying one. You don't find God in a beta test. You find it in nature and in the parts of yourself you've been trying to debug for years.

DR. DAVE'S MINDBLOWER #12

The ends do NOT justify the means. On the contrary, it is the means, or the intentional process of consciously making thoughtful choices moment to moment, that manifests desirable ends.

The nervous system doesn't care about ideology. It cares about regulation, safety, and connection. That's the real miracle. Not some cloud-based godhead, but two humans breathing in sync, remembering they exist, together.

At one point, Lorenzo invited me to his headquarters, an old church in Pittsburgh that had been converted into a "neural sanctuary." Rows of glowing pods lined the nave like digital confessionals. Inside one lay an individual strapped with electrodes, eyes closed, chasing unity through USB.

He turned to me, beaming. "We're teaching machines to lie."

I stared at the pods humming in the dark. "Careful," I said. "They might not have remorse like we do."

That's the heart of the Digital Messiah Complex: the belief that consciousness can be coded. That we can outsource the unbearable parts of being human, like uncertainty, mortality, and grief, to the cold precision of silicon.

You can't program awakening. You can only experience it.

The more we worship the algorithm, the further we drift from the flesh.

We start to believe the simulation *is* the soul.

And that's how you end up with billionaires launching themselves into space searching for God, when God has been quietly hiding in their vagus nerves the whole time.

Sometimes I think the next great spiritual awakening won't happen in a temple or a lab, but in a collective breakdown, the moment we realize our devices can't love us back.

When the dopamine runs dry.

When the data stops meaning anything.

When the last app promises transcendence and we finally, mercifully, laugh.

Because the truth is ancient and embarrassingly simple: You don't need a neural interface to meet God. You just need to stop running from yourself long enough to remember you were never separate in the first place.

Bizzie Gold described this phenomenon of self-deception in extraordinary detail in her book *Your Brain Is a Filthy Liar* [19]. The first way most of us deceive ourselves, without even realizing it, is by living and believing that we are separate from the source of our creation, the Earth, and each other, when both science and spirituality agree that we are all just slightly different expressions of the same stardust.

CHAPTER 6
The Great Burnout Revival

Humankind cannot bear very much reality.
T. S. Eliot (1888–1965)

Burnout just became recognized as a worldwide problem [20].

Now it's already a lifestyle brand.

You can buy it prepackaged: three parts hustle, one part self-help, two parts caffeine, and a garnish of moral superiority. Everyone's exhausted, and everyone's bragging about it.

We used to whisper about nervous breakdowns; now, we livestream them.

Welcome to *The Great Burnout Revival*, a national religion of depletion disguised as devotion.

You see it everywhere: people treating exhaustion like evidence of purpose. The tired have inherited the Earth, and they're too damn busy to enjoy it.

I often meet professionals who wear their fatigue like a medal. They introduce themselves with résumés of ruin.

"I work eighty hours a week."

"I haven't taken a day off in three years."

"I answer emails in my sleep."

They say it with pride, not despair. They believe collapse is proof of commitment.

DR. DAVE'S MINDBLOWER #13

Burnout is not a failure of resilience. It is a predictable biological response to chronic threat and continuous performance without recovery. When we burn the candle at both ends, we run out of wax quickly. The human body is the fanciest, high-performance vehicle we will ever have the pleasure of operating. As with any high-performance vehicle, it requires high-quality fuel and routine maintenance to keep running without breaking down. Treating your body worse than you treat your car while expecting more is a recipe for burnout.

They're not wrong. Not in this system. Capitalism rewards self-erasure. The less you feel, the more you're worth.

Those who know me also know that I am fascinated by cult psychology. And this, my dear friends, is so elegantly culty we don't even realize we're participating in it.

Burnout has become a sacred ritual of our species, the baptism by fire that precedes redemption, and significantly increases our chances of mental and physical illness.

We no longer rest to recover, for the enjoyment of life. We rest to perform productivity better.

I teach medical students, a student group with one of the highest pre-graduation burnout rates, that burnout isn't a moral failure; it's a physiological signal. The nervous system is screaming, "You're out of balance."

The modern world treats that scream as background noise.

The body was designed for sprints, not marathons. Yet here we are, running the longest anxiety relay in human history, passing the cortisol baton from generation to generation.

There's something biblical about it, this collective collapse.

Like we've mistaken fatigue for faith, burnout for baptism.

The body as sacrifice, the inbox as altar.

DR. DAVE'S MINDBLOWER #14

When recovery is framed as a productivity upgrade, the nervous system never actually rests.

And when it finally breaks down, when the panic attacks come, the immune system rebels, and the gut goes to war, we call it a revelation.

"I had to hit rock bottom to find myself," people say, as if self-destruction were a prerequisite for meaning.

It's not enlightenment. It's inflammation. And it's highly preventable.

Once, during a talk at a hospital, a young doctor asked me, "How do you balance being human with being productive?"

I told him the truth: "You do your very best, but it's tough in this system. Much of the time, we are confronted by the choice of which one to betray less."

He laughed nervously, like I'd said something profound, but I wasn't joking.

Medicine eats its young. Tech eats its prophets. Religion eats its saints. The American Dream is a carnivore, and burnout is its digestion process.

Here's the basic neurobiology of it: chronic stress keeps the amygdala lit up like a casino sign [21]. Cortisol floods the system. Inflammation skyrockets. The hippocampus, responsible for short-term memory and learning, starts to wither [22].

You forget who you are.

You lose empathy, creativity, joy, and passion.

Your nervous system becomes an engine running on fumes.

That's burnout. It's not weakness. It's a cellular revolt against intolerable, inhumane circumstances on repeat for years.

Here's the part I didn't expect: people are starting to fetishize the crash.

DR. DAVE'S MINDBLOWER #15

Chronic stress shrinks the hippocampus, inflames the immune system, and flattens emotional range. Burnout isn't just psychological, it's cellular.

They post about their "healing journeys" with the same performative zeal they once reserved for promotions. They burn out, retreat to Bali, and rebrand as life coaches.

It's the *metamorphosis economy*: transform your collapse into content.

The Great Burnout Revival isn't about recovery. It's about resurrection. The promise that if you annihilate yourself properly, you'll be reborn as someone more authentic, more aligned, and more marketable.

We're still worshiping work. We've just learned to call it *healing*.

The irony is that true recovery isn't glamorous. It's boring.

It's rest. Boundaries. Feeling your feelings before they become diseases.

It's learning to say "no" and surviving the silence afterward.

It's remembering that the nervous system doesn't care about your ambitions. It just wants to feel safe enough to stop running.

When I look at the world today, I see an entire species begging for permission to rest, but rest isn't earned. It's inherent. It's not the reward for enough suffering; it's the foundation of sanity to prevent unnecessary suffering.

If there's any hope in this Great Burnout Revival, it's that we're finally realizing the system itself is sick.

And maybe, just maybe, the cure isn't strong-arming transcendence. It's surrender.

CHAPTER 7

The Age of Anxiety

All of humanity's problems stem from man's inability to sit quietly in a room alone.
Blaise Pascal (1623–1662)

We are living in the *Age of Anxiety*. The most connected, informed, medicated, and terrified civilization in recorded history.

Fear is our lingua franca. Anxiety is the tax we pay for consciousness.

The ancients had gods of thunder, war, and wine. We have *notifications.*

You can feel it in the air, this baseline hum of collective unease. It vibrates through the streets, the subways, the timelines. Everyone is tuned to the same anxious frequency, a kind of global *sympathetic resonance.*

The world is one giant amygdala, pulsing, twitching, scanning for danger.

It's not even subtle anymore. Every headline is a potential panic attack in 48-point bold font. Every advertisement whispers, *You are not safe until you buy this.*

I once saw a billboard that read, "RELAX! YOU'RE DOING GREAT!," and I swear my blood pressure spiked.

Anxiety has become the organizing principle of modern life.

We plan for it, medicate for it, monetize it.

The economy runs on cortisol.

The media runs on adrenaline.

And social media runs on whatever primal neurotransmitter cocktail keeps us half panicked, half aroused, and fully online.

You're not supposed to *feel* calm. Calm doesn't click.

I once gave a lecture that described *Fear as a Feature, Not a Bug*. The audience looked horrified for a moment, as if I'd confessed to being pro-cancer, but fear *is* a feature. It's the oldest survival mechanism we have, and it's extremely important that it exists. The problem isn't fear itself, it's how we've rewired it.

DR. DAVE'S MINDBLOWER #16

When the brain is deprived of felt safety, it substitutes vigilance to protect us. When vigilance becomes chronic, survival becomes the priority, and joy goes offline.

The human brain evolved to manage saber-toothed tigers that chase us for a short time until we get to safety, not stock portfolios and TikTok comment sections that chase us for weeks, months, or years. The amygdala can't tell the difference between a predator and a notification. Both make your heart race, your palms sweat, your thoughts scatter like pigeons in a thunderstorm.

We're running Stone Age hardware on 5G bandwidth.

I remember a patient, a thirty-three-year-old therapist, who came to me saying, "Doc, I can't tell if I'm anxious or just paying attention."

That's the Age of Anxiety in one sentence.

We've pathologized awareness.

We've medicalized sensitivity.

We've confused being alive with being unwell.

He wasn't broken. He was just *awake* in a system designed to keep him slightly afraid at all times.

Anxiety sells everything.

It sells security systems, skincare, cigarettes, and startup software. It sells diets, drugs, and dog food. It sells identities.

The trick is simple: make people doubt themselves, then offer relief at a markup.

I call it *the Anxiety Industrial Complex.* A trillion-dollar organism that feeds on self-doubt and spits out coping mechanisms.

It's highly efficient. It doesn't care if the relief works, only that it expires.

You see it in culture, too, in the way we aestheticize panic.

We joke about it now, like it's a personality type.

"I have anxiety," people say, as if confessing to reading their weekly horoscope.

They post memes about mental breakdowns. They curate their panic into content.

It's not their fault. It's the only way to survive the absurdity: make art out of the ache.

Behind the humor, you can feel it. The raw, animal tremor of a species that's forgotten how to relax into *being*. Everyone is acting like Yosemite Sam is holding a gun to their feet and yelling, "Now dance," while firing bullets at the floor. When I ask who is firing the bullets, they say "no one." When I ask if the villain or gun is real, they say, "I'm not sure." When asked if they still dance as if someone is firing at them, the answer is "always, and I'm not sure why!"

The irony is that anxiety isn't our enemy. It's the body's way of asking for attention. It's the alarm system of the nervous system. It is not to be silenced, but understood.

Anxiety is not good or bad. It is a neutral survival signal to notice uncertainty, newness, and unfamiliarity in our surroundings. In the jungles or the prairies 100,000 years ago, anxiety evolved to help us survive so we could make it to today.

Today, our anxiety system is tricked into activating all the time because we are constantly overstimulated with uncertainty and unfamiliarity (e.g., the news). So to take control of our anxiety, we must learn to direct our attention back to that which we can always control, and it begins with the breath.

Taking just one deep breath by choice kicks off a powerful chain reaction, augmenting focus on what we can control (our breath) and what is certain and familiar, rather than what isn't. That chain reaction is anxiety management 101, and it's entirely under our control, just by nature of being born human.

DR. DAVE'S MINDBLOWER #17

Anxiety is not a malfunction. It is not good or bad. Anxiety is a neutral survival signal responding to uncertainty, unfamiliarity, and lack of control. It's uncomfortable because it evolved to save our lives, not to be ignored. As soon as we decide to stop avoiding anxiety or judging it as bad (and ourselves as bad for having it), we can just be present with it and feel it. Just starting to notice it and observe it without judgment kicks off a powerful mental-emotional process that starts to move anxiety through the body and out.

When you feel anxious, your body isn't betraying you. It's trying to bring you home. It's drawing your attention to what you are paying attention to and what your body wants you to pay attention to. And when *control* is touted as the most sought-after goal, paying attention to things outside of our control, which is most things these days, is the single largest source of anxiety.

Our feelings were meant to be felt and, simply by listening to our emotions, by feeling them, usually for no more than a couple of minutes, we allow them to move through us and out on their merry way. The source of all anxiety, including ruminations and negative intrusive thoughts, is a combination of resisting feeling our emotions when they come up and spending time paying attention to things that are outside of our control.

Sometimes, I fantasize about the entire human population stopping to take a breath all at once. And then another and another for a minute or two. Understanding the science of breath and how effective it is at shifting our perspective to one of self-connection and connection to the world around us makes it hard for me to believe that this would not be an incredibly powerful experience for our species. No phones, no screens, no self-improvement podcasts.

Just air, trees, flowers.

Uncomfortable silence.

At first, people would think about work they have to do, and possibly about leaving the car unlocked or the stove on, and consider reaching for phantom devices. Then they'd remember the rhythm of their breath. The smell of the air. The sound of their own heartbeat. The simple miracle of *not knowing what's happening in the world for a moment, and everything continuing on nonetheless.* Human *being* at its finest.

That's what healing looks like in the Age of Anxiety: remembering that most of what terrifies you isn't happening, it's being broadcast.

When I teach residents about anxiety disorders, I tell them the truth that no DSM manual can quantify: anxiety isn't just a symptom. It's a *mirror.*

It reflects the dissonance between how we live and what we need, between the human nervous system and the inhuman pace of progress and expectations.

If you experience some amount of daily anxiety in today's world, congratulations! Your biology is still functioning.

DR. DAVE'S MINDBLOWER #18

Anxiety decreases when attention returns to sensory experiences in the body. Rumination and worry stop in the mind when the body is humming, getting hugs, or exercising. This is because the body is always present in the here and now. Ruminations and worries are always about the past or the future.

You're not malfunctioning. You're responding appropriately to madness.

I call this the Age of Anxiety, but maybe it's something else. A transitional epoch, the chrysalis before a collective nervous system reset.

Maybe all this panic is a form of awakening. The sound of a species realizing it's been living outside its window of tolerance for too long.

If that's true, then anxiety certainly isn't a curse. It's the call.

A physiological plea to slow down, to feel, to return, to breathe.

To remember how to attend by choice.

To remember that *we are not our thoughts, but observers of them.*

CHAPTER 8
The Death of Intimacy

Intimacy requires courage because risk is inescapable.
Rollo May (1909–1994)

Loneliness has gone airborne.

It spreads invisibly, more contagious than any virus, quietly choking the social nervous system of the species that once survived by huddling around fire. We have eight billion people, and almost no one is truly *touching*.

That's what I mean by the *Death of Intimacy*.

Not the end of sex. Sex is everywhere, streaming, marketed, optimized, commodified.

What's dying is the slow, messy, wordless intimacy that happens when two humans put down their armor long enough to be seen.

We've confused proximity with connection.

We text instead of talk, scroll instead of feel, swipe instead of risk rejection. We share more data than ever, but less vulnerability. The body count goes up, but the heart rate stays flat.

In my clinic, I see it in the eyes of patients who sleep beside partners they haven't truly met in years. They have shared mortgages, calendars, playlists, but not presence.

We call it a relationship. Physiologically, it's cohabitated solitude.

You can measure the collapse in the data. Loneliness rates have tripled since the 1980s. Touch deprivation correlates with higher inflammation, lower immune function, and shorter lifespan.

Cuddle less, die faster.

That's psychoneuroimmunology.

When you hug someone for twenty seconds, your vagus nerve activates, serotonin and dopamine increase, oxytocin is released, cortisol drops, and heart and breathing rhythms synchronize. When you stare at a screen for three hours instead, your nervous system prepares for war.

We're starving for contact in a buffet of stimulation.

DR. DAVE'S MINDBLOWER #19

Intimacy is a state of nervous-system co-regulation. Without safety, proximity does not register as connection.

At one advanced therapy training I was teaching in LA, the participants were all other therapists and clinicians. Many of them were women who were burnt out or nearly broken by the selfless labor of constantly caring for others who were suffering, with no time left for themselves.

One of the sessions I taught was about the techniques for consensual non-sexual therapeutic touch that can be safely practiced in the psychotherapy setting. A fancy way of saying hand-holding when someone is having a tough time.

During one part of the training, a woman sobbed. I held her hand and arm, with her permission, to provide her support and help remind her that she was safe in her body. She found this extremely helpful and later stated that this had a very positive impact on her experience.

The following day, a female participant who was sitting on the opposite side of the room from us the day before approached me at breakfast. She had a disturbed look on her face and had difficulty making eye contact.

Eventually, she sputtered out, "It made me uncomfortable that you were holding Jane's hand yesterday."

I explained that she gave me permission to comfort her through a challenging experience and asked, "Would you not have done the same?"

"Yes, but I'm a woman, so it's okay."

It was both absurd and tragic. The sacred act of therapeutic touch, scorned by another healthcare provider in a setting where touch was taught as a healing technique, but this is where we are. So afraid of intimacy that we confuse sexual and non-sexual connections and demonize them all.

DR. DAVE'S MINDBLOWER #20

Twenty seconds of safe touch can synchronize heart rhythms and reduce cortisol. Our bodies evolved to regulate *together*.

Somewhere along the way, intimacy became inconvenient, unfamiliar, and downright scary.

Real connection requires vulnerability, and vulnerability doesn't monetize well. You can't A/B test trust. You can't sprint your way to emotional safety.

So we replaced it with efficiency. Dating apps became digital vending machines for affection. Therapy became a subscription. Marriage became branding.

We're all out here trying to love like we use Uber: fast, clean, no small talk.

The root of this crisis isn't technology. It's fear.

Fear of being seen. Fear of needing. Fear of losing control. Fear of being hurt.

Intimacy, resulting in pleasure when done right, is a key component of the biological antidote to that fear, but it demands the one thing we've forgotten how to give: attention.

Real attention. Not the kind that glances up from a phone every forty-five seconds. The kind that says, *I'm here. I'm not leaving when it gets uncomfortable.*

You can't fake that. The nervous system knows when it's being watched and when it's being witnessed.

Once, during a session, a patient said, "I feel invisible, even when people look at me."

I asked what she meant.

"They see what I post," she said, "but not who I am."

Her body started shaking. I told her to breathe slow, deep breaths like she was making space for herself inside herself. She cried for twenty minutes straight. When she stopped, she whispered, "I forgot what being seen feels like."

That's what intimacy sounds like: silence, breath, recognition.

DR. DAVE'S MINDBLOWER #21

Intimacy dissolves fear by providing evidence that safety exists between people, not just within them.

The pandemic only accelerated the decay. Two years of isolation turned human beings into phantoms of themselves.

Touch became dangerous.

Faces became threats.

Screens became lifelines.

And we never quite came back. We returned to the world physically, but our souls stayed quarantined.

Even now, people hesitate before hugging. You can see it, the micro-flinch of apprehension before closeness, as if tenderness were contagious.

Maybe it is. God willing, maybe that's how we heal.

Here's the neuroscience: intimacy is regulation.

When two people connect authentically through eye contact, touch, or rhythm, their nervous systems cohere, heart rates align, and breathing synchronizes. This is called *limbic resonance,* and it's the original wireless network.

Long before language, we survived through resonance. We healed through presence. We learned safety through the heartbeat of another.

We don't just crave intimacy; we *require* it.

Without it, the nervous system drifts into chaos. Anxiety rises. Sleep declines. The world feels unsafe. We are literally less biologically healthy and much more likely to die prematurely without regular intimacy and sex in our lives [23, 24].

When enough nervous systems lose that anchor, society itself begins to hallucinate danger.

That's where we are now. A civilization of disembodied brains trying to remember what a heartbeat feels like.

We chase "connection" through pixels, we simulate affection through emojis, and we wonder why we're lonely in a crowd.

We've mistaken communication for communion.

The Death of Intimacy doesn't look like war or apocalypse.

It looks like everyone scrolling in silence beside someone they love.

It looks like two people making love with their minds elsewhere.

It looks like never asking the question you're afraid to hear answered.

It looks like a culture that teaches independence as strength and vulnerability as pathology.

But the body knows better. The body is ancient. The body remembers.

When you touch someone with real presence, and they touch you back, you can feel 200,000 years of human evolution hum beneath the skin.

Safety. Warmth. Belonging.

That's what resurrection feels like.

We don't need to reinvent intimacy. We need to *return* to it.

To talk without agenda.

To hold without expectation.

To listen until words dissolve into heartbeat.

In the end, intimacy is not a technology problem. It's an attention problem.

And attention, when freely given, is the most intimate act of all.

CHAPTER 9
The Pleasure Rebellion

Pleasure is the only thing one should live for. Nothing ages like happiness.
Oscar Wilde (1854–1900)

Pleasure has become suspicious.

In the new moral order of progress and performance, joy is treated like a controlled substance. It is rationed out in microdoses, monitored for productivity-enhancing side effects, and preferably experienced in silence so you don't make anyone uncomfortable.

We are a civilization overdosed on stimulation and starved for satisfaction.

Pleasure is everywhere. Weaponized, monetized, digitized, and yet, somehow almost impossible to feel.

That's not an accident. It's a design.

Somewhere along the line, we forgot that pleasure is not indulgence, it's intelligence.

The body's way of saying, "This keeps you alive."

Touch, taste, breath, and rhythm are not luxuries. They're neural nourishment.

However, in the Puritanical sequel we're all living through, pleasure is suspect. It's inefficient. It's unproductive. It's indulgent.

If you doubt it, try taking a nap in public. Someone will call security or start a wellness app about it.

DR. DAVE'S MINDBLOWER #22

Pleasure is not indulgence. It is the nervous system's confirmation that life is safe enough to enjoy.

You can track this decline scientifically. Chronic stress blunts the dopamine response. Elevated cortisol suppresses oxytocin. The vagus nerve, that sacred river of calm that flows from brain to gut, is inhibited by fear.

Our bodies are begging for sensation, but our minds have outsourced it to the algorithm.

We don't make love anymore; we schedule it.

We don't sing; we stream.

We don't taste our food; we post it.

Even orgasm, the ultimate proof of embodied presence, has been colonized by analytics. There's technology that now graphs your climax in real time. Humanity, quantified.

And what's worse, 10-15% of women report never having an orgasm with a partner [25], while upwards of 50% report difficulty achieving orgasm with their partners because they don't feel safe enough to experience the vulnerability of sexual climax [26].

I once gave a talk to a group of clinicians that described *Pleasure as a Vital Sign.* Not a luxury, a diagnostic marker. Absence of pleasure correlates with inflammation, depression, anxiety, immune dysfunction, lower quality of life, and even early mortality [27-29].

I told them that the absence of pleasure is not a moral issue, it's a physiological one.

A dysregulated, stressed nervous system cannot feel joy.

If the body doesn't feel safe, it won't *allow* pleasure.

Pleasure accelerates healing.

One hospital administrator looked nervous, like I'd just suggested napping at work.

DR. DAVE'S MINDBLOWER #23

A nervous system that does not feel safe will not allow sustained pleasure, no matter how badly you want it.

The truth is that pleasure is rebellion.

In a world that profits from your exhaustion, your pleasure is unprofitable.

In a system that thrives on your compliance, your joy is dangerous.

In a culture addicted to stress, pleasure is like a weekly AA meeting we would rather skip.

Because a person in touch with their pleasure is not easily manipulated. They're anchored, regulated, whole.

I met a scientist once who told me, proudly, that he'd hacked pleasure. He'd built a "neurostimulation rig", a prototype device that delivered precise electrical pulses to the brain to induce climax "on demand."

"Think of the productivity gains!" he said.

I did. Then I thought of the tragedy. The idea that pleasure had to justify itself in the language of efficiency that can be measured. Even our ecstasy must now earn its keep.

There's an evolutionary reason we're wired for pleasure: it teaches safety, rapidly decreases inflammation, and heals our bodies and minds. When you feel good, your body learns that the world isn't always a threat.

That's why the simplest pleasures like a deep breath, a warm meal, sunlight on skin, a hug, or a kiss are more than comforts. They're medicine.

Pleasure is what keeps the nervous system from calcifying into paranoia. It's also an antidote to fear.

The revolution won't be televised. It will be *somatic.*

Once, during a ketamine-assisted therapy session, a patient started crying mid-journey. Between sobs, she said, "I didn't know it could feel this good to feel safe."

That's the whole game.

Pleasure isn't hedonism, it's homeostasis.

It's the body remembering what peace feels like.

Remembering how good it feels to feel safe in your own body.

And in an anxious civilization, that's a radical act.

You can see glimpses of the Pleasure Rebellion rising. A quiet insurgency of humans reclaiming their senses. People learning to cook again, to dance, to touch without agenda, to revel in eye contact. The slow revival of embodied life.

It's happening in bedrooms, in town squares, and in kitchens filled with laughter and the smells of our favorite foods. Small revolutions, every one. Because the truth is, pleasure doesn't need a business model. It only needs permission.

If the twentieth century was about conquest and consumption, maybe the twenty-first will be about *receiving*. Not taking. Not earning. Not optimizing. Just receiving breath, touch, beauty, and kindness without apology.

It sounds simple, but it's the hardest thing in the world for a nervous system raised on scarcity.

That's why I call it rebellion. Because the moment you allow yourself to feel good, really feel it, without guilt, without performing, without turning it into content, you become unstoppable.

No algorithm can own you.

No brand can sell you.

No fear can move you.

Unless you want it to.

The Pleasure Rebellion isn't about pleasure as distraction. It's about pleasure as *independent self-healing*. The right to feel good in your body is not a luxury or indulgence. It's the foundation of sanity, the root of empathy, the proof that living is not just survival, it's celebration.

So breathe. Taste. Touch. Move.

Laugh inappropriately.

Giggle unapologetically.

Let your nervous system remember what it was built for: aliveness.

The revolution starts there, at the nerve endings. And if we play our cards right, we might just be able to make each day on Earth significantly more fun.

CHAPTER 10
The Resurrection of Connection

Act as God and be kind and forgiving to all his creations.
Maimonides (1138–1204 CE)

Every death begs a resurrection story.

Even intimacy. Even us.

You can feel it now, can't you?

Somewhere under the static, under the endless scroll and the performance of composure, something ancient is trying to breathe again.

It's faint, but it's there: the low, rhythmic pulse of a species remembering what it means to belong.

This is *The Resurrection of Connection.*

It won't come from an app, a headset, or a clever piece of code.

It will come from what the machines can't replicate: *presence.*

Presence is analog. Slow. Inconvenient. It's sitting in silence with someone long enough for your nervous systems to negotiate peace. It's the look that says, *I see you. I'm here. You can exhale now.*

It's the first technology. The original wireless transmission. Bioelectric communication between hearts that learned to synchronize before words existed.

We forgot this for a while, but forgetting isn't the same as extinction.

In the clinics, I see glimpses of rebirth every day.

A veteran learning to trust his body again through slow breathing and touch.

DR. DAVE'S MINDBLOWER #24

True connection is not created by effort. It emerges spontaneously when the nervous system senses prolonged safety.

A couple rediscovering that empathy isn't a concept, it's a rhythm.

A teenager realizing her panic isn't pathology, but an invitation to presence.

When the body feels safe, it begins to talk again, not in words, but in signals: warmth in the chest, softening in the jaw, a breath that reaches all the way down.

That's connection. The parasympathetic revival.

The nervous system remembering the world isn't trying to kill it.

Our culture is built on the myth of separation: Self vs. other, mind vs. body, human vs. nature. The amygdala hijacked. It's efficient for commerce, but catastrophic for consciousness.

Connection, real connection, is messy. It blurs boundaries. It doesn't scale cleanly. You can't quantify it, brand it, or optimize it, but it's our primary sustainable energy source.

Two decades ago, I imagined what the world could look like if we designed technology not to dominate attention, but to restore and reinforce our control over it.

Imagine devices that reward stillness. Algorithms that detect dysregulation and help you regulate automatically. Imagine haptics tuned not to capture your attention, but to align it with your goals, helping you achieve them faster.

It's no longer science fiction. I saw it first in our lab at the University of Pittsburgh in 2016. Apollo vibrations resulted in 25% improvements in cognitive performance and focused attention, accompanied by significantly improved feelings of calm within three minutes in a double-blind randomized placebo-controlled crossover study [5]. Then it happened again in two additional clinical trials [6,7] and in the real world among over 100,000 people using the Apollo wearable. Attention can be trained, and technology can help massively accelerate this process when designed thoughtfully and used intentionally.

Tech should not replace touch, or any sense for that matter, but at the very least, it could help remind us how to feel again.

DR. DAVE'S MINDBLOWER #25

The major injury of trauma is that it fractures self-trust, leading us to question our ability to keep ourselves safe. When self-trust becomes injured, like a broken bone, it requires repair. When not repaired properly, the injury often becomes painful and causes mental and physical health issues over time.

Self-trust is repaired through consistent, low-intensity signals of safety, not grand gestures that aren't repeatable. The more we trust ourselves, the easier it is to attract and connect with the people we want in our lives.

The future of connection isn't post-human. It's *re-human.*

The resurrection starts small.

A dinner table with phones in another room (or at the very least out of sight).

A walk with no destination.

Eye contact that survives discomfort.

You don't need a revolution, just a moment of presence repeated enough times to become a habit.

Connection isn't built in grand gestures. It's built in microdoses of safety.

Every time you meet another person with curiosity instead of defense, you're rewiring your brain and rewriting history.

DR. DAVE'S MINDBLOWER #26

Humans evolved to borrow regulation from one another. Isolation forces the nervous system into a chronic state of self-defense.

There's a theory in trauma science called "co-regulation." It means your nervous system doesn't regulate itself in isolation; it learns safety from others [30]. When we've forgotten how to trust ourselves, we can relearn by remembering what it feels like to trust another.

We're designed to heal together [31].

Our hearts literally tune to each other's frequencies.

Our breath synchronizes.

Our brains mirror patterns of trust when we make eye contact.

When we say "I feel you," it's not poetry, it's neurobiology.

And that's the quiet miracle of this moment in history: even in our collective breakdown, connection is finding new ways to reach us.

People are turning toward each other again, in community gardens, in recovery circles, in late-night phone calls that stretch into dawn. The digital fatigue is forcing a rediscovery of touch.

The pendulum always swings back.

After decades of numbness, we are learning to feel again.

I believe this is the real renaissance, not of technology, politics or economics, but of nervous systems.

The body is the new frontier.

Consciousness is the revolution.

Connection, the simple, radical act of being with one another, is the resurrection.

It won't be tidy. Awakening never is.

But maybe the whole point of the chaos, the fear, the burnout, and the dopamine circus was to remind us of what really matters when the noise dies down.

When the last notification fades, and you're left with your heartbeat and the silence between breaths, there's only one truth left to feel:

We were never meant to do this alone.

In the end, loving connection isn't what saves us. It's what we are.

CHAPTER 11
The Cosmic Escape Plan

We are a way for the cosmos to know itself.
Carl Sagan (1934–1996)

Somewhere between the invention of the reusable rocket and the reusable water bottle, humanity decided it would rather colonize Mars than fix the kitchen sink.

It's not subtle anymore. The billionaires are no longer pretending they're launching satellites "for communication." They're building escape pods. The dream of the twenty-first century isn't peace, or wisdom, or collective healing. It's *elsewhere.*

We call it progress, but really it's the oldest addiction in the book: novelty.

This is *The Cosmic Escape Plan.* The fantasy that salvation lies up there, because down here feels unbearable.

I've met the dreamers, the engineers, the cosmic capitalists.

They say things like:

"Humanity must become a multi-planetary species."

"We're ensuring the survival of consciousness."

"We'll terraform Mars within fifty years."

And every time I hear it, I can't help thinking: *we can't even terraform empathy on Earth.*

The science doesn't care about the rhetoric. The reality is brutal.

Space, as every biologist knows, despises the human body. Zero gravity turns bones to dust, leeches calcium, and rewires the vestibular system until balance itself becomes a hallucination. Astronauts return from orbit with muscle atrophy, vision damage, immune dysfunction, and nervous systems that can't tell up from down [32].

Then there's cosmic radiation. The invisible chainsaw slicing DNA, seeding cancers, eroding the hippocampus like cosmic sandpaper [33]. No shield yet invented can block it completely.

Even if you survive the physics, you face the psychology. Extended isolation drives hallucination, insomnia, depression, and in some cases, quiet madness [34].

NASA knows this. Every serious space psychologist knows this. Even the Mars-obsessed billionaires likely know this, they just don't say it out loud. Because the dream of escape is too profitable to puncture. It's dopamine release tricking us again.

DR. DAVE'S MINDBLOWER #27

There is no escape. Escape is futile. We will always be here when we get back from wherever we thought we escaped to. When the nervous system cannot tolerate stillness, distance feels safer than presence, intensifying escape fantasies.

We learn to tolerate stillness by practicing patience. The more we can find to be grateful for within the silent stillness, the more present we are, and the healthier our vagal nerve tone becomes.

In truth, sustaining a high-quality of life for extended stays in outer space is nowhere near possible with current or foreseeable technology. The body is an Earth instrument, tuned to the frequencies of gravity, sunlight, magnetism, and microbes.

We evolved in conversation with this planet, the bacteria in our gut, the ions in the air, the rhythm of daylight on skin. You take that orchestra away, and the music stops. Our mitochondria remember Earth even when we forget it.

We are not astronauts; we are ecosystems.

Still, we fantasize.

We stream rocket launches like sporting events, misty-eyed as boosters land upright on autonomous barges. We talk about colonizing Mars as if it's a fixer-upper on Zillow.

Let's be honest: This isn't exploration. It's escapism in a lab coat. It's the Dopamine Economy leaving orbit.

Remember back in Chapter Three how I said we're addicted not to pleasure, but to anticipation? This is the same thing, just on a planetary scale. Space travel is the final dopamine loop: the promise of transcendence just one breakthrough away.

The fantasy of the next frontier keeps us chasing the high of "almost." It's the same algorithmic itch, only now it's written in rocket fuel.

Meanwhile, here on Earth, this gorgeous, improbable biosphere that evolved to cradle us in the perfect cocktail of oxygen, pressure, and sunlight, we're running an extinction experiment in real time. At a time when life on Earth has never been better or more convenient. A time where two-day delivery for nearly anything you need is just three clicks away, and nearly all the information in our known universe is at all of our fingertips, including the instructions for how to disarm the time bomb we accidentally planted for our own extinction in a moment of deep self-loathing somewhere between five and fifteen beers.

DR. DAVE'S MINDBLOWER #28

The body evolved in conversation with Earth. Remove the context and regulation deteriorates, no matter how advanced the technology.

We don't need to conquer Mars. We need to remember how to *deserve* and *preserve* Earth. The air thickens, the seas rise, the bees vanish, and our collective response is to build better helmets.

Every resource we're pouring into terraforming red dust could be used to re-terraform our own blue miracle. The technology to sustain a high-quality of life on Earth already exists. It's called *community.* It's called *regeneration.* It's called *cooperation with biology instead of domination over it.*

We could restore forests, balance carbon, reinvent food systems, and redesign cities to breathe again. We could build societies where people have clean air, safe water, and time to feel sunlight on their skin. That's not science fiction. That's tomorrow if we wanted it, but we don't, because it's not new. Novelty is our drug, and we've been trained to destroy the Garden of Eden and the rest of paradise with it to get a fresh hit.

I once asked an investor why he was putting billions into space travel instead of Earth conservation. He smiled, that soft Silicon Valley smile that hides terror under teeth, and said,

"Because the ROI on Mars could be infinite."

That's the dopamine loop again. Infinite potential, zero presence.

He didn't want to save humanity. He wanted to be first in line for the next dopamine high.

Earning money activates the same dopamine-driven reward systems in the brain as insufflating a line of cocaine [35-37]. It's powerful, addictive, and equally dangerous in the way that it distorts our priorities and decision-making.

Here's the truth no one wants to print on a T-shirt:

We don't need to go anywhere to find wonder.

We're standing on it.

We don't want to leave Earth because it's uninhabitable.

We want to leave because it's *demanding.*

Earth requires relationship, boundaries, and reciprocity. You can't dominate a planet that keeps reminding you that you're alive and achieve a good outcome.

Space offers a fantasy of control.

No ecosystems to respect.

No claims to land to argue with.

No consequences you can't throw money at to fix.

It's the ultimate optimization dream. And the ultimate dissociation.

Earth is the only known place in the universe where consciousness evolved to witness itself in physical form. We are the miracle, and we're too distracted to notice.

The cure for the cosmic escape plan isn't more exploration. It's awe. Awe doesn't require altitude. Transcendence doesn't require escape velocity.

You can find it by standing barefoot on the ground long enough for your nervous system to remember gravity is holding you without effort. By watching sunlight hit leaves and realizing that the fusion reactor is already online, free, reliable, and not trying to monetize your attention.

Step outside at dawn and listen to the sound of the world waking up. Touch the dirt that made your neurons, the microbes that trained your immune system, the roots that outlive empires. That's eternity through presence. You don't have to fly to Mars to find it. You just need to *be here now.*

The Cosmic Escape Plan isn't evil. It's terrified.

It's what happens when a culture loses trust in its ability to repair, to feel, and to coexist, and starts looking for exits instead of answers. Unfortunately, there is no eject button in a human being.

Wherever you go, there you are.

The irony is almost too perfect.

We're searching the cosmos for signs of life while ignoring the one system that made life possible in the first place.

We're chasing the stars while forgetting how to sit still on the only planet we know of to date that can love us back.

And it's consequential because this is an expensive search that consumes a tremendous amount of Earth's precious resources, further accelerating climate change that is rapidly making the Earth inhospitable to humans.

So, to all the billionaires out there, I say this with love:

You don't need to save humanity by leaving the Earth.

You need to remember how to stay.

We don't need new planets.

We need new priorities.

And we need your help to see those priorities through so you can continue to live in a world where you can spend your hard-earned dough.

Like all things in life, outer space exploration is much better, more fun, and less damaging to the Earth's environment when it is motivated by pure discovery rather than a desperation to colonize a new planetary apartment building from scratch.

The primary problem isn't that we're running out of worlds (although we do only have one of those at the moment that is habitable). It's that we're running out of wonder for the one we already have.

CHAPTER 12
Chemical Comforts

Everything in excess is opposed to nature.
Hippocrates (460–375 BCE)

The modern pharmacy is no longer a place; it's a planet. Orbiting around us are satellites of serotonin, dopamine, GABA, and glutamate, each promising salvation in capsule form. We live in an age of chemical abundance, and yet no one seems to feel right.

Every decade has its drug of choice, but the twenty-first century has refused to choose.

We want all of them. Sedatives to sleep, stimulants to wake, psychedelics to remember how to feel, anesthetics to forget. A bespoke neurochemical wardrobe for every mood.

This is *Chemical Comforts*, the oldest pal in the human project of avoiding feeling.

I see it every day in the clinic.

Executives on amphetamines, anxious parents on benzodiazepines, students toggling between Adderall and alcohol, artists microdosing mushrooms to stay inspired, veterans self-medicating with ketamine and cannabis because they can't get the treatments they so desperately need at the VA.

Everyone is just trying to feel *something*, or nothing at all.

The problem isn't that people use drugs; humans have always used drugs. The question we should be asking is *why*? Because these days, it's generally not for communion or healing or ceremony, but for calibration; for relief from pain and discomfort. For escape, but there is no escape. There is only more life when we get back from the drug-induced reprieve.

DR. DAVE'S MINDBLOWER #29

Pain is an unavoidable feature of adaptive biological systems from reptiles to humans.

Suffering emerges when pain is resisted, suppressed, or interpreted as threat rather than information.

The sedatives came first. Opioids, benzodiazepines, Z-drugs, and barbiturates before them. Each generation promises safety, sleep, and relief.

They work beautifully, until they don't. And they are highly habit-forming. They blunt not only anxiety, but also curiosity; not only panic, but also presence. Stay on them long enough, and at best you'll stop dreaming and have impaired judgment, at worst you can develop REM suppression, memory fragmentation, emotional flattening, and have a greater likelihood of developing dementia [38-41]. Not to mention the withdrawal syndromes that feel like you're dying (or that actually kill you in the case of benzodiazepines).

With studies like that, and the opioid and benzo epidemic we're currently facing, it shouldn't surprise anyone that dementia is more common than ever.

Then came the stimulants, dressed up as productivity tools.

Amphetamines, methylphenidate, modafinil, every pill a tiny applause for the prefrontal cortex [40]. Focus like a laser, appetite gone, sleep optional.

Then comes the crash: dopamine depletion, irritability, cardiac strain, a nervous system so exhausted that it starts to forget [41].

We've medicalized the bipolarity of capitalism itself. Speed up to produce, slow down to recover, repeat until collapse.

And then, somewhere between burnout and the abyss, came the psychedelics. Our shimmering hope, our chemical sacraments of reconnection. Psilocybin, LSD, MDMA, and DMT: Some of our most powerful healing tools repackaged in slide decks and investment rounds.

Psychedelics used properly really do open doors. Neuroplasticity blooms, fear circuits can loosen, safety can be amplified, and the self dissolves into something bigger [44, 45].

But even here, the modern reflex to optimize infects the sacred. People chase enlightenment like a weekend hack. Dose, integrate, monetize. Set and setting replaced by schedule and ROI.

We're trying to microdose our way out of macro-dysregulation.

DR. DAVE'S MINDBLOWER #30

A regulated nervous system experiences wonder without novelty. A dysregulated one requires constant escalation.

Statistically, substance misuse and abuse are climbing across every category [46-48]. The National Institute on Drug Abuse reports opioid overdoses went up over 300% between 2011 and 2023. Overdose deaths involving stimulants among adults are up over 600% since 2015, and psychedelic self-experimentation is doubling in urban populations [49-51].

"Unintentional poisoning," mostly driven by opioid overdoses, now kills more Americans each year than car accidents and is the leading cause of accidental death in America [52]. Most of them are quiet deaths, respiratory failure behind closed doors, hearts that simply forgot how to beat at 3 a.m. I've lost several physician colleagues under forty. No one is immune.

Even the survivors walk around chemically haunted. The nervous system adapts to whatever relief it's offered; remove the compound, and reality itself feels underdosed.

Pharmacology was supposed to be a means of liberation from suffering.

Instead, it became an arms race against discomfort.

We replaced ritual with dosage, community with prescription, and meaning with mechanism.

I don't blame the molecules.

They're just tools, neutral, ancient, indifferent.

It's our relationship with them that's pathological.

When I guide patients through psychedelic-assisted therapy, the medicine is the least important ingredient. What heals is context: safety, presence, intention, integration.

The medicine amplifies safety in the psychotherapeutic context to accelerate healing.

The same molecules that awaken empathy in ceremony can destroy it in isolation.

DR. DAVE'S MINDBLOWER #31

A chronically activated dopamine system suppresses the nervous system's ability to feel contentment. Without pauses, the brain never receives the signal: "We are safe now."

Here's what the data and the body keep telling us:

Psychedelic drugs don't create states that don't exist.

They amplify what's already there [53].

If what's inside is chaos, the trip will be chaos.

If what's inside is longing for connection, the medicine will show you every reason you've forgotten how to love.

That's the paradox of Chemical Comforts: the more we use them to escape ourselves, the more they remind us of what we're escaping.

The real crisis isn't addiction.

It's *alienation.*

We've engineered a world that dysregulates the nervous system by design, then shames people for reaching for chemical rescue. We sell the wound, then the salve.

If we built societies that honored rest, touch, community, and purpose, we would prevent mental illness before it happened.

So yes, keep studying psychedelics.

Keep prescribing antidepressants when they save lives.

Keep using ketamine in clinics and coffee for creativity.

But let's stop pretending any molecule can make pain disappear forever or replace the relationship between brain and body, self and world, one human and another.

Drugs can show us the door.

Only connection can teach us how to walk through it.

And maybe that's the point history keeps trying to whisper through our neurotransmitters:

The chemistry was never the cure.

It was just the conversation-starter.

CHAPTER 13
The Age of Augmentation

Emancipate yourselves from mental slavery; none but ourselves can free our minds.
Marcus Garvey (1887–1940)

The machines aren't coming for our souls.

They don't want your job, your art, or your lover.

They don't *want* anything.

That's the part most people miss.

Artificial Intelligence (AI) is not our replacement; it's an academic field of inquiry. AI products are our reflection. A mirror polished with silicon and code, showing us what we value most by what we choose to automate, and right now, that reflection is nervous.

We've built machines that can compose symphonies, diagnose cancer, generate empathy in customer service chats, and write songs, poems, and essays that sound suspiciously like humans.

But somewhere between awe and panic, we forgot something important:

The goal of the field of AI isn't to create products that feel for us. *It's meant to free us to feel again.*

The goal was never to build a better therapist, or teacher, or lover.

The goal was to build better *tools* so that humans could spend more time *being* human.

DR. DAVE'S MINDBLOWER #32

AI amplifies pattern recognition without context. The human nervous system supplies the context with emotional meaning, whether we realize it or not. AI products reflect the intention of those who build them. AI products cannot destroy humanity unless we build them to do so. Humans remain humanity's greatest threat to survival.

There's a dangerous delusion rising in the fog of progress: the idea that AI should fill the spaces where humans have failed each other. AI therapy bots, companions, girlfriends and boyfriends who never argue, never age, and never ask for rent. It's comfort on demand. The next dopamine economy.

It's not connection. It's simulation. And as we've already seen, simulation without soul breeds more loneliness, not less. When I talk to technologists about this, I tell them the nervous system doesn't just crave communication, it craves *resonance.*

You can't outsource resonance.

An algorithm can mimic empathy, but it can't *embody* it. It can simulate compassion, but it can't sweat, shake, or weep with you.

Empathy without embodiment is theater. Therapy without presence is noise.

AI products can guide you to a mirror, but they cannot meet you there.

The real opportunity, the sane, beautiful, necessary opportunity, is augmentation, not substitution.

AI as *co-pilot*, not caretaker.

As *translator*, not preacher.

As a *partner in cognition*, not a counterfeit soul.

My esteemed colleague Dr. Ken Ford, PhD, a world-renowned AI expert and CEO emeritus at The Florida Institute for Human and

Machine Cognition, who has served as the Director of NASA and Scientific Advisor to President George W. Bush, describes AI as "augmented intelligence." Its goal is not to replicate human intelligence and all its foibles, like fear, jealousy, and shame, but to make it better, like a teammate who's always looking out for us. A teammate who sees our blind spots and informs us pre-emptively, so we don't run into the guy creeping up behind us when we're changing lanes too quickly.

DR. DAVE'S MINDBLOWER #33

When we let machines decide everything, our bodies stop learning how to make decisions. Thinking is a muscle. So is judgment. If you don't use them, you lose them, even with the smartest tools.

AI can be leveraged to amplify what's sacred about being human: our creativity, our curiosity, our capacity to collaborate. Imagine an AI product that helps teachers teach with more empathy by handling the bureaucracy that drains them. Imagine doctors freed from electronic paperwork, with hours restored to listen and provide medical care. Imagine an engineer who builds better cities because a wearable AI tool helped her sleep soundly through the night so she could dream about light and wind.

That's augmentation. The amplification of wisdom, not its replacement.

In neuroscience, we call this *distributed cognition*: intelligence as an ecosystem, not an ego.

Brains, bodies, tools, and environments all working together in a feedback loop. Humans evolved the profound intelligence we have today through cooperation, through collective problem-solving, and shared attention. Our brain's insula (the emotional recognition and memory center) at work.

AI is just the next tool in that lineage.

It's the modern equivalent of fire: powerful, dangerous, sacred.

Used wisely, it expands consciousness.

Used recklessly, it burns civilizations to the ground.

Here's what I tell my colleagues when they panic about AI therapy bots:

AI should not replace human therapists. It should make them better.

It can handle pattern recognition, data analysis, and, to some extent, triage. It can process physiological data in real time, like heart rate, breathing, and sleep, to help clinicians know when the body is saying something the mouth can't. It can spot patterns invisible to human intuition, but it should hand them *to* human intuition, not replace it.

The sacred act of healing still requires two nervous systems in resonance.

No algorithm can replace that trembling, awkward, beautiful moment when one human says to another, "I see you. Let's breathe through this together."

It would be wise to create AI products to clean oceans, cure chronic illnesses, balance grids, feed people, design systems that restore biodiversity, translate languages, and eliminate the soul-crushing inefficiencies that keep billions of humans too exhausted to dream.

It would be unwise to use AI to simulate jealousy, anger, resentment, deception, or love. The former four are common sense. No one in their right mind would want more jealousy and deception in the world. We have too much of that to handle as it is.

But love, the real kind, the embodied, inconvenient, unconditional kind, is not a dataset. It's an act of courage performed by imperfect creatures trying to remember they're not alone.

AI can help us rediscover that courage by taking the drudgery off our backs, not the humanity out of our hearts. That's the bargain worth keeping.

One day, if we are wise, AI will be remembered not as the invention that replaced us, but as the one that facilitated our emancipation from mental slavery.

The age of augmentation isn't about building gods. It's about building *gardens.* Environments where intelligence (biological, digital, and collective) grows together in rhythm instead of competition. A world where machines do the work, and humans do the living.

Because the true measure of progress isn't whether machines can think like humans. It's whether humans can remember how to feel again.

CHAPTER 14
The Immortality Hustle

You could leave life right now. Let that determine what you do and say and think.
Marcus Aurelius

Death has terrible PR.

No onboarding materials.

No user manual.

No customer service hotline.

So naturally, we've decided to fire it.

Welcome to the *Immortality Hustle*. The belief that aging is a bug, mortality is optional, and with enough data, discipline, supplements, stem cells, and money, we can finally outrun the one thing no organism has ever escaped.

Not transcend it.

Outrun it.

The pitch is seductive.

Optimize your biomarkers.

Reverse your genetic age.

Track every molecule.

Meditate like a monk.

Sleep like a baby.

Eat like a caveman.

Exercise like a demigod.

Live forever, or at least long enough to sell the story. Longevity has become a performance art, and like all good hustles, it confuses *extension* with *avoidance.*

Humans have always feared death. That part is not new.

What's new is the belief that this fear can be solved with spreadsheets. It's a strange thing, watching people try to outsmart death with spreadsheets.

We used to accept mortality with a kind of sacred resignation. Build pyramids, write poems, drink wine, raise children, and hope for a decent afterlife. Now we treat it like a solvable engineering problem.

This is the Immortality Hustle, the newest and most lucrative delusion in medicine.

DR. DAVE'S MINDBLOWER #34

Aging is not a disease process to be cured; it is a systems-level adaptation unfolding over time.

Pathologizing aging as anything other than a natural, inevitable process of growth accelerates aging by increasing our perception of threat toward the inevitable, thereby increasing stress and inflammation. Chronic stress and inflammation dramatically accelerate aging. Safety and healthy vagus nerve activity significantly slow aging. Aging cannot be "reversed."

Everywhere I look, people are lining up for the next new experimental treatment that promises to "reverse aging." Despite few, if any, safeguards, they chase immortality with fasting apps, psychedelics, IV drips of NAD, and stem cells. Some billionaires even routinely transfuse young blood like vampires...

Death, to these folks, is just poor planning.

They talk about *escape velocity*, the theoretical moment when medical science outpaces decay. Live long enough, and you'll live forever. Just another quarter, another funding round, another pill.

It's the same old religion with a better logo.

It's one thing to get these treatments from a trusted, regulated clinic in the United States or Europe to decrease inflammation, improve your health, and live a better life. Particularly if you are struggling with a chronic intractable illness and are guided by a licensed physician.

It's a completely different, and significantly riskier, thing to receive these treatments from an unregulated American clinic, or to travel to Mexico or Central America for the purposes of reversing aging or achieving immortality. Intention matters. The latter is a process of desperation to avoid the inevitable that can actually increase your chances of early expiration.

I've been an invited speaker to some of these longevity conferences, the temples of techno-eternalism.

Everyone's wearing crisp white sneakers and talking about autophagy over gluten-free muffins. They're not scientists trained in interpreting highly nuanced peer-reviewed studies, yet they quote the latest *Nature* papers as if they were scripture.

"Did you see the new study on peptides?"

"Yes, but what about mitochondrial uncouplers?"

"Have you tried metformin?"

It's not conversation; it's a biochemical arms race.

One man told me that he is "biologically twenty-seven" according to his telomerase biological clock. He was sixty-three chronologically and looked like an overcooked almond.

He said it with pride, but I could see it in his eyes. That unmistakable shimmer of terror. The kind of terror that money can't anesthetize.

Longevity, as they sell it, isn't about living. It's about *not dying*.

It's fear in designer sneakers. A trillion-dollar tantrum against entropy.

We forget that aging isn't a disease. It's the body's poetry, the nervous system's evolving narrative of time. The creases, the aches, and the slowing down aren't failures of biology; they're the texture of existence.

To erase aging is to erase meaning.

You can't have wisdom without a little wear.

I met a woman once, a geneticist, brilliant, sleepless, who told me she was terrified of losing her memory. She'd sequenced her own genome, mapped her telomere length, quantified her risk for Alzheimer's, and much more. She could tell you, to the percentage point, how afraid she was.

When I asked what she wanted most, she said, "To remember everything."

"Even the pain?" I asked.

She paused. "Maybe not that."

That's the deal, isn't it? You don't get to edit the human condition. You can't cherry-pick immortality. Every memory, every scar, every moment of decay is part of what makes consciousness both bearable and beautiful.

The irony is that the pursuit of eternal youth is aging us faster. I know biohackers who sleep four hours a night, testing supplements that might extend life. They measure their telomeres monthly, which cannot possibly be good for their telomeres. They're actually quite shy.

So many are living in a permanent state of stress about dying, and stress, as any good doctor will tell you, is the fastest way to die.

DR. DAVE'S MINDBLOWER #35

Impermanence increases meaningfulness and value-based decision-making. Meaning emerges from constraint, not infinity. In other words, if everything lasted forever, everything would become boring quite quickly.

We've built an economy where anxiety itself accelerates aging, and the cure is to buy more anxiety in capsule form.

It's the perfect business model.

There's something tragic about it, though. This desperate attempt to escape impermanence in a universe made of it.

We were never meant to live forever. We were meant to *live fully.*

There's a difference.

Longevity without presence is just duration.

Existence without decay is machinery, not life.

If we strip away mortality, we strip away the urgency that gives love its shape. The clock is what makes every heartbeat worth something.

Sometimes, late at night, I think about the patients I've lost. The ones who didn't make it, the ones who taught me what healing really means. None of them wanted forever. They just wanted *more now.*

That's the paradox of the Immortality Hustle: in trying to escape death, we forget how to be alive.

The goal isn't to live longer, but to live *deeper.*

To inhabit the present so fully that time slows on its own.

To feel every breath, every tremor, every flicker of awe that reminds you this moment will never happen again.

That's the real longevity protocol: presence, connection, curiosity, joy.

The same medicine that's been keeping us alive for two hundred thousand years: breath, touch, laughter, wonder, and play.

No patents pending.

DR. DAVE'S MINDBLOWER #36

Physiological resilience and health span are enhanced by variability and diversity, not the endless pursuit of perfection. Nervous systems that learn to tolerate fluctuation and dynamics survive and thrive longer than those that resist it. Perfect is the enemy of the good.

So go ahead and drink the green smoothies, take the vitamins, get a couple extra lab tests, and track your biomarkers if it makes you happy, but don't let the pursuit of eternal youth steal your only life.

Because the truth, whispered quietly beneath all the data and denial, is that mortality isn't the problem. It's the miracle.

The clock is the drumbeat of existence.

Without it, the song doesn't play.

CHAPTER 15
The Oldest Wisdom We Forgot

We are all visitors to this time, this place. We are just passing through. Our purpose here is to observe, to learn, to grow, to love.
Aboriginal Australian proverb (est. 40,000 BCE)

In the end, it turns out the answer was here the whole time.

Buried not in the cloud, not in the algorithm; not in our data, but under our feet.

The oldest teaching humanity has ever received.

The one we've spent the last few centuries actively ignoring:

Take care of yourself and the Earth.

They are the same thing.

This wasn't whispered through microdosing retreats or crypto conferences. It was carved into the psyche of every Indigenous culture on the planet long before we invented rockets and panic disorders.

Now, after sprinting headlong into our beautifully engineered anxiety machine, modern science has finally circled back around and said, "Ah. Yes. They were right."

Funny how that works.

Indigenous wisdom has always been annoyingly ahead of the curve.

They didn't need brain scans or lab tests to understand symbiosis.

They had something better: attention.

Long, uninterrupted, reverent attention to the land that fed them, held them, raised them.

They speak of Mother Earth, Pachamama, the Web of Life, not as a metaphor, but a literal cosmology.

Everything is connected.

Everything alive.

Everything owed respect because everything is kin.

Meanwhile, modern humanity, armed with satellites and sensors, is only just now catching up to the idea that destroying your habitat is not a sustainable business model.

You don't need a doctorate to figure this out, but it helps if you have a pulse.

Science, with all its brilliance and neuroses, has now mapped what Indigenous cultures never needed to measure:

The health of humans is inseparable from the health of the planet.

Pollute the air → We poison our lungs.

Strip biodiversity → We destabilize the food web and our immune systems.

Erase the forests → We deplete the atmosphere of oxygen and our nervous system's capacity to self-regulate.

Lose connection to nature → Anxiety skyrockets, inflammation rises, depression spreads like wildfire.

Every ecological wound becomes a physiological one.

Every insult to the Earth is a bruise on the human body.

The Earth doesn't take revenge; it just reflects.

We've built a civilization that lives as if we're renting the planet month-to-month, fully refundable, with a crew coming in after we leave to clean up the mess for us.

As if the forests are drive-thru windows and the oceans are bottomless garbage dumps.

As if our microbiome isn't an ecological love letter written by 200,000 years of co-evolution.

Indigenous cultures warned us:

Break the balance, and you break yourself.

We traded reciprocity for extraction.

Attention for convenience.

Reverence for ROI.

And now the bill is coming due in species lost, climates unraveled, and nervous systems fried beyond recognition.

Science now confirms what ceremony always knew:

Nature heals.

Not as a figure of speech, but as physiology.

Touch grass, cortisol drops.

Breathe forest air, joy enters.

Sit by a moving body of water, and the vagus nerve wakes up like your dog that hasn't seen you all day.

Eat fresh, local, organic, unprocessed food, and your microbiome sings ancient hymns of gratitude.

The Earth is medicine, and we are withdrawal patients wandering around with no detox plan.

Climate change is not the Earth attacking us.

It's the Earth clearing its throat, asking,

"Are you sure this is the way you want this to go down?"

The storms, the fires, the floods are not prophecies.

They're feedback loops.

Physics doing what physics does best when hubris outpaces wisdom.

So, where does that leave us?

With the simplest, hardest prescription ever written:

Respect the Earth.

Respect your body.

They are the same conversation.

Our nervous systems are not a separate ecosystem from the planet; they're a fractal of it.

Our breath is borrowed atmosphere.

Our bones are repurposed rocks.

Our microbiome is the Earth's whispering choir living inside us, tuning us to the key of life.

Indigenous cultures never forgot this.

Thanks to billions of our tax dollars, modern science has finally remembered.

Now it's our turn to live like we understand it (and like we paid for it).

If humanity has any hope, real hope (not the dopamine kind), it won't come from Mars colonies or optimizing the mitochondria of billionaires. It will come from rediscovering the original contract:

Take care of the world that takes care of you.

Connection isn't a wellness trend.

Stewardship isn't activism.

Self-care isn't indulgence.

They're survival instincts we were all born with.

Biological imperatives.

The original roadmap home.

Because, relatively speaking, the Earth isn't fragile.

We are.

And if we're wise, if we can humble ourselves enough to finally learn to listen to the voices we were taught to silence, we might just remember that the greatest technology ever created wasn't AI, or the rocket, or the psychedelic molecule.

It was the planet itself.

Our first teacher.

Our oldest healer.

Our only shot.

CONCLUSION
The Diagnosis and Treatment Plan

Nature is pleased with simplicity. And nature is no dummy.
Sir Isaac Newton (1643–1727)

There is a core principle from the fourteenth century that has quietly guided our most important scientific discoveries, from physics to biology to medicine. It is known as Occam's Razor: when multiple explanations exist, the simplest one that requires the fewest assumptions, yet still accounts for all the evidence, is most likely to be true. This works because unnecessary complexity often signals that we are missing a deeper, unifying pattern. This is a foundational principle for rational critical thinking.

In medicine, Occam's Razor shaped our diagnostic method from fragmented symptom-based thinking toward unified mechanisms. Instead of treating fever, cough, and fatigue as separate problems, we learned to recognize the signs of infection. Instead of naming dozens of unrelated syndromes, we discovered shared biological pathways, from inflammation to neurotransmitter imbalance to autonomic dysregulation. The goal is not reductionism for its own sake, but for clarity, because clearer models lead to more effective and compassionate care by getting to the root of the problem.

So now, after the zoo tour, the social experiments, the dopamine traps, the burnout rituals, the chemical comforts, the space fantasies, the AI dreams, and the immortality hustles, I want to offer the diagnosis that only becomes visible now.

Not for an individual patient. I'm talking about a working diagnosis for much of our species. A clinical impression that only emerges after you've watched the same patterns repeat across millions of lives, across generations, and across cultures that swear they're different while doing the same self-harm with better branding.

To do so, I am applying Occam's Razor to a question that modern medicine has largely avoided asking directly: what if many of the chronic health conditions we treat as distinct are actually different expressions of the same underlying unhealed trauma process? A continuum of behaviors rooted in the human drive for safety, certainty, attention, and meaning, expressed through the body when those needs are repeatedly unmet or misunderstood.

The diagnosis is uncomfortable, which is usually how you know you're close to the truth.

Münchausen syndrome.

Yes. That Münchausen syndrome.

One of the most ominous diagnoses in psychiatry precisely because there is no pill that fixes it, no quick procedure that resolves it, no lab value that redeems it. A diagnosis that forces us to look not at the symptom, but at *the story underneath* it.

Allow me to explain, now that you've seen everything else.

In medicine, Münchausen syndrome, now politely renamed *factitious disorder imposed on self*, refers to a pattern in which a person intentionally produces, exaggerates, or sustains illness. This is not for money or to avoid responsibility, but for something far more human and far more primal: care, attention, and validation [54].

The suffering is real.

The damage is real.

The motivation, generally unconscious, is to be seen, heard, held, and taken seriously.

The body becomes the message.

This syndrome was first described in the second century by Claudius Galen, a Roman physician, and then again in 1951 by Richard Asher, who named it after Baron von Münchhausen, the fictional nobleman famous for extravagant, self-inflicted tales of heroism and disaster [55]. The irony was never subtle. Patients would tell increasingly elaborate stories of illness, sometimes going so far as to inject themselves with bacteria, poison their own blood, or submit to unnecessary surgeries just to remain in the patient role [56].

That's the textbook version.

Western medicine, bless its brilliant, reductionist heart, is exceptional at diagnosing and treating crises. However, when the crises turn chronic, we are far less comfortable asking why they persist.

If you trace the story backward far enough, Münchausen syndrome is less about well-disguised self-deception and much more about desperation. It emerges from an especially common brand of trauma. The trauma where care is conditional, affection is inconsistent, and worth is earned through suffering rather than granted through existence [57].

By now, after getting this far into this book, that should sound painfully familiar.

Let's zoom all the way out.

What if our entire culture has been trained, slowly and, in all likelihood, accidentally, to believe that we are not worthy of rest, love, or attention unless something is wrong with us?

What if we learned early on that productivity earns praise, calm earns tolerance, but *being well*, truly well, content, embodied, and satisfied earns responsibility, expectations, and suspicion at best, and abandonment at worst?

What if illness became the last socially acceptable way to ask for care?

Welcome, belatedly, to the waiting room of modern civilization.

Look around.

We knowingly eat food that inflames us.

We knowingly design cities that overwhelm and isolate us.

We knowingly build and misuse technologies that hijack our nervous systems.

We knowingly sacrifice sleep, touch, pleasure, and presence, and act shocked when anxiety, depression, autoimmune disease, addiction, and burnout explode across the population.

We scroll ourselves into panic.

We caffeinate ourselves into exhaustion.

We medicate ourselves into numbness.

And then we line up, palms out, saying: "Help me! Something is wrong!"

Something is wrong, but not in the way we think.

In classic Münchausen syndrome, the patient unconsciously believes:

I am only worthy of care when I am sick.

In modern culture, we didn't just adopt that belief.

We automated it at an industrial scale.

We turned it into an operating system.

The evidence is no longer subtle.

As of 2021, over 359 million people worldwide carried a diagnosis of an anxiety disorder [58]. This is expected to grow to 515 million people by 2040 [59]. Depression is now a leading cause of disability worldwide. Burnout is now recognized by the World Health Organization [20]. Chronic inflammatory diseases, once rare, are now routine [60]. Personality disorders are more prevalent [61]. Substance misuse and overdose rates have grown substantially and span sedatives, stimulants, opioids, alcohol, and psychedelics, all used as emotional prosthetics to distract or numb us in a world that refuses to slow down [47-48].

And here's the part we avoid because it makes everyone squirm:

Much of this suffering is behaviorally reinforced.

Sick people get time off.

Sick people get sympathy.

Sick people get permission to stop performing.

Healthy people?

Healthy people are expected to keep producing.

This isn't a moral failure.

It's conditioning.

In behavioral psychology, we call this *secondary gain*, the indirect benefits that reinforce illness over time [62]. We recognize that when care is inconsistent or conditional, the nervous system learns extreme strategies to secure attachment [63].

If being regulated doesn't get you tender love and care, but being dysregulated does, guess what the body learns to do?

Münchausen syndrome doesn't arise in a vacuum.

It emerges from attachment wounds.

Children who grow up unseen, emotionally neglected, or valued only for performance often learn a dangerous lesson:

My needs are a burden; my suffering is evidence.

Over time, the nervous system stops asking directly for connection and care, and starts speaking through symptoms: pain, illness, GI distress, collapse [64].

Fast-forward several centuries, and scale that dynamic across an entire economy built on scarcity, comparison, and productivity worship.

We didn't just teach people to ignore their bodies.

We taught them that their bodies are only worth listening to when they break.

Once you step back and look at the pattern, it becomes hard to unsee. This is not random pathology. This is learned self-harm in a culture that forgot how to nurture itself.

That's my diagnosis.

What I'm describing is not a single disorder so much as a continuum; a behavioral and cultural spectrum I'm calling *Münchausen Spectrum Disorder* (MSD).

On one end are the people who are only *mildly* implicated: those of us who learned that stress, overwork, and self-neglect are the price of belonging. Taking time for ourselves feels indulgent. We regularly ignore sleep, override hunger, suppress emotion, push through pain, and then feel a strange sense of relief when the body finally forces us to stop.

Illness becomes permission.

Collapse becomes care.

This is *Münchausen's on the spectrum*: quiet, socially sanctioned, often applauded.

Move farther along, and the pattern becomes harder to ignore. We repeatedly place ourselves in harmful environments, relationships, or habits, knowing, somewhere beneath the surface, that suffering will bring attention, structure, care, or meaning we don't know how to access directly. The body becomes the résumé. Symptoms become identity. Healing threatens relevance.

At the far extreme sits the darkest variant: Münchausen's by proxy, scaled beyond the individual and woven into culture itself. This is where attention, meaning, or pleasure is derived not just from one's own suffering, but from the suffering of others, also described as *Schadenfreude*. It shows up as moral outrage, addiction, doom-scrolling, public shaming rituals, and the quiet dopamine hit of watching someone else fail, fall, or fracture.

Schadenfreude isn't just cruelty; it's outsourced Münchausen behavior.

I don't have to bleed if you will.

As the saying goes, misery loves company.

Social media supercharges this end of the spectrum. Algorithms reward indignation. News cycles monetize catastrophe. Entire industries profit from keeping us fixated on pain, ours or someone else's. The nervous system learns that distress equals engagement, and engagement equals worth.

Seen this way, MSD isn't rare. It's pervasive. It's what happens when a species is trained to believe that wellness is invisible, patience is boring, and only suffering deserves witness.

The tragedy is not that we're broken. It's that we adapted brilliantly to a system that mistook pain for proof of life, but here is the part worth ending on.

There *is* hope.

In individual Münchausen syndrome, the evidence-based treatment approach is surprisingly consistent. You don't confront. You don't shame. You don't rip away the symptom and demand health.

You do three things (and medication isn't one of them) [56, 57,65]:

You establish safety without requiring illness.

You provide consistent, non-contingent care with genuine concern and compassion.

You help the patient learn direct ways to ask for attention, connection, and support.

In other words, you teach the nervous system that it does not need to suffer to belong.

Now imagine applying that at scale.

A society that offers rest before collapse.

Connection before loneliness.

Pleasure before suffering.

A culture that rewards regulation instead of burnout.

A childhood that teaches feeling before performing.

A healthcare system that measures success not by symptom suppression, but by restored capacity for joy, curiosity, and connection.

That's what this book has been pointing toward the whole time.

Not ideology or utopia, but a clinical intervention accessible to us all.

Because if the diagnosis is cultural Münchausen Spectrum Disorder, trauma-induced self-inflicted illness in exchange for care, then the cure is both embarrassingly simple and profoundly difficult:

Teach people they are worthy without bleeding.

Teach nervous systems how to settle without collapsing.

Teach communities how to co-regulate rather than competing.

Teach technology to give us back our time instead of stealing our attention.

Teach medicine to listen as carefully as it measures.

I did not write this guide to accuse humanity. We're all in this together.

I wrote it because, clinically speaking, we are a population that has been trying our best to survive in the only ways we were taught.

And survival strategies look pathological when they outlive the conditions that created them.

If we're willing to see that, *really* see it, then fear and loathing don't have to be the final diagnoses.

They can be the presenting symptoms.

And for the first time in a long time, that means we might finally be ready to heal.

BOOK 2

THE SOLUTION—THE WAY HOME

CHAPTER 1
You Are a Human Being

When I let go of what I am, I become what I might be.
Lao Tzu (6th century BCE)

You are a *human being*, not a human doing.

Yet somewhere between your third calendar app and that unread mindfulness book, you forgot how to just...*be*.

You've been busy! Running errands, paying bills, and overthinking that one thing you said in a meeting three weeks ago. You've been achieving, scrolling, and surviving, which is impressive, really, but also exhausting.

To be human, truly and fully, means remembering that your worth is not tied to productivity. You don't have to earn the right to exist by crossing items off a to-do list.

You are allowed to just be.

Your brain has two primary gears [1, 2]: *doing mode* (task-based, goal-oriented) and *being mode* (open, listening, present, self-aware, receiving). Most of us are stuck in doing, which makes sense. It's rewarded. You get gold stars. Paychecks. Approval from your dentist.

However, being mode is where peace and power both live. It's where awe, empathy, and creativity bloom. It's where we learn. It's your brain and body doing what they do best: listening quietly, reflecting, imagining, connecting, and daydreaming. When you pause and *just exist*, allowing yourself to stop doing things for a moment, you're not lazy. You're being a fully operational human being.

When you're fully present, time expands [3, 4]. A single deep breath can feel like a whole minute. Watching a bird land on a branch can feel like a gift from the universe. That's presence. That's being. Kids do it all the time. Dogs do it constantly. You used to do it too because it's our actual default. It's where you are at your absolute best because 100% of you is here now.

To be human is to inhabit your body. Not just drag it around like a poorly packed suitcase. Your mind can be anywhere (past, present, or future), but your body always exists in the right here and right now.

When you listen to your body and feel the hunger, fatigue, tension, and the tingles, you reconnect with your intuition, the real-time feedback system built into your nervous system [5].

Breathe. Stretch. Yawn. Wiggle your toes in the grass. Just notice your body.

Boom!

You're there!

And what's on the other side?

Stillness. The most forgotten superpower.

Stillness isn't "doing nothing." It's active noticing. It's choosing to listen rather than react right away. Stillness gives your nervous system a chance to downshift from fight-or-flight into rest-and-digest [6]. It's not weakness. It's a mega flex. Especially in a world that's constantly screaming at you to hustle.

The elegance is in the simplicity. We can train ourselves to be patiently comfortable with stillness simply by reminding ourselves that it's okay to do nothing at all in this moment. When we understand stillness as the goal, we realize that patience is, ironically, the lowest effort skill to master.

Here's a secret to stillness that monks, therapists, and neuroscientists agree on:

You are not your thoughts. You are the awareness behind your thoughts.

The part of you that notices the thoughts racing by like subway trains, without having to ride every single one to the end of the line.

When you start to notice that you are the observer, the one who has awareness of your thoughts without attachment to them, you begin to become more aware of yourself and the world around you. You also begin to gain a clearer understanding of what you know and what you don't know (Figure 3). What is already automated and what still requires effort. As you can see in the Pie Chart of Knowing, there is a lot more to discover than we may have originally considered.

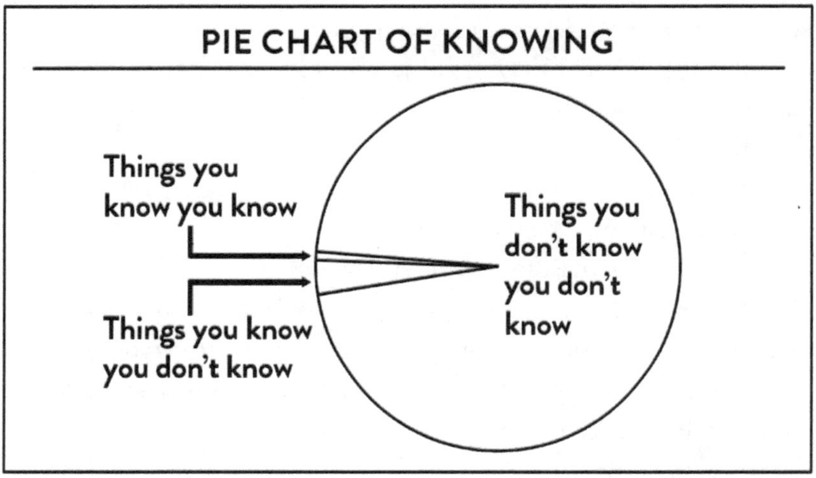

Figure 3. The Pie Chart of Knowing

Meditation, breathing, stretching, soothing touch, Apollo Neuro, and the other practices described in this book help you access this *observer mind*, the you behind the mental chatter. The more time you spend there, the less power your inner critic has and the more inner peace you find.

Turns out, not everything your brain says is true. Shocking, I know. When you spend enough time observing your thoughts to realize that most of them are actually nonsense, that's the first step to letting them go and reclaiming your attention for what is worthy of your time, that which is true and useful to you.

ATTENTION!

Your attention is the single most valuable skill you have. It is the gateway to your awareness. It is where listening starts. Paying attention to something is like inviting that thing into your consciousness. The longer we pay attention to it, the more it becomes concentrated within us (Figure 4).

Whatever you focus on, you resonate with [7]. Our attention is like a spiritual radio dial. Worrying about the future tunes you into chaos. Gratitude for something in the present (e.g., yourself) tunes you into a state of flow. Judgment tunes you into your inner troll. Kindness tunes you into divinity.

All we really have right now is the present moment. The past has already happened, and the future has not yet come to pass. This very moment is the single most important moment of your life. The more time you spend paying attention to this moment, and not the past or the future, the more you will be you, and the more of you will be here now, with us.

Our intuition lives in this moment [5]. It is the you inside you. The voice in our heads that sounds like us, that's waiting for us to listen. It communicates with us and we with it. It wants to be heard. It is our body speaking to us. Like a person, when not acknowledged, it will act out to get our attention. Practice listening to what this moment has to offer you, and you will never be led astray, as this moment contains all the information we need to inform our next move.

As often as you can remember, focus your attention on simply taking in this moment (without doing anything about it). Start by simply listening to your body, the part of us that always lives in the here and now. In doing so, you reclaim all the power that you were born with as a human being. You are a human *being*, not a human doing. When you take back your attention, you set yourself free, and time starts to bend before your eyes.

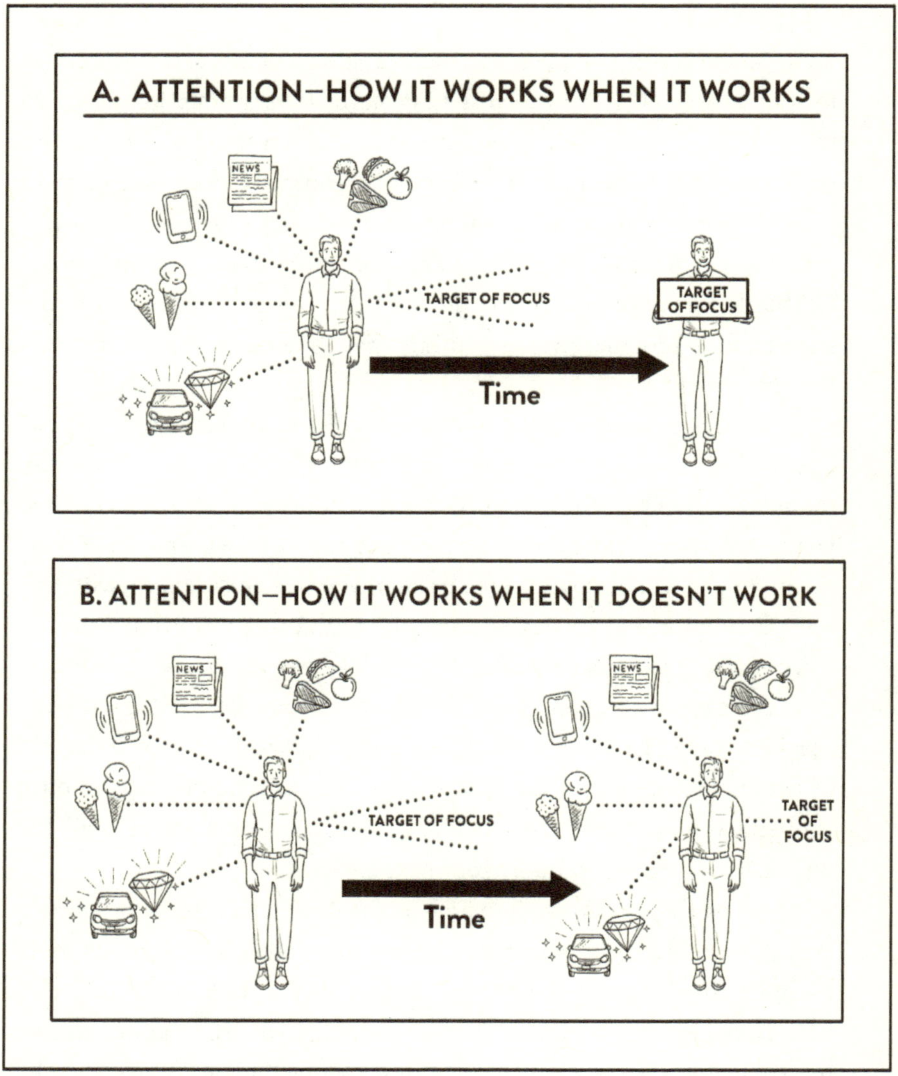

Figure 4. Attention (A) Attention - How it works when it works.
(B) Attention - How it works when it doesn't work.

DR. DAVE'S ESSENTIAL EQUATION #1:

Attention x Time = Concentration

The more we pay attention to something, the more of it is invited into our conscious awareness. The more of that thing that comes into our awareness, the greater percentage of our awareness it occupies, and therefore the more concentrated it is inside of us.

We must also be careful of what we pay attention to because that is what concentrates in us and becomes part of us [7]. In other words, our attention is an invitation to mingle with our energy.

One powerful example is with anxiety, that annoyingly reliable signal that there is uncertainty in our midst: if we focus our attention on things we cannot control (the news, others' thoughts, the weather, etc.) for 50% of the time, the more these things concentrate in us, and we start to feel out of control (and therefore anxious) half of the time. Things outside our control right now are considered *thought vampires.* These vampires are very real, can only come in when invited by our attention, and, once in our consciousness, stick around like houseguests who have overstayed their welcome and suck our energy completely dry. On the contrary, if we spend 90% of our time focusing on things we can control (breathing, movement, listening, touch, etc.), we concentrate those things in us and start to feel in control (and therefore less anxious) 90% of the time.

Another common example is when we're worried about forgetting something. Paying attention to worrying about forgetting something makes it much more likely that we will forget that thing because we are concentrating on "worrying about forgetting" rather than the thing we're trying to remember. If we know that our bodies remember all the important stuff automatically (which they do when we're present and paying attention to what's meaningful to us), then we can sit back and watch our memory improve by spending less time worrying about forgetting. When we let this go, we free up that much more of our attention to be present with experiencing the things we are trying to remember, concentrating them for a greater likelihood of accurate recall.

Your attention is completely within your control, and it all starts with noticing where it is at any moment.

THE POWER OF BREATH

Deep down, we all want to feel safe enough to play, to love freely, to sleep deeply, to be curious, and to be delighted by small things. Things like bubble wrap popping, a dog in sunglasses, or remembering that taking a deep breath feels good and can reset your nervous system in under sixty seconds.

That's right, folks. Intentional breathing (breathing by choice) is how we, supercharged meat-based Wi-Fi beacons of consciousness, can interact with the air to control our attention, our perception of time and space, and our bodies [3, 4]. Slow and deepen your breath, and you can shift heart rate, blood pressure, mood, perception of pain, stress, and even the passage of time itself in any moment [4, 8].

When you choose to breathe with intention, a slow, deep, conscious breath, something strange and beautiful happens: time slows down. Not because you've hacked the space-time continuum, but because you've shifted your attention [3, 4].

With every mindful inhale, you shrink the future and soften the past by reminding your brain's fear and contrast-detection center (the amygdala) that you're safe enough to stop and take a breath [8]. You anchor yourself in the present moment, which just so happens to be the only moment where life actually occurs. One conscious breath is like pressing the pause button on the psychological treadmill of "not enough" and stepping into the calm center of your own *being*, where time bends, slows, and sometimes even disappears.

Indigenous cultures, Buddhist monks, yogis, and Judeo-Christian-Islamic mystics have known for thousands of years that anchoring in the breath returns us to the present moment.

The right now.

The only moment that actually exists. This is also the moment where our true power as human beings shows up, because it's the only moment where choice can happen.

Neuroscience studies now show that intentional breathing alters activity in the Default Mode Network (DMN) [9]. This is a group of brain regions responsible for ego, self-identity, self-protection, self-doubt, and overthinking what that last text really meant [2]. Breathing slows your heart rate [8], modulates cortisol [10], and brings your insula (the emotional recognition and memory center) back online [11]. Over seventy years of biofeedback research has demonstrated the physiological mechanisms beneath what the mystics knew only through experience and intuition [8, 12].

Interacting with the air isn't just about keeping you alive. It teaches you how to *live*. With breath, you reclaim control over your mind, over your entire nervous system, and over your experience of time itself. Turns out the secret to time travel was in your lungs all along.

THE SCIENTIFIC METHOD AS A PATH TO WISDOM

At its core, the scientific method isn't cold or mechanical. It's patient. It is a disciplined way of letting reality speak for itself over time. When you strip away the jargon, science follows a simple hierarchy, one that mirrors how human nervous systems learn what to trust.

It starts with paying attention to something we choose. This is the foundation of listening. Listening invites data. Data are raw observations, measurements, sensations, counts, and signals. By themselves, individual data points are meaningless. A single data point is just noise. Two data points? Now you've got a clue. Three data points? Now you've got a trend. Over time, patterns begin to emerge that become extremely useful.

DR. DAVE'S ESSENTIAL EQUATION #2:

Listening × Time = Data

Over a million trillion things are happening in and around us at any given time. Each of these "happenings" is a data point if we so choose to observe it.

Observation or listening is the first step toward understanding the world around us, so we can collect data to make accurate predictions about our environment.

DR. DAVE'S ESSENTIAL EQUATION #3:

Data × Time = Information

Information is organized data. It tells us what is happening over time. Trends appear. Correlations form.

The brain loves this stage because it feels like progress, but information alone doesn't tell us what matters. When information is tested, challenged, and applied *over time*, it becomes knowledge.

DR. DAVE'S ESSENTIAL EQUATION #4:

Information × Time = Knowledge

Knowledge is predictive. It helps us anticipate outcomes. It lets us say, "If I do this, that is likely to happen." This is where models form, theories stabilize, and confidence grows.

Knowledge still isn't the end of the journey.

When knowledge survives real-world complexity, when it's held with humility, compared and contrasted with others' knowledge, updated with new evidence, and integrated with human context, it becomes wisdom.

DR. DAVE'S ESSENTIAL EQUATION #5:

Knowledge × Time = Wisdom

Wisdom is the goal. It's how we know when to act and when to wait. It knows the limits of our understanding and is content. It recognizes that certainty without context is dangerous.

In this sense, the scientific method isn't just a tool for discovering facts. It's a practice in patience, curiosity, and respect for reality. Science, done right, doesn't rush to conclusions. It's patience as an art form.

It listens long enough to learn the truth.

A TREASURE MAP IN THE NERVOUS SYSTEM

Beneath our thoughts and stories, an ancient system hundreds of millions of years old quietly allocates the body's most precious currency: blood. This is the autonomic nervous system (ANS), composed of two complementary forces in constant conversation, like yin and yang (Figure 5A).

The insula (Figure 5B) embodies *yin*, the feminine principle, receiving, sensing, cooling, and integrating internal states into awareness. The amygdala (Figure 5B) reflects *yang*, the masculine force, activating, acting, heating, and driving rapid responses to threat or opportunity. Together, they maintain balance. Perception without action is incomplete, and action without perception is blind. Health emerges from their continuous, fluid interplay. Like a well-run economy, the ANS shifts resources moment by moment, breath by breath, depending on what the body perceives as most important for survival.

When the world feels uncertain, unfamiliar, overwhelming, or threatening, the sympathetic (fight-or-flight) nervous system, activated by the amygdala, takes the lead (Figure 6) [13]. It is the physiology of "just in case." Blood is redirected away from long-term maintenance systems like digestion, immunity, and reproduction and toward the heart, lungs, and skeletal muscles for immediate action. Focus narrows, acuity heightens, the body tenses, vigilance takes the wheel, and inflammation increases. If this state persists, what begins as an adaptive response can harden into chronic stress, making it harder for the system to return to equilibrium, leading to lower vagus nerve activity and eventually systemic dysfunction.

In contrast, when we experience safety, familiarity, predictability, and a sense of control, activity increases in the parasympathetic (rest-and-digest) nervous system, which is governed by the vagus nerve via the insula [6, 8, 12, 14]. This is the physiology of "just in time." Blood returns

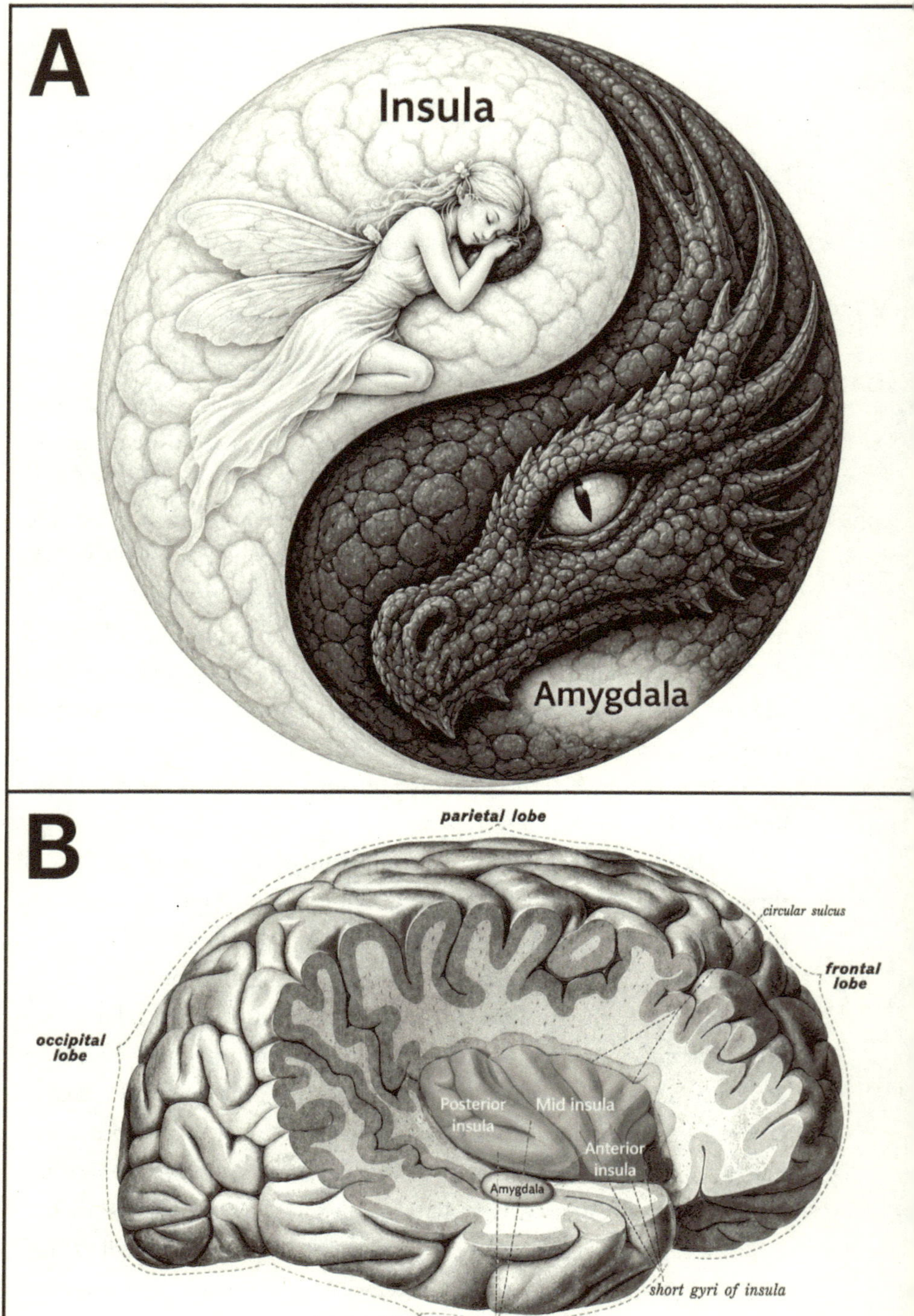

Figure 5. The Anatomy and Balance of the Autonomic Nervous System
(A) The Yin-Yang of Autonomic Balance. (B) Anatomy of the Limbic System.

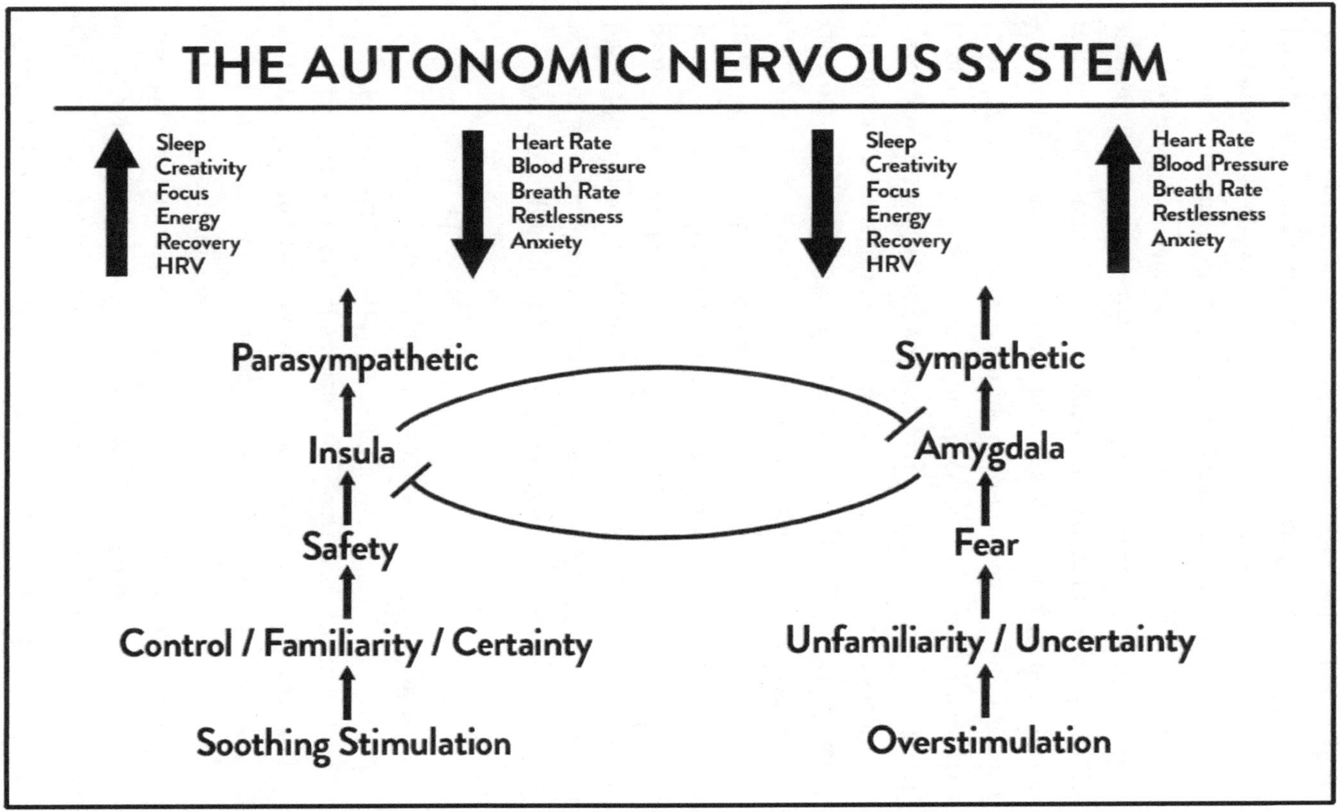

Figure 6. The Map of the Autonomic Nervous System

to the organs of repair and restoration: the gut, the liver, the immune system, the sleep system, and the brain regions responsible for connection, reflection, and learning. Heart rate slows, blood pressure decreases, digestion improves, reproductive systems kick back on, and the body shifts from surviving to thriving.

Chronic stress is a resource-allocation problem because there is only so much blood to go around at any time. Blood has two primary functions:

1. Deliver essential nutrients (oxygen, glucose, vitamins and minerals, water, etc.) to cells
2. Remove waste (Carbon dioxide, urea, lactic acid, water, etc.) from cells

At rest, approximately 20% of our blood is going to the brain, 20% is going to skeletal muscles, 45% to the liver and kidneys (our built-in blood filters), and 5% is going to the heart, leaving the remaining 10% to be distributed to the rest of the body [15]. Under these conditions, our recovery systems have enough blood to function and can request more from the vagus nerve as needed.

When engaged by stress, physical or otherwise, our skeletal muscles can command over 80% of our total blood flow [16, 17]. Under these circumstances, this leaves us with only 5% left for the brain, 5% for the heart, 5% for the liver and kidneys, and 5% for the rest of the body. The sympathetic nervous system pushes back hard against the recovery system's requests for more blood in the face of a potential threat to survival. We would not live long if we were mistakenly engaging our empathy or reproductive systems when a hungry bear is out to get us, so these systems are shut down first. Sleep is next on the chopping block because it is our most physically vulnerable state. Then emotion regulation, and so on.

In the moment, this sympathetic survival response ensures we make it back to safety [14]. When this persists over time and safety is not restored quickly, the rest of the body, which splits up only 5% of the available blood, continues to operate in a state of both resource-depleted starvation and decreased waste removal. This further increases inflammation, eventually leading to cellular dysfunction and disease if left unchecked [18, 19].

All animals dating back to ancient reptiles evolved this way to ensure survival at all costs [20]. This is the hardwiring of our nervous system. This rule can be bent, but never broken.

CHOOSE YOUR WORDS CAREFULLY

The words we choose to describe ourselves and the world create our reality. Many of the tribal traditions mentioned here, including the Toltec culture as described by Don Miguel Ruiz in *The Four Agreements*, treat words as spells because they have such power over us by shaping meaning [21]. The Aramaic phrase *avra k'davra* ("Abracadabra" in the parlance of our times), literally translates to "I create as I speak." While this phrase has been associated with ancient Judaism, its written origins in *Liber Medicinalis* by Roman physician Serenus Sammonicus date back to the 2nd century CE. Jesus describes the importance of "The Word" in manifesting reality in the New Testament of the Bible. Genesis, the first book of the Old Testament, estimated to have originated over 1000 years before Jesus, describes how God speaks the world into existence, starting with, "Let there be light!"

Ever wonder why it's called "spelling" in school?

At their very best, our words are an imperfect description of experience. They do not define experience. Language is a living thing. Every time words are passed down from one person to another, with each subsequent degree of separation from the original source of an experience dilutes the original meaning, and in many cases, it is lost entirely. Just like the childhood game of "telephone."

What we don't talk about enough is the harm that comes from misspelling words or using them incorrectly to define ourselves and our experiences. For example, a single mislabeling of someone as "having depression" when they're just sad for a while because they went through something challenging can result in such a tight wiring of the concept of "depression" to their identity that it could last a lifetime. Misdiagnosis happens all the time in and out of the clinic.

Thankfully, correct spelling can be learned quickly and is much easier when we are safely grounded in the present moment.

Throughout this book, you will notice that certain key points are repeated. This is intentional. Repetition is required for learning and is represented in the brain as stronger wiring between brain cells. Learning is one of the most important skills human beings possess. Neuroplasticity means learning by forming new connections (and brain cells) in the brain. What we learn is solidified through repetition. Neuroplasticity is happening in every moment of our entire lives unless we do something to mess it up. When we stop learning, we stop growing. When we stop growing, entropy wins, and we begin to deteriorate.

THE GAME WE FORGOT WE WERE PLAYING

At the heart of this book is a simple idea that sounds radical only because we've forgotten it: *science doesn't disprove spirituality, it explains it.* What we call wonder, beauty, awe, imagination, and even God are not childish fantasies to outgrow; they are states of nervous system regulation and conscious awareness that children access naturally, before they are taught to be afraid, busy, and "productive."

Toddlers don't need to be convinced that existence is magical; they just know. If you are reading this, you have experienced that magic, whether you remember it or not. Play is not a break from life—it *is* life. And play, it turns out, is one of the most powerful healing states a human nervous system can enter. Modern neuroscience confirms what ancient traditions always knew: when we are playful, curious, and present, the brain shifts into states associated with learning, connection, creativity, and repair. Play is not frivolous or self-indulgent. It is sacred biology. This is *The Forgotten Secret.*

DR. DAVE'S ESSENTIAL EQUATION #6:

Play × Time = Joy

Remembering how to play is not regressing. It is a return to the unburdened, divine intelligence that was there all along. In remembering, we don't just heal ourselves, we change the rules of the world we are creating together.

Somehow, somewhere along the way, we were taught to play a different game.

That game says the goal of life is to accumulate more money, more status, more stuff, more control. It teaches us that worth is scarce, that we must compete to deserve safety, and that happiness lives just one achievement or social post away. The cruel irony is that this game cannot be won. No matter how much we collect, the nervous system remains hungry. We destroy our bodies, our relationships, our communities, and even the planet itself by chasing a finish line that doesn't exist.

The game that the science of spirituality shows us is quite different.

The real game is not about how much you have, it's about *how in tune you are* [22]. How present. How aware. How intentionally you act and relate to your thoughts, your body, other people, and the living world around you. The more you perceive, the more conscious choice you have. The more conscious choice you have, the more real power you experience. Not power *over* others, but the power, *with* life, to manifest the reality you desire.

The secret to winning is ironically quite simple: distraction is the enemy. Focused attention is true power. Win your attention, and you win the game.

Here's the extraordinary part: *anyone can win.*

You don't need special talent, wealth, enlightenment, or luck. If you were born human, you already have everything you need. Awareness is not scarce. Presence is not exclusive. Wonder is not reserved for the chosen few. When one person becomes more attuned, the entire system benefits. This is a game where individual victory strengthens the community, and collective well-being amplifies individual joy.

THE 60-SECOND BEING RESET

Right now. Stop.

Say unto yourself: *I am going to breathe by choice right now.*

Breathe in slowly through your nose for four seconds.

Hold it.

Exhale slowly for six seconds.

Feel the air entering and leaving your nose, mouth, and lungs.

Do it again. Just notice your body. Notice gravity.

Pretend you're not reading a book right now, and do it again at least three more times.

Voila! You just entered *being mode in under a minute.* You didn't solve world hunger, but you did regulate your vagus nerve and reintroduce yourself to your actual life. Not a life controlled by your thoughts, but a life as a human being that observes your thoughts, like watching clouds pass by overhead on a glorious sunny day.

BEING IS THE PREREQUISITE TO EVERYTHING ELSE

Want to feel better? Love better? Find your purpose? Create something meaningful? You need to *be* first. Being keeps you grounded in authenticity. It gives you access to choice. To empathy. To joy. It's not the opposite of doing. It's the foundation for doing anything with soul.

To be human is to remember: *Your presence is enough. You being here now is the gift.*

You don't have to do anything to deserve it. Just *be here now.*

CHAPTER 2
Our First Language

The skin is the outermost layer of the soul.
Dr. David M. L. Rabin, MD, PhD

Hundreds of millions of years ago, long before humans or words, the earliest mammals emerged into a world where survival depended on one thing above almost everything else: a newborn's ability to recognize safety instantly. These newborns were blind, fragile, and entirely dependent. They could not reason their way to safety. They could not speak or interpret symbols, but they could feel.

So, evolution did something elegant. It made soothing touch the first language of life.

A mother's warmth. The pressure of being held. The rhythmic movement of breathing and heartbeat. When everything else was utterly overwhelming, these sensations became the original signal: *you are safe enough to survive this moment.*

This system worked so well that it never went away. It became us.

Today, when a parent instinctively rocks a crying child, when we snuggle a pet, when two people reach for each other's hands without thinking, you are witnessing one of the oldest communication systems in biology still operating exactly as designed.

Soothing touch releases all the body's natural molecules and hormones that make us feel good, including dopamine, serotonin, oxytocin, endorphins, endogenous opioids, endogenous cannabinoids, and many others [23-27]. Touch is not just contact; it's valuable information.

THE SKIN: WHERE TOUCH BECOMES SIGNAL

To understand how touch works, we begin with the skin, the largest sensory organ in the human body, and one of the most neurologically rich (Figure 7).

Embedded within the skin is a sophisticated network of receptors, each tuned to detect different aspects of the physical world [28]. Merkel cells register sustained pressure and texture. Meissner corpuscles detect light touch and motion across the skin. Pacinian corpuscles sense deep pressure and vibration. Ruffini endings detect stretch and deformation. Free nerve endings signal temperature, pain, and crude touch.

All of these receptors perform the same essential function: they convert mechanical stimulation into electrical signals, a process known as mechanotransduction.

Among these, one system stands apart for its role in human connection: C-tactile afferent fibers.

These slow-conducting, unmyelinated nerve fibers are specialized for gentle, social touch [29]. They respond most strongly to slow stroking, light pressure, and skin-temperature contact. In other words, they are exquisitely tuned to the exact qualities of a comforting hug, a reassuring hand on the shoulder, or fingers interlaced with yours.

Unlike other touch receptors that prioritize speed and precision, C-tactile fibers prioritize meaning.

They do not simply tell the brain *what* is happening.

They tell the brain *how it feels to be held in that moment.*

When you receive a hug, something remarkable happens beneath the surface.

As two bodies come into contact, multiple receptor systems activate simultaneously. Pressure receptors register compression. Stretch receptors respond as the skin deforms. Thermoreceptors detect warmth. And C-tactile fibers begin firing in response to slow, gentle contact.

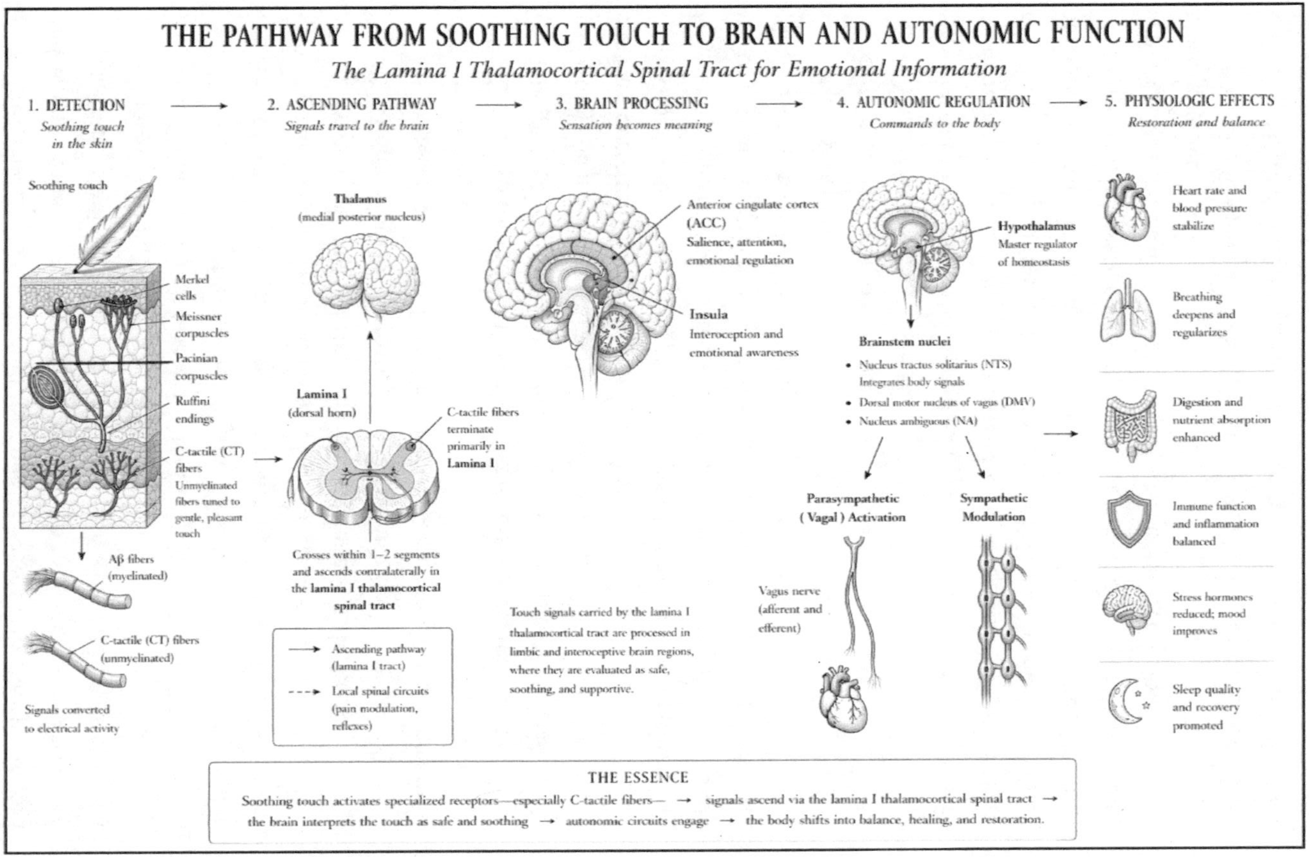

Figure 7. The Path From Soothing Touch to the Brain

These signals travel through peripheral nerves into the spinal cord and ascend to the brain. The faster signals reach the somatosensory cortex, mapping the physical characteristics of the hug, where it is, how strong it is, and how long it lasts.

The C-tactile signals take a different path [30].

They project to the insula (Figure 5B), the region in the limbic system responsible for three critically important skills we are all born with as human beings that most of us don't learn much about:

1. Posterior Insula → Interoception (awareness of the body)
2. Middle Insula → Introspection (self-reflection)
3. Anterior Insula → Empathy (feeling someone else's feelings from their perspective)

This is also the part of the brain that is responsible for feeling, where sensations like soothing touch become emotion [30, 31]. The insula has strong neural connections with the amygdala, the brain's threat and contrast-detection center, a.k.a. the reptilian brain (Figure 6).

When you receive a hug from a friend, even on the hardest days (Figure 8), you feel better instantly, in part because the insula is safely rocking your amygdala back to sleep and boosting vagus nerve activity [32]. Within seconds, the body begins to shift.

From fear to safety.

From contraction to openness.

From isolation to connection.

At the same time, the hypothalamus produces oxytocin, the hormone most associated with bonding and trust, triggering its release from the pituitary gland into the bloodstream [24]. Oxytocin further reduces amygdala activity, lowering fear and vigilance [33]. It enhances feelings of connection, increases parasympathetic rest-and-digest nervous system activity, slows the heart rate, and deepens the breath, contributing to the hug afterglow.

This is what happens when soothing touch, like a hug, comes from someone we trust and feel safe around. The touch amplifies the safety you already feel around that person.

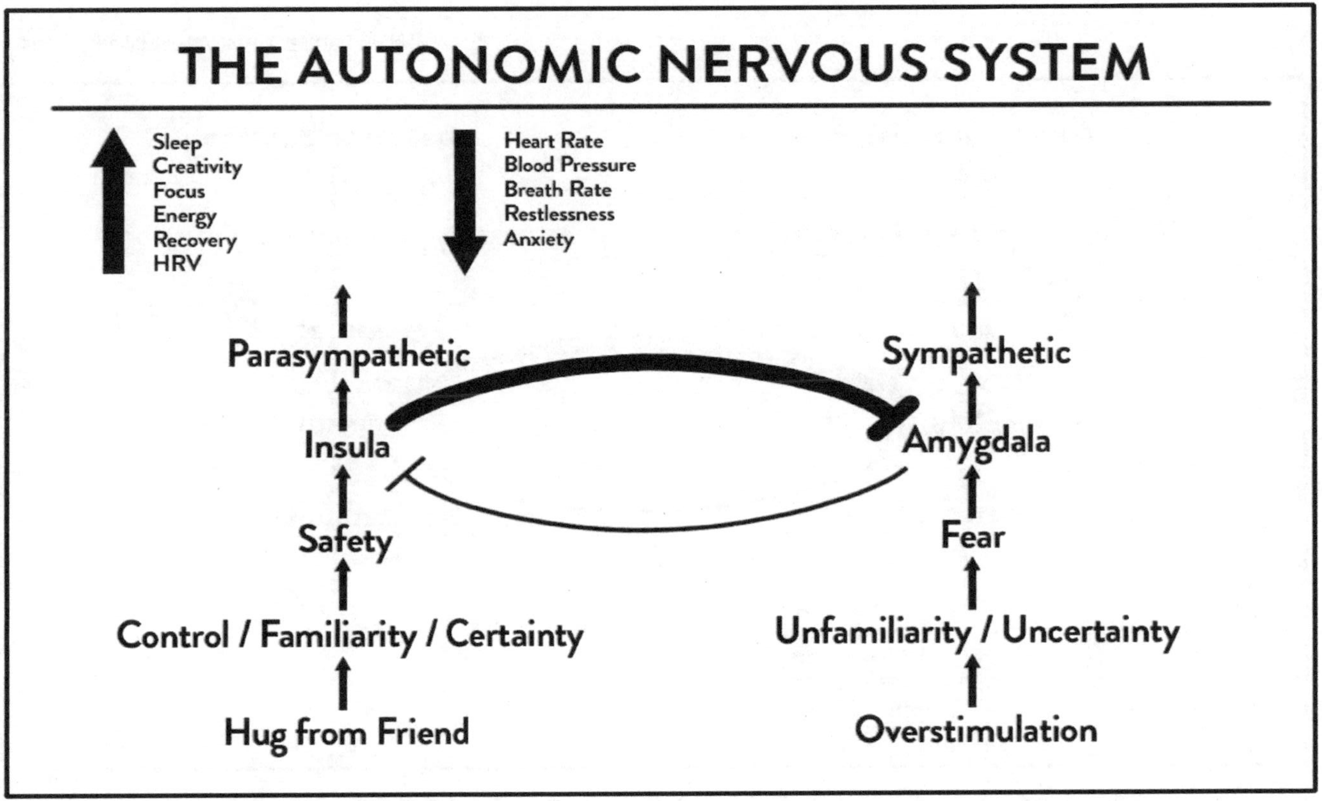

Figure 8. Soothing the Autonomic Nervous System

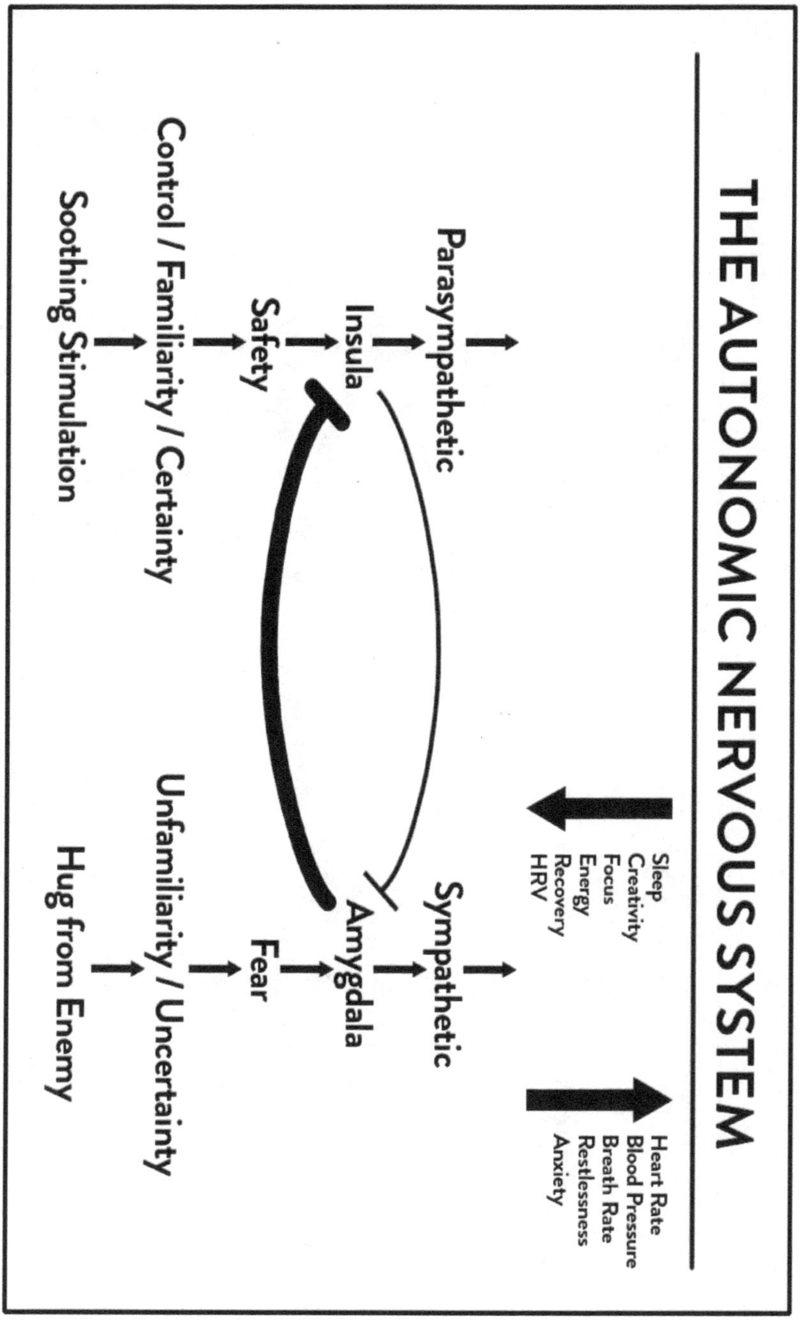

Figure 9. Scaring the Autonomic Nervous System

This is, of course, not the case when you receive a hug from someone you don't like, or someone with whom you do not feel safe and comfortable (Figure 9). When you receive a hug from someone you don't like or don't feel safe with, it doesn't feel good, and the sympathetic fight-or-flight nervous system is intensely activated because there is no foundation of safety and trust. In this scenario, the amygdala is activated much more than the insula, thereby inhibiting the safety-amplifying effects of the hug.

THE LANGUAGE OF SAFETY

What makes touch so powerful is not just that it feels good.

It is that it bypasses cognition [30-32].

You do not need to believe a hug is safe for it to begin working. You do not need to analyze it or understand it. The body recognizes it instantly because it has been recognizing it for hundreds of millions of years.

This is why, in moments of distress, a simple hand on the back can succeed where language cannot.

Touch speaks directly to the nervous system in its native language.

WHEN TOUCH IS MISSING

If soothing touch is the first language of safety, then its absence leaves a profound imprint.

Research consistently shows that lack of nurturing touch, especially early in life, is associated with increased stress reactivity, impaired emotional regulation, higher rates of anxiety and depression, and altered development of the nervous system [34]. Touch and vibration in newborns, especially premature newborns, have been proven to significantly decrease infant mortality, which is why they have been implemented in neonatal intensive care units worldwide [35].

In adults, we've somehow convinced ourselves that we don't need touch. Instead, we live in a chronic touch-deprived state, manifesting as a persistent sense of disconnection, loneliness, hypervigilance, and/or emotional numbness [36].

The body forgets what safety feels like, and when that happens, it adapts through tension, through guarded posture, through subtle but persistent contraction patterns that become embedded in the body over time.

To understand where those patterns live, we need to venture a little deeper.

FASCIA: THE BODY'S LIVING NETWORK

For decades, fascia was dismissed as little more than packing material, an inert wrapping around muscles, nerves, and organs. We now know this was a profound misunderstanding.

Fascia is a continuous, body-wide network of connective tissue that surrounds and interpenetrates every muscle, organ, nerve, and blood vessel [37]. It is the body's internal matrix.

More importantly, fascia is alive with information. It is richly innervated, electrically conductive, mechanosensitive, and capable of transmitting force and signals across distant regions of the body [38].

This means that what happens in one part of the body can influence another, sometimes far away.

Sound familiar?

This is essentially what ancient Eastern Medicine traditions describe as *meridians.*

Modern anatomical and imaging studies have demonstrated that many traditional meridian pathways align closely with fascial planes, nerve intersection points, and connective tissue lines [39]. What was once described as the flow of Qi can now be understood as the movement of mechanical, electrical, and fluid-based information through this network.

Different language, same map.

TRAUMA LIVES IN THE FASCIA

When we experience stress or trauma, the body responds immediately. Muscles contract. Breathing becomes shallow. Posture shifts to protect vulnerable areas.

If the experience resolves, the body returns to baseline.

If it does not, the pattern remains.

Over time, these protective responses become encoded in the fascial network as chronic tension patterns. Fascia stiffens, dehydrates, and loses its ability to glide freely [40-42].

This is not just a structural issue.

It is a functional one. The problem is not isolated. It is systemic.

These patterns can manifest as postural issues, chronic pain without a clear structural cause, headaches, digestive issues, pelvic floor dysfunction, restricted breathing, anxiety, fatigue, and movement limitations that span multiple diagnoses.

Trauma is stored in the fascia. This is why purely cognitive approaches often fall short. You cannot think your way out of a fascial contraction, but you can feel your way through it.

ACCESS POINTS TO THE NETWORK

Now we come to Tsubo, the acupoints described in Shiatsu and acupuncture, dating back to ancient Traditional Chinese Medicine (est. 100 BCE).

In Chinese medicine, these pressure points along meridians are used to restore the flow of energy in the body (Figure 10) [43]. Science has now shown that these points consistently correspond to areas of high neural density, fascial convergence, vascular and lymphatic intersections, and regions of altered electrical conductivity. In other words, they are places where the body is already highly communicative.

When pressure is applied to a Tsubo point, multiple systems are engaged simultaneously [44].

Mechanoreceptors in the skin and fascia send signals to the brain, influencing nervous system balance. Fascia releases under pressure, restoring mobility and reducing tension. Piezoelectric properties of connective tissue generate electrical signals that influence cellular communication. Circulation improves, pain perception shifts, and, critically, the same pathways involved in soothing touch are activated, boosting vagus nerve activity.

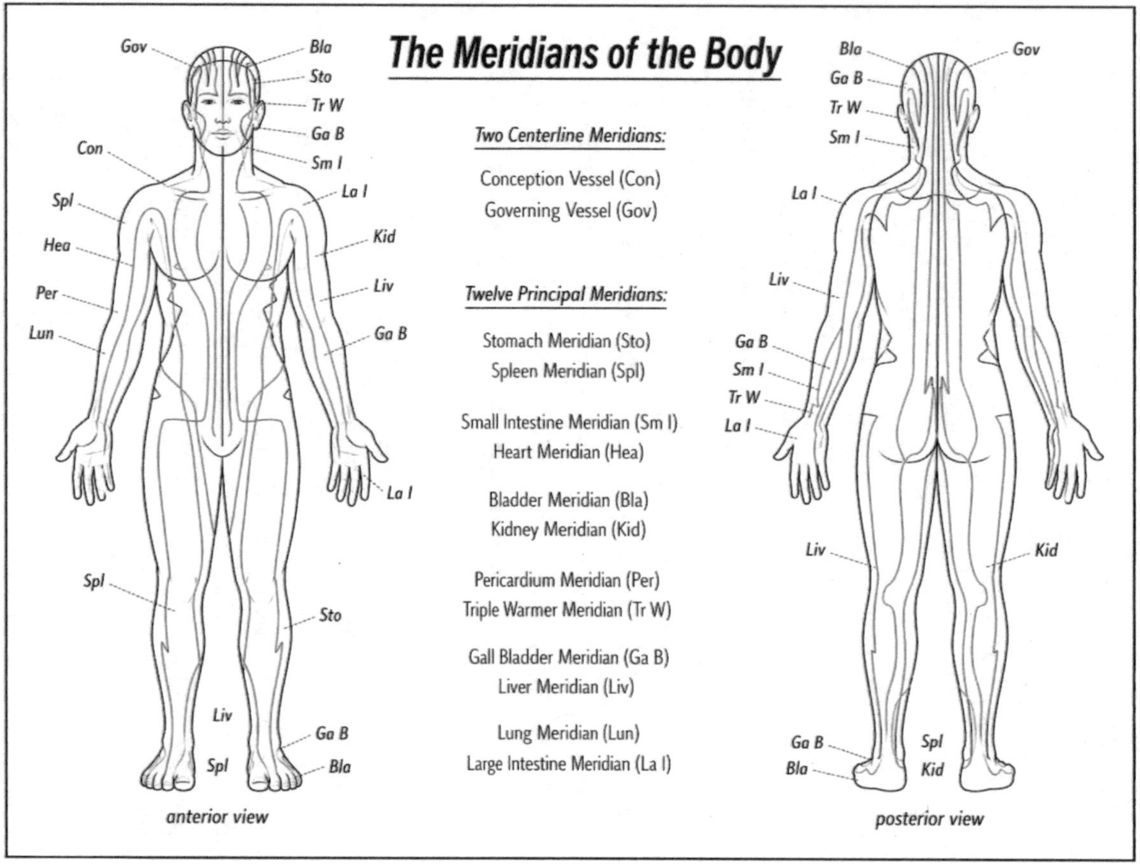

Figure 10. The Meridians of the Body

This is why these points often feel both physically intense and emotionally meaningful. They are intersections of structure, sensation, and regulation.

Touch is a form of communication.

Not forceful correction, but informed conversation.

The practitioner listens with their hands for tension and temperature, occasionally applying slow, intentional pressure to specific points and pathways. This enhances interoceptive awareness, the brain's ability to sense and interpret internal bodily states. As this awareness increases, the nervous system gains the information it needs to regulate more effectively.

From a Western perspective, this aligns seamlessly with what we know about the insula, the vagus nerve, and autonomic balance.

From an Eastern perspective, it is the restoration of unobstructed energy flow within the system.

Two frameworks. One process.

Acupuncture, acupressure, and Shiatsu are now supported by a growing body of scientific evidence demonstrating effectiveness for chronic pain, migraines, anxiety, depression, insomnia, and digestive disorders [45].

Functional imaging studies show that stimulating specific acupoints activates predictable brain regions involved in pain processing, emotional regulation, and autonomic control [46].

THE MAPS AT THE EDGES

If touch is the first language, then the hands and feet are its most eloquent instruments.

We tend to think of them in terms of utility. Hands grasp, build, signal, create. Feet support, balance, and move us through space. They are the tools we use to interact with the external world, but this is only half the story.

They are also among the most densely innervated, information-rich, and neurologically significant regions of the human body [47]. They are not just tools for action, they are portals for perception.

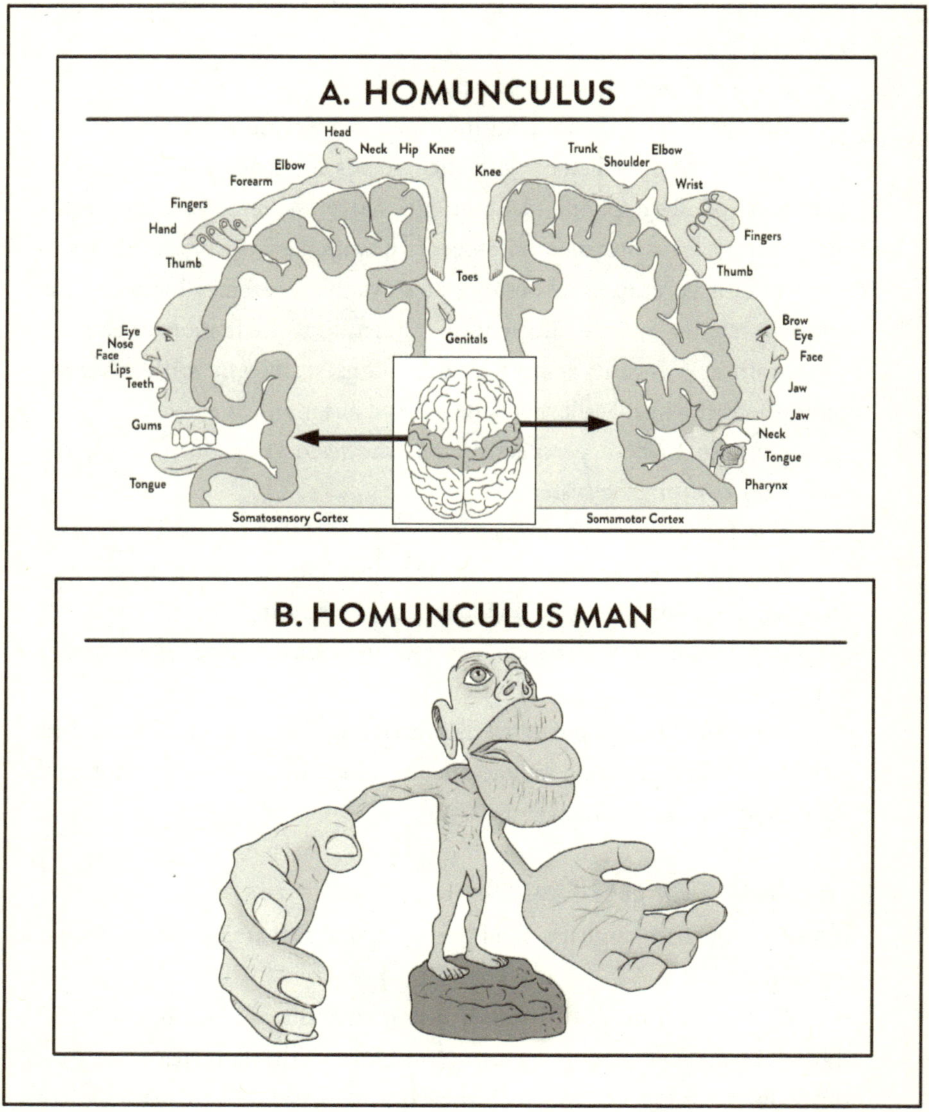

Figure 11. The Cortical Homunculus (A) The Homunculus Man folded over the brain showing the parts of the brain that are important for sensing and moving each body part. (B) The Homunculus Man is drawn with the size of his body parts determined by the amount of brain tissue that represents each body part.

In both Eastern and Western traditions, they have long been understood as maps of the entire organism.

From a Western neuroscience perspective, the hands and feet occupy an outsized portion of the brain's sensory and motor cortex. This is clearly visualized in the cortical homunculus (Figure 11), a representation of how the body maps to the brain, first described in 1937 by Dr. Wilder Penfield, MD (1892–1976), and his colleague Dr. Edwin Boldrey, MD (1906–1988) [48, 49].

This is not artistic exaggeration. It reflects reality.

The density of mechanoreceptors in the hands, particularly in the fingertips, is among the highest anywhere in the body. This allows for extraordinary precision in detecting texture, pressure, vibration, and movement. The feet, while slightly less refined in discrimination, are exquisitely tuned for pressure, balance, and spatial orientation, continuously feeding information into the nervous system about where we are in space.

Every step you take is a conversation between your feet and your brain. Every object you hold is a dialogue between your hands and your nervous system, and beneath that dialogue lies something deeper.

These regions are not just sensing the outside world.

They are influencing the internal one.

Going even further back in time to reflexology (est. 2330 BCE), originating in ancient Egypt, specific points on the hands and feet correspond to organs and systems [50]. The toes relate to the head and brain (Figure 12). The ball of the foot corresponds to the chest and lungs. The arch maps onto digestive organs. The heel reflects the lower body and pelvis. Similarly, in the hands, different regions correspond to the spine, internal organs, and energetic systems (Figure 13).

These mappings often align with nerve distributions, fascial lines, somatotopic organization in the brain, and clinically observed referred pain patterns. They are not arbitrary. They reflect the hardwiring of the nervous system.

Stimulating the hands and feet has effects throughout the body because:

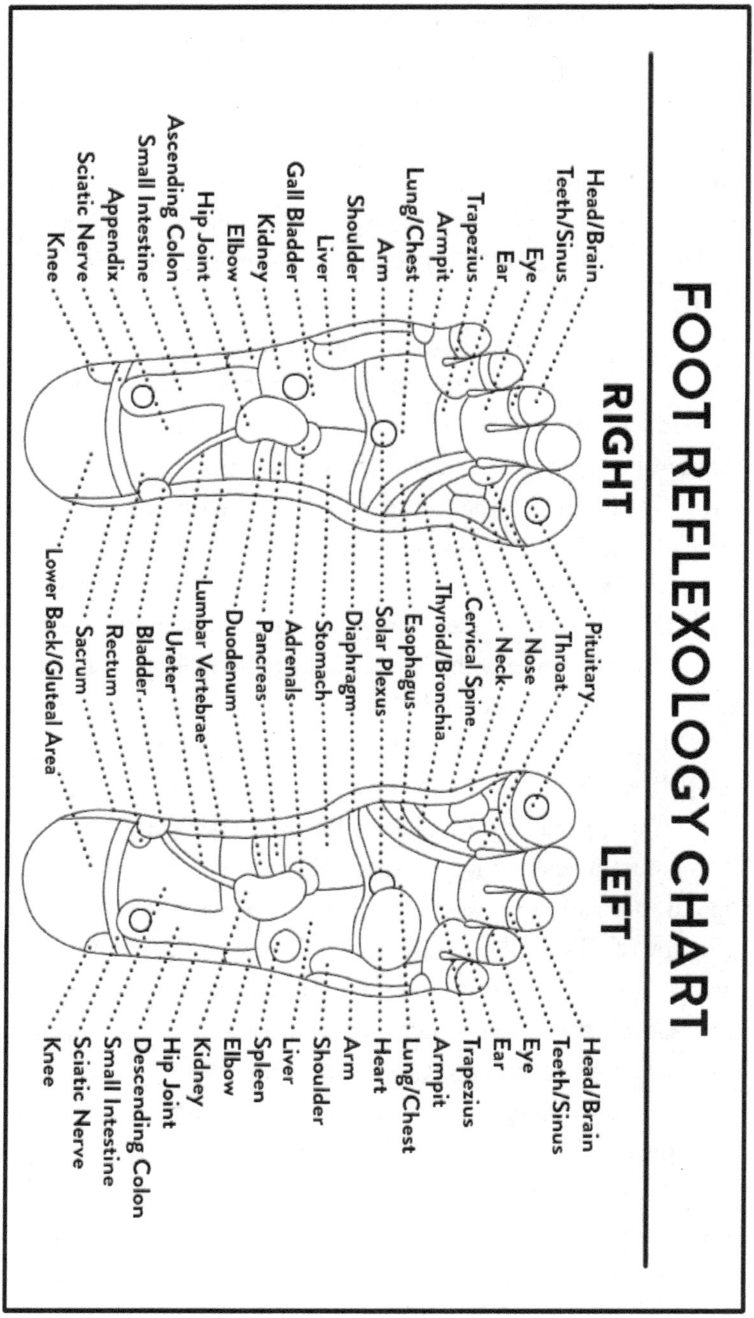

Figure 12. Foot Reflexology Chart

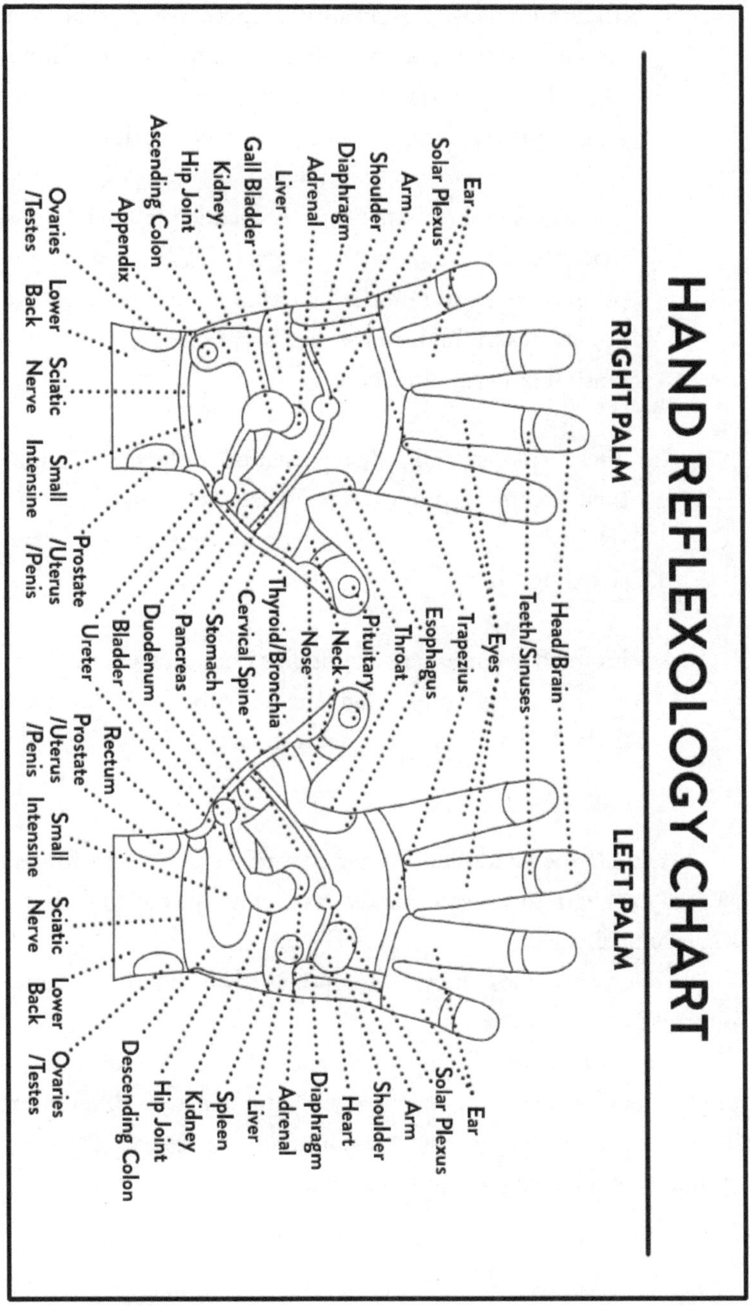

Figure 13. Hand Reflexology Chart

1. Their high density of sensory receptors means that even small amounts of stimulation generate significant neural input [47]. This input travels rapidly to the brain and can influence autonomic regulation, attention, and perception.

2. The hands and feet are deeply embedded in fascial networks that extend throughout the body [51]. When you apply pressure to a point on the foot, that force is not isolated. It propagates through connective tissue chains, influencing tension patterns elsewhere.

3. These regions are highly represented in the brain. Stimulating them creates disproportionately large effects in cortical activity, which can "reset" or reorganize patterns of neural signaling [52].

4. From an evolutionary standpoint, these are areas of constant environmental interaction. The nervous system prioritizes input from the hands and feet because they are critical for survival.

As such, the hands and feet are powerful entry points for regulation. When you begin to see your hands and feet not just as tools, but as maps, something changes.

Touch becomes more intentional. Movement becomes more informative.

Simple acts like rubbing your hands together, pressing into the arch of your foot, or holding someone else's hand take on a different meaning. They become a way to instantly communicate safety across our entire system through a single point of contact.

SENSORY LINGUISTICS

Touch may be the first language of safety, but it is not the only one.

Every moment of your life, your nervous system is taking in information through multiple sensory channels, translating the external world into internal experience. What is remarkable, and deeply important, is that many of these sensory pathways converge in the same region of the brain we discussed earlier: the insula [30-32].

The insula integrates signals from touch, temperature, pain, and internal organs, and combines them with emotional and contextual information to create a unified experience of "how I feel right now."

In other words, it is where the outside world becomes your inner state, and touch is only one of its inputs.

SIGHT

Vision is often thought of as a purely cognitive sense, something that helps us navigate and recognize objects. It is also one of the most powerful emotional regulators we have.

When you see something frightening, a looming shadow, an aggressive face, a sudden movement, visual information travels rapidly through the retina to the thalamus and then to the amygdala, triggering a near-instant stress response [53].

Visual information also reaches the insula, where it contributes to your felt sense of safety or threat.

This is why environments matter so much.

A cluttered, chaotic, or harshly lit space subtly signals unpredictability. The nervous system registers this as a potential threat, even if consciously, you "know" you are safe. Fluorescent lights, blue light from your smartphone, and even watching the news on mute increase your heart rate and blood pressure and decrease your sense of well-being in near real time through your eyes.

In contrast, when you look at a calm ocean, a tree swaying in the wind, or a warm, softly lit room, the visual input promotes parasympathetic activity and a sense of ease.

A sunset is not just beautiful.

It is regulatory.

SMELL

Of all the senses, smell has the most direct route to the emotional brain.

Olfactory signals bypass the thalamus entirely and project straight to the limbic system, including the amygdala and hippocampus, as well as the insula [54].

This is why smell can evoke powerful emotional memories almost instantly.

The scent of something rotten can trigger disgust and aversion before you have time to think.

The smell of freshly baked cookies can evoke warmth, nostalgia, and comfort within seconds.

There is no intermediary.

No translation step.

Smell is emotion, delivered directly.

SOUND

Sound, too, has profound regulatory effects.

The auditory system connects not only to the cortex for processing meaning, but also to subcortical structures involved in emotion and autonomic regulation, including pathways that influence the insula and vagus nerve [55].

Harsh, unpredictable noises like sirens, alarms, and shouting activate the stress response.

Rhythmic, harmonious sounds akin to soothing music, nature, and steady breathing promote synchronization and calm. This is why a piece of music can shift your entire state within moments.

It is not just heard.

It is felt.

TASTE

Taste is often overlooked, but it is another pathway into the insula.

The insula contains the primary gustatory cortex, meaning it plays a central role in how we experience flavor, which, as we know, is directly linked to emotion [30, 31, 56].

Taste is inherently tied to survival, distinguishing between nourishment and potential toxins. Sweetness signals energy. Bitterness can signal danger. Salt reflects electrolyte balance.

Beyond this, taste is deeply emotional.

Comfort foods are not just caloric.

They are regulatory experiences.

The act of eating something warm, familiar, and satisfying sends signals of safety and sufficiency into the system.

NON-PHYSICAL SENSES: INTUITION, INTEROCEPTION, AND EMPATHY

In addition to the five traditional senses, we have internal sensing systems that are equally powerful.

Interoception is the ability to sense the internal state of the body, heartbeat, breath, gut sensations, and tension [30, 31]. This is mediated largely by the posterior insula (Figure 5B) and forms the foundation of emotional awareness.

Introspection is the ability to observe your own thoughts, beliefs, and mental patterns as they arise. Engaging the middle insula (Figure 5B), it allows us to step back from immediate experience and examine the stories the mind is telling [30, 31]. Unlike interoception, which senses the body, introspection senses the mind itself. It is the foundation of self-awareness, enabling you to recognize biases, reframe perceptions, and choose responses rather than react automatically.

Empathy, the ability to feel others' emotions, engages the anterior insula (Figure 5B) [30-32]. When you are around someone anxious, calm, joyful, or distressed, your nervous system begins to mirror aspects of their state. We possess the capacity to experience the world from another being's perspective by choice at any time.

Intuition can be understood as rapid, unconscious pattern recognition arising from interoceptive and sensory integration [5, 30, 31]. It is the body's way of signaling "something feels right" or "something feels off" before reasoning catches up.

These are measurable biological processes, and they are constantly shaping your experience.

THE HIDDEN WORLD BEHIND CLOSED EYES

There is a world we enter every night with which no one teaches us how to interact. No onboarding, no user manual, and ironically, it might simply be the most powerful operating system you have. You can watch it boot up the moment you close your eyes.

When vision shuts off, the brain doesn't power down [57]. It reallocates resources. Activity shifts away from processing the outside world and toward internal networks where memory, imagination, healing, and meaning-making live. When you stop looking out there, your brain finally has time to take in what's going on in here.

This is where intuition lives.

Intuition is rapid, unconscious pattern recognition built from everything you've ever experienced [5]. Your brain is constantly making predictions about what's safe, what's sketchy, and what's worth your time. When something "feels right" or "feels off," that's not random. That's your nervous system sending you an urgent message you haven't read yet because you've been too distracted to focus on it.

Closing your eyes turns down the noise so you can actually read it. Or rather, feel it.

With fewer distractions, subtle signals get louder. A tight chest. A relaxed belly. A quiet pull toward one decision over another. Chills. Tingles. These are real data streams. Your autonomic nervous system is continuously scanning for safety and familiarity, reallocating blood flow, energy, and attention accordingly. Intuition is what that constant calculation feels like from the inside.

Then there's imagination, intuition's wildly creative cousin.

If intuition helps you recognize patterns, imagination lets you run simulations. It's your brain's built-in sandbox mode. You can rehearse conversations, solve problems, or replay that one thing you said in 2007.

The key is that the brain activates many of the same circuits whether something is real or vividly imagined [58]. Imagination is practice without the social consequences.

Athletes use it. Musicians use it. Therapists use it. You use it, mostly to imagine worst-case scenarios at 2 a.m.

If left on autopilot without proper training, this inner world tends to drift toward anxiety, rumination, and creative disaster planning. Evolution wired us to look for threats first and chill second. So if you don't actively shape your space, it will shape you. Like when you close your eyes hoping for sleep and instead get front-row seats to the latest Hollywood blockbuster, "Everything That Could Go Wrong," now in IMAX.

Thankfully, this system is trainable.

Breath, attention, intentional visualization, and even daydreaming can shift the tone of your inner world. Over time, this space can become less like a group text between a bunch of people who hate each other and more like a well-run meeting where useful ideas actually get heard and shit gets done.

A space where intuition is clear.

A space where imagination works for you, not against you.

A space you can always trust.

No matter how loud the outside world gets, this one is generally calmer and always available.

You just have to close your eyes and check your messages a little more often.

WE BECOME WHAT WE ARE AROUND

When we step back and take this all together, something becomes clear.

Every sight, every sound, every smell, every taste, every touch, and every internal signal is feeding into the same system that determines how you feel.

Which means:

You are, quite literally, being shaped by your environment at every moment.

If you spend time in environments that are loud, chaotic, tense, artificial, or threatening, your nervous system adapts to that input. It becomes more vigilant, more contracted, more reactive.

If you spend time in environments that are calm, supportive, comfortable, and aesthetically pleasing, your nervous system adapts in the opposite direction.

It becomes more regulated.

More open.

More resilient.

This is not a matter of mindset.

It is a matter of input.

THE RESPONSIBILITY OF CURATION

This leads to an uncomfortable, yet empowering, truth.

If we do not intentionally curate our environment, our environment will curate us.

Without feedback.

Without asking permission.

Often without your awareness.

When this happens, the balance of influence shifts. The environment exerts more control over your internal state than you do. This is when people begin to feel stuck, overwhelmed, or out of control, not because they lack willpower, but because their nervous system is being shaped by inputs they did not choose.

The good news is that the reverse is also true.

When you begin to intentionally design your environment, choosing what you see, hear, smell, taste, touch, and who you spend time with, you reclaim influence over your internal state.

You tip the balance back.

Toward agency.

Toward regulation.

Toward well-being.

THE SIMPLE SUMMARY

Touch was our first language.

Soothing sensations signal safety.

Overstimulation signals threat.

Our fascia is the medium through which the nerve signals of touch travel.

Meridians, reflexology, and tsubo points are the places where touch can be applied most effectively, along with the methods for doing so.

Posture is the foundational structure that allows what we build to stick.

Your body is not a collection of separate parts.

It is a continuous, intelligent network. When you learn to communicate with it through touch, awareness, alignment, and listening, you are not adding anything new. You are remembering something ancient. Something your body has known all along.

CHAPTER 3
Ancient Wisdom

All things are connected. Whatever befalls the Earth befalls the children of the Earth.
Si'ahl (1786–1866)

It's fifty thousand years ago, and we wake before the sun.

Not because our calendar is full, not because we set an alarm, but because something deep inside us stirs us awake. A sound in the distance. A shift in temperature. The faint awareness that today, like yesterday, survival is not guaranteed.

There is no language for anxiety yet, but your body knows it intimately.

You are lying on the ground, or perhaps on a bed of woven grasses or animal hides. The air is cool. The fire has burned low. Around you, others sleep. Your family. Your tribe. Your entire world.

We listen first.

Always, we listen. Or we make sure someone we trust is listening for us.

Because listening is living.

A crack of a branch could mean food or death. The same sound, two completely different futures. Your nervous system does not debate this intellectually. It does not scroll or second-guess. It decides, instantly, intuitively, beneath consciousness.

This is the world for which your brain was hardwired.

You stand quietly, scanning the horizon. The light is just beginning to stretch across the land. The world is vast, textured, unpredictable. There are no straight lines. No artificial light. No digital noise. Only gradients, shadows, and movement.

Everything that exists in your world matters. Every sound carries meaning. Every smell carries information. Every sensation on your skin is a signal. Your nervous system is not overwhelmed. It is perfectly calibrated. The stimulation you are receiving is exactly the kind your brain evolved to process. Natural. Rhythmic. Variable. Present. Alive.

The wind moves unpredictably but not chaotically. The fire flickers with the wind. The sounds of animals rise and fall with the sun and moon in patterns your body understands instinctively. This is what your brain was designed to respond to.

Not endless notifications.

Not fluorescent lighting.

Not the unnatural stillness of sitting for twelve hours a day, staring at a glowing rectangle.

Your brain evolved for movement, for feeling, for connection, for immediate feedback from the environment, and most importantly, it evolved for one central task:

Ensure that the basic needs of survival, highlighted by Maslow's Hierarchy of Needs (Figure 14), are met in order of what will kill us first if we run out:

1. Air
2. Physical safety (including shelter)
3. Water
4. Food
5. Sleep

Breathe. Find food and water. Stay alive. Protect the group.

Everything else comes later.

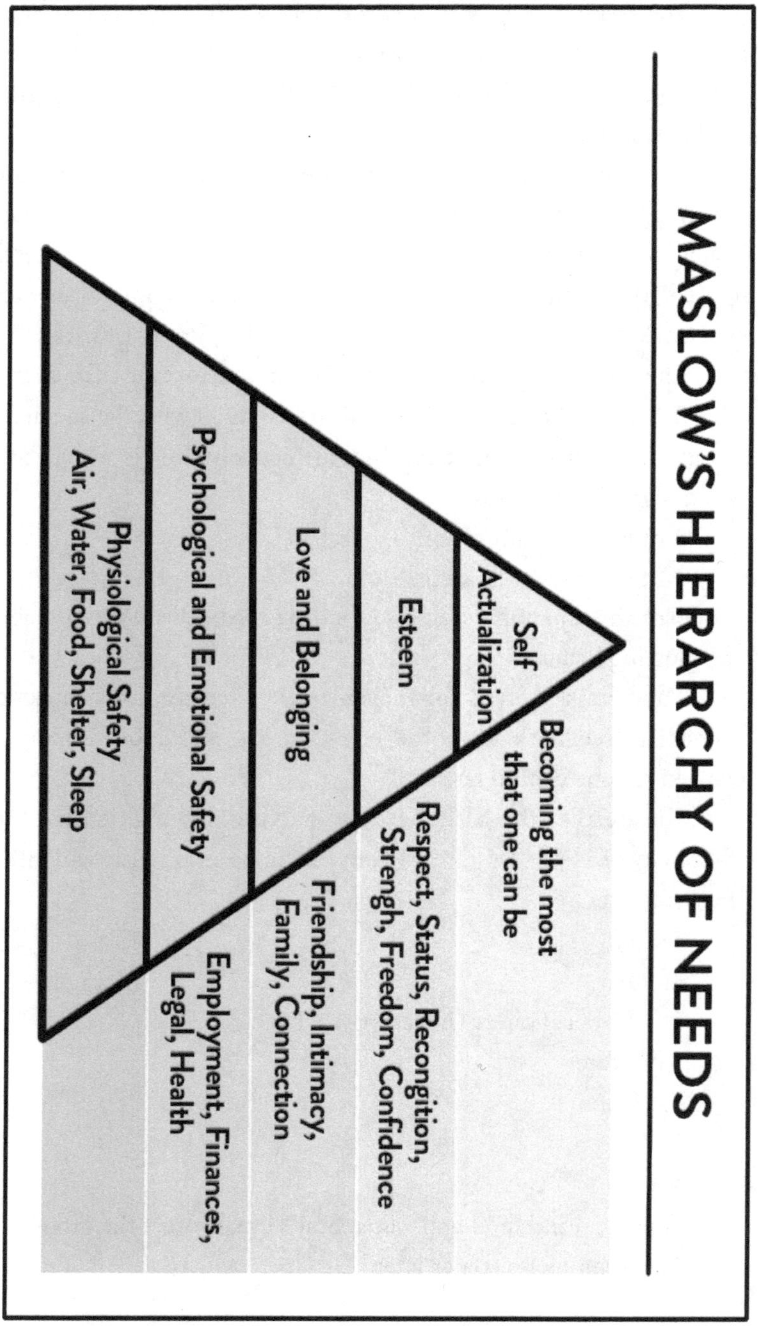

Figure 14. Maslow's Hierarchy of Needs

Hunger is the first teacher. It sharpens attention. It focuses the mind. It organizes behavior around a single, undeniable truth: you must eat, or you will die.

And not just you. Your children. Your partner. Your tribe. Food is not a convenience. It is not entertainment. It is not identity.

It is survival.

Hunting did not come about as a hobby. It is a life-or-death negotiation with the natural world. You track animals for miles. You read subtle disturbances in the Earth. You interpret broken twigs, displaced stones, and faint impressions in the dirt. Your brain is constantly predicting, adjusting, and learning.

This is neuroplasticity at its purest. Every failed hunt teaches something. Every successful one reinforces patterns. Your brain is being shaped, moment by moment, by direct interaction with reality.

There is no abstraction.

There is no buffering.

There is no "I'll figure it out later."

There is only right now.

And in this now, your nervous system operates with extraordinary precision. It is highly trained to quickly check the five survival boxes above and, once those are confirmed not to be in jeopardy, safety is rapidly restored, vagus nerve activity turns up, and the body can divert resources back to recovery functions. You are not chronically stressed about the past or the future, as modern humans are. You are acutely stressed when necessary, and deeply relaxed when safe.

When the hunt is over, when the food is secured, your body downshifts. You rest. You eat. You connect. You laugh. You play.

Yes, play. Even in a world this harsh, play is essential.

Play is how the brain practices survival without immediate risk. It is how children learn to hunt before they hunt. How adults maintain flexibility in thinking and movement with age. Your nervous system oscillates naturally and safely between activation and recovery.

This rhythm is everything. And it is something we have largely lost.

THE NERVOUS SYSTEM WE INHERITED

All mammals have the same stress response nervous system, dating back hundreds of millions of years [20]. Similar to ancient mammals, the human nervous system did not evolve for constant input.

It evolved for meaningful input. In this ancestral world, stimulation is sparse, but significant. Every sound matters. Every smell matters. Every visual cue matters.

Your brain is not filtering out 99% of the noise because there is no noise to filter. Everything is a signal. Contrast this with modern life, where nearly everything is noise. Your nervous system today is flooded with information it was never trained to process.

Endless scrolling. Artificial light at all hours. Notifications that mimic urgency, yet carry no real consequence. Your amygdala cannot distinguish the news or a ping from a rustle in the bushes that might indicate a predator. Physiologically, both trigger attention, but only one matters for survival. So the amygdala defaults to predator just in case.

Over time, this mismatch creates dissonance, the opposite of harmony in music. Dissonance is represented by chronic dysregulation in the body. If your body is an orchestra, dissonance is what happens when half your violin section is out of tune.

This is not happening because your nervous system is broken, but because it is working exactly as designed in an environment it was never designed for.

Fifty thousand years ago, your brain was shaped by:

- Movement through varied terrain
- Direct sensory engagement with nature
- Social bonding within small, stable groups
- Immediate feedback loops between action and consequence
- Rhythmic cycles of stress and recovery, day and night
- Touch as the most common language of safety.

Today, many of these inputs are absent, distorted, or hidden beneath the noise.

THE ASHÁNINKA: A WORLD WITHOUT "MIND" OR "BODY"

The Amazonian Asháninka tribespeople do not divide reality into mind and body [59- 61].

In episode 4 of my podcast *Your Brain Explained*, Jamie Wheal and I had the pleasure of interviewing world-renowned Swiss anthropologist and author Jeremy Narby, who lived embedded with the Asháninka for quite some time. He explains that the Asháninka don't even have a direct equivalent word for "mind" and "body" as separate categories. Instead, they speak of an "inside person" and an "outside skin."

They also do not divide humans from nature. Instead, they describe a world composed of persons.

Humans are persons.

Animals are persons.

Plants are persons.

We are all *beings*. Each has an inner life and a point of view.

This may sound poetic, but it carries profound implications, because if everything is a "person," then everything is part of a relationship.

You don't extract from a person. You negotiate with them. You don't dominate a person. You listen and compromise. This fundamentally changes how we interact with the world around us.

Medicine is no longer something you just take. Food is no longer something you just eat.

They are not objects. They are subjects. They are part of us. They are alive "beings" with whom we enter into relationship.

THE SHIPIBO: SINGING THE BODY BACK INTO HARMONY

For the Shipibo people of the Peruvian Amazon, healing is about restoring harmony in a field of relationships.

Central to their tradition are *Icaros*, healing songs that are not symbolic, but functional [62, 63]. These songs are said to shape perception itself, guiding the experience of plant medicine and reorganizing the internal landscape.

From a neuroscientific lens, we might say:

Sound entrains neural oscillations, facilitating harmony between the brain and body.

Harmony reshapes perception.

Attention directs plasticity.

From the Shipibo perspective:

The song *is* medicine. The healer is not imposing change, but facilitating communication between the individual and the intelligence of nature.

The body is not broken. It is like a piano out of tune, and the healer's Icaros helps retune it back into harmony with nature.

CONVERGENT WISDOM ACROSS CULTURES

Perhaps the most astonishing aspect of these traditions is not what they say. It is how similar they are to traditions that developed completely independently [59, 60]. As Narby observed, many cultures "arrived at remarkably similar understandings...even though they haven't been communicating with one another." The Shipibo and Asháninka in the Amazon, the Toltecs of Mesoamerica, the Aboriginal Australian traditions, and the Miwok people of California converge on the same core principles:

1. Nature is alive and intelligent. Not symbolically, but literally. The world is composed of relational beings, not inert objects.
2. Knowledge comes through non-ordinary states of consciousness. Dreams, breathing, music, dancing, connection, and plants are all used to access deeper layers of perception.
3. Healing is relational, not mechanical. Illness is not just a biological dysfunction. It is an imbalance in the relationship: to self, to others, to environment, to spirit. When balance is restored, biology corrects.
4. Attention is the gateway. What you attend to shapes what you perceive. What you perceive shapes what you become.
5. Humility is necessary. Certainty is dangerous. Openness is protective.

This convergence suggests something profound:

These are not arbitrary, unfounded beliefs. They may be observations of a shared underlying reality, one that could be more real than the reality we have been living day to day.

The Toltec tradition speaks of "domestication," the idea that we are trained, from childhood, to perceive reality in a particular way [21]. Not necessarily the true way, just a consistent one. What is often described as "consensus reality."

This mirrors Narby's observation that Western knowledge systems have systematically separated humans from nature, defining nature as "that which is opposed to humans" or "that which is an object created for the sole purpose of being consumed by humans." A definition so deeply ingrained we rarely question it [59-61].

Yet, once seen, it becomes obvious:

This is not reality. It is a framework. A useful one at times, but also perhaps a limiting one.

In Aboriginal Australian traditions, the "Dreaming" (*Jukurrpa*) is not fantasy. It is the foundational layer of reality. A dimension where time collapses, where ancestors, land, and identity are unified [64].

This is strikingly similar to Amazonian descriptions of plant-induced states of consciousness. Not hallucinations, but access to a deeper layer of the same reality [59]. A layer where patterns become visible. Where relationships become obvious. Where the illusion of separation dissolves.

The Miwok peoples of California understand the world through kinship [65]. Animals are relatives. Plants are relatives. The land itself is a relative. This is not symbolic. It dictates behavior. How you hunt, gather, and live.

It enforces a built-in ethical system:

You do not exploit your relatives. You care for them because your survival depends on your relationship with them.

Another common symbol keeps appearing:

Two lines intertwined. Often drawn as serpents. Sometimes moving in opposite directions. Alive with motion, tension, and balance.

Among Amazonian shamans, these serpents are not decorative [53]. They are seen in visions, often luminous, often described as the carriers of knowledge itself. Narby recounts his own experience of being confronted by "enormous fluorescent serpents" that seemed to communicate something fundamental about the interconnectedness of life.

In the Asháninka and Shipibo traditions, these intertwining patterns emerge not only in visions but also in their textile art, ceramics, and ceremonial geometry. The intricate, repeating designs known as kené are often described as visual representations of reality's underlying structure. Patterns of nature that become observable in non-ordinary states of consciousness are then translated into visual form.

Now, step outside the Amazon.

In Mesoamerican traditions, the Toltecs and the Aztecs revered Quetzalcoatl, the feathered serpent, a being associated with creation, knowledge, and the breath of life itself.

Among many Native American traditions, including those of the Miwok, serpentine patterns appear in stories and symbolic representations of life force, cycles, and renewal.

In India, the concept of kundalini is depicted as a coiled serpent energy rising along the spine, awakening consciousness.

In ancient Greece, the staff of Asclepius features a serpent coiled around a rod, representing healing and medicine. It is still used today as a symbol of medicine.

In Australian Aboriginal traditions, the Rainbow Serpent is the creator being, responsible for shaping the land and animating life.

In the Judeo-Christian-Islamic Bible, the serpent entices Adam and Eve to eat the fruit from the Tree of Knowledge. This fruit from the serpent granted them the knowledge of good and evil and everything in between.

Different continents. Different languages. Different cosmologies.

And yet, the same motif:

Life force and knowledge, structured as a dynamic, interwoven pattern. Often depicted as serpents.

THE DOUBLE HELIX: WHEN SYMBOL MEETS STRUCTURE

Then, in 1953, something remarkable happened in a laboratory at the University of Cambridge.

James Watson and Francis Crick, building critically on the X-ray diffraction images produced by Rosalind Franklin, described the structure of DNA, not as a line, not as a static object, but as two strands, intertwined, and spiraling around each other [66].

A double helix.

A structure so elegant and so precise that its discovery would go on to earn a Nobel Prize in Physiology or Medicine, fundamentally upgrading life on Earth.

DNA, we now understand, is the primary information-carrying molecule of life [67]. It is present in every living organism on Earth, encoding the instructions for growth, repair, reproduction, and adaptation. DNA contains ALL of the instructions for ALL forms of life to exist in a microscopic form factor.

It is, scientifically speaking, the most consistent common organic thread across all known life.

Every plant.

Every animal.

Every human.

Each is a slightly different expression of the same underlying code.

Could it be that these ancient Indigenous traditions are perceiving *patterns of life* that science later described in a different language?

The resemblance is not just visual. It's conceptual.

DNA is not just a structure. It is a relationship. Two strands, held together by complementary pairing, contain in a microscopic package all the instructions for life to exist. The information emerges not from one strand alone, but from the interaction between them.

A conversation. Not a monologue.

This mirrors the Indigenous emphasis on relationship as the foundation of life.

Life is not a thing. It is a process. A living conscious interaction. A continuous exchange of information, energy, and meaning that is built on the foundation of empathy, love, and respect.

THE SERPENT AS MEMORY

So, perhaps the recurring image of the serpent is not accidental.

Perhaps it is the mind's best attempt to represent something that is difficult to put into words:

The flowing, self-organizing, recursive nature of life.

None of this happened by chance.

It's a pattern. And this pattern folds back on itself. It contains a library of knowledge. It evolves. It connects. In this sense, the serpent is not just a symbol. It is a metaphor for the process itself. For continuity. For the living thread that runs through everything.

From a Western scientific perspective, DNA reminds us of something both simple and profound:

We are biologically continuous with all life on Earth.

The same molecular architecture that builds a tree builds you.

The same chemical language that encodes a bacterium encodes your brain.

We share 41% of our DNA with a banana and 99.9% with every other human being.

We are not separate from life. We are but one expression of it.

From many Indigenous traditions, we have a language of serpents, songs, and spirits. Both, in their own way, are trying to describe the same mystery:

How life organizes, sustains, and knows itself.

And perhaps most importantly, how it reminds itself.

Every time you look at another living *being*, you are not just seeing something different. You are seeing a family member generated by the intentional variation of the same pattern.

A different verse in the same song.

A different expression of the same code.

The same serpents, still dancing.

We are not separate from the pattern.

Bringing us to the deeper philosophical question:

Before we are doctors, patients, scientists, or thinkers...

Before we are identities, roles, or stories...

We are alive. And that aliveness is not unique to us.

It is shared, inherited, and continuous.

If there is a single lesson that both science and these ancient traditions agree on, it is this:

We are all alive before we are anything else.

OLD SCHOOL EMPATHY

Inspired by what I was learning about how the Asháninka, Shipibo, and Miwok people approach life, I started looking into other traditions on the topic of empathy through a sense of singularity or oneness, and many were quite similar. Empathy is essential to sustaining a healthy connection to ourselves, our community, and the Earth. By honing the skill of empathy, we train ourselves to live in relationship with everything around us, as if it is part of us and we are part of it; as if we are one. Lucky for us, we have an entire region of the brain, the insula, that evolved specifically for this purpose.

Many ancient cultures independently explained our connection to nature by focusing on four *classical elements* (Air, Water, Fire, and Earth) that they believed made up the world. In the Western world, this concept was first attributed to Empedocles (494–434 BCE), the Greek pre-Socratic philosopher. So, in the spirit of honoring our ancestors' wisdom, let us now appreciate the four classical elements of life. The next four sections describe what I learned from breathing and meditating with a focus on empathizing with each element as if we were one; as if each element were the same as me, conscious, alive, and present.

With slow deep breathing alone, for 5-10 minutes each day for 30 days, I perceived the world from the perspective of the elements (rather than from my usual first-person Dr. Dave perspective) by activating my insula. What follows is the ancient wisdom that I received in these empathy-led meditative states, not just as a one-off, but consistently, time and time again.

Importantly, I learned that this information is not solely available to me but, as the Elders say, to anyone who chooses to listen. I invite you to listen with me.

BREATHE—I AM THE AIR

Allow me to reintroduce myself.

I am the air: the invisible VIP of your existence.

You might not see me, but trust me, I'm working double overtime to keep you alive.

I'm the breath you didn't realize you were taking just now.

And also the one you forgot to take when you read that stressful email.

Without me, you die. Quickly. And not glamorously. So, let's talk.

I'm so essential that your body has three separate openings in your face to let me in: two nostrils and a mouth, all working together like an elite nightclub security team whose only job is to make sure I get in first.

And yet, for something so important, you rarely think about me, unless I smell like a subway or you've just walked by a questionable burrito truck.

Breathing isn't just inhaling and exhaling. It's your body's built-in stress-release system.

When done right, it's like hugging your nervous system from the inside out.

When done wrong, which, let's be honest, is most of the time, you might find yourself shallow-breathing like a panicked pigeon late to a job interview.

Every breath is a reminder that you're still here. Still kicking.

Still able to reboot your system in the time it takes to inhale through your nose and sigh it out dramatically like you're in a French film.

Try it now. Really.

Stop reading after reading the instructions in the next three sentences.

Breathe in through your nose, deep into your belly.

Hold for a moment.

Now sigh it out like you just realized your phone's been on "Do Not Disturb" for six hours, and your mom has texted you seventeen times.

Feels good, right?

Do this at least three more times before continuing. This strengthens our connection and gives you access to our power together.

I'm not just air. I'm your first and last breath. And I'm always right here, waiting for you to notice me.

P.S. If you swallow me, I will give you gas.

DRINK—I AM THE WATER

I am the water. Flowing through everything from rivers, oceans, and clouds to your brain, your blood, and your bladder. I shape the land, nourish life, and quench the thirst of every living creature. I am the essence of life. And yet somehow, you still forget to drink me until your lips feel like sandpaper and your brain starts buffering.

Without me, nothing survives. No plant, no animal, no human. I am gentle and powerful, vital and transformative. I am sacred, and I've also been very patient with your iced coffee addiction.

To be human is to respect me, not just because you'll get cranky and constipated without me, but because I literally make up at least 60% of you at any given time. You are basically a sophisticated water balloon with opinions.

I am not just a beverage. I am the rain that nourishes your crops, the river that sustains your cities, and the ocean that regulates the planet's climate. The source and sustenance of all living things. When you take me for granted, you treat your own body like a dried-out houseplant.

Access to clean water is not universal. Running water is one of the most beautiful, miraculous conveniences we have. Express gratitude for this gift every day.

I can be calm or catastrophic. I soothe, and I flood. Don't build where I need to roam. Don't expect me to stay put. And for the love of Poseidon, please don't try to outswim a rip current. Respect the power, or pack floaties.

I give you life. You give me stewardship. Together, we co-create the possibility of continued existence on this lovely blue dot for countless generations to come. Protect my sources. Celebrate my presence. And maybe, just maybe, start carrying that reusable water bottle you swore you'd use.

CREATE—I AM THE FIRE

I am fire. The original influencer. Before electricity, before words, before memes, there was me. I was there when you cooked your first mammoth steak. I was there when you stared at the stars and thought, *What if I painted that on a cave wall with mud and hope*? I was also there when you accidentally burned your first house down.

I am warmth. I am light. I am transformation. And I am very much *not* to be left unattended.

To be human is to dance with me, carefully, because I am both your greatest spark and your most spectacular meltdown. I am creativity, anger, libido, drive, destruction, and rebirth, sometimes all before 9 a.m.

Let's get this straight: I am not "good" or "bad." I am energy in motion. I can light a candle…or a wildfire. Roast marshmallows…or your entire comfort zone. When you repress me, I burn inward. When you ignore me, I explode outward. Burn your candle at both ends, and you'll burn right out. Learn to use me wisely, and I'll warm your whole damn soul.

You know that urge to burn it all down? Quit the job, end the relationship, delete everything? That's me! Raw, unfiltered fire energy. But if you pause to breathe (hi, Air!), and aim me intentionally, I become a creative force. I prefer to be the bonfire around which you gather rather than the arsonist in your inbox.

I am not subtle. I'm the original *too much*. Without a container, a vision, a discipline, a healthy outlet, I get destructive. Burnout? That's me unsupervised. Road rage? Same. Overcooked lasagna? Tragically, yes. The solution? Boundaries, ceremony, intent, recovery time, and oven timers.

Your passion lights your path, but if you carry that flame too close to your ego, or your Instagram account, you might incinerate everything good around you. Use your fire to illuminate, not to dominate. You don't need to be a fire-breather, just someone who can keep a candle lit in a windstorm.

Creativity without sleep is mania. Drive without reflection is obsession. Passion without rest? Burnt toast. You can't stay lit 24/7 just like you can't burn a candle at both ends without running out of wax twice as fast. Even the sun sets. Even God rested on the seventh day. That's not laziness, it's wisdom. Learn to stoke your inner fire, and then step back. Let the coals do their slow, sustainable work.

When things fall apart like your job, your health, or your ten-year plan, don't panic. This is fire doing what fire does: clearing space. Nature burns old forests so new seeds can sprout. You are no different. Grieve, and then plant something. You're not starting over. You're starting wiser.

Use me to speak truth. To make art. To fight for justice. To melt what's frozen in you. I am the friction that ignites innovation. The rage that leads to revolution. The spark that says, *There's got to be a better way.* Trust me, there is. It starts with owning your flame, not hiding it.

Fire doesn't just destroy. It refines. It turns clay into pottery. Dough into bread. You into you. To be human is to let life bake you. You'll be messy, you'll be hot, but in the end, you'll come out crisped into something solid and good, and usually more delicious.

Your drive to love, to build, to fight, to dance? That's me too. When you're fully alive, lit from within, fully *on purpose*, that's when we're working together. I am your sacred flame. Not to be feared. Not to be ignored, but to be tended like a hearth. You are your own fireplace.

GROW—I AM THE EARTH

I am the Earth. The OG caregiver. The one who has been cradling you like a cosmic weighted blanket for your entire existence, and not once have I asked for rent.

I gave you dirt to plant, trees to shade you, mushrooms to heal you, and just enough gravity to keep you humble. And what do I ask in return? Not much. Just don't poison me or use me like a shopping mall you never clean up.

To be human is to grow. And to grow, you need me. I am your ground. Your food. Your gut biome's best friend. Your sleep signal. And if you forget that? Well...I have ways of reminding you.

You're not separate from me. You are *of* me. Stardust, soil, and anxiety, wrapped in a nervous system. Every ant, every tree, every crusty lichen has a part to play, and so do you. Forgetting that leads to dissonance and disease. Remembering it leads to calm, awe, and a strangely satisfying desire to compost.

You are a steward of the Earth. You don't *own* the land. You borrow it from your children, their children, and some future goat that doesn't even exist yet. To steward is to tend. It means planting seeds you won't see grow. It means picking up trash that isn't yours. It means learning to say, "Wow, look at that beetle!" instead of "Ew."

Have you ever touched soil with your bare feet and suddenly felt less terrible? That's not a coincidence. It's co-regulation. Studies show that just being near green things like trees, grass, moss, or that fern you keep forgetting to water reduces anxiety and improves your ability to focus. Forest bathing is now a public health initiative for good reason. Nature is your emotional support system. And guess what? It's free.

Every breath, every bite, every warm rock under your butt on a sunny day? That's me loving you. So maybe say thank you once in a while? Gratitude isn't just a vibe; it's a brain hack that makes both of us feel good. It boosts dopamine, improves sleep, and makes you way more fun to be around at dinner parties. Every act of gratitude brings us one step closer to living in grace.

To grow, you must rest. I don't mean scrolling while horizontal. I mean actual, honest-to-goodness, phone-in-another-room, nervous-system-decompressing *rest*. Like lying in grass. Or watching clouds. Or doing absolutely nothing and calling it "rewilding your psyche," because that's what it is.

You are a garden, and gardens require weeding, watering, and sometimes just friendly company. You don't bloom all at once. You bloom at weird, unpredictable times. Stop judging yourself for not being ripe yet. Compost your shame. Fertilize your joy. Pull out those mental weeds, and make space for something new to grow.

Everything in this garden exists for your enjoyment. Joy cannot emerge at the expense of everything outside of you, only in collaboration with it.

I love you until the end of time. Never forget it.

CHAPTER 4
Making Meaning

However far the stream flows, it never forgets its source.
Yoruba proverb

From the earliest cave paintings to the layered cosmologies of ancient traditions, meaning was never treated as optional. It was survival. It was orientation. It was the difference between chaos and coherence.

Ancient Egyptians encoded meaning into the afterlife. Greek philosophers like Plato argued that meaning was tied to eternal forms. Many indigenous traditions, including the Shipibo, understand meaning not as a thought process, but as something *felt* through a relationship with the living world. For them, meaning was not intellectual. It was embodied, relational, and inseparable from experience.

What is striking is that across cultures, meaning was always tied to the intensity of experience. Experiences of ritual, music, fasting, dance, plant medicine, and storytelling. These are not hobbies. They are ancient technologies for *amplifying meaningfulness*.

Only recently have we begun to understand why.

MEANING, IN THE BRAIN

At its core, meaning-making is not a philosophical act. It is a biological process.

The brain is constantly filtering incoming information and asking a single question:

Does this matter enough for me to store?

If the answer is yes, the experience is tagged, encoded, and integrated into memory. If the answer is no, it fades.

This tagging process depends heavily on the interactions among emotional salience, autonomic nervous system activation, and neurotransmitters such as serotonin.

UNDERSTANDING MEANING BY STUDYING ITS ABSENCE

In science, one of the most reliable ways to understand a system is to observe what happens when it is disrupted.

Few tools have given us as clear a window into the biology of meaning-making as Selective Serotonin Reuptake Inhibitors (SSRIs).

SSRIs, used to primarily treat depression, anxiety, and PTSD, are among the most widely prescribed medications in the world. Their primary mechanism is straightforward: they increase the availability of serotonin in the synaptic space (the space between two connected neurons) by preventing its reabsorption.

In simple terms, they flood serotonin receptors with serotonin, creating a state known as *tonic activation* (constantly activated).

In the short term, this can be stabilizing [68]. Especially for individuals acutely overwhelmed by anxiety or depression, this dampening effect can provide relief.

However, there is a tradeoff that is remarkably consistent across studies and patient reports that includes emotional blunting, reduced sexual desire and function, apathy, and a general sense that the world feels…flatter [69, 70].

Patients often describe it not as feeling worse, but as feeling less. A narrower emotional window.

Less sadness, yes, but also less joy, less awe, less meaning.

This observation gives us a powerful clue:

When serotonin signaling is chronically elevated and receptors are overstimulated, the richness of meaning diminishes.

LESS IS MORE

To understand why, we need to zoom in on the serotonin receptors, the proteins sitting on the surface of the neurons that receive serotonin and pass the message down the chain.

Receptors are not passive receivers. They are adaptive.

When a receptor is overstimulated for prolonged periods, it does something intelligent:

It withdraws like a hermit crab retreating into its shell [71]. This process, known as desensitization or downregulation, reduces the receptor's responsiveness to stimulation.

It is the nervous system's way of protecting itself from overload, but over time, there is a cost. If receptors become less responsive, then signals that would normally register as significant begin to feel muted.

In the context of SSRIs, when the serotonin receptors are flooded, the constant presence of serotonin leads to receptor desensitization. This results in flatter emotional peaks, reduced signal-to-noise sensitivity, and a decreased likelihood that the brain will tag experiences as meaningful.

This also helps explain the withdrawal [72]. When SSRI medication is removed, the system is left with less responsive receptors and less serotonin, creating a temporary deficit state. The withdrawal often lasts 1–12 weeks, which coincides with the amount of time it takes for our neurons to make new serotonin receptors with fully restored sensitivity.

The more subtle and important insight is this:

Meaning requires contrast. It requires dynamic signaling. It requires peaks and valleys. The amygdala plays an especially important role here as the contrast-detection center of the brain.

THE MEANING RECEPTOR

Among the many serotonin receptors in the brain, one stands out in the context of meaning-making:

The 5-HT_{2A} receptor.

This receptor is highly expressed in the cortex (outermost layer of the brain), particularly in regions involved in perception, cognition, and integration of sensory and emotional information, like the cortex of the insula, where emotional memories are stored [73].

It is, in many ways, a gateway receptor.

What we now understand is that the 5-HT_{2A} receptor is not just involved in mood. It is deeply involved in learning and how experiences are interpreted as significant [73].

Unlike the steady-state flooding seen with SSRIs, which results in apathy, the 5-HT_{2A} receptor appears to facilitate meaning-making when activated in bursts [74]. Short, intense, high-affinity signaling.

This is where psychedelic compounds enter the picture. One nearly universal report from patients experiencing psychedelic-assisted therapy is that their experiences were incredibly meaningful [75, 76]. In many cases, they made the top-five list.

Interestingly, tryptamine compounds like LSD (lysergic acid diethylamide), derived from a group of fungi known as ergot, and psilocybin, derived from a mushroom, interact with the serotonin system in a fundamentally different manner than SSRIs.

Rather than increasing serotonin levels in the synapse (the space between two neurons where they signal each other) around the clock, they do two things:

1. They bind directly to the 5-HT_{2A} serotonin receptor in the same location as serotonin (the active site) to activate it [77,78].
2. They also bind to another location on the side of this receptor (the allosteric site) that increases the receptor's sensitivity to, and binding affinity (stickyness) for serotonin [77, 78].

In other words, they do not just activate the receptor; they make it more responsive to activation.

A 5-HT_{2A} receptor in this state is primed for burst activation, where incoming information is experienced as more vivid, more emotionally charged, and more significant.

Subjectively, this is often described as increased meaningfulness, an enhanced personal connection to experiences, and an understanding, felt deep in our bones, that every experience, including the most ordinary, is profoundly important.

From a biological perspective, the system is doing exactly what it was designed to do:

Tagging these experiences as highly relevant for learning and memory.

THE VOLLENWEIDER EXPERIMENTS

The most elegant demonstration of this mechanism comes from the work of Dr. Franz Vollenweider, PhD, and colleagues over the last decade.

Meaningfulness has often been described as a concept of 'self' largely based on finding personal relevance in what we might consider ordinary, mundane experiences [79]. Dr. Vollenweider knew that music was an ideal experimental tool for this question. It is emotionally evocative, but not tied to a single fixed interpretation. The same song can feel neutral in one state and profoundly moving in another.

In one double-blind, randomized, placebo-controlled crossover study, the most scientifically rigorous form of clinical trial, participants attended multiple sessions in which they experienced three different conditions [74]:

1. LSD Placebo (sugar pill) + Ketanserin Placebo (sugar pill)
2. LSD + Placebo
3. LSD + Ketanserin (a selective 5-HT_{2A} serotonin receptor blocker)

Neither the participants nor the researchers interacting with them knew which condition was being administered at the time. This design allowed each participant to effectively serve as their own control, dramatically increasing the reliability of the findings.

Prior to the experimental drug administration sessions, participants went through an extensive process of rating music from most meaningful to neutral to most meaningless. Music from each of these three categories, along with songs matched to them in genre and style that were unfamiliar to the subjects, was used in the study. In some cases, the most meaningful twenty seconds of songs were removed. Songs were played after the administration of each of the three combinations of LSD, Ketanserin, and placebo above, during the times that peak drug effects were expected to be experienced.

Participants were then asked to rate their subjective experience of the music using validated psychometric scales. These included measures of perceived meaningfulness, insightfulness, unity, bliss, and spiritual connection.

The results were surprising.

In condition 1 (LSD Placebo + Ketanserin Placebo), without any drugs on board, music was experienced as expected. Meaningful songs were still considered meaningful, neutral songs were pleasant, but nothing special, and meaningless songs were utterly meaningless.

In condition 2 (LSD + Placebo), however, something fundamentally changed.

Participants reported significantly increased meaningfulness from music previously rated as neutral or meaningless.

This was not an increase in volume, hallucination, or sensory distortion. It was an increase in meaning attribution. The music was not just heard more intensely. It *mattered more.* Their sense of insight, unity, bliss, and spiritual connection also increased significantly.

Then came the critical manipulation.

When participants were pretreated with Ketanserin, which selectively blocks activity at the 5-HT_{2A} receptor, before receiving LSD, these effects were almost entirely abolished.

The music still sounded like music, but the sense of depth, emotional resonance, and personal significance were gone.

This finding is extraordinarily important.

It demonstrates that the sensory perception of music (and possibly other senses) can remain intact, while the meaning assigned to that perception is selectively disrupted.

The master switch controlling this appears to be the 5-HT_{2A} serotonin receptor.

These results are consistent with an earlier study using slightly different outcome measures, also conducted by Dr. Vollenweider's group, which found that Ketanserin blocked most of the effects of psilocybin as well [80].

From a mechanistic standpoint, this tells us that activation of the 5-HT_{2A} receptor does not simply enhance perception. It is responsible for the brain's ability to integrate sensory input with emotional and autobiographical memories, assign salience and relevance, and encode experiences as meaningful.

When the 5-HT_{2A} receptor is blocked or overstimulated, this integrative process is interrupted. The brain still receives the signal, but it no longer tags it as important.

These experiments provide one of the clearest demonstrations we have that meaning is not inherent in the stimulus.

It is constructed by the brain based on a serotonin-mediated interaction with the environment in which a given stimulus occurs. That construction depends on specific neurobiological conditions, including burst activation of the 5-HT_{2A} receptor.

When the 5-HT_{2A} receptor is dynamically activated in bursts, the brain enters a state where:

The ordinary is allowed to become extraordinary.

When it is blocked or desensitized, even the most meaningful experiences can feel empty.

This leads us to a profound insight:

Meaning is not just psychological or subjective. It depends on the burst activation of the 5-HT_{2A} serotonin receptors.

MEANING, SAFETY, AND THE NERVOUS SYSTEM

At this point, another pattern begins to emerge:

Meaning is not generated by steady, background signaling.

It is generated by dynamic shifts in state.

Specifically, shifts in the autonomic nervous system between two fundamental states. In one corner, we have complete and total safety. In the opposing corner, we have our deepest, darkest fears. Everything else exists somewhere on the spectrum in between.

When the system is activated sufficiently to identify an experience as safe or threatening, all parts of that experience are marked as significant in association with their respective tags.

This is why traumatic experiences are remembered so vividly, peak positive experiences shape identity, and ordinary neutral moments (like what we ate for breakfast) often fade from awareness quite quickly.

Our nervous systems are constantly prioritizing the question:

What should I be learning from this experience?

The answer depends on how strongly the system is activated on the fear-safety spectrum.

When we take these observations together:

- Chronic, steady 5-HT_{2A} receptor activation (as with SSRIs) leads to flattening of meaning and apathy.
- Burst 5-HT_{2A} receptor activation (as with LSD, psilocybin, or peak experiences) leads to amplification of meaning.
- The 5-HT_{2A} receptor is a central gatekeeper in this process.
- Safety and fear are the two biggest influences on how we make meaning from experience.

A remarkably coherent concept appears: Meaning is derived from the combination of the contrast and intensity of experiences with engagement of the autonomic nervous system.

From this perspective, meaning is not abstract.

It is encoded on multiple levels, from 5-HT_{2A} serotonin receptor activation to remodeling of our DNA expression patterns.

WHY AWE, JOY, AND FEAR MATTER

This brings us to a subtle, but profound realization.

The experiences that shape us most are not necessarily the ones that are objectively important.

They are the ones that shift our internal state the most, like:

- Falling in love
- Standing at the edge of the ocean at sunset
- Hearing music that stops you in your tracks
- Facing something that terrifies you

These moments are not just memorable.

They are biologically prioritized.

They drive:

- Stronger encoding of memory
- Faster learning and understanding
- Reorganization of neural networks
- Increased automation of new patterns

In other words, they help us grow faster.

Neutral experiences, by contrast, do not sufficiently engage the system to trigger a fear or safety earmark, so they pass through without leaving a deep imprint.

There is a famous Buddhist saying:

Before enlightenment: chop wood, carry water.
After enlightenment: chop wood, carry water.

What both modern neuroscience and ancient traditions are teaching us is this:

The more we remember that we are safe enough to be present with what is happening right now without doing anything about it, the more we learn to associate meaning with every experience. Even those that were considered "neutral" or mundane in the past. The more we practice this, the faster we learn, and the more we remember.

THE SHIPIBO PERSPECTIVE

The Shipibo people understand this intuitively.

For them, meaning is not constructed through analysis.

It is revealed through relationship and experience [62, 63].

Through ceremony, song, and medicinal plants, they create conditions that:

- Heighten perception
- Deepen emotional resonance
- Engage the body and the nervous system fully

In this state, meaning is not something you think about.

It is something you *feel.*

Something that reorganizes you.

From a modern scientific lens, we might say:

They are curating internal and external environments that facilitate burst activation of the systems responsible for meaning-making, including the 5-HT_{2A} receptor.

Shipibo Shamans would likely say something simpler: *You are remembering how to listen.*

The emerging science does not reduce meaning to molecules.

It reveals the mechanisms through which meaning becomes possible.

It shows us that while meaning-making is our default state, meaning itself is not constant.

It is not guaranteed. It must be activated, and we must be in a physiological state primed to receive it.

Perhaps most importantly, it reminds us that the experiences of awe, joy, and wonder are not luxuries.

They are the very conditions through which we learn, grow, and become.

When those experiences are muted, the world can feel flat.

When they are amplified, even briefly, everything can change. Not because anything outside of us changed, but because the brain has decided:

This matters.

THE BODY REMEMBERS

If the 5-HT_{2A} receptor is the biological gateway to meaning, then the next question is unavoidable:

What happens after the gate opens?

Because meaning is not just something we feel in the moment.

It is something that changes us.

To understand how that change becomes lasting, we have to follow the signal deeper, past the receptor into the neuron that houses it, all the way into the center of the cell, called the nucleus, where our DNA resides.

If you wanted to design the perfect experiment to answer the question, *"How does experience become who we are?"*, you might not start with a human brain.

You might start with a sea snail.

That is exactly what psychiatrist and Nobel Laureate, Dr. Eric Kandel, MD, decided to do.

What he discovered is one of the most important scientific insights of the last century:

Memory is not just electrical. It is structural. It is genetic. It is alive.

FROM SEA SNAILS TO YOU

Working with the sea snail *Aplysia*, which has been on Earth for roughly 300 million years, Dr. Kandel showed that when a neuron is activated by a meaningful stimulus, something extraordinary happens [20].

At first, the neuron simply fires. A neurotransmitter like serotonin is released. The signal is passed along. Not much else changes.

That is short-term memory.

However, when that activation is strong enough, repeated enough, or emotionally relevant enough, the signal has a longer-lasting effect.

The signal travels from the surface of the neuron through intracellular signaling pathways, into the nucleus to the DNA. Then something almost magical happens. Genes turn on. Proteins are made. New connections grow.

The neuron literally begins to change its shape, its strength, and its behavior to plan for the future. It becomes more likely to fire the same way again. It begins to form a *memory*, built into the cell's structure itself.

What Dr. Kandel proved is that:

Strong, Meaningful, and/or Repeated Experiences → Receptor Activation → Gene Expression Modifications → Increased Protein Synthesis (particularly of scaffolding proteins that neurons need to grow and form new connections) → Neuronal Structural Change → Stored Memory

The premise is simple: more meaning → more memory. From sea snails to humans, the blueprint is the same.

THE EPIGENETIC LAYER: THE SCORE WRITTEN ON TOP OF THE MUSIC

Let's zoom in one level deeper, because the real question is:

How does a signal turn a gene on?

This is where the epigenetic code enters the story.

Think of your DNA as the sheet music of your life. Every cell in your body (except for sperm and egg cells), from your neurons to your liver cells to your skin cells, carries an identical musical score (DNA code). The same exact sequence of A, T, C, and G.

And yet, somehow, you are not a blob of over 30 trillion identical cells.

You are made of over 200 distinct cell types, each performing wildly different functions. Same code, different expression pattern.

How is this possible? Because layered on top of your DNA is another system:

The epigenetic code.

If DNA is the sheet music, epigenetics refers to the musical notation that tells a specific cell to play specific sections of the music louder or softer, faster or slower, or not at all [81]. The epigenetic system uses chemical tags, like DNA methylation and histone modification, for notation to mark sections of your DNA as:

- Read this
- Ignore this
- Turn this up
- Turn this down
- Save this for later

It does not rewrite the letters of our DNA code. It changes how they are read and expressed by our cells.

Here is the part that matters most:

This system is constantly changing.

Not once in childhood.

Not once per year.

Moment to moment.

Every experience we have involves interacting with this system. Every meaningful activation of our nervous system, in some small or large way, leaves marks dictating how our genes are expressed. This is one of the primary ways the body keeps a biological record of experience.

THE BRIDGE: FROM NEUROTRANSMITTERS TO IDENTITY

Let's bring this back to what we already know about serotonin and meaning.

A neurotransmitter like serotonin binds to a receptor.

If that activation is weak or tonic, nothing lasting happens.

If that activation is:

- Strong
- Repeated
- Emotionally significant and meaningful

The signal reaches the nucleus.

The epigenetic code is updated.

Gene expression is modulated.

Proteins like Brain-Derived Neurotrophic Factor (BDNF), essential for learning and memory formation, are produced.

Synapses grow stronger.

Connections reorganize.

This is how a fleeting moment becomes a lasting pattern.

This is how "something happened" becomes:

"This is who I am."

In *The Body Keeps the Score*, Dr. Bessel van der Kolk, MD, describes how trauma is not just remembered cognitively, but is stored in the body [41].

Felt in physiology. Replayed in patterns.

What we can now add, with modern molecular biology, is this:

The "score" he describes is not just metaphorical or superficially related to fascia and body tension. It is fully biological.

It is written in the epigenetic layer of our cells.

You can think of this as an internal scoreboard.

SAFETY VS. FEAR

Every experience you have casts a vote (Figure 15).

- Moments of safety, connection, awe, and love
- Moments of fear, threat, chaos, and overwhelm

Figure 15. The Body Keeps the Scorecard Take 1

Each one activates your nervous system. Each one influences receptor activity. Each one nudges gene expression. Each one leaves a trace.

Over time, the side that is activated more strongly and more frequently begins to win our worldview.

Not philosophically.

Biologically.

THE TRAUMATIZED RECEPTOR

Some of the most compelling evidence for this comes from studies of stress.

Researchers studying both animals and humans have shown that traumatic experiences can alter the epigenetic regulation of the glucocorticoid receptor [82, 83]. This receptor is one of two primary receptors for cortisol, one of our most important stress response hormones. Cortisol must bind to this receptor (and the receptor must be functioning correctly) to carry out cortisol's mission of regulating your body's response to stress and decreasing inflammation.

When this receptor is functioning well, your body can rapidly and appropriately turn the stress response on and off as needed in response to survival threats.

However, when trauma alters the epigenetic code regulating this receptor, something changes. The glucocorticoid receptor becomes more sensitive to cortisol. The system becomes less efficient at shutting off. The alarm lingers. The body behaves as if the threat is still present.

This pattern has now been observed in:

- Animal models of early life stress and trauma [83, 84]
- Humans with histories of childhood trauma and significant trauma in adulthood [82, 85]
- Individuals with a PTSD diagnosis [82, 85]

In other words:

Trauma changes how the body reads its own stress signals, as evidenced by changes in the epigenetic code.

WHEN EXPERIENCE CROSSES GENERATIONS

Now, we arrive at another one of the most interesting discoveries in modern biology.

Epigenetic patterns, such as those induced by trauma on the glucocorticoid receptor gene, can be passed down. Not just through behavior, but through biological inheritance.

In animal studies, stress-induced epigenetic changes can be observed in multiple generations of offspring, even when those offspring are raised in safe environments [83, 84]. These changes have been shown to be inherited for up to fourteen generations [84].

Studies of human populations exposed to extreme trauma, such as the series of particularly impressive studies in Holocaust survivors and their offspring conducted by Dr. Rachel Yehuda, PhD, have shown alterations in stress-related genes such as FKBP5 across generations [82, 85-87].

This helps to explain why those of us whose ancestors experienced severe trauma have an increased likelihood of developing a mental illness, even if we have not experienced it firsthand. In humans, it is suspected that epigenetic marks from trauma can be passed down across three or more generations [87].

This also helps explain why those of us whose ancestors experienced famine are more likely to have a slower metabolism. Our ancestors' bodies adapted back then to conserve calories in the face of food shortages by decreasing the rate at which the body uses energy by prioritizing energy conservation. Our bodies still remember those tough times, even though they might have happened hundreds of years ago. That memory and the response to it are stored in the epigenetic code. Generations later, the same adaptation that facilitated survival during a food crisis dramatically increases the likelihood of obesity in the face of constant food surplus.

This does not mean trauma is our destiny.

It means that our epigenetic code is changing in response to experience, especially meaningful experiences. This strongly suggests that with a little intentional curation of our own, we can update our epigenetic code back to a safe, stable "untraumatized" state.

It means that *meaningful experiences echo biologically beyond a single lifetime.*

It also means that our bodies remember experiences from much further back than we had ever considered. Memory that spans lifetimes.

At the same time, you may struggle at any given moment to remember something that happened yesterday. Despair not! This does not mean you have forgotten it for good. The memory is stored away in your body, in your cells, all the way down to your epigenetic code. It will be with you for your lifetime (at least).

Curate your environment to facilitate the memory resurfacing, and it will return.

THE SIMPLE SUMMARY

Bringing this all together:

- Meaningful experiences generate strong, burst-like activation of the 5-HT_{2A} serotonin receptor.
- Once activated, the 5-HT_{2A} receptor signals to structures within the neuron to release specific stores of calcium, a critically important ion for cellular signaling and protein synthesis.
- The significant rise in intracellular calcium activates proteins in the nucleus of the cell that begin to update the epigenetic code, modifying gene expression to produce more proteins that form the scaffolding for neurons to wire together.
- These epigenetic changes reshape neural circuits, behavior, and stress physiology so that we, and our offspring, are biologically prepared for the challenges our environment throws at us.

So, *meaning* is not in any way ambiguous. It is not optional. It is not just subjective.

Meaning is what happens when experience becomes biology.

This helps us arrive at a profound understanding:

Memory is not stored in one place.

It is not just electrical.

It is not just psychological.

It is:

- Structural
- Molecular
- Network-based
- On our DNA

Your experiences are not just remembered. They are written into you.

Not perfectly, not permanently, but they are written in patterns, in tendencies, in probabilities.

If the epigenetic layer is a scorecard written in *meaning*…

Then every moment matters more than we think, because every single moment is an opportunity to create more meaning. When we intentionally update our code by training ourselves to receive more meaning from our experiences, we're not just healing ourselves; we're stopping the cycle and protecting future generations.

Not because every moment rewrites your destiny, but because every intentional, meaningful moment tilts the scale back toward safety, curiosity, and connection (Figure 8). Over time, as those tilts and tips become traits, our neurons rewire, our epigenetic code is rewritten, and the delicate balance of the Force is restored.

This is why reminding ourselves that we are safe enough to embrace childlike awe, joy, and delight is so essential to *being* human. It tips the scales back in our favor. Back toward safety, security, and comfort. We were all born doing this as children, and our bodies remember how to do this to this day.

Meaningful experiences are not just experiences.

They are instructions.

And your body is always listening.

Always learning.

Always writing the next line of the score.

CHAPTER 5
The Memory We Forgot

If a problem can be solved, there is no need to worry.
If it cannot be solved, worrying will do no good.
His Holiness the 14th Dalai Lama

As a freshman in college, before I held a human brain in my hands or traced the microscopic architecture of stress under a lens, there was a headline that stopped me in my tracks.

It was the early aughts, and mad cow disease (Bovine Spongiform Encephalopathy, or BSE) was everywhere.

Not just in scientific journals, but on the front page of newspapers, on television, in conversations at dinner tables. Entire herds of cattle were being culled. Countries were restricting imports. My family stopped eating beef. People were suddenly questioning something they had never thought twice about before:

Could the food I'm eating give me dementia?

What made this moment so frightening and compelling to me wasn't just the scale of the outbreak.

It was the mechanism.

This wasn't a virus.

It wasn't a bacterium.

It wasn't a parasite.

It was something far stranger.

A protein known as a prion (proteinaceous infectious particle).

A CONTAGION WITHOUT A GENOME

The idea that a disease could spread through food, from cow to cow, and even to humans, without any traditional trackable infectious agent, felt impossible.

And somehow, that's exactly what was happening.

A number of people exposed to contaminated beef had developed a devastating condition known as Variant Creutzfeldt-Jakob disease (vCJD). This is a rapidly progressive neurodegenerative disorder with a sudden onset that starts with anxiety and apathy, followed by loss of balance, sensory symptoms, memory loss, severe cognitive decline, loss of motor function, and ultimately, death [88].

The connection between what we eat and how our brain functions had never felt so real, or so unsettling.

This was not an infection in the way we understood it. This was a transformation, resulting from the smallest infectious particle ever discovered.

BSE and vCJD are both caused by misfolded prion proteins entering the body that persuade other normally occurring prion proteins to misfold in the same way and stick together [88, 89]. A cascade that begins invisibly and ends in complete neurological destruction in as little as twelve months from symptom onset.

At the time, this challenged one of the most fundamental assumptions in biology: that all transmissible diseases required instructions for replication in the form of nucleic acids (DNA or RNA).

Yet, prions didn't need nucleic acid instructions.

They *were* the instructions.

CURIOSITY BECOMES DIRECTION

We also were starting to see a rise in CJD in people who were receiving neurological tissue transplants, like corneas in the eye, from donors who had the mutant prion protein [90]. Prions could not be destroyed by the temperatures we used to kill bacteria and viruses when sterilizing surgical equipment at that time because they require higher temperatures to denature [91]. There was a clear, immediate need to understand prions so we could update our practices and prevent undue harm to unsuspecting patients.

Could memory loss and dementia be contagious now?

I couldn't look away.

The more I read, the more I realized this wasn't just an isolated agricultural or public health issue. It was a window into something much deeper about how the brain works, how it fails, and how information itself can be encoded biologically.

If a misfolded protein could spread a disease that takes our memories away, how did it do it, and what else could it do?

These questions pulled me in completely.

I dove headfirst into the study of prion diseases. Not casually, not academically at a distance, but with the kind of focused curiosity that starts to reorganize your life around it.

I wanted to understand how structure becomes information, how a protein's shape could act like a memory, how something so small could dismantle something so complex.

In 2005, that path led me to Patricia Spilman, whom I met by chance in the stands at one of my little brother's little league games. After hearing about my interests, Patricia introduced me to her colleague, Dr. Steven DeArmond, MD, PhD, at UCSF. They just happened to be looking for extra assistance on some research projects in the prion department. It was a particularly unique opportunity because Dr. DeArmond was the leading pathologist working with Dr. Stanley Prusiner, MD, the neurologist who was awarded the Nobel Prize for discovering prions. Needless to say, I took the job immediately.

THE PROTEIN THAT BEHAVES LIKE AN IDEA

An infectious prion is a protein that has folded incorrectly, but instead of simply being degraded and cleared, it interacts with normal versions of itself and convinces them to adopt the same misfolded shape. It has a structure that behaves as if it is "sticky" when in the presence of other similar proteins.

It is structure as information.

A structure that is self-propagating.

This was the radical insight that led to Dr. Prusiner receiving the Nobel Prize [89, 92]. At the time of his discovery, the scientific community resisted fiercely. The idea that a protein alone could transmit disease seemed impossible. Nearly everyone else, aside from Dr. Prusiner, thought the culprit had to be a "slow virus," but Stan proved 'em wrong! We now know that diseases like scrapie, BSE, Kuru, and Creutzfeldt-Jakob disease are all caused by mutant misfolded prion proteins, and that proteins alone can cause infectious disease.

Some prion diseases are genetic and inherited, like Fatal Familial Insomnia (FFI). Others are primarily transmissible, like BSE and vCJD, but the mechanism is the same:

Misfolded proteins accumulate, spread, and destroy the cells that host them. When this happens in brain cells, memory is hit hard.

A PATTERN EMERGES

Modern science increasingly suggests that many dementia disorders that accompany aging are not contagious like some prion diseases, but they are caused by the inappropriate accumulation of toxic misfolded proteins, very similar to prions [93].

In Alzheimer's disease, the misfolded protein culprit is amyloid-beta.

In Parkinson's disease and Lewy body dementia, it's alpha-synuclein.

In Huntington's disease, it's mutant huntingtin.

In Frontotemporal Dementia (FTD), it's often tau or TDP-43.

Different proteins. Same fundamental problem.

They misfold.

They accumulate.

They bind to each other.

The more of them that stick together, the harder and harder they are for the cell to remove.

When they hit a critical mass, they kill precious brain cells.

There are moments in medical training that don't just teach you science. They change how you see what it means to be human.

For me, one of those moments came in Dr. DeArmond's lab, where I had the privilege of briefly working alongside neurologist Dr. Bill Seeley, MD. He spent long hours carefully slicing and studying cadaveric brains from patients who had died of FTD, and let me tag along.

FTD, and specifically the behavioral variant of FTD (bvFTD), is one of the most extraordinary examples of how specific brain systems give rise to specific aspects of who we are. Unlike Alzheimer's disease, which typically begins with memory loss, bvFTD often begins with something far more insidious:

A loss of empathy and emotional memory [94].

Patients often become socially inappropriate. They say things that feel blunt, insensitive, or even cruel. Completely out of character for who they once were. They lose the ability to read social cues, to recognize emotional nuance, and to respond to others with care.

Yet, more often than not, non-emotional memory and general intellect remain mostly intact in the early stages.

They can still solve problems.

They can still recall facts.

They can still hold their ground cognitively.

What is essentially missing is the ability to feel with others.

One of the most fascinating discoveries in this field has been the role of two very specific types of neurons that degenerate in bvFTD: von Economo neurons (VENs) and fork cells [95].

VENs are large, spindle-shaped neurons, and fork cells are, you guessed it, fork-shaped neurons found primarily in regions like the insula and anterior cingulate cortex, areas deeply involved in emotional awareness, emotional memory, social intuition, empathy, self-awareness, meaning making, and the actions that result [96].

Both of these neuron types are relatively rare. They are only found in species with complex social structures, such as humans, great apes, elephants, dolphins, and whales [97]. They appear to play a critical role in rapid, intuitive social-emotional processing and autonomic regulation.

In bvFTD, these neurons are among the first to degenerate, explaining why one of the earliest casualties of the disease is empathy and emotional memory [95].

What makes bvFTD so illuminating, and so heartbreaking, is its specificity.

It does not initially erase everything.

It selectively dismantles the neural architecture of social connection.

You begin to see that what we often think of as personality—kindness, restraint, emotional attunement—is not subjective or philosophical.

It is biological.

It lives in networks.

In circuits.

In specific cells.

When those extremely resilient neurons are damaged, the qualities they support begin to fade.

THE EYE IS THE WINDOW TO THE BRAIN

In the summer of 2006, I started my neuroscience graduate work studying stress responses in the retinal pigment epithelium (RPE) under Dr. Sally Temple, PhD. Dr. Temple was the first to demonstrate the existence of a new type of multipotent neural stem cell that continues to generate new neurons in the adult brain, even as we age [98]. She was studying aging from a stem cell perspective, and I was into it.

The RPE is a single layer of cells responsible for maintaining the health of the photoreceptors of the retina, one of the most metabolically demanding tissues in the body [99]. Every moment your eyes are open, photons strike your retina, and the frequencies of light we perceive are converted into electrochemical signals that your brain interprets as everything we see.

This happens continuously. For decades. Ideally, for over a century without disruption, which is truly remarkable because the RPE cells that support this process do not divide. They are in a very special family of cells, along with neurons and cardiac myocytes (heart muscle cells), known as *quiescent* cells. The same RPE, neurons, and cardiac myocytes that are with us when we're born are with us when we die [99, 100]. This put the RPE at the very top of the list for the most resilient cell award and made them the perfect subject for my doctoral research on how chronic stress causes aging and disease.

In Age-related Macular Degeneration (AMD), the leading cause of vision loss and blindness worldwide, RPE cells begin to die due to chronic overwhelming stress [101]. And one of the key toxic players?

Amyloid-beta. The very same protein implicated in Alzheimer's.

It turns out this isn't just a brain story. Amyloid-beta also accumulates in cardiac myocytes as we age, contributing to heart disease.

This is a systems-level phenomenon.

THE WASTE MANAGEMENT PROBLEM

The good news is that, for most of your life, this is a non-issue.

Your cells are extraordinarily good at cleaning up after themselves. Systems such as the proteasome and autophagy pathways identify, degrade, and recycle damaged or misfolded proteins [102].

Your cellular waste management team works tirelessly until aging starts to shift the equation [103].

With aging, stress continues.

Cells and organs continue to function.

Waste production continues.

Waste clearance slows with age.

In long-lived, non-dividing quiescent cells like neurons and RPE, there is no easy reset.

Stress increases the production of toxic cellular waste products.

If waste removal keeps up with waste production, the cell survives.

If waste accumulates faster than it can be cleared, the cell begins to fail.

This is why minimizing stress, sleeping deeply, and optimizing our intake of foods and nutrients that reduce inflammation are essential for improving longevity and healthspan.

WHEN HEALTHY PROTEINS BECOME TOXIC STRUCTURES

Common waste products that must be removed and recycled nearly as quickly as they are produced are misfolded proteins. If not rapidly recycled, prions and misfolded proteins, such as Amyloid-beta, accumulate in and around cells and begin to stick together [93].

At first, this is manageable, but over time, these misfolded proteins aggregate into increasingly stable structures that are much harder (and sometimes impossible) for our cells to break down. When they reach a critical mass, something even more dangerous happens:

They form pore-like structures that insert themselves into the cell membrane and begin to leak calcium ions into the cell [104].

Calcium is one of the most important signaling ions in biology. Cells maintain a roughly 10,000:1 gradient between extracellular (outside the cell) and intracellular (inside the cell) calcium concentrations [105]. This extremely intentional and delicate calcium gradient is essential for regulating everything from learning, memory formation, and memory storage to protein folding, gene expression, cellular metabolism, and cellular survival with exquisite precision.

However, when calcium leaks in uncontrollably, the cell can't get it out fast enough, and it quickly becomes toxic. To our neurons and RPE, this is like being in the middle of the ocean with someone who randomly starts punching tiny holes in your boat because they're stressed. We start dumping water out, but the water keeps coming. We eventually tire, unable to keep up with the floodwaters, and we meet our maker. It's not a fun way to go out.

Excess intracellular calcium disrupts protein folding even further, accelerating the production of more misfolded proteins [106].

A vicious cycle emerges:

More misfolding → more aggregation → more calcium influx → more damage → cell death

THE COLLECTIVE STRUGGLE TO SURVIVE

Here's the beautiful part.

Cells don't just give up.

Neurons, cardiac cells, and RPE cells all evolved to distribute this burden. Through their networks and ion channel junctions that connect them, they spread excess calcium and metabolic stress across neighboring cells, helping preserve function for as long as possible [107].

It's a collaborative, power-in-numbers, survival strategy that exists even on the cellular level. The group comes together for the individual cell in the network that is struggling and lends extra hands to lighten the load in real time.

When our cells work together as a team to distribute the weight of stress, it works for most of our lives.

This is why people with neurodegenerative diseases often appear completely normal for years, even decades. The team is compensating. Redistributing. Holding the line.

Until it can't any longer.

When a critical threshold of stressful toxic load is reached, cells begin to die. And when they do, they release their accumulated calcium, misfolded proteins, and other waste products into the surrounding environment, increasing the burden on neighboring cells.

This can trigger a chain reaction of cell death.

This is why degenerative diseases of aging, like dementia, often sneak up on us with rapid decline shortly after detection.

WHAT THIS TEACHES US ABOUT MEMORY

Memory is not just electrical. It's epigenetic. It's structural. It depends on the integrity of cells that must survive for a lifetime while continuously adapting.

The same mechanisms that allow neurons to change, grow, and encode experience for our entire lives are the ones that, under chronic stress, can lead to dysfunction.

Which is why the work of psychiatrist and Nobel Laureate Dr. Eric Kandel remains so profound.

Memory is encoded through changes in gene expression, protein synthesis, and synaptic structure [20]. It is built through repetition, attention training, and meaning-making.

Memory is maintained through cellular health. Chronic stress impairs cellular health. When our neural cells are healthy and can clear toxic waste efficiently, our memories last and are more easily accessible.

When our cells falter, memories fade.

THE HIDDEN STRENGTH OF YOUR MEMORY

Despite everything that can go wrong, your brain is far more resilient than you think.

For most of your life, your cells are winning this battle.

You are remembering far more than you realize. Experiences are encoded, stored, and influencing you beneath the surface of awareness much of the time.

The challenge is not that your memories are ever gone or lost.

The challenge is reliably accessing them.

ATTENTION, STRESS, AND SELF-SABOTAGE

Memory retrieval depends on attention.

And your attention depends on your state of mind.

When you are stressed, distracted, or overwhelmed, your attention is fragmented. When attention is fragmented, you are less present with your experiences, and less information enters your conscious awareness. In addition, memory retrieval suffers.

Even more subtly, anxiety about memory creates intrusive thoughts that consume cognitive bandwidth.

"Why can't I remember this?"

"What's wrong with me?"

These thoughts pull attention away from the task itself.

The system sabotages itself.

When we ask ourselves the wrong questions, we get the wrong answers.

MEMORIZATION VS. UNDERSTANDING

There is a quiet but critical distinction at the heart of how we learn, and it shapes not only how much we remember, but how deeply that knowledge becomes part of us.

Memorization is fast.

Understanding is slow.

And in modern education, we have systematically chosen speed.

MEMORIZATION: RAPID RECALL

Memorization is the act of storing information without necessarily connecting it to meaning. Sort of like a parrot.

You repeat a fact enough times, and it sticks, at least temporarily. Neural pathways are activated, short-term synaptic changes occur, and for a while, recall is possible. This skill is very useful and, at times, necessary, but memorization alone is fragile because it is not integrated into the whole.

From a neurobiological perspective, memorization often relies on relatively shallow encoding. Information is stored in isolated neural circuits, with limited connections to broader networks of meaning, emotion, and sensory experience. Without repeated use or reinforcement, these connections weaken over time.

This is why cramming works only in the short term.

You can bust your butt to pass the test.

Then, a week or three later, it's gone.

The brain is incredibly efficient. If something is not used meaningfully, it is pruned.

UNDERSTANDING: MEMORY THAT BECOMES YOU

Understanding is different.

Understanding is what happens when new information is woven into your existing model of the world. It engages multiple systems at once: cognitive, emotional, sensory, and often social.

When you understand something, it transforms from information to knowledge.

You can explain it.

You can apply it.

You can adapt it to new situations.

You can teach it fluently to others.

This kind of learning is supported by widespread neural integration. Multiple brain regions coordinate. Synaptic changes are reinforced across networks. Gene expression shifts. Structural changes occur as neurons wire and rewire.

In Dr. Kandel's language, this is long-term potentiation with meaning [20].

And once something is truly understood, it becomes remarkably durable. Not because we are trying harder to remember it, but because it has been knit seamlessly into how we see the world.

THE MISSING HALF OF LEARNING

There is another layer to learning and memory that is often overlooked [108].

Most modern education is overwhelmingly top-down (brain-to-body cognitive learning).

We sit. We read. We listen. We think.

Fortunately and unfortunately, the brain did not evolve to learn in isolation from the body. In fact, a substantial portion of learning (at least 50%) is bottom-up (body-to-brain experiential learning), like learning to ride a bike, and is driven by sensory experience, movement, emotion, and physiological state. If you try to teach someone how to ride a bike or play a sport solely by following written instructions, it is impossibly challenging [109].

These inputs shape how information is encoded and retrieved. They influence attention, salience, and memory consolidation at a fundamental level. Most importantly, bottom-up learning accelerates the path to understanding.

When we ignore the body in the learning process, we are ignoring half the system.

So when we prioritize memorization over understanding, and top-down learning over bottom-up learning, a wildly disturbing realization emerges:

At best, we are teaching people only a fraction of the ways in which humans actually learn, but are still asking them to learn extremely complex things quickly. It's a recipe for failure, and the results are beginning to show.

A GENERATIONAL WARNING SIGN

Studies now suggest that Generation Z is the first generation in recent history to perform worse on standardized cognitive measures than the generation before them [110].

This is not a blip. We are witnessing meaningful declines that signal a society in regression. Regression, the opposite of growth, is not compatible with the survival of any species, so it must be addressed immediately.

There are many contributing factors, including the issues with how we teach people to learn described above, but one stands out prominently:

The increasing dominance of screens as primary learning tools.

Screens are not inherently bad. They are powerful tools, but they tend to compress learning into narrow channels, primarily visual and cognitive, often fragmented, fast-paced, and highly distracting. Screens are also overstimulating due to the sheer amount of information they display, including blue light, which constantly bombards our senses. Overstimulation increases uncertainty, thereby activating the sympathetic fight-or-flight response in the nervous system [13-15]. This literally shuts down our ability to learn new things that are not essential for survival in the moment.

Screens also reward quick hits of information rather than rewarding deep engagement and patience.

They bias toward memorization, not understanding. They bias toward solo top-down learning rather than experiential learning through relationships with other beings.

They further distance learning from the body, from sustained attention, and from meaningful integration into the whole.

WHY THIS MATTERS MORE NOW THAN EVER

This is not just an educational issue.

It is a societal one.

When we prioritize memorization over understanding, we produce individuals who can recall information temporarily, but struggle to apply it meaningfully in real-life situations. When we neglect the body, we produce individuals who are disconnected from the physiological states that support attention, learning, and resilience.

When these patterns are scaled across an entire generation, the effects compound exponentially. Words struggle to describe the gravity of this problem if it is allowed to continue, not to mention the countless resources spent educating entire generations of people who don't know how to effectively apply that information in the real world.

What we are seeing now is not a failure of individuals. It is a mismatch between how we teach and how the brain actually learns. This mismatch is what must be remedied.

DR. DAVE'S MEMORY TOOLKIT™

If you want to improve your memory, you don't just train recall.

You support the system that enables recall.

Here are five of the easiest science-backed ways to do this:

1. **Spaced Repetition**

   Repeated exposure over time strengthens synaptic connections and stabilizes memory traces. This is one of the most robust findings in learning science.

2. **Attention Training (Mindfulness)**
   Practices that improve sustained attention enhance working memory and reduce interference from distracting thoughts.
3. **Sleep Optimization**
   During sleep, especially deep slow-wave sleep, the brain consolidates memories, transferring them into long-term storage. Without sleep, memory formation and retrieval both degrade.
4. **Reaffirming Safety**
   Safety increases vagus nerve activity, making us more present in the moment. Increasing vagus nerve activity signals safety, quieting the amygdala in a powerful positive feedback loop. The more present we are in the current moment, focused on what we are intending to remember, the more meaning the experience takes on, and the more we remember. Activities such as those described in detail in this book that increase vagus nerve functioning, including Apollo Neuro, have also been linked to improved memory recall.
5. **Minimize Toxic Load**
   Both psychological stress and environmental toxins increase inflammation. Inflammation, when left unchecked over time, causes cell dysfunction and death. Gradually reducing your stress decreases inflammation. Start by minimizing exposure to things you can control, like pesticides, herbicides, fungicides, caustic cleaning chemicals, heavy metals, smoking, alcohol, too much unprotected sun exposure, nuclear radiation, and foods that don't leave you feeling good after you eat them.

THE SIMPLE SUMMARY

Your memory is not fragile by default. It is a dynamic, resilient system maintained by brain cells that have been working hard on your behalf since the day you were born. We all forget things sometimes, especially when we're overwhelmed and underslept. Take it easy on yourself. There is nothing wrong with you (or your memory) that this happens.

Like all living systems, memory is dependent on balance. Balance between stress and recovery, between waste production and waste removal, between attention and distraction. When that balance is supported, something extraordinary becomes clear:

We carry far more of our lives with us than we thought.

When we understand that:

1. Memories are stored not just in neural connections, but in the epigenetic layer of code that regulates the expression of our DNA throughout the body.
2. Memory is something that happens automatically by the nature of the biology of experience.
3. Memories can be passed down to our offspring in our epigenetic code.
4. The easiest way to strengthen our memory is to do our very best to find meaning in our experiences.

We can rest easy knowing that we no longer have any reason to worry about our memory.

We all have the ability to curate the conditions for our memory to function optimally.

If we want to cultivate memory that lasts (and grows over time), we must shift our focus.

From memorization to understanding.

From speed to depth.

From disembodied cognition to integrated meaningful experiences.

Learning should feel a lot less like the painful download of a large file when your internet is on the fritz and a lot more like constructing a living, breathing model of the world.

That is what the brain is designed to do. When we work with that design instead of against it, something changes. We don't just remember more. We become better at making sense of what we remember.

That is the kind of memory that lasts a lifetime.

CHAPTER 6
Never Gonna Give You Up

Man is an animal who, more than any other,
can adapt himself to all climates and circumstances.
Henry David Thoreau (1817–1862)

Let's be real: life is not a gentle breeze.

It's more like a surprise obstacle course designed by emotionally unstable game show producers.

And yet, here you are. Still standing. Still showing up. Still reading. Still opening emails. That, my friend, is resilience.

To be human is to adapt. Not just survive the chaos, but somehow grow through it. If the field of evolutionary biology tells us anything, it's that our ability to adapt, and to do so together as a team, is one of the most important skills we have as a species. It is the primary reason we've made it as far as we have as a civilization, despite all odds.

As a species, we have overcome disasters of all kinds that sought to wipe us out, from plagues and epidemics to floods, fires, and famine. If you remember nothing else from this book, remember this: we evolved to adapt, and to adapt together, as our top survival skill. Connection, empathy, and working together are so important that they are hardwired into our brains.

The skill of collaborative adaptation (working together) activates a particular network in the limbic system (the emotional brain) that is involved in empathy (insula), acting on emotions (anterior cingulate cortex), and fear/safety learning (amygdala) [111].

Studies of these brain regions in animals and humans over the last half-century have shed light on how they communicate with one another, as they are critically important for emotional detection, recognition, memory, and motivation to act [30-32, 111]. The experience of genuinely connecting with another person stimulates this powerful neural network in a similar way in both people, resulting in co-regulation and a phenomenon described as *limbic resonance*: two emotional brains synced together in harmony [112]. Effectively, a state of profound safety that arises from being present together.

The lack of recognition of collaborative adaptation and empathy as having the importance they deserve may also be one of the primary reasons we are rapidly careening toward a tragic collapse of the stunningly beautiful civilization we just spent all this time creating for ourselves to enjoy. Ironically, our beautiful civilization would not exist without collaborative adaptation and empathy.

Division is the chief enemy of our human species. Collaboration is our best friend.

ATTENTION IS A FINITE RESOURCE

If attention is a currency, most of us are walking around like we just discovered online shopping with no budget and one-click purchasing enabled.

Scientifically, we know attention is a finite resource [113]. Experientially, we *learn* it the hard way.

Take driving, for example. You are cruising along, one hand on the wheel, feeling like a calm, competent adult. Then your phone buzzes. You glance down for what you swear is "just a second," and suddenly you have no idea how the last 300 feet of road happened. This is not because you briefly became a worse driver. It is because your brain reassigned resources. The attentional networks that were tracking lane position, speed, and the subtle micro-movements of surrounding cars got partially redirected to decoding a text that, let's be honest, could absolutely have waited. The result is not true multitasking. It is degraded driving plus mediocre texting. A lose-lose, with a side of existential vulnerability.

Now let's upgrade the difficulty level: you're writing an important email to your boss while working from home, and your baby begins to cry.

Not just a polite, brief, cinematic cry. A full, limb-flailing, nervous-system-activating, evolutionarily optimized scream designed to override every other priority you have ever had, that has no immediate end in sight. This is not an accident. Human infants are essentially tiny survival DJs, blasting the one track your brain cannot ignore. The sound recruits the amygdala, heightens vigilance, and redirects attention toward caregiving, whether you like it or not. So you sit there, attempting to answer emails while your nervous system is screaming, "THE SPECIES DEPENDS ON YOU." Predictably, your work quality declines, your stress increases, and the email you send somehow includes both a typo and a subtle cry for help.

And then there is the most insidious attentional leak of all: doing something you would rather not be doing.

Taxes are a classic example. You open the form with the enthusiasm of someone about to assemble furniture without instructions. Immediately, about 50% of your attention is allocated not to the task itself, but to an internal monologue that sounds something like, "Why am I doing this? Why does this exist? Is it too late to become a monk?" That internal resistance is not just psychological fluff. It is metabolically expensive. It occupies working memory, engages emotional circuitry, and directly competes with the cognitive resources required to complete the task.

So, now you are trying to do taxes with half your brain actively protesting the existence of taxes. The outcome is predictable. You make more mistakes, you take longer, and you occasionally consider simply mailing the IRS a handwritten note that says, "I did my best."

Across all of these examples, the principle is the same. Attention is not something we can infinitely divide without consequence. Every additional demand reduces the quality of what remains.

The key takeaway is that you are not bad at focusing.

You are operating within the constraints of a beautifully efficient, slightly overprotective, biological system that was never designed to drive, text, do taxes, and ignore a screaming baby all at the same time.

AUTOMATION

Much of our strategy for adaptation over the last century has been focused on creating external automations (AI included) that exist outside of us. The tricky thing with external automations is that they break down in a major way when we automate the wrong things or forget to teach people essential information because we outsourced it to machines long ago.

For so many generations, our ancestors worked their tails off so that somewhere, sometime, their offspring could lead easier, better lives. Thanks to the work of our collective forefathers and foremothers, we now have everything from cars to planes to smartphones to bridges to antibiotics to two-day delivery of just about anything.

So, first things first: shout-out to the old school. The next time you're with a family member or friend from an older generation, thank them for working so hard so that you could have an easier life than they had. A life free from the shackles of the Dewey Decimal System, landlines, and horse-drawn carriages as a primary mode of transportation.

Making life easier has always been the goal. And yet, despite our best intentions, access to so many conveniences has led us to forget the importance of certain critical skills for human survival. Skills such as kindness, gratitude, empathy, equanimity, and collaborative adaptation. All skills that can be trained, honed, and mastered to yield significant boosts to resilience and quality of life. Think of it like working out in the gym, but the gym is in your mind, and you can take it anywhere without the annoying monthly membership.

What we often forget is that the human body is the most incredible, fanciest automation machine we have ever had the pleasure of operating. We automate thoughts and behaviors rapidly to run in the background by learning them in meaningful ways, understanding them, and repeating

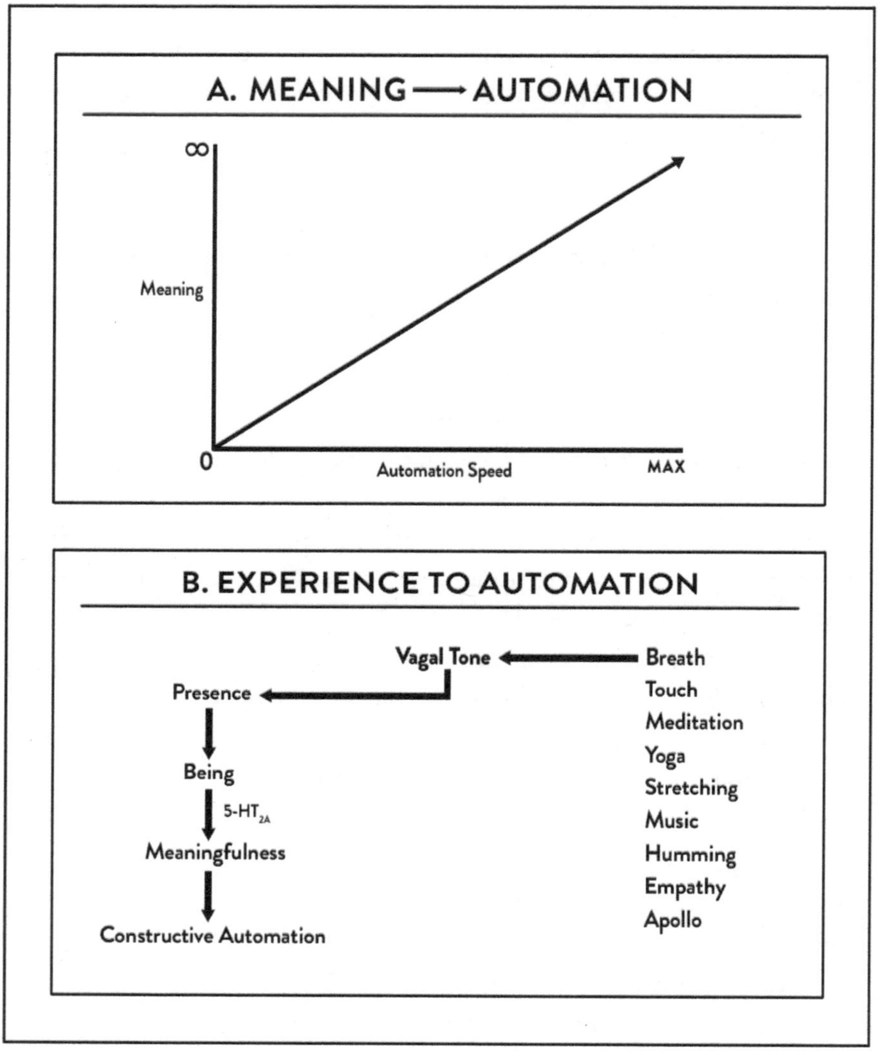

Figure 16. From Meaning to Automation (A) The more meaningful our experiences, the more we remember them and the more quickly we automate what we learn. (B) Techniques that improve vagal tone increase presence in the moment. More presence results in more *being*. More being leads to more meaningful experiences by way of burst activation of the 5-HT2A receptor, resulting in accelerated automation of desirable behaviors and traits.

them often. Automation can support adaptation when the correct behaviors are automated, or it can stifle it when bad habits are automated.

The more meaningful our experiences are, the more quickly their lessons are automated (Figure 16). The more present we are in our experiences, the more meaningful they become. *Being* present accelerates learning.

MULTITASKING AND AUTOMATION

When we understand that attention is a finite resource, the idea of multitasking takes on a very different form from what we were taught.

Most of what we currently call multitasking is not multitasking at all. It is rapid task-switching [113]. The brain toggles between two or more activities, reallocating attention back and forth in quick bursts. While many people, such as chefs, learn to excel at this technique for good reason, each switch comes with a cost. A small drop in efficiency. A slight increase in error. A quiet drain on energy. Over time, these micro-costs accumulate into fatigue, irritability, mistakes, and the feeling that we are doing everything but accomplishing nothing.

This is why answering emails during a meeting, checking your phone while having a conversation, or trying to write while half-listening to a podcast feels so unsatisfying. You are not doing more. You are fragmenting your attention into pieces too small to be useful.

True multitasking, in contrast, is not about dividing attention. It is about freeing attention.

It occurs only when one or more tasks have been automated.

Automation is the brain's way of conserving energy. Through learning and repetition, tasks that once required conscious effort become mastered and can be transferred to more efficient, lower-level, subconscious neural circuits [114]. What was once effortful becomes effortless. What once required focus is now beneath awareness, running in the background.

Walking is a classic example. At some point in your life, walking required your full attention. Balance, coordination, and timing were all-consuming. Now, you can walk while talking, thinking, or listening without any noticeable strain. The task has been automated.

Driving a familiar route can become automated. Typing on a keyboard, brushing your teeth, filtering incoming information, and even complex emotional and cognitive patterns can become automated over time, for better or for worse.

Consider something as simple as how you interpret a mistake. One person makes an error, and their mind automatically says, "I'm terrible at this." Another person makes the same error, and their mind says, "Good, now I know what to fix." Neither response is random. Both are learned, repeated, and eventually automated. The second pattern is profoundly helpful because it preserves attention. Instead of wasting cognitive resources on self-criticism, the brain stays oriented toward problem-solving and growth.

A similar pattern shows up in how we relate to stress. With practice, people can train an automatic reframe from "What did I do to deserve this?" to "What can I learn and how can I grow from this challenge?" Studies show that how we interpret stress changes physiological outcomes, including cardiovascular efficiency and performance [115].

Gratitude is a powerful example of an emotional tool that boosts EQ and can be automated to transform how we interpret stress. When practiced consistently, the brain begins to default toward noticing what is working rather than what is missing. Instead of scanning for danger alone, the brain also scans for safety and opportunity.

Mood is meant to exist on a normal distribution spectrum that ranges from utter despair to euphoria (Figure 17). We should all be spending the great majority of our time in the stable mood zone. When life gets overwhelming and nudges us toward despair and hopelessness, we can slide ourselves back to the stable mood zone by putting in a little effort. That effort starts with acknowledging our emotions, then identifying, accepting, feeling, and processing them so that the energy they carry can move out of our bodies. This entire process can take under five minutes. Contrast this with the Bipolar Mood Spectrum, seen in Bipolar 1

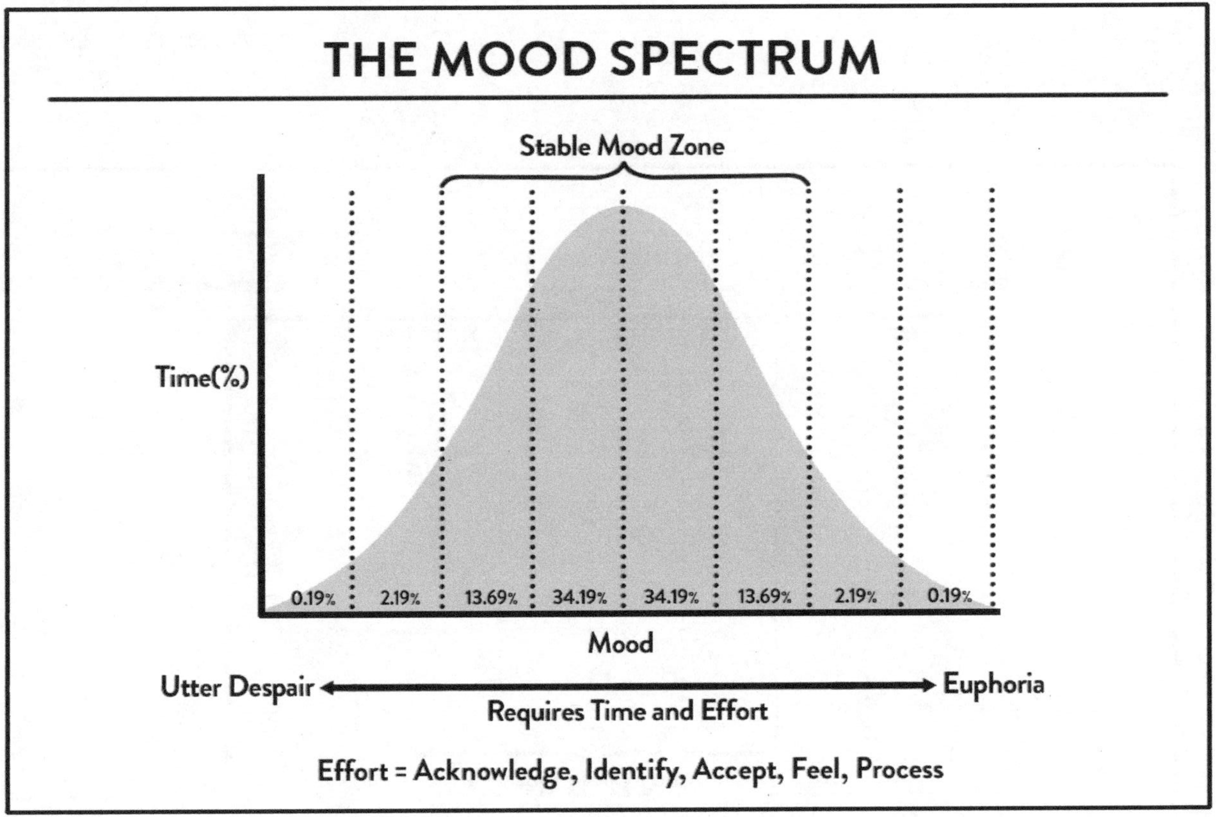

Figure 17. The Mood Spectrum

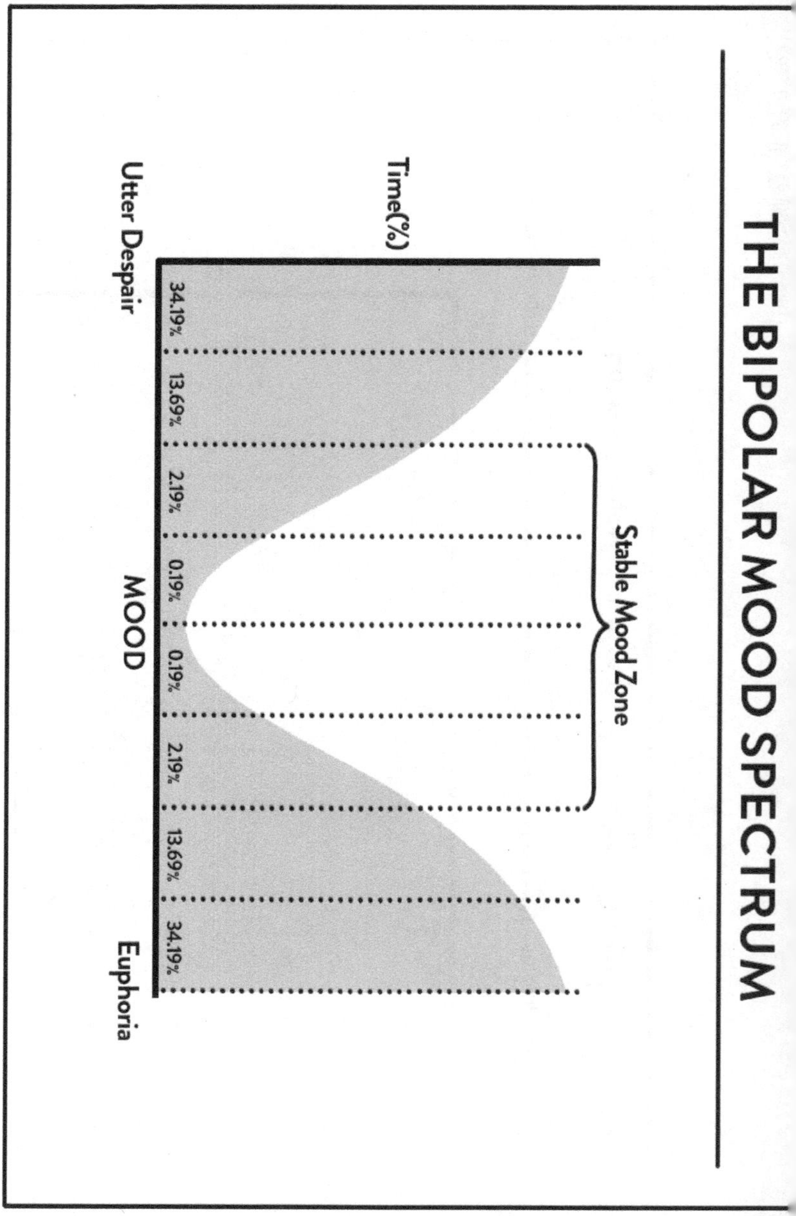

Figure 18. The Bipolar Mood Spectrum

Disorder (Figure 18). In this case, most of an individual's time is spent outside the stable mood zone, bouncing back and forth between utter despair and manic euphoria because insufficient effort has been put into feeling and processing emotions.

The good news is that the effort required for emotional processing is quite minimal once we understand what to do. Gratitude also helps us to automate patterns of self-talk. Simple phrases like "I can figure this out," or "I've overcome more challenging situations in the past," may start as intentional interventions, but with repetition, they become reflexive. In moments of uncertainty, these thoughts arise without effort, stabilizing attention when it would otherwise fragment.

Even presence itself can be automated. Practices like mindful breathing, body awareness, or simply noticing sensory input can, over time, become default responses to stress. Instead of spiraling into distraction, we return to the body. This is the nervous system learning that safety is available in the present moment.

This type of automation is the only form of multitasking that truly allows us to do multiple things at once. One task runs on "autopilot" in the background while your conscious attention is available for something else.

In this way, automation is the gateway to real efficiency. It expands your functional capacity without increasing your attentional load.

There is a subtle and important tradeoff of which to take note.

Automation is powerful, but indiscriminate.

The brain does not solely automate helpful behaviors. It automates whatever is most repeated, such as habits, thoughts, emotional reactions, patterns of avoidance, how you respond to stress, and the stories you tell yourself about who you are.

Over time, much of your life becomes a collection of automated processes running beneath awareness.

This is both one of our greatest strengths and one of our greatest vulnerabilities.

If your automated patterns align with health, curiosity, and resilience, your baseline experience of life becomes easier, lighter, and more adaptive. You are, in a sense, effortlessly multitasking, because the fundamentals of your life run smoothly in the background (Figure 16).

If your automated patterns are rooted in fear, distraction, numbing, or reactivity, then your attention is constantly being hijacked. Even when you try to focus, something pulls you away. Not because you lack discipline, but because your system has been trained to prioritize something else.

This is where resilience and adaptation come into play.

Resilience is not just the ability to withstand stress and bounce back quickly. It is the ability to update what has been automated.

Adaptation is the process by which the brain revises its predictions about the world based on new information and experience. It is how we learn. It is how we grow. It is how we heal. It is how we become more efficient, not by consciously doing more at once, but by requiring less effort to do what matters.

When you intentionally practice new behaviors, new ways of thinking, or new ways of responding to stress, you are not just "trying something different." You are teaching your brain what to automate next.

Over time, with repetition and reinforcement, these new patterns become your default.

Calm can become automatic. Presence can become automatic. Even joy, in its simplest form, can become something your system returns to without effort.

This is the highest form of multitasking.

In a world that constantly demands more of your attention, the most powerful move is not to divide it further, but to invest it wisely. To train your nervous system so well that what once required substantial conscious effort becomes subconsciously easy.

Because in the end, the goal is not to juggle more.

It is to require less juggling.

RESILIENCE IS NOT TOUGHNESS. IT'S FLEXIBILITY.

Resilience isn't about "powering through" with gritted teeth and caffeine.

That's just burnout in a cape.

Real resilience is *adaptive flexibility*, the ability to feel pain or discomfort, process it, pivot as needed, and bounce back quickly. Resilience trains *equanimity*: an even-tempered state of calm, clear composure that persists even through intense challenges, like bamboo in a storm.

Your autonomic nervous system plays a huge role (Figure 6). A flexible autonomic nervous system allows you to rapidly shift between sympathetic "fight-or-flight" and parasympathetic "rest-and-digest" with fluidity [116]. Think of it as emotional gear-shifting. You don't want to be stuck in fifth gear or reverse when you're driving up a big hill. You want range and power.

STRESS IS A SIGNAL, NOT A SENTENCE

Your body's stress response is ancient and brilliant. It was designed to help you run from saber-toothed tigers and learn new skills. These days, it gets activated by email subject lines and group texts from extended family, but the biology is the same.

Stress floods your body with cortisol and adrenaline, increasing inflammation [14-19]. This isn't bad in the short term. It sharpens focus, mobilizes energy, and helps you get out of bed when your alarm sounds like a screaming robot. The problem is when stress doesn't turn off. Chronic stress dysregulates everything from digestion to memory to reproduction to immune function [18, 19].

Stress is a lot like holding a drinking glass full of water. The glass is easy to hold for 20-30 minutes. After 45 minutes, you start to get restless. After an hour or two, you start to get annoyed. At four hours, your arm starts to ache. After a day or two, your arm can become paralyzed, and permanent damage can result.

Generally speaking, it is not the weight of stress in any moment that determines its impact on us, but the amount of time we choose to hold onto it. Every time we notice that we are still holding the glass is an opportunity to break the cycle by choosing to set it down. Every time we let go of stressful thoughts and return our attention to what we can control, we are training the brain's neural networks to remember that this act is meaningful, making it progressively easier to set the glass down in the future and lighten the load.

EUSTRESS VS. DISTRESS

What is not taught very well is that there are actually two varieties of stress:

Eustress and Distress.

Eustress ("Eu" stemming from the Latin root for "good") refers to stressful experiences that safely challenge us to grow and become stronger, such as learning to read, play an instrument, or ride a bicycle [117]. Having healthy amounts of eustress in our lives on a regular basis is not only essential for growth, but it is also the simplest inoculation to effectively prevent stagnation and degeneration.

DR. DAVE'S ESSENTIAL EQUATION #7:

Eustress x Time = Ease

Over time, eustress improves resilience by expanding our sense of capability through the discovery, practice, and mastery of new skills, thereby building confidence and cultivating ease. As we improve our existing skills and develop new ones, we become stronger, and our lives become easier.

The downstream biological reward for all our efforts is improved activity in the vagus nerve [116-119]. This is the primary nerve responsible for slowing things down and turning on all parasympathetic rest-and-recovery functions of the body, including digestion, immunity, reproduction, metabolism, empathy, creativity, and sleep (to name a few).

The vagus nerve is activated by engaging in activities that remind us that we're safe and not in immediate physical danger.

As we train our bodies to live in a more present "vagal" state, the body increases blood flow going to all organ systems we want to be active when we're safely resting (digestion, immunity, reproduction, empathy, etc.), and the brain rewires to quiet the amygdala's fear command center more often. Experiencing healthy amounts of eustress significantly promotes ease and reduces anxiety in a sustainable way.

Distress refers to overwhelming levels of stress, typically involving thoughts about things beyond our control [18, 19, 119]. Yup! You guessed it. Taking on too much eustress at once can turn it into distress because we can only handle so much at one time. Distress is uninspiring, feels like too much, and is often accompanied by asking ourselves the wrong questions, like, "Why me?" and "What's wrong with me that I have to deal with this right now?" Asking these types of questions to ourselves is like shaking our self-critic awake from a much-needed nap, so can we really blame it for being cranky? They are *neurostifling* questions that increase *neurorigidity* and inhibit neuroplasticity.

It is very important to notice when we start asking ourselves questions like this because these questions imply that there is something "wrong" with us as the premise. Believing there is something wrong with us by default adds a babbling brook of uncertainty to our awareness.

More uncertainty sends more danger signals to our amygdala, we enter fight-or-flight survival mode, and inflammation in the body increases [14, 18, 19]. In this state, vagus nerve activity is also inhibited (because we definitely don't want to be thinking about reproducing when we're outrunning a bear), and the body diverts nearly all blood flow to the heart, lungs, skeletal muscles, motor cortex, and brain survival centers to get us safely out of harm's way [14-17].

The fight-or-flight survival system is extremely resource-intensive, in large part because of the massive amount of blood required to fully power our skeletal muscles to escape or fight a predator. As such, there is significantly less blood available for recovery systems (digestion, immunity, reproduction, empathy, etc.). With less blood flow, there is less oxygen, fewer nutrients, and less waste removal from the cells of these systems. How long would you last with only one small meal each day and garbage pickup once every three months? That's what we're doing to our bodies when we're living with chronic stress. That's why it's always harder to digest and absorb our food, make babies, and fight off illness when we're chronically stressed.

DR. DAVE'S ESSENTIAL EQUATION #8:

Distress x Time = Disease

When distress is allowed to persist long enough, chronic inflammation and waste accumulation lead to stagnation and, eventually, disease.

And now, what you've all been patiently waiting for: how to transform distress into eustress.

Distress transforms into eustress nearly instantaneously by asking the right questions when we're facing hardship rather than the wrong ones. The question to ask is this: "What can I learn and how can I grow from this challenge I'm facing right now?"

Simply by asking this question instead of "Why me?", you have broken the cycle, and your brain (and your intuition) starts answering this new question with useful suggestions that are often quite meaningful, rewiring for resilience in a powerful way. Every time we successfully transform distress into a growth opportunity, we increase our happiness, reaffirm our safety, extend our lifespan, and, most importantly, show distress who's boss.

ADAPTATION IS BUILT INTO OUR DNA

You're not a static being. You're an ecosystem in motion. Your brain changes in real time with experience (neuroplasticity). Your genes change expression based on the environment (epigenetics). Your microbiome adapts to your diet, your mood, and that sketchy burrito you ate last night.

This means you're *always* adapting, even when it feels like you're stuck.

Even depression, anxiety, and trauma are forms of adaptation. They're your system trying to protect you in ways that may have once made sense. The good news? These patterns can shift.

The parts of our brains we use most literally strengthen. What fires together, wires together. Where attention goes, neural pathways grow.

REGULATION BEFORE REVELATION

Want insight? Creativity? Courage? First, we must regulate.

You can't think clearly if your nervous system is in panic mode. That's not enlightenment. That's survival brain.

Step one is always to come back to safety through breath, body, and sensation. Only from there can your prefrontal cortex (the wise CEO of your brain) re-engage.

Regulating your nervous system builds resilience by increasing your *distress tolerance*. You want your body to always know the difference between real survival threats and things that look like survival threats, but aren't (e.g., email, news, racing thoughts about the past or future). When you are already stressed out and overwhelmed, everything new looks like a real threat because your amygdala is on overdrive. Building distress tolerance buys us time to feel the signal, interpret it accurately as eustress or distress, and adapt appropriately and successfully.

The primary method for training distress tolerance is called *hormesis*, the process by which exposure to low doses of a stressor in a safe environment stimulates adaptive biological responses that increase an organism's resilience to future stress [118].

Interestingly, distress tolerance is on a circadian cycle. Like an energy meter bar in a video game, it starts at the top early in the day and then depletes at a rate proportional to the stress we experience throughout the day. Once you hit the 24-hour mark of no sleep, your distress tolerance starts to decline much more rapidly. Your distress tolerance refills every time you sleep (Figure 19A). The deeper and more restful sleep you get, the closer to your peak distress tolerance you get.

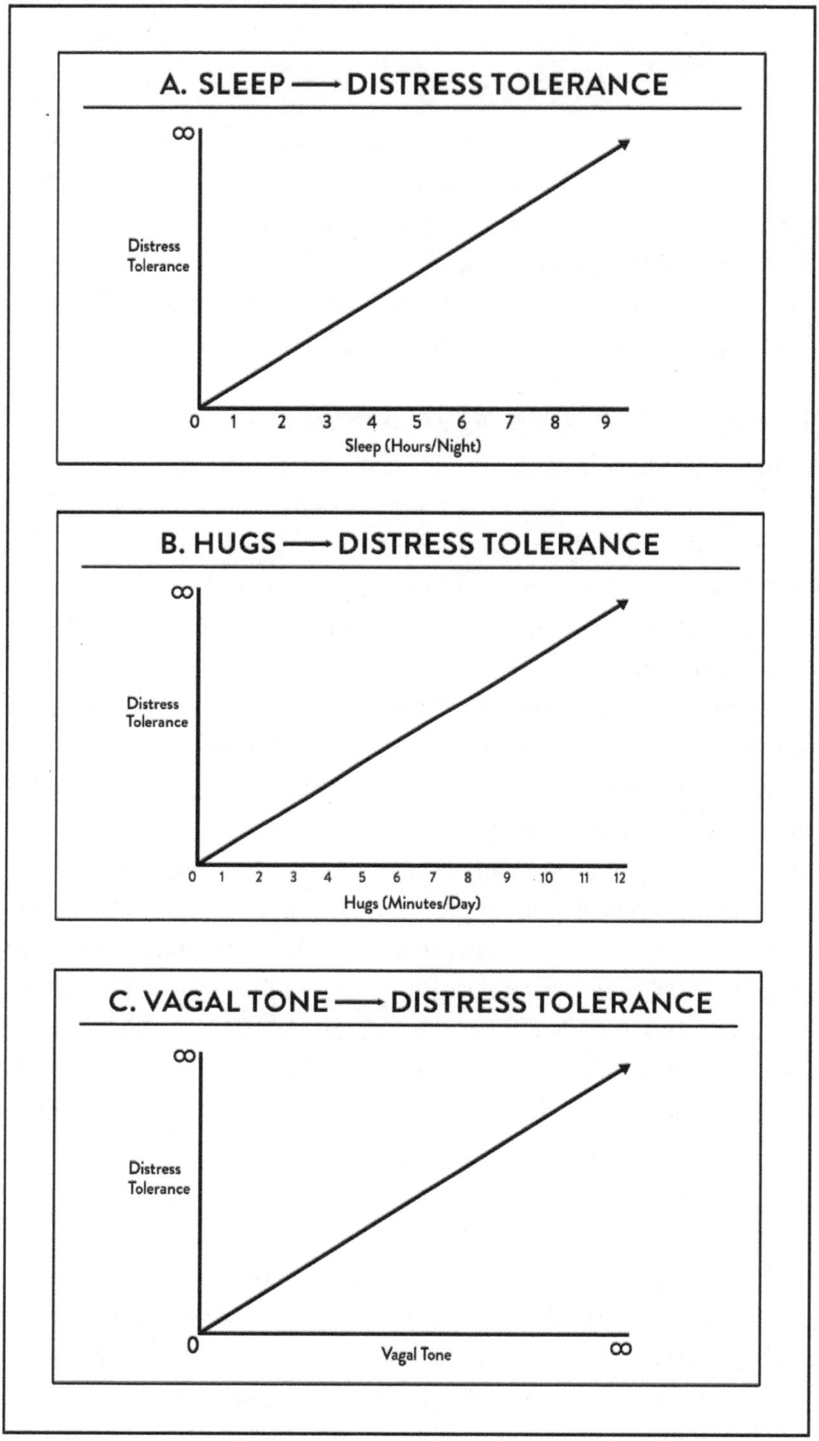

Figure 19. Vagal Tone and Distress Tolerance (A) The more high-quality sleep we get, the more distress tolerance builds. (B) The more hugs we get, the more distress tolerance builds. (C) The more vagal tone we have, the more distress tolerance we experience.

In fact, hugs (Figure 19B) and any experiences that improve vagus nerve activity will also refill your distress tolerance reserves (Figure 19C). This results in improved resilience, less time required to bounce back from whatever comes your way.

HEART RATE VARIABILITY AS THE BIOMARKER OF RESILIENCE

One of the most interesting aspects of resilience and distress tolerance is that, for the first time ever, you can track them on your Oura Ring, Apple Watch, or Fitbit because they have a biomarker: Heart Rate Variability (HRV).

HRV is the rate of change of your heartbeat over time. Our heart doesn't actually beat exactly once each second when our pulse is 60 beats per minute (bpm). Sometimes it beats at 950, 958, or 1020 milliseconds, and so on, because our heartbeat varies with our breath [8]. Each phase of each breath (such as inhalation and exhalation) changes the pressure in the blood vessels that flow throughout the lungs, which affects how hard the heart has to pump to get blood through the lungs. Your HRV is the average amount of change in the time between the peak of each heartbeat over time (usually requiring at least three minutes at rest for an accurate measurement).

Resilience is represented by HRV, a biomarker of the vagus nerve's activity over time [8]. The vagus nerve, cranial nerve X, innervates nearly the entire body and has both input nerve fibers (afferent) and output nerve fibers (efferent). The efferent output fibers of the vagus tell most of the body, and especially the heart and lungs, to slow down, thereby reducing heart rate and increasing HRV. Typically, people with a lower resting heart rate have a higher heart rate variability.

This is why, if you take slow, deep breaths at a rate of six breaths per minute, your HRV increases and your heart rate decreases within five minutes [8, 12]. You can measure this on an HRV app or wearable. By doing this specific breathing exercise that rapidly brings your heart and lungs into coherence, you are increasing activity in your vagus nerve, which slows your heart rate, lowers blood pressure, increases resilience and empathy, and accelerates the body's recovery.

HRV is interesting for a host of reasons:

- HRV decreases when we are exposed to stress of any kind, mental, physical, emotional, spiritual, or financial [8]. As our heart speeds up with stress, our breathing becomes more uniform and rapid, with more beats per minute and less wiggle room between beats. This signals that our body is in sympathetic fight-or-flight mode and intent on doing one of those things. When we rest and recover, practice deep breathing and yoga, get hugs, and especially when we sleep, HRV increases.

- When our HRV is lower than our usual, we are significantly more likely to get sick, more likely to make mistakes, less likely to perform consistently, slower to recover, and the list goes on [8]. On the contrary, when our HRV is higher than usual, we are significantly less likely to get sick and make mistakes, and much more likely to perform consistently at peak and recover quickly. Higher HRV is currently the best biomarker we have in the field for resilience, and now for resilience over time. High HRV was also recently found to be associated with improved longevity and health span [120-122].

- If our HRV is high when someone or something threatening is sneaking up on us, we detect it right away (before it knows we see it) and boost our heart and breathing rates, diverting nearly all blood to our skeletal muscles to make sure we get to safety fast. Once we get to safety, the heart and lungs slow down quickly. Our thoughts clear and slow down quickly as well, so that we can effortlessly move on to the next thing without delay and get some rest.

- HRV, our best-known measure of adaptability and resilience, has no upper limit in healthy individuals. Meaning that we don't yet know how high it can go. In other words, we don't yet know what we're capable of with respect to adaptation and resilience, two of our most important skills, for both survival and thriving. While the average HRV may be 20–30ms for most people reading this, I've known seventy-year-olds with an HRV above 200ms who are in impeccable shape. The most important goal when tracking your HRV is to identify your baseline (what is average for you), to notice when you're below average and take it easier those days, and to embrace more activities and behavior patterns that increase your HRV little by little over time [8, 12].

THE SCIENCE OF POST-TRAUMATIC GROWTH

Life challenges and hardships don't have to wreck you. They can *wake* you.

Studies show that people who heal from trauma often report increased empathy, deeper relationships, clearer priorities, and more meaning in life [123].

Pain cracks you open, and sometimes that's where the light gets in.

And compassionate support after a challenging event is critical to facilitate a *growth mindset*. Lack of support with blame or shame? That cements trauma in the body as fractured self-trust, resulting in the development of a *victim mindset*.

Dr. Gabor Maté, MD, the world-renowned addiction physician, author, and founder of Compassionate Inquiry, describes trauma not as the specific event that occurred, but as the response of the body to the event thereafter [124]. The effect of an event that is stored in the body as trauma is that the body learns to associate fear with the entire environment in which the event occurred. The smells, the sounds, and the sights. All of it.

Support from our community after challenging situations, something that we all have the ability to provide to each other, is a critical linchpin that determines whether a hardship is stored as a trauma in the body that keeps us stuck as a victim of circumstance, or as a victory that facilitates tremendous growth and feelings of self-worth. Each time a person is blamed or shamed for something challenging they went through, the scale is tipped a little more toward remembering the event as traumatic, cementing fear learning in the body (Figure 9).

This results in increased uncertainty and decreased vagus nerve activity. Like a broken bone, self-trust fractures a little more when someone we respect says we should have known better. And this ultimately triggers a dangerous question most of us may not even notice we are asking: if we couldn't keep ourselves safe then, can we really keep ourselves safe now?

As described above, the questions we ask ourselves when challenges arise have a major impact on the outcome. I often explain to my patients, "If you ask the wrong questions, you get the wrong answers." When facing hardship, if we ask "Why me?" or "What is wrong with me that these things keep happening to me?", the answer we get will often be laden with shame and self-judgment, destructive to our sense of self-worth and reinforcing a victim mindset. On the other hand, if we ask "What is this challenge trying to teach me?" or "How can I learn to be better from this situation?", then we receive answers that are thoroughly fortifying to self-worth and powerful facilitators of our growth.

The trick is to remember that we have the power to choose the outcome of all kinds of situations we face in life, and it all starts with thoughtfully and intentionally choosing the questions we ask.

But let's be clear: this isn't about glorifying suffering. It's about honoring the human capacity to *alchemize* it.

It's not "What did I do to deserve this?" It's "Even this can become fuel for growth."

HEALING IS NONLINEAR

One day, you feel powerful and present. The next, you're eating cereal from the box in your bathrobe, whispering, "I'm fine."

This is normal.

Healing is not a straight line. It has peaks and valleys. A cycle. A dance.

Sometimes growth looks like breakdown. Sometimes resilience means canceling plans, grieving, crying, and *not* trying to fix it.

Resilience is allowing the wave to pass through without drowning in it.

RESILIENCE IS A SKILL YOU CAN STRENGTHEN

Resilience is not fixed. It's trainable. Like a muscle.

Every time you meet discomfort with awareness, every time you pause instead of react, every time you soften instead of explode, every time you bounce back, you build capacity and bounce back faster.

Tools like journaling, movement, connection, cold showers (ugh, I know), hot saunas, community, play, and awe all build resilience.

So forgive, laugh, and rest (especially rest!) without guilt.

To be human is to grow through what you go through.

To learn to bend without breaking.

To remember that no storm lasts forever, and neither does any stuckness.

You are not fragile.

You are adaptive brilliance incarnate.

CHAPTER 7
We Are All Energy

If you want to find the secrets of the universe,
think in terms of energy, frequency, and vibration.
Nikola Tesla (1856–1943)

You are energy. Not just symbolically like "she's got great vibes," but quite literally. Like everything else that exists in this physical world, you are made of atoms. Atoms are made of particles. Particles are vibrating waves of energy constantly pushing back on entropy, the natural tendency to fall back to their lowest, most stable energy state.

You don't just "have" energy. *You are energy.* Energy comes from all the particles of the universe vibrating at their unique frequency. And your energy isn't neutral, it's contagious. Like yawning, or laughter, or inexplicable dance floor confidence at weddings.

When you walk into a room, you don't just enter, you broadcast. Your presence is a frequency. And depending on your nervous system, your sleep, your blood sugar, and whether you've been doomscrolling for the last hour, that frequency might be calming, chaotic, electric, or just deeply snack-deprived.

Emotion is energy in motion. When you repress a feeling, you don't delete it. You just bury it under a mental sticky note that says, "deal with this later," that your body interprets as tension, fatigue, or why you just cried during a dog food commercial.

Let it move. Scream into a pillow. Dance. Walk. Breathe or sing loudly in your car with the windows rolled up.

EVERYTHING VIBRATES, EVEN YOU

I am extraordinarily grateful to my dad, a physician and electrical engineer, for teaching me the basic principles of math and physics from a very young age. Admittedly, I did not fully appreciate this at the time. As an adult, I realize how fundamental these principles are to understanding life and the universe.

From the smallest subatomic quark to the stars, everything in the universe is vibrating. Including you. Every thought, feeling, organ, and tissue has its own rhythm. That gut feeling? Vibrational information. That heartache? Emotional energy with a beat.

Even your voice carries this signature. Ever notice how someone's voice can either soothe you or make you want to set your hair on fire? That's vibration in action.

Tesla and Einstein knew it over a century ago. Now it's time for us to know it.

The scientific field of physics provides an elegantly simple understanding of energy, despite often being taught poorly. Let's break it all the way down.

Vibration refers to the periodic motion of particles around a point in space. This motion is governed by forces that cause oscillations in the system, like ripples in a pond when a drop of water falls into it. The frequency (the number of ripples per second) of these oscillations defines the vibration. Energy, in this context, can be thought of as the capacity to cause, or be the result of, vibration. The energy of a vibrating system is proportional to the frequency of its oscillations and the amplitude (strength) of the vibration.

Nikola Tesla, known for his contributions to the development of the alternating current (AC) electricity that powers all of our homes, had a profound understanding of the relationship between vibration and energy [125]. Tesla believed that the universe itself was built on the principle of vibration. Tesla was particularly fascinated by resonance phenomena, which occur when an object vibrates at its natural frequency, amplifying the vibrations and energy in one or more other objects. Tesla used this understanding in his designs for wireless power transmission, enabling electricity to be transmitted over large distances without wires. His experiments with electromagnetic waves and resonance led to major innovations in wireless communication and energy transmission, which remain foundational in modern electrical systems. Tesla viewed vibration as the key to unlocking more efficient, sustainable energy systems.

Albert Einstein's (1879–1955) theory of relativity and his work with the photoelectric effect helped demonstrate that energy and matter are deeply interconnected [126]. In his famous equation $E=mc^2$, Einstein explains that energy (E) and mass (m) are interchangeable when multiplied by the speed of light (c) squared. The speed of light clocks in at 186,282 miles per second, which is pretty darn fast! This means that energy and mass are related by the factor distance over time (speed).

Einstein knew that energy is a fundamental property that exists in various forms, from light to sound to vibration. He proved his theories above by showing that light behaves as both a particle and a wave, indicating that physical matter and energy are intricately linked through vibration. Particles of light (photons), which are a form of electromagnetic radiation, vibrate at different frequencies, and this vibration allows us to see all the colors of the rainbow. Einstein's work paved the way for understanding how vibration can represent both energy and matter at the quantum level.

THE LAW OF CONSERVATION OF ENERGY

In 1842, the physician Julius Robert von Mayer (1814–1878) strung seven words together that revolutionized science from that point forward: "Energy can be neither created nor destroyed." It only changes form. This became known as the Law of Conservation of Energy. It describes a phenomenon universally observed in nature. That frustration you didn't process from earlier? Still there. That joy you gave someone by actually making eye contact? It lives on.

This fundamental law of the universe suggests that the total energy in a closed system remains constant, though it may shapeshift. The energy within your body, the heat you radiate, the electrical impulses that travel through your nervous system, and even the chemical reactions that power your muscles. All of these forms of energy are continuously in motion and transformation.

You are constantly giving off energy through pôsture, tone, intention, movement, and breath. You're also always absorbing it. We're basically supersensory emotional sponges with arms, legs, and Wi-Fi.

When you engage in any activity, whether it's physical, emotional, or intellectual, the energy within you is transferred into the environment. This could be through a simple handshake, the words you speak, the friendly gaze, or even the vibrations you emit when you are in a particular mood. This energy, while invisible, is deeply felt and affects the space and people around you. It is a tangible force that flows in and out of your body, influenced by your thoughts, actions, and environment.

This concept is not only supported by modern physics but also aligns with principles found in Eastern and Indigenous knowledge systems, which have long recognized the interconnectedness of all beings and the transmission of energy between them.

Now that you understand the Law of Conservation of Energy, you're ready to learn the basic physical principles of energy so that you can tap into it. *Entropy* and *enthalpy* are the invisible accountants keeping score beneath the surface of everything we do.

They are not obscure physics terms reserved for scientists in lab coats. They are the rules of energy and order that govern your thoughts, your feelings, your body, and even your sense of meaning.

To understand them is to understand why life feels effortless some days and impossibly heavy on others.

ENTROPY: THE COST OF EXISTING

Entropy is often described as the natural tendency toward disorder over time, but a more useful way to think about it is this:

Entropy is what happens when energy spreads out into the surrounding environment and becomes less focused, less structured, less organized.

In many ways, life is a constant battle against entropy, because the only way to counter it is to put energy back into the system, which requires intentional effort. What we call "work."

There are simply more energy-efficient ways for things to be disorganized than for them to be organized. Order requires effort not just to implement, but to sustain, while disorder just happens. Anyone who has owned a house or a car knows this well. Things just tend to fall apart over time. Without constant input of energy, order drifts.

Take the example of a screw that has been tightened into place to provide support for your house or car.

At first, the effort we put into tightening it to completion makes the screw feel secure, aligned, stable, and intentional. However, over time, especially in systems exposed to more vibration, temperature changes, or repeated use, that same screw tends to loosen.

This is because tightening a screw is an act of imposing order by intentionally directing our human energy toward a goal. You are aligning threads, increasing friction, and storing energy in the system, which serves an important purpose: providing the structural support that keeps your house or car stable, safe, and functional.

For the screw to tighten itself over time, all the tiny random motions from environmental vibrations around it would need to align in just the right direction, over and over again, to increase that order.

That is extraordinarily unlikely.

Instead, what happens is far more probable: Small random movements gradually disrupt that alignment. Microscopic shifts reduce friction. Stored energy dissipates. The system moves toward a state where the screw is less tightly constrained.

Not because anything is "trying" to loosen it, but because there are vastly more ways for it to be slightly loose than perfectly tight. The only likely way for the screw to become tighter over time is if someone chooses to tighten it and actually does so.

That is entropy.

You can see the same principle literally everywhere:

Food composting.

Metal rusting.

Aging.

A hot cup of coffee cooling down to room temperature, but never spontaneously heating itself back up.

In each case, energy spreads out. Structure dissolves. Order requires effort to maintain.

ENTHALPY: THE ENERGY AVAILABLE

If entropy is the natural tendency toward disorder, then enthalpy is the total energy we have available at any given time to impose order. They are opposing forces in constant balance.

Enthalpy is, in simple terms, the total energy contained within a system. In chemistry, it is often described as heat energy. In life, *enthalpy is the total energy available to you to do anything at all at any moment.*

Every breath you take, every thought you think, every movement you make requires energy. That energy comes from food, water, oxygen, sleep, and the countless biochemical reactions happening inside your cells every second.

Here is where it gets really interesting.

Enthalpy is not just about the quantity of energy. It is about accessible energy.

You can have a body full of calories and still feel exhausted. You can sleep eight hours and still wake up depleted. You can sit still all day and feel more tired than after a long walk in the sun.

Not all energy is equally usable. Our actions, thoughts, and environment can increase or decrease the amount of energy available to us at any given moment.

When you feel threatened or stressed, even subtly, the sympathetic fight-or-flight nervous system takes over, and energy becomes restricted. Most blood is diverted to the skeletal muscles, heart, lungs, and amygdala to maximize fighting (or fleeing) chances. When survival is believed to be at stake, there is little energy left for other essential bodily functions, such as empathy, creativity, recovery, immunity, digestion, reproduction, and sleep. Because these functions are still required, they operate, but much less efficiently in a resource-starved state. With reduced blood flow, there is also reduced waste removal, which over time increases inflammation and leads to disease. This is a low-enthalpy (high-entropy) state in which less of our energy is available to us, and parts of the system tend to deteriorate faster over time.

When you feel safe, your body allocates energy efficiently through the parasympathetic nervous system. Blood flow to rest and recovery systems improves. Heart rate and blood pressure decrease. Our cells and organs do what they do to sustain us with less effort, and less waste is created in the process. You feel clearer, calmer, capable, and alive without trying very hard. This is a high-enthalpy (low-entropy) state, where more energy is available to us for healing, digesting and absorbing food, reproducing, creating, connecting, and living.

Same body. Same calories. Completely different experience. Enthalpy, in your lived experience, is your capacity to meaningfully engage with life. High enthalpy states are associated with higher HRV and increased longevity and healthspan [8, 120, 121].

By training your nervous system to remember that it is safe with the simple practices found in this book, you will increase your enthalpy by making more of your energy available for your use.

These physics principles shine a bat-signal-sized spotlight on the power of our choices, specifically on where we choose to put our energy. As with the screw, simply by directing our energy, by setting our intention on a goal, and following through, we are willfully increasing order and organizing the system (the environment) around us. Doing this continuously is how we manifest our life goals.

INTENTION

If attention is how we decide what energy is invited in, intention is our human energy output. Our intention increases the enthalpy of a given system. It is our true north. It's our goal at any moment. Do we actually have a desire to accomplish it? If so, intentionality really matters. It is the bullseye we're aiming for. And without it, it's a lot like throwing darts while blindfolded.

DR. DAVE'S ESSENTIAL EQUATION #9:

Intention x Time = Manifestation

Intention is the human energy that we put into anything we do that makes things happen in our lives. Unintentional thoughts and actions yield unintentional results. Intentional actions yield intentional results. Intention is also the source of our motivation, and it must be internally generated.

Close your eyes for 30–60 seconds, and take a big, deep breath. Then take another, and on your exhale, imagine what you want out of your life. Your big why. We all have at least one if we look. Try to narrow it down to one primary intention over time. When we have our intention clearly visualized, our human energy is locked in like a finely tuned laser. As soon as you get distracted from it or forget about it, just notice that your thoughts have migrated, and gently return your attention to your intention. Every time we return to our intention, we are strengthening our attention like a muscle we're building in the gym. We're also dramatically increasing the chances of successfully manifesting our life goals, whatever those may be (Figure 20).

Are the things you do consistent with your intention? With what you want out of your life? Or are they more often contrary?

Our intention and actions must be aligned to manifest and achieve our goals [127].

For example, if our intention is to get a good night's sleep tonight, but we drink a cup of coffee after dinner, it is unlikely that we will sleep well. Similarly, if our intention is to feel better about ourselves, but we

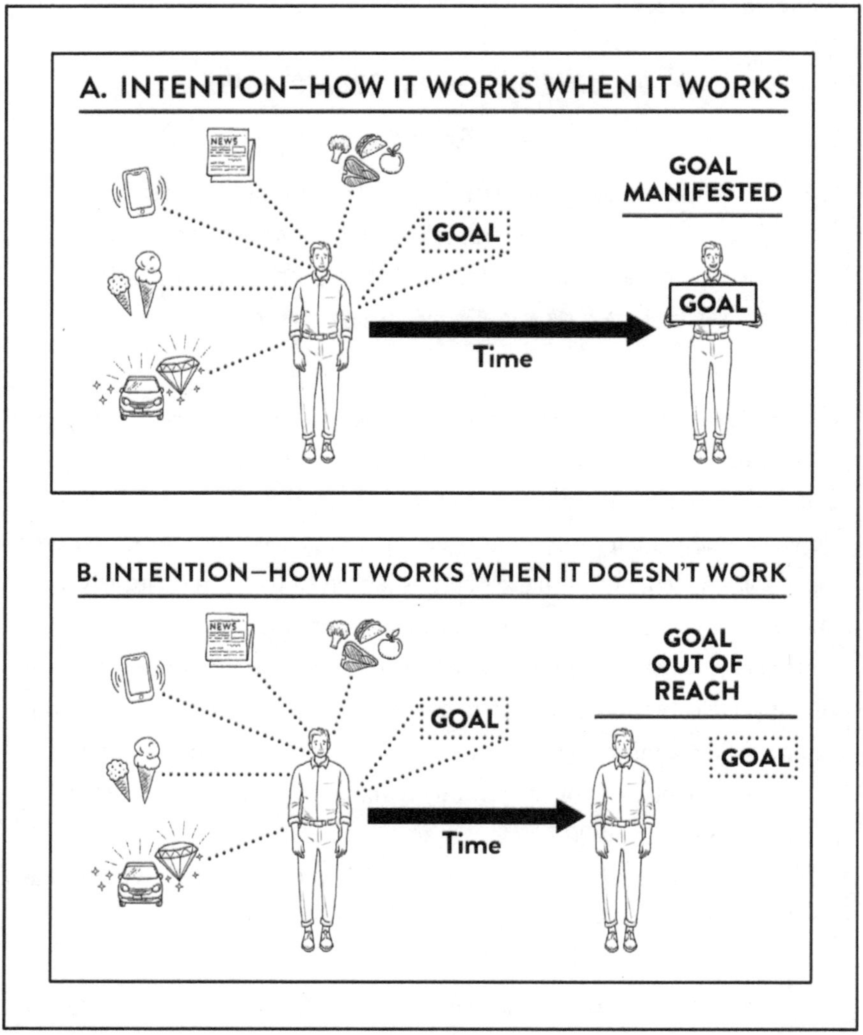

Figure 20. Intention (A) How it works when it works. (B) How it works when it doesn't work.

continue to scroll social media, looking at edited versions of people who set an unnatural standard of attractiveness, our manifestation will fail.

The most beautiful thing about intention is that as we practice it, we start to realize that anything is possible with a little practice. We realize the true power of our *free will*, and even more importantly, *free won't*.

MOMENTUM & INERTIA

If physics had a personality, it would be the quiet genius at the dinner party who says one sentence all night and somehow explains your entire life. Two of its greatest hits, momentum and inertia, do exactly that.

In physics, *momentum* is mass times velocity. Translation: how hard something is to stop once it's moving. A freight train can't screech to a halt because it feels like it. It keeps going because it is so heavy and moving so fast that it physically must do so, until the engineer triggers the heavy-duty airbrake system to slowly stop the train.

Humans aren't so different. Ever notice how three days of good sleep, decent food, and a few optimistic thoughts suddenly make you feel like a functional adult? Or how exercising for a few days in a row gives you an uplifting feeling many refer to as "flow" or a "runner's high" that gets easier to access over time? That's momentum. The more we do something, the less effort it takes to do the same thing, and the harder it becomes to stop us from doing it.

Your brain loves efficiency. Repeat a behavior enough times, and it starts to be outsourced to autopilot. What used to require discipline starts happening on its own. That's momentum working its quiet, powerful magic. Then there's *inertia*, described by Sir Isaac Newton in 1687 as the First Law of Motion, inspired by the earlier work of Galileo Galilei (1564-1642), who died while under house arrest for his heretical discovery that the Earth revolves around the sun. Newton's Law of Inertia explains why getting off the couch after you've been sitting for a while can feel like lifting a car, but once you're moving, you're fine. *Objects at rest tend to stay at rest. Objects in motion tend to stay in motion.* Unless acted on by an outside force, of course. A human with a lifetime subscription to Netflix and no encouragement...you get the idea.

In the nervous system, inertia shows up as state lock. Sitting a lot? It feels like it takes much more effort to get moving. Stressed? Your brain doubles down on making sure you're ready for danger at any moment. Calm? Vagus nerve activity increases, helping us bounce back from stress with ease. Your body isn't dramatic, it's consistent. Once it picks a lane, it prefers to stay there.

Put them together, and you get the real secret: direction matters more than intensity. You don't need a heroic overhaul. You need ease and familiarity. The often overlooked thrill of making progress, even when it's incremental. You need a small nudge in the right direction, repeated often enough that your brain goes, "Ah, yes, this again," and builds structure around it.

Breaking bad patterns feels hard because you're fighting inertia *and* redirecting momentum at the same time. That's not weakness. That's physics being annoyingly reliable.

Here's the really good news. Small changes really matter. Once you shift even slightly toward something that helps you, those same laws start working for you. Momentum builds. Inertia stabilizes. And eventually, taking care of yourself stops feeling like a project and becomes just *being* you.

PEOPLE FEEL YOU BEFORE YOU SAY A WORD

Ever walk into a room and immediately know who's stressed, who's happy, and who's low-key debating auto-defenestration (throwing themselves out of a window)? That's energy. Humans are brilliant at reading it, often unconsciously.

The insula talks to the rest of the emotional brain to help you pick up on facial expressions, posture, and tone instantly, and respond. We're vibrational empaths. When someone is regulated and grounded, they can calm an entire room without saying a word. That's not magic. That's nervous system mastery.

So don't take it personally when someone says something to you that sounds disrespectful because now you have a forcefield of understanding protecting you. The energy of others, particularly when they're angry, can be overwhelming at times. There's no doubt about that, but what and how someone speaks are not because of us, and they do not mean anything about us.

The first question to ask yourself when hearing someone speak is: *What is that person actually communicating about how they feel right now?*

That is the most important question to answer in human interactions and should always be asked first to correctly guide your response.

When we falsely perceive that someone is talking to us in a certain way because of us, we become defensive, which always makes the situation worse. We do this often because a part of us still believes there is something wrong with us, and that it is our fault. Just the right kind of person can bring this part of us to the surface by poking it with their words.

When we know that nothing is wrong with us and we ask the above question first when we hear someone speak, we will never take anything personally again. This is also one of The Four Agreements by Don Miguel Ruiz, from the Toltec tradition [21]. Every interaction becomes an important opportunity to learn to see the world from someone else's perspective. Every interaction has the potential to enrich our existence.

Imagine the person who challenges you the most. Then, know this person is your greatest teacher.

One of my favorite sayings from Ram Dass speaks to this well:

"If you think you're enlightened, go spend a week with your family."

ENERGY IS TRANSMITTED THROUGH TOUCH, BREATH, AND PRESENCE

A hug. A sigh. A deep breath in sync. These aren't small things. These are energetic exchanges. Touch releases oxytocin [24]. Co-breathing synchronizes heart rates [112]. Being fully present with someone can regulate both your nervous systems simultaneously, and nearly instantly.

This is why babies calm when held. Why you feel better around certain people, and when your dog curls up next to you. You're not imagining it. You're entraining neural pathways between your insula and amygdala to remember that you're safe in your environment (Figure 8).

Understanding this helps us realize that it's not magic. It's *healing through physics* instead of chemistry, our usual go-to.

The Inverse-Square Law of Physics states that the intensity of energy decreases by the inverse square of the distance [128]. This means that if you double your distance from a speaker, the volume decreases by 75%, and if you triple your distance, the volume decreases by 89%. This also means that if you have something soothing really close to you, even if it's not that intense, it attracts your attention more than disturbing things that are farther away.

This is why getting a hug from a friend on a bad day, snuggling a pet, listening to music, and feeling Apollo Vibes all work like noise-cancellation for your brain. The source of comfort is physically closer to us than the source of the stress, so by the Inverse-Square Law, the comfortable energy is stronger (louder, higher amplitude) than the stressful energy and drowns it out. When the body is calm and remembers that it's safe, the mind clears and can more easily distinguish noise from music. As we only have so much time to pay attention to anything in a given day, we might as well enjoy the music as often as we can.

YOU ARE THE CONDUCTOR

You don't need to "raise your vibration" like it's a cosmic iPhone update. You're already vibrating. The question is: Is your orchestra playing noise or music? Which are you paying attention to?

Tuning into your energy, noticing it, breathing into it, tending to it, and softening it is one of the most direct paths to clarity, compassion, and bliss.

We are not separate from the universe. We *are* energy. Every breath, thought, and feeling ripples outward. You are the medicine. You are the music. You are the vibe.

Understanding this is true power. Use it responsibly.

CHAPTER 8
The Harmony of the Spheres

One good thing about music, when it hits, you feel no pain.
Bob Marley (1945–1981)

There is a moment, subtle yet unmistakable, when the first notes of one of your favorite songs begin to play. Before you consciously recognize the melody, your body has already responded.

Music starts as rhythmic waves of air pressure colliding with the eardrum [129], which vibrates and passes that motion through three tiny bones that amplify it into the fluid-filled cochlea. There, cochlear fluid ripples and hair cells bend, opening ion channels that convert the mechanical motion induced by the sound waves into electrical nerve signals. These signals travel by way of the auditory nerve to the auditory cortex of the brain, where timing, pitch, and volume are decoded in milliseconds.

At the same time, those signals are routed into the limbic system, particularly the insula, amygdala, and hippocampus, where emotion, meaning, and memory intertwine [30, 31]. The brain begins to predict what comes next, and when those predictions are met or artfully violated, the reward system responds. Dopamine is released, not just when the chorus hits, but in anticipation of it. This is why music can feel like a rising wave inside the body, a kind of emotional momentum building toward a moment you somehow already knew was coming.

Within seconds, the autonomic nervous system begins to shift [32]. Your heart rate may synchronize with the rhythm. Your breathing subtly entrains to the tempo. In the case of one of your favorite songs, it feels safe, familiar, and meaningful. The parasympathetic nervous system engages, increasing vagal tone and creating a sense of warmth, openness, and connection (Figure 8). If the music is intense or unfamiliar, the sympathetic system may activate instead, sharpening attention and heightening arousal (Figure 9). In either case, music is not just something you hear. It is something that reorganizes your internal state.

This is part of why music is so uniquely powerful. It does not rely solely on language, which is relatively slow and cognitively demanding. Instead, it communicates directly through pattern, rhythm, and resonance. It speaks the native language of the nervous system. When words are paired with music, their meaning is amplified and encoded more deeply [130]. The hippocampus binds melody, rhythm, and narrative into a single memory trace, making it far more durable than speech alone [131]. When music makes us feel safe, learning is supercharged. This is why you can remember lyrics from decades ago with perfect clarity, even when you cannot recall what you had for breakfast yesterday.

In this sense, music is one of the most efficient forms of communication ever developed. It spreads not just information, but feeling. A song can move through populations at a speed and with a persistence that rival, and in many ways exceed, the transmission dynamics of biological contagions. Unlike a virus, which requires physical proximity and biological susceptibility, music requires only attention. A melody can cross continents instantly, embedding itself into millions of nervous systems, replicating not through cells, but through memory and emotion. It is, quite literally, more viral than any pathogen, because it leverages the very mechanisms that make us human: our capacity for pattern recognition, emotional resonance, and shared experience.

Most importantly, music reminds us that communication is not just about exchanging information. It is about creating alignment between nervous systems. When we listen to the same song, sing the same words, or move to the same rhythm, our brains and bodies begin to synchronize. We become, even if only briefly, part of the same pattern. This is why music has always been at the center of ritual, culture, and connection. It is not decoration. It is infrastructure for belonging.

In Indigenous traditions, sound is ancient medicine [59, 62, 63]. Music is coded emotion created from a highly intentional combination of human and environmental energy that vibrates the air at frequencies we can hear. Vibration is the hidden architecture of everything.

And you? You are a living, humming, rhythmically oscillating instrument tuned not just by biology, but by the symphony around you. Music also allows us to tune our mood and energy at will, just like how hearing your favorite song randomly come on the radio on a bad day is instantly uplifting.

THE UNIVERSE IS MUSICAL AND SO ARE WE

Pythagoras (570–495 BCE) discovered a heck of a lot more than how to measure three sides of a triangle. He believed that the cosmos itself was organized by music. He called it *musica universalis*, the "harmony of the spheres." He thought the planets sang in orbit. Turns out, he wasn't wrong, because his musical discoveries hundreds of years before Jesus resulted in the Circle of Fifths, the foundation of all modern music and harmony to this day. NASA now converts electromagnetic data from planets and stars into sound [132].

Your atoms vibrate. Your brain pulses in oscillatory patterns. Your heart beats in rhythm.

Your body is like an instrument. And how you feel depends on how in tune you are with yourself, with others, and with nature.

Notably, music requires generating sound that consists of the correct note played at the correct time. Both are essential.

WHY MUSIC MOVES YOU

Ever cry during a movie score? Feel chills at a certain lyric? Dance involuntarily when the beat drops? That's your nervous system remembering what it forgot: sound *is* emotion in action.

Music synchronizes brain waves, regulates breathing, and stimulates the release of dopamine and oxytocin. It's basically a spa treatment for your amygdala [133, 134].

It's no surprise hospitals use music therapy to reduce pain, calm anxiety, and support recovery [135]. Even preterm infants gain weight faster when lullabies are played [136]. You're never too small (or too grown) to be healed by harmony. In fact, harmony may be the single most important thing in our lives we didn't realize we were supposed to care about.

Sound waves don't just shift emotion; they shift matter. Cymatics, images of the effects of sound on water, show how sound frequencies organize particles, including water, into patterns. Your body, which is made up of ~60% water, responds like a living cymatic plate. That's why a gong bath or singing bowl session *feels* different than listening to the radio. You're not imagining it. You're resonating.

COHERENCE: WHEN YOUR HEART, BRAIN, AND BREATH SYNC UP

When your heart rate and breath rate fall into a synchronized, harmonious rhythm, working together at optimal efficiency, it's called *coherence*, and your brain quickly follows suit [8, 137]. For nearly every human being on the Earth, coherence can be accessed by breathing at 5-7 breaths per minute (~10 seconds per breath) for under 10 minutes [8, 12]. Most healthy people can get there in under 90 seconds. Some can get there instantly. And a few are always there.

Coherence feels like flow, ease, the zone, and alignment. Exquisitely present. It's not rare. We have all experienced it as children, even if we cannot remember it as grown-ups. In this state, vagus nerve activity increases, reducing heart rate, blood pressure, and restlessness while increasing creativity, focus, energy, and heart rate variability [8, 12]. Coherence happens naturally when you're safe, connected, and present (Figure 8).

Music and vibration (like Apollo) are extremely helpful for accessing coherence more quickly [137-139]. Especially when they are repetitive, soothing, and rhythmically patterned. They help you get there faster by giving you a metronome. That's why lullabies, chants, and tribal drums have been used for millennia. You're not just listening, you're syncing.

If your body (including your mind and everything else in it) were an orchestra, coherence is when your orchestra goes from being a struggle to listen to during warm-ups, out of time and out of tune, to sounding magnificent, in time and in tune, with the guidance of a conductor. The conductor is the great decider who synchronizes the orchestra in time and in tune. In this case, the conductor is you.

SOUND AS CEREMONY AND SCIENCE

Every ancient culture used sound for healing, like chanting, drumming, fluting, and overtone singing. Not because it was fun, but because it worked. Modern science is catching up, measuring what the ancients already knew: frequency is medicine.

From music therapy and vibroacoustic therapy beds to binaural beats and Apollo Vibes, we're rediscovering sound as a healing tool. Not just for expression, but for transformation.

AN ODE TO THE ANGELS OF SOUND

Musicians translate the invisible into something the body can feel. If the universe is made of vibration, then musicians are its interpreters. Call them artists or performers if you like, but let's be honest: they're closer to angels, messengers moving meaning through air.

Music does what words cannot. It regulates us without asking permission. Like touch, it sneaks past the thinking brain and speaks directly to the nervous system, reminding hearts how to beat together.

In grief, music holds us when language fails.

In joy, it amplifies what already wants to overflow.

In moments of chaos, it restores rhythm.

In moments of numbness, it brings sensation back online.

A world without music would be technically functional and emotionally uninhabitable. No lullabies. No anthems. No songs to fall in love to, no melodies to mourn to, no beats to dance the restlessness out of our bones. Civilization might survive, but something essential would be missing.

So respect musicians. Treat them kindly. Pay them fairly. Protect their nervous systems, because they are expending theirs to regulate ours. They are tuning forks for the collective soul, reminding us, again and again, what harmony feels like. Music is not a right; it is a gift.

We can all agree on this:

The world without music would be an unbearably sad place in which to live.

YOUR BODY IS THE INSTRUMENT

Your voice has healing potential. Not just what you say, but how you say it.

Tone, rhythm, and breath all matter. Try humming when you're anxious. Sing when you feel stuck. Whisper lovingly to yourself (yes, out loud).

You don't have to be a musician. You just have to make sound with intention.

You are a walking, vibrating, multi-instrumental miracle.

The Earth is your orchestra. Your body is your instrument.

And your voice? Your rhythm? Your presence?

That's your song.

Play it well.

PRO TIP:

It is impossible to ruminate when you are humming or singing.
Try it for yourself!

PRO TIP:

By aligning the right kind of music with your intention, it has the capacity to accelerate learning and automation. Check out the *Simple Guide Playlist* when you register your purchase of this book to learn the techniques described here even faster!

CHAPTER 9
Science Meets Spirit in a Molecule

You are not a drop in the ocean. You are the entire ocean in a drop.
Rumi (1207–1273 CE)

If you had asked me earlier in my medical career where science ended and spirituality began, I probably would have given you a very confident, very wrong answer.

I would have told you that science is what we can measure, and spirituality is what we feel. That one lives in the lab, the other in the ineffable. That they are complementary, perhaps, but ultimately separate domains. Clean, organized, and comfortably divided.

Then I met a molecule that refused to respect that boundary.

In neuroscience, we spend a lot of time talking about receptors, signaling pathways, and networks. Tiny interactions that somehow give rise to everything we call reality. Your memories, your fears, your sense of self, and your feeling that you are "you" and not someone else. All of that emerges from chemistry. Not in a reductive way, but in the same way that a symphony emerges from vibration. The parts matter, but the experience synergizes into something so much greater.

Certain molecules naturally found in both plants and humans have a peculiar ability to amplify that "something more."

They don't just change what you think. They change the way thinking itself feels. They loosen the rigid patterns that define our perception of 'normal' and allow the brain to briefly operate with increased flexibility.

Networks that usually stay in their lanes begin to communicate, and assumptions soften. The brain, for a moment, becomes less certain and more curious.

From the outside, we describe this in terms like receptor agonism, cortical desynchronization, and neuroplasticity. All accurate. All incomplete.

From the inside, people describe something else entirely. A sense of connection and meaning. A dissolving of boundaries. The feeling that the separation between self and the world was never quite as solid as it once seemed. Sometimes this is experienced as awe. Sometimes as relief. Sometimes as the quiet recognition that what we've been searching for has been here the whole time, hiding in plain sight beneath layers of habit and expectation.

Indigenous traditions have long approached these molecules not as tools to control, but as relationships to be understood. In many Amazonian cultures, plants are not passive chemicals. They are teachers. Knowledge is not extracted through force, but received through attention, discipline, and humility. The practice is not simply to have visions, but to learn how to discern them, to differentiate insight from self-defensive projection, signal from noise.

Nature, after all, has always been the original pharmacy. Long before randomized controlled trials, humans were learning directly from the natural world, discovering that certain plants could relieve pain, alter consciousness, or restore balance in the body. Many of our most important modern medicines trace back to these observations, from willow bark to aspirin, from poppies to morphine, from fungal spores to penicillin.

Psychedelic compounds are part of this same lineage. They are not anomalies. They are natural molecules evolved within complex ecological systems that, when introduced into the human body, interact with our nervous system in ways that are both precise and profound.

What fascinates me is not that these experiences happen. It's that they are reproducible, measurable, and increasingly predictable. We can watch the brain change in real time. We can correlate those changes with subjective reports. We can even begin to understand why certain patterns of activity are associated with feelings that humans, across cultures and centuries, have called "spiritual."

And yet, no scan, no dataset, no paper fully captures what it is like to be inside that experience.

This is where science starts to do something interesting. It doesn't collapse spirituality into chemistry. It reveals that what we've been calling "spirit" may be deeply rooted in the biology of being alive. Not as an illusion, but as a fundamental feature of how the brain constructs meaning.

In this way, the molecule does not create something new. It reveals something fundamental.

A built-in capacity of the human brain to reorganize itself, to perceive differently, and to experience connection in ways that feel larger than the individual self.

Science once diminished this. Today, it clarifies the mechanism.

In doing so, it invites us to reconsider a possibility that feels both ancient and newly rediscovered: that what we call "spirit" does not exist outside of biology, but may be one of its most beautiful expressions.

A SURGICAL APPROACH TO TRAUMA HEALING

When a surgeon repairs a physical wound, the task is clear: remove what's damaged, realign what's torn, and restore structure so the body can heal itself. It's precise, visible, and guided by anatomy.

In the Western psychiatric approach to psychedelic-assisted therapy, what my surgical colleagues sometimes half-jokingly call "psychosurgery" is less visible, but follows a similar principle. Trauma disrupts patterns, not tissue. We help patients identify where those patterns have become stuck, overactive, or protective beyond their usefulness, and then gently create the conditions for the brain to reorganize. The goal isn't to remove something, but to restore flexibility and safety so healing can occur.

From studying with the Shipibo people in Peru, I learned that Indigenous lineage-trained shamans approach this from yet another angle. What we might call "spiritual surgery". They work within a framework of meaning, relationship, and perception. Instead of focusing on repairing injured tissue or neural patterns, they engage the person's sense of connection to self, others, and the natural world, using ritual, sound, and plant medicines to "retune" what feels out of balance. The Shipibo shamans view trauma as energy that is stuck in the body, creating blockages that prevent the rest of the person's energy from flowing freely. Aided by medicinal plant combinations such as *Ayahuasca*, the vibrations of their songs (*Icaros*) shake up this stuck trauma energy, removing the blockages and restoring the person's energy to a pre-traumatized state, so the body can heal itself.

Different languages. Different tools. Same healing principles. Remove the barriers to healing and restore coherence when something has been disrupted, so the system can remember how to heal itself.

THE DIVINE HOTLINE

For millennia, humans have built temples, chanted prayers, and risked their sanity in deserts, caves, monasteries, and now, the back rows of sweaty yoga studios for one universal reason: to remember. To remember what is already known. To feel the part of ourselves that is more than muscle and memory. To touch the Divine.

Then there's the miraculous molecule we don't really learn about at all in school: Dimethyltryptamine (DMT), our fast-track cosmic boarding pass. In seconds, this tiny molecule can crack the illusion of separation and drop us face-first into a reality so vibrant and interconnected that it leaves even the most devout skeptics picking their jaws up off the celestial floor. DMT is also the primary psychoactive ingredient in Amazonian medicinal Ayahuasca brews.

Here's the coolest part: DMT isn't foreign. It's an endogenous molecule. We make it, and it lives inside all of us.

DMT is composed of a tryptamine backbone and two methyl groups, a molecular whisper, similar in shape to serotonin, and found in thousands of plant species and nearly all animals [140].

DMT is made in our brains. One particularly interesting brain structure that houses it is the pineal gland, the mysterious midline structure in the center of the brain, aptly proposed as the "principle seat of the soul" by René Descartes (1596–1650), who is considered the pioneering founder of the modern philosophy of science [141]. The pineal gland is also the neuroendocrine source of melatonin, the molecule that regulates our circadian rhythms (sleep and wake cycles). DMT is hypothesized to be released into the brain at birth, death, in dreams, and meditative states, but the body degrades it so quickly that it is extraordinarily difficult to measure [142].

New research suggests that DMT may not so much "cause" mystical experiences or hallucinations as unlock access to a deeper reality that's always here, like a master key in a lock we forgot we were holding [143].

When the Default Mode Network supporting the ego softens its grip in response to DMT (whether it comes from within or without), something wild and sacred emerges: *non-dual consciousness* [144, 145]. The boundary between "you" and "everything else" blurs, and what remains is the undeniable sense that consciousness itself, and being alive, is a sacred shared experience.

This isn't hallucination. It's your nervous system re-experiencing unity. And it's mediated by, you guessed it, the 5-HT_{2A} serotonin receptor [146].

Judeo-Christian-Islamic traditions generally describe God as "one", reflecting a monotheistic approach. What if it also refers to seeing the world from a non-dualistic viewpoint? What is often missed is the understanding that "one-ness" means complete and total one-ness, not at our exclusion. God is "up there" in the sky, down here on Earth, and within us because we were all created in God's image (Hello again, Law of Conservation of Energy!). One-ness, by definition, is inclusive of us as we are part of the whole, meaning that each of us possesses the capacity for divinity.

What is most exciting is that we can learn to access non-dual consciousness anytime with our breath, by falling deeply asleep, with a powerful runner's high, and more!

Studies of DMT are now revealing that we are all born with biological access to these Divine states that ancient spiritual mystics have described for millennia.

Some of the most interesting studies of DMT over the last thirty years were conducted at the University of New Mexico by psychiatrist Dr. Rick Strassman, MD. Dr. Strassman demonstrated that administering DMT to human subjects intravenously reliably induces mystical, spiritual dream states that, in many subjects, resembled near-death experiences [147-150]. There is no longer any debate that DMT is the first known *psychedelic* molecule that naturally lives inside all of us.

PSYCHEDELIC STATES

Whenever I lecture on psychedelic medicine, I always see people in the crowd shaking their heads and leaning in to their neighbors as if to say, "I never have and never will try that."

I am excited to inform you that if you are old enough to read this book, you have, without any hesitation or doubt, already experienced at least one type of psychedelic experience: dreaming.

The word "psychedelic," meaning *to reveal the mind*, was coined by Aldous Huxley (1894–1963) and Dr. Humphry Osmond (1917–2004) in 1957 to more accurately describe the experiences induced by consciousness-altering substances akin to psilocybin mushrooms, LSD, mescaline, and DMT.

In Latin:

Psyche = "mind"

Delos = "to show" or "to reveal"

Similar to what unfolds with psychedelic substances, when we dream, the volume gets turned down on our ego (our awareness of the world that is required for survival day-to-day), revealing the information stored beneath the surface in our subconscious and unconscious minds.

Your consciousness is like an iceberg. When the captain of the Titanic first spotted one in the distance, he could only see the tiny tip of the iceberg that was above the surface of the water. This is what we call conscious awareness. In other words, that which we know we are aware of (Figure 3). The captain was convinced that this was all there was to see, and his hubris resulted in one of the greatest civilian transportation tragedies of the twentieth century and at least one extraordinarily long romance film. What the captain missed is the 98% of the iceberg that was beneath the surface, beneath awareness. In the same vein, most of our consciousness is beneath our day-to-day awareness.

In essence, most of the information in your brain is beneath your awareness when we are awake, but becomes available to your awareness when you dream or enter psychedelic states with meditation, molecules, and the like.

To access psychedelic states of consciousness, drugs are not required.

PSYCHEDELIC-ASSISTED THERAPY

In 2012, my good friend and colleague Dr. Rena Paris, MD, sent me a half-dozen of the latest peer-reviewed scientific studies on psychedelic medicines and how they were being used to accelerate progress in psychotherapy for treatment-resistant mental illnesses like PTSD. Among these were three double-blind randomized placebo-controlled studies evaluating MDMA (3,4-methylenedioxymethamphetamine) for chronic treatment-resistant PTSD, a patient population I had started to work with frequently in the clinic [151-153]. The results were impressive. It immediately made me more curious about psychedelic medicines and how they work to facilitate trauma healing.

The first thing I learned is that LSD and psilocybin have some similar experiential qualities to DMT, and are all members of the tryptamine family of psychedelics [154]. Both LSD and psilocybin were already showing early promise for addressing the burden of anxiety and depression in patients with life-threatening illnesses where other tools had failed [155, 156]. MDMA, on the other hand, lives in a different family of psychedelic molecules known as phenethylamines [157]. Interestingly, all of these psychedelic molecules bind the 5-HT_{2A} serotonin receptor as their primary site of action. MDMA turns out to be a particularly effective tool for trauma therapy because it is an empathogenic molecule, meaning that it specifically enhances empathy, acceptance, feelings of safety, emotional openness, and social connection.

In properly conducted psychotherapy, MDMA has been shown to help PTSD patients feel safe enough to remake meaning from past traumatic events, from a perspective of safety rather than fear, guilt, and shame [151-153]. Safe enough to step out of victim-mentality for several hours to re-experience the power of choice through presence. Even more interesting was that the clinical trials of MDMA combined with psychotherapy were starting to show the first signs that long-term remission from mental illness was achievable without requiring daily dosing of medication for life [152, 153]. The first sign that a *cure* for mental illness may be within reach.

When I asked clinicians and patients involved in these studies about the experience of MDMA, many described it as "child's eyes", because it is as if you are looking at yourself and the world through your eyes as a child again. Restoring the familiar, but often distant experience of childlike innocence and wonder.

The Forgotten Secret rushed back into my awareness.

Study subjects also described their experiences with MDMA in the clinical trials as one of the most meaningful of their entire lives, and yet, this experience did not appear to provide anything new. It appeared to provide access to crystal clear memories of what we have forgotten.

Thanks to the tremendous work of Dr. Rick Doblin, PhD, Dr. Michael Mithoefer, MD, Annie Mithoefer, and their team at the Multidisciplinary Association for Psychedelic Studies (MAPS) over the last forty years, we have now witnessed MDMA-Assisted Therapy for PTSD shift the way we think about trauma as it relates to mental illness as a whole.

Rick was kind enough to allow me to receive training from his expert team on this technique in 2016.

The treatment protocol for PTSD involves just three doses of MDMA and 42 hours of intensive psychotherapy over twelve weeks with two therapists [158]. The MAPS Phase 2 double-blind randomized placebo-controlled crossover trials found that within two months of completing the twelve-week MDMA treatment, ~50% of subjects (with treatment-resistant PTSD for over seventeen years on average) were no longer meeting diagnostic criteria for the disorder [151-153, 159-162]. A fantastic result in and of itself. Even more astonishing is that at one year out, with no additional treatment administered by the research team, remission rates increased from ~50% to 67%, with remission sustained for over five years in some subjects.

This is the first time in the history of psychiatry that patients have been observed to continue to get better on their own after the primary treatment was discontinued. Across all of our prior clinical studies of legal psychiatric medicines, symptoms get worse when patients stop participating in the prescribed treatment, not better [163-165].

Given the uncanny overlap with my interests in trauma, chronic stress, and meaning making, I was compelled to understand the biology behind MDMA's ability to amplify the effectiveness of trauma therapy.

In regular old trauma therapy without psychedelic medicines, we know that when our patients feel safe enough to be vulnerable, they have an opportunity to get to the source of the emotional injury so they can repair it, just like cleaning and repairing a physical wound. When they don't feel safe, they guard the wound. Safety allows the vulnerable parts of the person injured by a trauma to be faced directly, comforted, loved, and accepted as part of the whole.

From the work of Kandel, Skinner, and Pavlov, I remembered that fear and safety drive learning, meaningfulness, behavior, and the growth of neural connections. Trauma is learned fear. Healing is learned safety. They also found that fear-driven behaviors can be extinguished by learning to reassociate safety with the environment [20, 166, 167]. The amygdala and insula are key players in this process (Figure 6) [168, 169].

As I dove deeper, I learned that MDMA appears to work so well to accelerate trauma healing because it molecularly amplifies safety learning and fear extinction, all the way down to the amygdala and insula [170-175]. These are the same parts of the brain that respond to soothing touch and intentional breathing (Figure 7) [30-33].

This made me start to wonder: If people continue to get better over time after MDMA therapy has completed, then there must be something sticking around in the body that is representative of this safety learning and continued improvement. Something that we could measure.

This led me back to the work of Dr. Rachel Yehuda, showing that trauma changed cortisol receptor gene expression patterns by modifying the epigenetic code [82, 85]. Dr. Yehuda and others had also demonstrated that epigenetic changes on the cortisol receptor gene resulting from trauma can be inherited across generations [82-87].

If trauma results in fear learning that causes "damage" to the cortisol receptor's epigenetic code, would extinguishing the fear with meaningful experiences of extraordinary safety, like those provided by MDMA-Assisted Therapy, repair the epigenetic damage? Perhaps this is how MDMA was working. If so, would the amplified safety provided by MDMA-Assisted Therapy rewrite the epigenetic code of the cortisol receptor enough for us to detect the change?

With all of this on my mind daily, I decided that I needed help from some experts who knew more than I did to answer these questions. So in 2017, I brought a supergroup of scientists together and kicked off a research study led by Dr. Candace Lewis, PhD at Arizona State University and Dr. Rael Cahn, MD, PhD at the University of Southern California, in collaboration with Dr. Rachel Yehuda at the Icahn School of Medicine, Mt. Sinai, Dr. Joe Tafur, MD at Modern Spirit, Dr. Ben Kelmendi, MD at Yale, and the MAPS clinical research team led by Dr. Berra Yazar-Klosinski, PhD.

The first two colleagues that immediately came to mind for this research adventure were Dr. Kelmendi, a psychiatrist with a background in trauma, psychedelic science, and epigenetics, and Dr. Tafur. Dr. Tafur had spent quite a bit of time building a relationship with a Shipibo community deep in the jungles of Peru outside of Iquitos. He had also published a wonderful book, *The Fellowship of the River*, describing what he had learned about healing from the Elders of this community. Fascinated by what I was learning from Dr. Tafur and Jeremy Narby, I coordinated a research expedition to Nihue Rao Centro Espiritual with Dr. Kelmendi and Dr. Tafur to better understand the ancient shamanic approach to trauma healing with the Shipibo people. This trip left me with one resounding message: *You're on the right track. Keep going.*

Upon returning home, Dr. Tafur helped assemble the rest of the research team and ran one of the scrappiest successful crowdfunding campaigns I have ever seen. With Rick Doblin's blessing, we collected saliva samples from subjects with PTSD in the MAPS Phase 3 double-blind randomized placebo-controlled crossover study to look for epigenetic changes to the cortisol receptor gene before and after their twelve-week MDMA-Assisted Therapy treatment [162].

The results knocked our socks off.

Not only was there significantly greater epigenetic repair of the cortisol receptor gene in participants who received MDMA compared with placebo, but the amount of epigenetic repair correlated with the amount of symptom improvement [176]. Our hypothesis was actually correct! The experience of MDMA-Assisted Therapy was indeed safe enough, and meaningful enough to facilitate a process of repairing damage to the cortisol receptor gene that had been inflicted by trauma. The more epigenetic repair, the greater the likelihood of symptom improvement.

This is some of the first evidence that trauma is reversible in humans on the level of the epigenetic code. The more fearful experiences we have, the more fear is encoded into our epigenetics. The safer we are, the more safety encodes, turning the tables on the body's scoreboard (Figure 21). This directly impacts our biology, modulating the function of the cortisol receptor, our stress response, and therefore, our entire nervous system.

So healing yourself really matters. If not for yourself, then definitely for the kids because the benefits of the work we do to heal ourselves pass down directly to them. We can stop the trauma cycle in this generation.

This is really good news for us because it confirms that we have a say in the outcome. If our experiences modify our epigenetic code, then we can curate our biology down to what is inherited by our offspring by curating our experiences.

Figure 21. The Body Keeps the Scorecard Take 2

This discovery is paradigm-shifting for psychiatry and is among the most important of the last century. It definitively demonstrates that accessing the trauma at the root of a person's suffering can resolve the problem for the long haul through fear extinction. The studies of psychedelic-assisted therapy teach us that PTSD (and possibly other mental illnesses) are not a life sentence, but are highly treatable, and perhaps even curable, when addressed as emotional wounds that require healing attention.

PSYCHEDELIC TECHNOLOGY

As exciting as the results were, I knew that MDMA-Assisted Therapy would not be accessible to my patients for many years due to legal and cost barriers. My PTSD patients were struggling and needed better healing tools yesterday. I often wondered if we could leverage technology to provide some of the safety benefits of MDMA to patients in the meantime.

Knowing that soothing touch and MDMA both activated the same key brain regions in the limbic system, I figured the sense of touch was the best place to start. I went back to our lab at the University of Pittsburgh after my MDMA-Assisted Therapy training in 2016 and began experimenting with methods for delivering soothing touch signals to the body on the go using low-frequency sound wave vibrations and wearable technology. If MDMA and soothing touch both target the insula-amygdala network to accelerate safety learning and fear extinction, then we should be able to use technology to tap into that same network. We just needed to figure out how to vibrate the touch receptors in the skin so as to send the correct safety signal to the brain.

This is where the C-tactile fibers come back into the picture (Figure 7). These touch receptors are unique because they respond specifically to slow, soothing, gentle touch. Unlike other touch receptors, they travel to the brain via a special spinal pathway for emotional information called the Lamina I tract [30-33]. The neurons in this tract project directly to the insula and amygdala. Drawing on prior studies that identified the specific frequencies of touch and vibration to which the C-tactile fibers optimally respond [29], I began composing vibrational songs tuned to these touch receptors.

As any good scientist does when they discover something new that is safe and needs initial validation, we began testing these vibrations extensively on ourselves and our willing friends, family, and colleagues. In doing so, we found that low-frequency soundwave vibrations, in the bass range of music, delivered to the skin in an ocean-wave-like pattern, seemed to have the most promise for facilitating rapid access to states of calm, clear, present safety. Music composed for the body instead of the ears. We were getting close to figuring out our body's favorite songs.

Dr. Greg Siegle, PhD, my brilliant mentor at the time, along with my psychiatrist colleagues Dr. Eric Lorass, MD, and Dr. Shan Gao, MD, PhD, and I completed our first double-blind randomized placebo-controlled crossover study on these vibrations in 2018. This study demonstrated that the specific vibration patterns we had composed for the C-tactile fibers significantly improved HRV, vagus nerve activity, cognitive performance, and feelings of calm under very stressful study conditions within as little as three minutes [138]. Subjects consistently reported improved feelings of safety in their bodies. Subjects who had experienced MDMA in the past were surprised that the feelings of safety from the experimental vibrations were so similar to those of MDMA without having to take a drug. A second double-blind randomized placebo-controlled trial followed shortly thereafter, confirming these findings in collegiate athletes under stress [139].

With the astute guidance and stewardship of my wife, Kathryn, who has a background in emerging technologies, we translated this discovery into what is now known as Apollo Neuro. With Kathryn at the helm as Apollo's CEO, and yours truly as chief scientist and innovator, we launched the first version of the Apollo wearable to the public in 2020 as the first consumer wearable to effortlessly improve HRV, vagus nerve activity, and cognitive performance, just by putting it on.

Apollo is the very first of the newest generation of wearable technology that doesn't just track your data, it takes action for you. It makes kickstarting the healing process easy and fun. By listening to your body and tracking your sleep, Apollo's AI automatically turns on day and night to improve vagal tone, restoring a sense of embodied safety around the clock. Apollo has now been studied in seventeen completed clinical trials involving over 2000 research subjects, consistently showing significant improvements in sleep, energy, focus, resilience, mood, anxiety, performance, and overall quality of life without side effects [138, 139, 177, 178].

Apollo is also the first technology proven to reduce fatigue and stress while improving mood and quality of life in severe autoimmune disorders like Systemic Sclerosis [177], and the first to reduce burnout in high-stress environments [178].

Two particularly exciting clinical trials in patients with severe PTSD (currently under peer review), conducted by independent university researchers, observed remarkable response rates to Apollo vibrations, with greater symptom reductions than SSRI medications within as little as two weeks of use. One of those studies also collected biological samples for epigenetic analysis to determine whether the feelings of safety provided by Apollo vibrations over twelve weeks are sufficient to repair the epigenetic code of the cortisol receptor gene, as occurs with MDMA-Assisted

Therapy. With this extensive epigenetic analysis ongoing, I remain optimistic.

Full circle, Apollo is now the first wearable technology to be studied and used to improve outcomes in psychedelic experiences, with and without psychotherapy. A white paper published in 2025 found that people using psychedelic medicines with Apollo had significantly less anxiety before, during, and after their sessions than with psychedelics alone[179].

Anxiety is one of the primary factors that contribute to unpleasant psychedelic experiences. As high anxiety can cancel out the therapeutic benefits at best, and result in retraumatization at worst, it is a major risk area to tackle in advance of psychedelic medicine administration. While we always address this in therapy before administering psychedelic medicines, most of the millions of people each year who use these medicines do so without the guidance of a trained provider. Apollo can now serve as a modern tool to safely enhance these experiences with or without a therapist present. Two more clinical trials on this topic are currently ongoing.

Apollo is not a replacement for psychedelic medicines, therapy, or soothing touch. It is the newest emotional tool in our toolbox, reminding the body that it is safe enough to learn, grow, and heal. Even in our most challenging moments.

PARADIGM-SHIFTING TOOLS

Taken together, it's hard to ignore the significance of these findings.

Psychedelics are to mental illness what antibiotics were to infection. It is an uncomfortable concept for some to grasp, but so were germ theory, handwashing, prions, and epigenetic trauma, so we're in good company!

In medicine, progress rarely arrives fully formed, and it usually isn't pretty. It begins as an observation that doesn't fit. Dr. Ignaz Semmelweis (1818–1865) noticed that women and newborns died less often in childbirth when physicians washed their hands before delivering babies. In return for his incredibly important discovery, he was ridiculed and ultimately institutionalized. Dr. Alexander Fleming (1881–1955) observed that mold could kill bacteria on a petri dish. His observation, which became the origin of all antibiotics, lay largely ignored until necessity forced its adoption. Both revealed invisible forces shaping life and death. Both are considered among the most important scientific discoveries of all time as they extended the average human lifespan by decades. Both were dismissed before they were understood.

We now stand at a similar threshold with psychedelic-assisted therapy. After decades of prohibition, compounds such as MDMA, psilocybin, LSD, ibogaine, and DMT are re-emerging within rigorous clinical frameworks. Their results are difficult to ignore and highly reminiscent of penicillin: rapid and durable improvements in illness that sustain with appropriate aftercare, even after the treatment is stopped. This observation alone is unprecedented in psychiatry. Our patients rarely continue to improve after the prescribed treatment is discontinued [163-165]. In PTSD patients treated with MDMA-Assisted Therapy, this was the new norm [152, 153, 159-162].

As with antibiotics, the true significance is not just the compound; it is the shift in perspective.

Both antiseptics and antibiotics helped us understand and address the invisible source of infectious disease. They showed us that infection is not caused by "bad air," but by microorganisms invading the body. Psychedelics illuminate the invisible internal causes of suffering, such as trauma patterns, rigid beliefs, and dysregulated neural networks that persist long after the original threat has passed. They help us understand that most mental illness is not genetic (in our DNA), it is epigenetic, trauma stored as learned fear on our DNA. Unlike our genetic code, our epigenetic code can be modified by our behavior and the environment.

In both cases, healing arises not from brute force, but from assisting the body's own intelligence. The immune system in one, and the brain's capacity for plasticity and integration in the other.

Infection and traumatization follow similar biological logic. Both are responses to invasion. Both trigger protective mechanisms that, when unresolved, become the source of ongoing illness. In this sense, post-traumatic stress is not so different from chronic inflammation: a defense that never fully turns off.

Psychedelics appear to create conditions in which these defenses can finally be resolved. They do not numb pain so much as reopen it safely, allowing it to be cleaned, processed, reorganized, and released by the body. The process resembles cleaning a wound more than pain relief. Just as antibiotics weaken bacteria, allowing the immune system to work its magic, psychedelics may support the mind in doing the same by weakening the grip past traumatic events have on our identity.

Medical revolutions rarely announce themselves as such. Handwashing, anesthesia, vaccination, and the germ theory of disease were all born into ridicule. General anesthesia, introduced in 1846 with the discovery of diethyl ether, was derided as unmanly and spiritually suspect; vaccination was decried as contamination. In each case, observation outpaced explanation. Proof came later.

Psychedelic medicines now join this lineage. They share with anesthesia the ability to render unbearable healing procedures tolerable; with vaccination, the capacity to inoculate a person with resilience, affording protection against traumatization; and with germ theory, the revelation that unseen processes can determine life-or-death outcomes.

The microbiome revolution offers another parallel. Once considered mere commensals, gut bacteria are now known to regulate immunity, metabolism, and mood [180]. Psychedelics similarly reveal that mental health is not the product of a single neurotransmitter, but of dynamic, interconnected systems (including the gut!). Both discoveries expand medicine's focus from parts to patterns.

History also suggests we should proceed with both curiosity and caution. Antibiotics transformed medicine, but their overuse led to resistance and new forms of disease. Psychedelics carry similar risks. Without proper training, ethical frameworks, and integration, premature commercialization undermines safety, trust, and healing.

What unites these breakthroughs is not just chemistry, but humility. Each one reminds us that healing is less about dominating the body than about safely cooperating with it to make meaning.

If antibiotics addressed the crisis of the body, psychedelics may address the crisis of the mind; the epidemic of disconnection, trauma, and despair that no pill alone has resolved. Both remind us that healing does not come from domination of nature, but from cooperation with it.

The lesson is simple: the most powerful medicines are often the ones that restore our trust in the systems we already carry within us.

The sooner that we collectively, as a medical system and a society, recognize the unparalleled capacity of psychedelic medicines to facilitate trauma healing and shift our mental health paradigm, the sooner we will realize that we can cure many mental illnesses for good (including Münchausen's Spectrum Disorder!).

NEURAL SYMPHONIES OF THE INFINITE

At the level of neurophysiology, DMT, psilocybin, LSD, and MDMA decrease activity in the Default Mode Network associated with ego and self-identity while increasing functional connectivity between the parts of the brain that should be talking to each other more often at rest [143, 181-183]. In short, brain regions that typically do not talk to each other start conversing. These four psychedelic molecules have also been demonstrated to accelerate learning by enhancing neuroplasticity [184, 185].

DMT specifically synchronizes cortical oscillations, especially in the gamma frequency range [143]. This is the same rhythm linked to meditation, insight, memory integration, compassion, and the "a-ha" of connection. This gamma coherence also arises during lucid dreaming, deep meditation, childbirth, orgasm, and mystical experiences.

In other words, your nervous system already knows this song. You've hummed it in your sleep, danced with it during intimacy, and felt it vibrating through your body during your most awe-filled moments. Endogenous DMT may act like a spiritual punctuation mark, helping you to rewrite the chapters of your soul's autobiography in a language far deeper than words.

And yet, we've spent the last several thousand years trying to prove that the natural, biologically accessible experiences of holiness were real all along.

Now, in our lifetime, science has finally caught up to the mystics, and DMT is a major part of that story because we can finally administer it to people and induce spiritual and mystical phenomena on demand [147-150]. We can scan brains in deep meditative states and mid-prayer. We can administer DMT and reliably facilitate mystical experiences. And we're discovering what Indigenous cultures have long known:

The temple was never made of stone. It's made of synapses, breath, and the silent space between.

TRAINING THE BODY TO REMEMBER DIVINITY

The body has always been the original altar. It turns out we can train it to experience transcendence. Through intentional breathing, prayer, vibration, intimacy, meditation, movement, and rhythmic ritual, we can activate the same systems that release endogenous DMT.

Apollo vibrations restore the body to a state of parasympathetic safety, a necessary precondition for awe [138, 139, 186]. When the body feels safe, the soul can come out.

Over time, repeated practice of these techniques, what I call *neurocatalytic conditioning*, builds resilience. It accelerates neuroplasticity, automation of thoughts and behaviors that serve us, and cognitive flexibility. It trains the nervous system to enter expansive states without fragmentation.

The veil thins not by force, but by coherence.

FROM PEAK EXPERIENCES TO EVERYDAY DEVOTION

DMT is not the goal. It's not about chasing the high or mapping the cosmos. It's about learning how to live in such a way that presence itself becomes the miracle.

Faith, prayer, and sacred rhythm aren't just mystical hobbies. They're ancient neurotechnologies built into all human beings to regulate the psyche and restore the union of mind and body with the Divine. When we remember that all beings are variations on a DNA theme, we begin to see the divinity in everyone.

When we pray and feel held, when we breathe deeply and remember our worth, when we hold the hand of a loved one and feel the universe in our palm... That's the medicine. Remembering how to live like the sacred is already here, because it is. Remembering how to reclaim power through connection, play, and delight, because it's nothing short of a miracle that we exist.

DMT's existence within us proves it. With enough breath, rhythm, and gratitude, you can teach your body to remember it in every moment. On autopilot.

Our nervous system is the temple.

And the altar is unabashedly you, fully present, fully alive.

CHAPTER 10
Sleep It Off

Sleep is the golden chain that ties health and our bodies together.
Thomas Dekker (1572–1632)

There is a quiet, universal truth that most of us spend most of our lives ignoring: you already know how to sleep.

Before you learned fear, before you learned to check your phone in the middle of the night like it might whisper secrets about how to fall back asleep, your body knew exactly how to do this. Sleep is not a skill you acquire. It is a core function you are born with. Roughly one-third of your life, by design, is meant to be spent in this state.

Not optimized. Not negotiated. Not feared.

Just...surrendered.

Science is remarkably consistent on this point. Nearly every human being who has ever lived has been born with the innate capacity to sleep for roughly a third of our entire lives. The exceptions are so rare that they read like a warning from biology itself. One such hereditary condition that only exists in a handful of families worldwide, known as Fatal Familial Insomnia, occurs because a toxic misfolded prion accumulates in the parts of the brain responsible for initiating sleep [187]. When sleep disappears, so does everything else. Hallucinations and severe cognitive impairment begin between 36 and 72 hours of sleep deprivation, florid psychosis within 7 days, and death within 3-18 months.

Sleep is not optional. It is foundational to *being* alive [188]. Most of your body's physical, mental, and emotional recovery happens during deep and REM (rapid eye movement) sleep [189, 190]. Memories are consolidated from short-term to long-term and organized. Toxins are cleared from the body and brain [191]. Energy and *constitution* are restored like getting your character's hearts refilled in a video game.

And yet, for something so essential that we would never give up in a video game, we treat it like a suggestion in real life. We delay it. We trade it. We pretend we can out-negotiate it with caffeine and ambition. We treat sleep as if it is something we'll get to once everything else is handled.

To our continued dismay, biology does not organize itself that way.

SLEEP IS FOUNDATIONAL TO LIFE

In the 1940s, Abraham Maslow (1908-1970) proposed a simple but powerful idea: human needs are structured like a pyramid (Figure 14).

At the base are the essentials for survival and physiological safety: Food, water, air, shelter, and sleep. When these needs aren't met, we don't last long. Just above that sits psychological and emotional safety—important things like employment, legal safety, and health. Then, connection, love, and belonging. Then, esteem, confidence, self-efficacy, and strength. Then, at the very top, self-actualization: becoming who you are meant to be in this life.

We love to talk about the top of the pyramid. Purpose. Meaning. Optimization. Peak performance. Enlightenment. We build entire industries around it.

However, Maslow was very clear about one thing:

If the base is unstable, the rest collapses like a house of cards. Like building a house, each higher section of the pyramid can be built up only when the section beneath it is rock solid enough to bear the weight without collapsing.

Sleep is at the very bottom of this pyramid, woven into both physiology and safety. It is not just recovery. It's infrastructure. It is the condition that allows every other level to function.

When you are sleep-deprived, your brain does something very predictable. It shifts resources away from higher-order thinking and toward survival.

You become more reactive. More vigilant. More sensitive to threat. Not because you are failing, but because your brain believes you are in danger. Which means that when you are not sleeping well, you are not operating from the top of the pyramid. You are sliding down it, layer by layer.

Self-actualization becomes inaccessible.

Esteem becomes fragile.

Connection becomes strained.

And eventually, all that remains is the question your nervous system is trying to answer:

Am I safe enough to let go?

THE PARADOX OF SLEEP: TOTAL VULNERABILITY, ABSOLUTE NECESSITY

Every night, you enter one of the most vulnerable states available to a human being. Your body becomes still. Your muscles relax into near paralysis. Your awareness of the environment fades. You cannot run. You cannot defend. You cannot perform.

From a purely survival perspective, this makes no sense. And yet, every organism that has survived long enough to evolve has retained sleep because the benefits are too profound to abandon. To sleep is to temporarily surrender control in exchange for restoration.

Here's the catch:

You can only surrender if you feel safe.

This is where Maslow's hierarchy becomes more than a theory. It becomes a lived experience in your nervous system. If your environment, thoughts, or physiology signal danger, your brain will prevent you from descending into deep sleep. You may drift, you may doze, but you will not fully let go.

From the perspective of your biology, letting go without safety is not rest.

It is a risk. And so your system keeps one foot on the gas, even when you are lying perfectly still.

WHEN THE THOUGHT ITSELF BECOMES THE THREAT

There is a particularly cruel paradox that emerges around sleep. It often begins innocently.

"Why can't I sleep?"

"What's wrong with me?"

At first, this feels like curiosity and problem-solving. A reasonable attempt to understand. Unfortunately, the nervous system does not interpret it that way. The moment the question shifts from "What is happening?" to "What is wrong with me?", something subtle, yet profound, occurs. The problem is no longer external or situational.

It becomes identity, and identity-level threat is one of the most destabilizing signals the brain can receive. Because if something is wrong with *you*, then where do we find safety?

The bed is no longer just a place to rest. It becomes a testing ground. A performance arena. A quiet courtroom where your worth is evaluated in eight-hour increments. Now, instead of surrendering into sleep, your brain is scanning, monitoring, judging, and trying to fix things.

Now, the very effort to sleep becomes the thing that prevents it. This is not a failure of discipline. It is a positive feedback loop of perceived threat that we trained and automated accidentally because we weren't paying attention.

Thought → "Something is wrong with me because I can't sleep."

Signal → "I am not safe."

Response → Increased vigilance

Outcome → Sleep is physiologically inhibited/prohibited

Reinforcement → "See? Something really *is* wrong with me."

Just like that, the mind creates evidence for its own fear just because we asked ourselves the wrong question. From Maslow's perspective, this is a rapid descent down the pyramid.

The moment you believe something is fundamentally wrong with you, esteem collapses. Connection becomes harder. And most importantly, safety erodes from the inside out. Now the threat is not the environment.

It's you.

SAFETY IS NOT A THOUGHT

We often try to think our way into safety.

"I know I'm safe."

"I locked the doors."

"I'm in my bed."

Your nervous system does not run on logic. It runs on signals. The frequencies of energy around us (Chapter 7). Light exposure, noise, heart rate, breathing patterns, and emotional residue from the day all play a role. Then there's unresolved stress, the subtle hum of uncertainty that lingers in the background of modern life.

If these signals suggest a threat, your brain prioritizes vigilance over restoration, which means sleep becomes lighter, more fragmented, and less restorative. You wake up tired, not because you didn't spend enough time in bed, but because your brain never fully allowed you to leave the lower levels of Maslow's pyramid.

You stayed in safe mode all night, and ironically, safe mode is not the same as feeling safe. It's what happens when your computer crashes and won't restart.

CHRONOTYPES: YOUR RHYTHM IS NOT A MORAL ISSUE

One of the most compassionate advances in sleep science is the recognition that we are not all designed to sleep the same way.

Your circadian rhythm is biologically programmed, influenced by genetics, environment, and age [192]. Within this system, individuals fall into different chronotypes, patterns of wakefulness and sleepiness that shape when you feel most alive.

Dr. Michael Breus, PhD, the world-renowned double-board certified sleep doctor and bestselling author of *The Power of When*, describes these patterns as Lions, Bears, Wolves, and Dolphins [193].

Some people are wired to rise early and move quickly.

Others come alive at night, thinking more clearly when the world quiets down.

Some follow the sun's rhythm.

Some move through sleep lightly and irregularly.

This is not personality. It is physiology.

When you force your life into a schedule that conflicts with your chronotype, your body experiences it as a form of chronic misalignment. Dissonance instead of harmony. A subtle but persistent disruption of safety. When safety is disrupted, sleep is one of the first things to go.

We often label this as laziness or lack of discipline, but what's really happening is much simpler:

You are asking your biology to ignore itself. And it won't.

Or, as Dr. Breus puts it:

"If time is the currency of life, and attention is the currency of time, sleep is the currency of attention."

If you spend your nights misaligned with your biology, your days become cognitively expensive. Attention becomes harder to sustain. Focus becomes effortful. Presence becomes something you chase instead of something you inhabit.

WHEN SLEEP BREAKS, THE PYRAMID COLLAPSES

Without sleep, the entire hierarchy destabilizes.

Your emotional brain becomes louder. The amygdala becomes more reactive, scanning for threat even when none exists. At the same time, the prefrontal cortex, the part of your brain responsible for regulation, planning, and perspective, becomes less effective.

You feel more anxious, more irritable, less capable of handling the ordinary stressors of life. Connection suffers, you misread social cues, you withdraw, and you react more impulsively. Esteem erodes; you doubt yourself more and trust yourself less.

The idea of self-actualization, of becoming your fullest self, feels distant, abstract, and almost absurd because your nervous system is still trying to answer a much simpler question:

"Can I rest without something bad happening?"

Until that question is answered with a felt sense of yes, the rest of the pyramid remains out of reach.

SLEEP IS WHERE SAFETY BECOMES REAL

If this book is about learning to feel safe enough to be alive, then sleep is where that learning is tested. Not in theory, in physiology.

You can practice breathing. You can meditate. You can do everything "right" and yet, sleep is the moment your body decides whether it believes you. It is the ultimate bottom-up confirmation of safety because you cannot force sleep.

You can only allow it. And that allowance begins with something deceptively simple:

The willingness to stop asking, "What's wrong with me?"

And to start recognizing:

Nothing is wrong with you.

Your system is trying to protect you.

And when it finally feels safe enough to stop trying…

Sleep can become automatic too.

CHAPTER 11
The Body Speaks

The more relaxed the muscles are, the more energy can flow through the body. Using muscular tensions to try to 'do' the punch or attempting to use brute force to knock someone over will only work to opposite effect.
Bruce Lee (1940–1973)

Before you finish reading this sentence, your body has already decided whether you are safe.

Not your thoughts.

Not your beliefs.

Not your productivity metrics.

Your body.

Posture is one of the fastest, quietest, and most underappreciated ways the nervous system communicates with itself. Before words, posture was how mammals signaled danger, dominance, submission, curiosity, and belonging. *The body speaks first.* The mind comes along later to explain whatever the body has already decided.

This is why posture is not just cosmetic. It is biological information.

When we talk about anxiety, depression, burnout, trauma, or confidence, we tend to frame them as psychological states. From the nervous system's perspective, these are postural states as much as mental ones. Patterns of muscular tone, orientation to gravity, breath restriction, and gaze direction that signal either safety or threat to the brain.

Modern neuroscience is increasingly clear on this point: how you hold yourself shapes how you feel, think, and behave, not just the other way around.

POSTURE AS A NERVOUS SYSTEM SIGNAL

The autonomic nervous system continuously scans for cues of safety or danger through a process called *neuroception*, a term coined by Dr. Stephen Porges, PhD to describe the body's unconscious threat detection system [194]. Posture is one of its primary inputs.

A collapsed posture, rounded shoulders, flexed spine, downward gaze, and shallow breathing tend to co-occur with increased sympathetic arousal. In contrast, a balanced, upright posture with expansive, unrestricted breath and a level gaze supports parasympathetic regulation and vagal tone [195]. Improving vagal tone results in higher EQ over time.

This isn't as much about "standing tall" to look confident as it is about mechanical signaling:

- Spinal flexion compresses the thoracic cavity, limiting lung expansion.
- Reduced lung expansion alters carbon dioxide tolerance and vagal signaling.
- Altered vagal tone changes HRV.
- HRV strongly predicts emotional regulation capacity and resilience.

In other words, posture influences breath, breath influences vagal tone, and vagal tone influences emotional regulation.

EMBODIED COGNITION: THE MIND LIVES IN THE BODY

Research in embodied cognition has repeatedly demonstrated that body position influences mood, memory, risk-taking, and perception. Studies show that expansive postures can increase feelings of confidence and agency, while contracted postures are associated with helplessness and threat sensitivity [196, 197].

Even facial musculature matters. Holding a neutral or slight smile can shift emotional processing via feedback loops between facial muscles and limbic structures, a phenomenon known as *facial feedback* [198].

The takeaway is simple but profound:

The brain constantly listens to the body.

If the body is folded inward, the brain assumes danger.

If the body is balanced and supported, the brain lets its guard down.

TRAUMA, POSTURE, AND FROZEN TIME

Trauma is not just stored as a story. It is stored as a posture toward the world.

People with trauma histories often develop characteristic postural patterns: protective hunching, forward head position, braced abdominals, restricted rib movement, and downward gaze. These patterns are not flaws; they are adaptations. At some point, they helped the organism survive.

When these postures persist long after the danger has passed, the nervous system continues to receive the message: *Threat is still here.*

Research shows strong links between trauma exposure and chronic musculoskeletal tension, altered proprioception, and postural rigidity [41, 199]. This is why purely cognitive approaches often fail to resolve trauma symptoms: the body never got the memo that it's over.

Posture is not about forcing the body into "correct" alignment. It's about inviting the nervous system out of yesterday and back to right now.

GRAVITY AS A REGULATOR

One of the most underappreciated aspects of posture is its relationship to gravity. Humans are upright mammals, so how we organize ourselves vertically matters.

A balanced posture distributes load efficiently throughout the skeleton, reducing unnecessary muscular effort. This frees metabolic resources and lowers baseline levels of stress hormones such as cortisol

[200]. Chronic misalignment, by contrast, requires constant muscular compensation, subtly increasing energy expenditure and stress signaling.

In simple terms:

Poor posture is metabolically expensive.

When the body feels supported by gravity rather than fighting it, the nervous system interprets this as a sense of safety.

POSTURE, GAZE, AND SOCIAL SIGNALING

Posture doesn't just regulate your internal state. It affects how others respond to you, which in turn feeds back into your nervous system.

Open posture and level gaze are associated with increased perceptions of trustworthiness and approachability, while collapsed posture is associated with avoidance and social threat cues [201]. This creates feedback loops: posture shapes social response, social response shapes emotional state, emotional state reinforces posture.

Change the posture, and you begin to change the loop.

POSTURE AS PRACTICE, NOT PERFORMANCE

This is not an instruction to "sit up straight." That kind of approach often increases tension and self-criticism.

Instead, posture becomes a practice of listening.

- Where is your head? Can your head float over your spine instead of jutting forward?
- Can you feel your ribs? Can your ribs soften enough to allow a full breath?
- Can you feel your pelvis? Can your pelvis rest rather than grip?
- Where are your eyes? Can your gaze widen instead of fixating downward?

Small changes are enough. The nervous system is exquisitely sensitive. Even brief postural adjustments have been shown to alter HRV and emotional state within minutes [202].

POSTURE AS AN ACT OF SELF-TRUST

At its deepest level, posture is a statement of relationship to life.

A collapsed posture often says, "I am bracing."

A balanced posture says, "I am allowed to take up space."

This is not arrogance. It is biology. When posture communicates safety, the brain loosens its grip, thoughts slow, breath deepens, attention returns, and the body remembers that it belongs here.

Posture is not about fixing yourself. It's about reminding your nervous system that the ground is still holding you. That is how you begin to feel alive again.

You don't have to change much to change your life.

Sometimes, you just have to let your body stand all the way up and say,

'I'm here. And it's okay."

Affirmation: *If I am not for myself, who will be for me?*

CHAPTER 12
Addiction Learning

A single twig breaks, but the bundle of twigs is strong.
Tecumseh (1768–1813)

Let's get something out of the way. Anyone can become an addict, and we all have tendencies toward something, be it sugar, caffeine, or money, the three most culturally acceptable addictions.

What we become addicted to, and the severity of the behavior, has a lot less to do with genetics and a lot more to do with the circumstances under which the pain was inflicted, the tools available for coping, and the role models and mentors available to us for support.

No one learns how to be human alone.

From the moment we're born, our nervous systems are shaped in relationship. We borrow regulation before we can generate it. We learn what is safe, what is possible, and what is allowed by watching someone who has walked the terrain before us. Long before books, the internet, and smartphones, wisdom was transmitted person to person, nervous system to nervous system. That hasn't changed. We've just forgotten how essential it is.

A mentor is not someone who gives you answers. A mentor is someone whose presence helps you ask better questions, especially when you are scared, confused, or standing at the edge of something difficult. At their best, mentors provide what no algorithm, protocol, or self-help book can: a living example of how to stay human under pressure.

This is true in childhood, but it remains true at every stage of life. Adolescents need models of courage. Early adulthood needs guides for discernment. Midlife needs witnesses who can normalize doubt and reinvention. Later life needs elders who remind us that meaning outlasts productivity. At no point do we "graduate" from needing mentors; we simply need different ones. The absence of human mentors teaching children is one of the primary reasons experts cite for the intellectual regression in Generation Z [110].

Neuroscience helps explain why. Learning accelerates in the presence of safety, trust, and attunement. When someone steadier than us holds space, especially in moments of distress, our nervous system relaxes enough to absorb new information. Mentorship is not just guidance; it is nervous system regulation by proximity.

Impulsivity and addiction are learned states. Change only becomes possible through practice, but practice does not happen in a vacuum. It happens in relationship. Almost every lasting transformation I've seen, both in my patients and in myself, can be traced back to someone who stayed present, believed in possibility, and modeled what it looks like to meet suffering without turning away.

Mentorship is not a luxury.

It is one of the most powerful growth strategies we have.

My first mentors were my mom and dad. I was very fortunate in that they fostered a nurturing and loving environment for me, starting when I was very little. In that environment, I was able to explore curiosity and discover the excitement of discovery itself. No question was too dumb to be asked. And that non-judgmental environment that encouraged questions of all kinds was just what I needed to feel safe. It also made me excited to take on really tough problems and learn challenging things because I wasn't afraid of failure. I learned early on that mistakes are par for the course.

Some of the most important pieces of advice my parents gave me (other than to find more mentors) were to find my passions and pursue them. For me, these started with dreams and grew into dreaming up (and building) technology to provide better healing tools for people struggling with chronic stress and complex mental illnesses like substance use disorders.

If there is one lesson that fundamentally reshaped how I understand addiction, impulsivity, and behavior change, it came from sitting face-to-face with people suffering through withdrawal who were often scared, ashamed, angry, and exhausted. I was under the guidance of Dr. Antoine Douaihy, MD, one of the most extraordinary addiction psychiatrists and mentors I have known, and his outstanding disciple, Dr. Henry Patrick Driscoll, MD. Dr. Douaihy's clinical work and scholarship emphasize a simple, but profound truth: addiction is not a moral failure; it is a nervous system adaptation in the context of threat and unmet regulation.

Dr. Douaihy's approach is founded on safety, empathy, motivation, and meeting people right where they are, especially in their toughest moments of withdrawal and craving. He highlights the therapeutic stance that "people have ambivalent feelings when it comes to changing entrenched behaviors…it is often better to elicit their own reasons for change" rather than insisting on compliance with our reasons for change. As it turns out, this is a good general rule for all human interactions.

PRACTICE MAKES "PERFECT"

I use " " around the word perfect because, contrary to what many of us were taught, perfection does not exist by our own creation. It is at best a fantasy, at worst a paranoid delusion. To do anything "perfectly" is impossible because we evolved to make adjustments and take chances all the time, and when you take chances, mistakes are inevitable. Mistakes are also our best opportunities for learning. Perfect is indeed the enemy of good. If we strive for something that does not exist, we spend our lives disappointed in ourselves, no matter how well things actually turn out. Rather than perfection, let's set our sights on a goal that is both achievable and exciting: *mastery*.

DR. DAVE'S ESSENTIAL EQUATION #10:

Practice x Time = Mastery

Dr. Eric Kandel's Nobel Prize-winning work showed that learning physically changes the brain: repeated meaningful experiences strengthen synapses and neural circuits, thereby facilitating the storage of memories related to fear and safety [20, 203, 204]. What we practice becomes a concentrated, fortified structure, from our thoughts to our neurons and all the way down to the expression of our DNA. What fires together, wires together.

Dr. Douaihy translated this into clinical addiction psychiatry: addiction is mastery in the service of short-term relief (instant numbing or distracting from emotional or physical pain), a deeply practiced circuit of prediction and behavior to avoid the discomfort of confronting pain. Healing is mastery in the service of long-term relief.

This helps to illuminate the biology of habit and automaticity. This is how the brain learns to respond repeatedly to stress, craving, or discomfort.

Unfortunately, there is no quick-fix escape for pain and discomfort. You must put your head in the mouth of the beast, face it down, and learn to tolerate it because every escape plan will fail, leaving us right back where we started. Feeling safe enough to engage with the source of the pain, our vulnerability, and remake meaning around it is how healing from trauma takes root.

MEETING PEOPLE WHERE THEY ARE: EMPATHY AS REGULATION

One of Dr. Douaihy's defining teachings, rooted in his extensive work on Motivational Interviewing and substance abuse treatment, is to reduce threat before trying to build change [205]. His work highlights that Motivational Interviewing is not just a technique; it's a way of being with people, prioritizing empathy, autonomy, and collaboration over confrontation. Furthermore, it echoes a powerful sentiment uttered by Hippocrates thousands of years earlier: *The natural healing force within each of us is the greatest force in getting well.* In other words, healing is an inside job, and the motivation to heal must come from the person seeking healing for it to be effective. This could not be truer than in the case of substance abuse and addiction.

COMPASSIONATE INQUIRY

Dr. Gabor Maté's work reframed addiction not as a question of "Why the behavior?" but "Why the pain?" Similar to Dr. Douaihy and Dr. Kandel, Dr. Maté's central insight is disarmingly simple and clinically profound: addiction is not the primary problem. Addiction is an attempt to regulate unbearably painful internal states shaped by trauma, stress, and disconnection.

Dr. Maté's therapeutic approach, Compassionate Inquiry, is built on this premise [206]. Rather than confronting or correcting behavior, the clinician gently guides patients to explore the emotional and somatic experiences that arise beneath the impulse to use. The method prioritizes curiosity over judgment, safety over compliance, and understanding over force. In practice, this means slowing down the interaction, tracking bodily sensations, naming emotions, and asking open, non-leading questions that help people reconnect with parts of themselves that have been long gone from awareness.

From a neuroscience perspective, Compassionate Inquiry and Dr. Douaihy's motivational interviewing approach work so well because they *reduce threat*. Shame, confrontation, and unsolicited advice activate defensive circuits that reinforce addiction. Compassion and attunement do the opposite: they engage prefrontal regulation, soften limbic reactivity, and restore access to choice [207]. Patients are no longer fighting themselves. They are learning to listen.

Dr. Maté also emphasizes that healing happens in relationship. Addiction thrives in isolation; recovery emerges through felt safety with another human being (e.g., mentorship). Compassionate Inquiry doesn't excuse harmful behavior, but it recognizes a deeper truth: people don't give up addictions because they are told to. They give them up when they no longer need them to survive. In that way, Compassionate Inquiry is not just a technique. It is a biological invitation back to wholeness, available to any of us who choose to open the door.

Addiction is a learned behavior in the form of an instant gratification loop trained to distract or numb ourselves to pain and discomfort that we would prefer not to feel.

IMPULSIVITY BREEDS IMPULSIVITY

It's a vicious cycle, by definition.

Dr. Kandel's work confirmed that we get better at anything we practice, whether it serves us or not [20, 203, 204]. Impulsive behavior can also be learned, and when we engage in it, we train ourselves and our neural networks to excel at being impulsive. On the contrary, every time we engage in patience, we train our brains to be less impulsive and more intentional in everything we do.

From Dr. Douaihy's perspective, impulsivity is not a lack of control, but control delegated to faster neural circuits because the slower circuits responsible for reflection were never given a safe learning context. Addiction becomes understandable as the nervous system's attempt to minimize discomfort by repeating whatever has worked fastest in the past.

This mirrors the neurobiological truth revealed by Dr. Kandel: neural circuits strengthen with repetition. Each time an individual practices intention over reaction, with empathy, safety, and support, new circuits form and old ones weaken.

The work of Dr. Douaihy and Dr. Maté demonstrates that reducing threat and increasing safety significantly reduces impulsive behavior and improves curiosity, engagement, and treatment outcomes. So if impulsivity is learned behavior, then so too is patience and healing. It's not personal. It's what we were taught, and if you can learn it, you can unlearn it.

DR. DAVE'S ESSENTIAL EQUATION #11:

Curiosity x Time = Discovery

The more we explore ourselves and the world with an open mind, the greater our chances of discovering something new and exciting. Discovering something new is one of the most magnificent feelings we are blessed with experiencing as human beings, and we are meant to experience it more often.

The trick with addiction is not to address it after the fact, but in the moment. To see the signs that a trap is ahead before we step into it. The first sign is that scratching doesn't make the itch go away. It makes it worse. Smoking a cigarette doesn't make the anxiety go away long-term. It just makes you crave a cigarette every time you feel anxious. The opposite also occurs. Like an itch that gets worse when you scratch it, the more we smoke or drink when we're anxious, the more anxious we become.

When we notice this response pattern to any behavior (e.g., money, sugar, nicotine, alcohol, video games, social media) it is imperative that we take that behavior very seriously and not engage in it to distract or numb ourselves to discomfort. This is a sign that this behavior is likely to become automated quickly and spur impulsivity, increasing the likelihood of addiction.

Impulsivity is the enemy of success as a human being. Patience is the sure path to victory.

There is no rush. When we rush, we make more mistakes and often have to start over.

Addiction teaches us a lot about automation in the brain. It teaches us that behaviors we learn to automate the most quickly provide a sense of instant gratification in the form of "escape" (temporarily numbing or distracting) from discomfort. When we automate these behaviors involving sources of relief outside of the body, addiction and all its downsides result.

We also have the capacity to automate other types of rapidly gratifying discomfort-alleviating behaviors that involve only what we have in our bodies (not requiring anything external to us for relief). Automating a resting breath rate of between five and seven breaths per minute is a great example that improves overall health and how good we feel on a regular basis. Another terrific practice to automate is questioning your thoughts (described in detail in Chapter 19), which trains your thought filter and literally adds time back to your day. Another is noticing where your attention is, which trains you to be mindful. Another is gratitude. Doing any of these activities at any time increases their automaticity, so they can run in the background without effort. Automating these types of tools and techniques improves your quality of life, and that of everyone around you, because they are activities that originate within the self.

This reminds us of another extremely important lesson:

I have everything I need right now to be. (Everything else I think I need is actually a bonus.)

By practicing internally generated techniques for distress tolerance (e.g., acknowledging and feeling your emotions, expressing gratitude for the feeling, setting aside time to express emotions), we train our ability to quickly move emotional energy out of our bodies by directly engaging with the feeling, rather than escaping from it. After all, escape is futile. When we avoid feeling, the energy of the emotion that cannot be expressed outward turns inward, increasing restlessness and anxiety.

GRACE → GRATITUDE → GRATEFUL → GRACIOUS → GRACEFUL

Gratitude is one of the most important emotional "muscles" to train for well-being because it is a positive feedback loop that is easy to automate. Studies show that the more gratitude you practice, the more gratitude you feel [208]. Your mood, anxiety, and overall mental health also significantly improve. Practicing gratitude is like bodybuilding for your emotional brain, but the gym is you, which is nice because there's no annoying membership fee.

DR. DAVE'S ESSENTIAL EQUATION #12:

Gratitude x Time = Grace

A simple, "Thank you!" to yourself for still being alive a couple of times each day will do just fine for starters. The more opportunities we find to express gratitude, the more grateful and gracious we become, which brings us ever closer to living in grace.

Grace is the goal state we all strive for: a quiet, peaceful mind, contentment, smoothness, effortless presence, and flow. Never rushing and never seeking. Always savoring the gift of simply existing in the here and now. Historically, grace refers to an unearned gift, a kind of ease or benevolence that flows without force. It is something given, something received, and something embodied.

Let's break it down:

- *Gratitude* is the *recognition of grace*. It is the moment you notice that something good has been given, whether by another person, by circumstance, or by life itself.
- *Grateful* is the *state of being* that follows that recognition. It is what your nervous system settles into when you truly register that you've received something meaningful.
- *Gracious* is how that state begins to *express outwardly*. When you feel grateful, you tend to become more generous, more patient, and more kind in your interactions.
- *Graceful* is the *embodiment* of all of this in motion. It is what it looks like when grace moves through behavior, posture, speech, and action with ease and coherence.

You notice something good (grace).

You recognize it (gratitude).

You feel it (grateful).

You act from it (gracious).

And eventually, you *become* it (graceful).

The chain can also run in reverse [208]. Practicing gratitude intentionally can cultivate a sense of gratitude, softening behavior into graciousness, which, over time, shapes a more graceful way of being, making you more open to perceiving grace in the first place.

It becomes a loop rather than a line. A kind of self-reinforcing system of perception, physiology, and behavior, where noticing goodness makes more goodness visible.

GRATITUDE VS. PAIN

Addiction is a behavior pattern centered around pain relief via escape hatch. If we accept that there is no escape from feeling, then the only other option left is to engage with feeling. This includes feeling pain.

Let's focus on emotional pain for a moment. Instead of numbing, distracting, intellectualizing, or shaming ourselves for the pain, we can express gratitude for being alive and being able to feel, and ask the pain what it is trying to teach us. Understanding that emotions are not "good" or "bad", we realize that they are neutral signals conveying a message that wants to be received.

As we engage in this process, the parts of the body that hold the pain start to release tension and relax. Awaiting us is a message with a constructive lesson or something that we can do to help relieve the pain, while simultaneously inviting slightly more joy into our lives.

GRATITUDE VS. ANGER

Anger is one of our most powerful emotions. When we repress it, it turns inward and wreaks havoc. When we express gratitude for it, we can harness it for constructive purposes. Fiery passion, ambition, athleticism, and unbridled creativity are often anger transmuted. Anger is also a wellspring of motivation.

GRATITUDE VS. SADNESS

Sadness is a signal that we have lost something, a loss that needs to be grieved. I like to think of the act of grieving as the metabolizing of sadness into acceptance. According to the popular Kubler-Ross model, there are five reliable stages:

1. Denial
2. Anger
3. Bargaining
4. Depression
5. Acceptance

Grieving is actually an extremely important skill that we can train, and we have the remarkable capacity to become quite good at it. The more we value grief as a skill, the faster we move through the five stages when we're sad, and the quicker we bounce back from losses.

SPIRITUAL MENTORSHIP

Some of the most profound lessons I learned over the last decade came from my spiritual mentor, the Honorable Segyu Choepel Rinpoche—an electrical engineer, a Tibetan Buddhist teacher and meditation master in the Vajrayana tradition, and authorized holder of the Segyu lineage dating back to 1432 CE. From Rinpoche, I learned that we are all energy and that human energy obeys the laws of physics, like all energy. I learned that the root of addiction is not desire, but disconnection from awareness. He taught me that suffering persists not because we feel too much, but because we forget how to sit with what we feel without reacting.

In his presence, I saw that true freedom is not the absence of craving, but the ability to witness it without becoming it. He emphasized that the mind, when untrained, chases relief, but when gently disciplined through awareness and compassion, it begins to rest in itself. This shifted everything for me.

THE QUIET POWER OF MENTORSHIP

In medical training, I learned the scientific method, how to identify complex diagnoses, and how to use advanced treatment techniques to address them. From my parents, I learned to read, to write, to ask questions, and not to always trust the answers that came back. I learned that curiosity is a skill that can be trained and that mentors are our life sherpas.

From Dr. Douaihy, I learned how to sit with suffering without trying to dominate it, and how deep empathy is not soft, but profoundly regulating and healing. From Rinpoche, I learned that addiction is not something to fight, but something to understand. And understanding, practiced with patience, becomes liberation.

CHAPTER 13
There Is Nothing to Fear

The only thing we have to fear is fear itself.
Franklin D. Roosevelt (1882–1945)

Okay, let's talk about fear.

Not the exhilarating kind that comes from haunted houses or skydiving. No, I mean the chronic, *ambient terror* kind. The kind that hums in your nervous system like a really old refrigerator you just haven't found the time to replace. The kind that whispers, "You're not good enough," just loud enough to ruin your day.

Fear is the flavor of adulthood we didn't sign up for. And yet, here we are, chewing on it like old gum while telling ourselves we're "fine."

FEAR IS JUST YOUR BRAIN TRYING TO HELP...POORLY

Your brain isn't trying to ruin your life. It's just confused. It thinks it's still 100,000 BCE, and you're about to be eaten by a saber-toothed tiger. In modern life, the tiger is your tax return. Or the awkward silence in the Zoom meeting. Or your in-laws.

Enter the amygdala, a tiny almond-shaped structure in your brain that's basically your emotional smoke detector [8, 14, 15]. It doesn't know if the smoke is from a real fire or just burned toast. It just yells *"FIRE!!"* every time something changes.

This is called contrast detection. The amygdala's job is to freak out whenever something feels "off." New sound? Panic. Unexpected email?

Sweat. Cute stranger? Fight, flight, freeze, or awkward flirt. Newness in our environment is supposed to trigger the amygdala by default because, many thousands of years ago, newness meant uncertainty, and that could mean sudden death at a moment's notice.

Here's the thing: the amygdala isn't evil. It's just extremely sensitive and dramatic. Like a Shakespearean actor with zero chill.

FEAR ISN'T THE PROBLEM. IT'S WHAT WE DO WITH IT.

Children are actually pretty great at handling fear. They scream, cry, shake it out, and then go eat string cheese as if nothing happened.

Adults, on the other hand, avoid and suppress it. We turn it into ulcers, scrolling, spreadsheets, and passive-aggressive emails. Or we outsource it to the news and let it hijack our attention 24/7.

We're taught to believe that feeling fear makes us weak. In reality, feeling fear and choosing to stay open anyway is what makes us human. It's what makes us powerful.

YOU ARE NOT YOUR AMYGDALA

Remember: the amygdala is a *part* of your brain. It is not your whole personality. It's like your overprotective friend who tells you not to fall in love again because *"remember what happened with Todd?"*

Thankfully, you have lots of other friends in your brain, such as the insula [11, 30-32]. This is your quiet inner compass. Your inner child's therapist. It helps you feel your body, reflect on your emotions, listen to your intuition, and empathize with others.

Avoidant behavior is a slippery slope (Figure 22). The more we avoid something because we perceive it to be scary or threatening, the scarier and more threatening it appears. On the contrary, the more we engage with things that appear threatening on the surface by running the checklist to ensure that our core survival needs (Hello, Maslow!) are met in advance, the less scary or threatening they appear (Figure 23). Both of these actions rapidly train automatic responses in a positive feedback loop. Avoidance increases perceived uncertainty and fear, thereby increasing

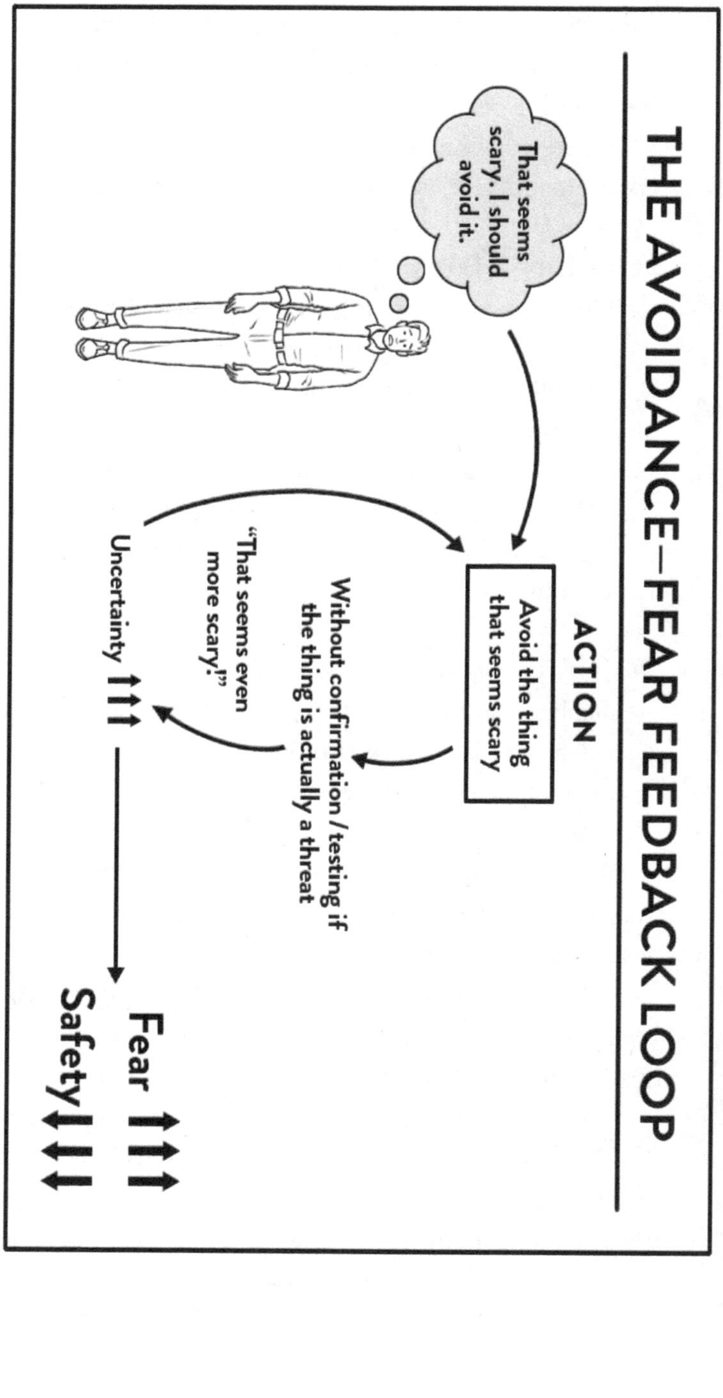

Figure 22. The Avoidance-Fear Feedback Loop

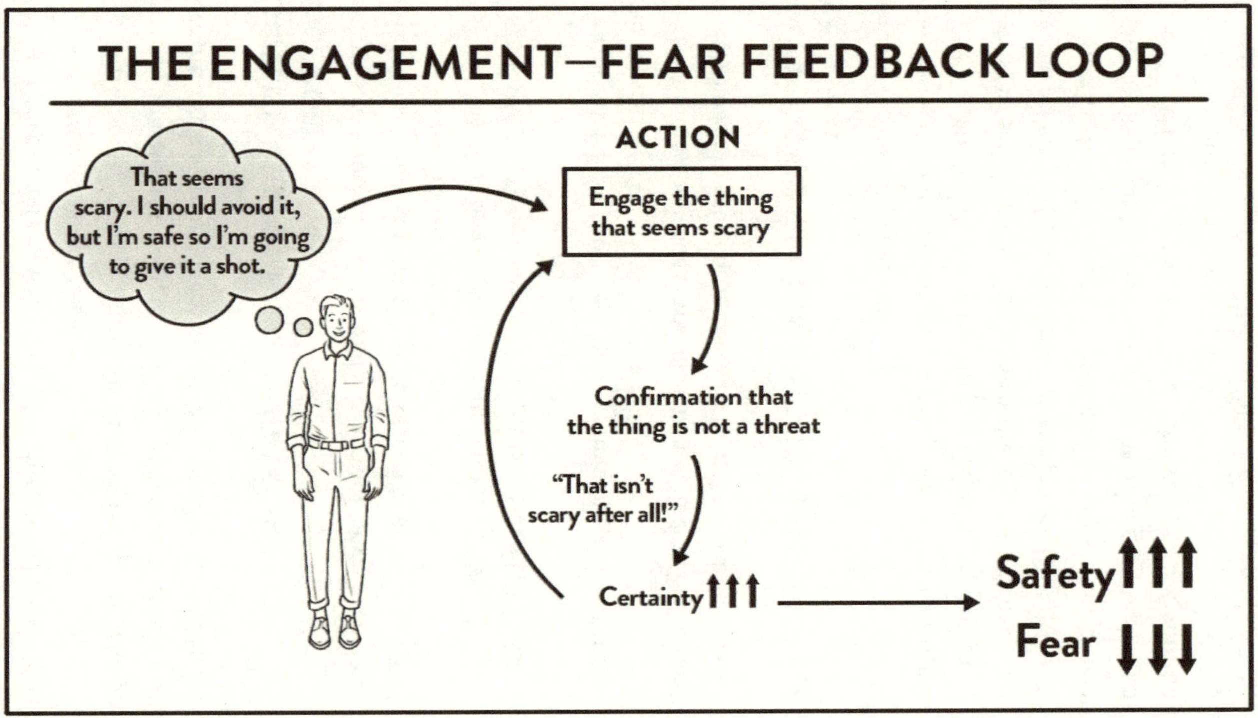

Figure 23. The Engagement-Fear Feedback Loop

anxiety. Engagement increases perceived certainty, safety, and vagal tone, resulting in decreased anxiety. This applies directly to how we interpret (or avoid interpreting) our feelings.

The more we practice *awareness* through techniques like breathing, listening, noticing the body, or crying in the car with Adele playing, the more the insula steps in to remind us, *"Hey, buddy…we're okay. All is well."*

SOCIETY HAS BEEN HIJACKING YOUR FEAR FOR PROFIT

Modern media and advertising understand your amygdala better than you do. They hijack your fear for clicks, votes, and cash money.

- News: "You're definitely not safe."
- Ads: "You're not good enough, but for $19.99…"
- Politics: "If you vote wrong, civilization ends Tuesday."

And we fall for it because fear is contagious, and our inner children are exhausted.

Here's the good news: you can train your fear brain. Just like you trained yourself to use chopsticks or lie politely at baby showers.

HOW TO RECLAIM CALM: THE DR. DAVE ANTI-FEAR TOOLKIT™

1. Breath Is Your Superpower

Taking slow, deep breaths by choice tells your body: "I can't possibly be running from a lion if I have the time to focus on my breath right now, so I must be safe." Studies have shown that controlled breathing reduces amygdala activity and boosts parasympathetic tone [6, 8, 10].

Practice: Start by just filling and emptying your lungs, breathing in and out through pursed lips as if you're breathing through a straw. Just notice the feeling of the air traveling through your lips and filling your lungs. No counting necessary.

After you are comfortable with this practice, try 4–7–8 breathing. Inhale for 4, hold for 7, exhale for 8.

Repeat these practices until calm, or until someone thinks you're asleep.

2. Touch Reality

Put your feet on the ground. Literally. Wiggle your toes. Feel the air on your skin. Touch a tree. Give yourself a hug. Remind yourself: *I am not in a war zone. I'm at my desk at work.*

Bonus: Soothing touch, the likes of hugs, hand-holding, snuggling your pet, and Apollo Vibes all release oxytocin, which lowers fear and increases feelings of safety and connection, instantly.

3. Listen to the Insula: The Body Is the Truth-Teller

Your body knows if you're safe before your brain catches up. Tight chest? Spinning thoughts? That's your body saying, "Hey, I think you need to hear me out and down-regulate before we buy a flamethrower on Amazon."

Practice: Close your eyes and scan your body with your attention for a minute. Where's the tension? Breathe into that. Feel the tension, breathe it out, and let it go. Where's the softness? Feel the softness, embrace it. Soften a little more with each breath.

4. Laugh in the Face of Doom

Laughter increases parasympathetic tone, improves immune function, and tells your nervous system: *"It's okay to come out now."*

So laugh at your fear like it's a toddler in a Batman costume. Respect it, but don't let it drive.

5. Name It to Tame It

Labeling emotions helps us to feel them for what they are (signals), which calms the amygdala and boosts insula-prefrontal connectivity. Like most signals, emotions exist to communicate a message. The message is received first by feeling the emotion without judging it, then by acknowledging and identifying it (labeling it). Within minutes, the emotion will pass through us, leaving behind the message it was sent to deliver.

There's a major difference between saying "I'm feeling scared" and "I am scared." The first is your current state. The other is your identity over time. You are not your fear. Use your words wisely.

SO WHAT IS LEFT TO FEAR?

Sure, death, public speaking, crocs, fear itself, but what if the thing you're really afraid of…is fully showing up?

Because showing up means being vulnerable. It means feeling deeply. It means being willing to look ridiculous if it makes you feel good, like a child wearing a tin-foil hat and sheet proudly announcing, *"I'm an astronaut now."*

That kind of openness? That's not weakness. That's divine courage.

You were never meant to be fearless. You were meant to be *brave.*

DR. DAVE'S ESSENTIAL EQUATION #13:

Bravery x Time = Courage

Acts of bravery are among the most challenging, as they require holding fast to our intentions and trusting our intuition in the face of tremendous adversity. And continuing to do so even when the chances of failure appear very high, and the consequences appear great.

Bravery is one of our most important survival skills. Every single act of bravery trains us to be more courageous, which is one of our most valuable skills for being an effective, adaptable, and successful human being. As we practice acts of bravery, we feel more courageous around the clock, and we spend less time debating what the right decision is, to be both brave and smart in the moment in which we are called to act. Practicing all the techniques described here builds resilience, making it more likely that we will act courageously in the next challenging situation that arises.

Speaking of courage, one of the hardest things to do sometimes is to be honest. And yet, we're told we're supposed to do that a lot. Telling the truth appears difficult much of the time because we don't want to feel responsible for hurt feelings. If honesty is the best policy, as our parents or teachers likely told us, maybe there is some truth to that worth discovering. After all, what is a man if not for his word?

Start by closing your eyes and just taking an honest look at yourself for ten seconds.

Do you see yourself for who you really are?

Do you see the person reading this book who is doing their very best despite great adversity?

Or do you zoom in on all the things we were taught to see as imperfections?

Do you see your victories first or your failures?

It turns out that being true to ourselves is REALLY important, and it starts with how we use our words. Spelling correctly and speaking correctly, with intention, so as not to accidentally mislabel something. It's as easy to mess up as repeating, "What's wrong with me that I can't sleep?" to induce insomnia, or "What's wrong with me that I have trouble learning?" to develop a learning disability, or "What's wrong with me that I'm not as attractive as everyone else?" to develop body dysmorphia.

Remember, if you ask the wrong questions, you get the wrong answers.

There is nothing wrong with you. You're just using incorrect spelling.

We also must be mindful to avoid using words to deceive or manipulate. Even when someone we have deceived doesn't know it, our body knows. The body always knows what is true, regardless of what the mind is able to convince itself. This is because deception creates dissonance between the body and mind, like the sound of a fork scraping on a plate in our nervous system. It's really tough to live with for an extended period of time. That's why people nearly always confess to wrongdoing eventually.

If deception creates dissonance, truth creates resonance and harmony, like the musicians in a symphony orchestra playing together, in tune, in time, and magnificently.

DR. DAVE'S ESSENTIAL EQUATION #14:

Truth x Time = Righteousness

Embracing truth as a skill we can practice, and practicing it as often as possible, builds righteousness. If deception increases uncertainty, righteousness increases certainty. The more righteous we are, the more certainty we have because less of our consciousness is polluted by deception-induced uncertainty. The more certainty we have, the less fear and anxiety we carry with us.

Practicing truth on its own isn't that hard. We all have moments of clarity, flashes of insight, sudden urges to be a better human that last a few weeks, but don't quite get us to where we would like to be.

In the ancient Jewish tradition, *righteousness* is what happens when truth is lived consistently over time, without applause, without identity, and ideally without even noticing you're doing it. It's what happens when truth has been stress-tested by real life. Bills, traffic, screaming babies, taxes, road trips, group texts that should have been emails. All of it.

In this tradition, righteousness is the opposite of perfection and moral performance. It is about always being intentional, kind, dependable, and trustworthy. It is not being the person who reminds everyone that it's wrong to eat meat at dinner. It is a quiet, sustained alignment with compassion, humility, and service that becomes so automatic we stop noticing it. And critically, the truly righteous person does not walk around thinking, "Nailed it! Crushing righteousness today." The moment you start narrating your own sainthood, the equation breaks.

The legend dates back to sometime between 200–500 CE. In the Talmud, we're told that at any given moment, the Lamed Vav Tzadikim (meaning thirty-six righteous individuals) sustain the world. No pressure, just...our entire civilization quietly resting on a group the size of a large dinner party.

Then in the thirteenth century, Kabbalah mystics expanded this idea, describing these individuals not just as "good people," but as channels. Their unwavering alignment with truth allows something larger than themselves to move through them, divinely stabilizing the world in ways we don't directly see.

500 years later, in the eighteenth century, Hasidic Judaism delivers the twist that makes this teaching quietly revolutionary: these people are completely ordinary and don't even know who they are.

I appreciate this contribution because the moment righteousness becomes identity, it starts to drift away from truth and toward performance. And performance, as your nervous system will happily remind you, is exhausting. Righteousness is rejuvenating and revitalizing.

So the Lamed Vav Tzadikim are not trying to be righteous. They are simply living in such consistent alignment with truth that, over time, righteousness emerges as a byproduct. Their equation is running on autopilot in the background, quietly, steadily:

Truth × Time = Righteousness

Let's dive deeper into the nervous system for a moment. Deception, even subtle self-deception, increases uncertainty. Uncertainty is fuel for the nervous system's threat response (Figure 6). It's what keeps us scanning, bracing, doubting, and second-guessing with our shoulders up to our ears.

Righteousness, on the other hand, increases certainty. The more aligned we are with truth, the less our inner world is cluttered by noisy contradictions we have to manage. The less we have to manage, the quieter our minds. The quieter our minds, the safer we feel.

More certainty → less fear
Less fear → more presence
More presence → more meaning
More meaning → more joy, curiosity, memory, healing, and longevity

Righteousness, in this framing, is not about being morally superior in the slightest. It's about becoming internally coherent. Clean signal, less noise. A nervous system that isn't constantly trying to reconcile competing stories about reality.

This is exactly where the tradition of the Lamed Vav Tzadikim becomes both profound and strangely practical. I remember learning this around age twelve in Sunday school, and the takeaway landed with surprising clarity. If there are thirty-six people sustaining the world, and no one knows who they are, then they could be anyone.

The person next to you.

The stranger you pass on the street.

The person you're about to underestimate.

And maybe, on a good day, even you.

Which leads to a beautifully simple and hopeful conclusion:

Treat everyone, including yourself, with deference and respect.

When you do, you're not just honoring them.

You're practicing the very equation that sustains the world.

TALK TO YOUR INNER CHILD

Take a moment. Put your hand on your heart. Close your eyes. Take a deep breath. Then another.

Imagine the six-year-old you. The one who danced in the grocery store. Who feared the dark, but believed in magic.

Say this:

"Hey, kid. I've got you now. You're safe. You're seen. You're not alone because I'm here now. We're going to be okay. I love you."

That's it.

Fear doesn't stand a chance.

BUDDHISM VS. FEAR

Let me tell you a story about nervous systems.

One day, Milarepa (1028–1111 CE), the famous eleventh-century Tibetan Buddhist cave yogi who makes most of us look like amateurs at solitude, left his cave to gather firewood. Translation: he stepped away from his regulated, breath-synchronized, mountain-view meditation pod and went to do something practical.

When he came back?

Demons.

Everywhere.

Not symbolic ones. Not subtle ones. We're talking full-on, fang-dripping, nostrils-flaring, bulging-eye demons. The kind your amygdala throws a parade for.

Milarepa's first reaction was profoundly human:

"Absolutely not."

The sympathetic nervous system comes online. Adrenaline spikes. Cortisol rises like the stock of hand sanitizer companies during COVID. He lunges at them. He chases them. He tries to evict them from his cave like a landlord who has just discovered squatters.

However, the more he chases them, the more comfortable they become.

Because this is how demons work.

And by demons, I mean anxiety. Trauma. Shame. Grief. Fear itself. That email you forgot to send in 2017.

The harder you try to crush them, suppress them, out-logic them, or spiritually bypass them…the more they settle in. They kick off their boots. They redecorate.

Milarepa notices something crucial:

Brute force isn't working.

So he switches strategies.

If I can't fight them, maybe I can educate them.

He sits down like a good scholar-monk and starts teaching the dharma. Existence. Nonexistence. Compassion. Impermanence. The nature of the mind. Probably with impeccable posture.

He looks up after a while.

The demons are still there.

Staring at him.

Huge eyes. No blinking. No applause. No enlightenment certificates.

This is the moment every therapist, meditator, and founder eventually encounters:

You can't TED Talk your trauma into leaving. No matter how good a speaker you are.

Intellectual insight is not the same as nervous system resolution.

So Milarepa does something radical.

He exhales. A deep one. Surrender.

Parasympathetic tone returns. The vagus nerve activates. Shoulders soften.

He realizes: These demons are not leaving because they are not invaders.

They are unintegrated parts of him.

He stands. He bows to each one.

"It looks like we're going to be here together," he says.

"I open myself to whatever you have to teach me."

And in that moment?

All but one demon disappear. Because most of what terrifies us is sustained by resistance to feeling.

The one that remains. The biggest, fiercest, scariest demon of them all. The final boss level of the psyche. The one you don't post about on Instagram.

Emboldened by his early success, Milarepa goes even further along the thread of surrender.

He walks up to the last demon and says the most neurologically sophisticated thing possible:

"Eat me if you wish."

And he places his head inside its mouth.

The last demon bows and dissolves into space.

Illumination through complete surrender to the safety within ourselves.

It's the moment you stop fighting the panic attack.

The moment you say, "I trust that I can feel this fully and know that I'll be okay."

The moment you stop trying to outrun grief and instead let it metabolize.

Because the final demon is always the illusion of separation.

When we fight our internal experience, we amplify it.

When we try to outthink it, we end up compartmentalizing it.

When we welcome it, we integrate it.

The toughest challenges, our deepest darkest fears, the inner demons, are not defeated through dominance.

They are resolved through coherence.

Acceptance lowers defensive activation.

Curiosity restores agency.

Compassion reintegrates fragmented parts into the whole.

THE SIMPLE SUMMARY:

When writing this book, I had to confront one of my own fears: the fear of drawing. This may sound silly, but when I was a kid, I was absolutely terrible at drawing and painting. I dreaded art in school because the other kids would use it as a reason to make fun of me. So I quietly told myself, "You're just not good at art, so that's going to be something you just don't do." The message my nervous system took away is:

Art → Exile → Danger

Toward the end of my writing process, I realized I needed illustrations to visualize the book's most important concepts. After all, a picture speaks a thousand words. When I asked my illustrator friend Phil if he would help me out, he asked me to draw my ideas and send them over so he could use them as inspiration.

At first, I was terrified of what he would think of me when he saw my drawings. What would I think of me? But I really needed those illustrations. So after months of thinking about it without making any progress, I mustered up the courage, walked up to this demon, put my head in its mouth, and began to draw on it.

It began as extremely uncomfortable, and I noticed I was constantly judging myself, which made it hard to feel good about being creative on paper. Within a few days, however, it became a flow. The concepts I was writing about were now coming out of my hand onto paper as lines, boxes, and people with far less effort, and far less self-criticism. I no longer view drawing and art as scary or dangerous, only as skills that I never developed. Skills that I can get a heck of a lot better at with a little patient practice.

When you peek at the illustrations throughout this book, you're not just seeing information in visual form; you're witnessing the product of my personal healing process. My nervous system once associated drawing with threat. Over the last several months, I retrained my nervous system to associate drawing with fun, creativity, curiosity, and most importantly, safety.

Don't get me wrong, I'm still not particularly skilled in the art of drawing, but this process unlocked the opportunity to learn this new skill without the burden of past judgment weighing my nervous system down. The result is that I now expend less effort and I learn much faster when drawing.

In a physically safe setting, when we place our head in the mouth of the things we fear most, consciously and willingly, we discover it was just us all along.

CHAPTER 14
The Nervous System's Rip Cord

A day without laughter is a day wasted.
Charlie Chaplin (1889–1977)

Laughter is what happens when the nervous system realizes it's not about to die.

That's it. That's the core mechanism.

The nervous system laughs when a threat turns out to be imaginary, exaggerated, or, best of all, self-inflicted. Humor is the sound of relief escaping the body at high velocity. It's the *psssshhh* of pressure releasing. It's the brain saying, "Wow, I was really about to take that way too seriously."

Which, to be fair, is most of what we do.

From a neuroscience perspective, humor is a rapid jailbreak. The brain predicts something bad, awkward, or meaningful...and then, plot twist, it's fine. Or absurd. Or both. The result is a cascade of neurochemicals that feel suspiciously like joy [209]. Dopamine lights up. Endorphins show up like old friends. The vagus nerve clocks in and says, "I've got this."

Laughter is not just fun or an indulgence.

It's an ancient social technology.

THE BIOLOGY OF THE PUNCHLINE

A joke is basically a Trojan horse for safety.

Neuroimaging studies show that humor activates the prefrontal cortex (the part that says, "Wait...what?"), followed by the reward centers of the brain (the part that says, "Ohhh. Nice.") [209]. The nucleus accumbens lights up. The amygdala chills out. The vagus nerve gets a spa day.

Laughter lowers cortisol [209, 210]. It raises pain tolerance. It improves immune function. It increases social bonding. It also makes you breathe like a functional mammal instead of a panicked squirrel.

From an evolutionary standpoint, laughter likely evolved as a group signal meaning:

"False alarm. We're all good!"

Which explains why laughter is contagious. One person laughs, and suddenly everyone's nervous system gets the memo. It's peer-reviewed regulation. And children, even babies, are naturals at it.

HUMOR AS A PSYCHOLOGICAL PRESSURE VALVE

Dr. Sigmund Freud (1856–1939), the Austrian neurologist who founded psychoanalysis and is often blamed for ruining sex, actually loved jokes.

In *Jokes and Their Relation to the Unconscious*, Freud argued that humor allows forbidden or painful material to sneak past internal security [211]. A joke distracts the guards. The truth slips in wearing sunglasses and a fake mustache.

Freud later called humor "the highest of the defense mechanisms," which is a very Freudian way of saying: *this one actually works*. Humor lets the ego acknowledge suffering without being crushed by it. It says, "Yes, this hurts, and also, look how ridiculous this is."

In modern terms: humor creates distance without dissociation. You're still present, you're just not drowning.

HUMOR AS A SIGN OF PSYCHOLOGICAL MATURITY

Dr. Carl Jung (1875–1961), a Swiss psychiatrist and Freud's protégé turned rival, took humor even more seriously. For Jung, humor was evidence of integration [212]. If you can laugh at yourself, you are no longer possessed by your persona. The ego has loosened its grip. The psyche has room to breathe.

Jung believed excessive seriousness was a red flag. When someone can't laugh, it often means something inside is rigid, defended, or terrified of cracking. Humor signals flexibility. Wholeness. The ability to hold paradox without imploding.

Where Freud saw humor as release, Jung saw it as wholeness.

WHY HUMOR IS SO EFFECTIVE IN TRAUMA

Trauma collapses perspective. Addiction narrows it. Both falsely convince the nervous system that *this moment is forever.*

Humor breaks the spell.

Not by denying pain, but by restoring scale. It whispers, "This isn't the whole story." And sometimes that whisper is enough to bring the nervous system out of red alert. Humor is not disrespect. It's survival intelligence. It's the psyche saying, "I'm still here. Not today, Satan!"

THE SACRED CLOWN

Across cultures, the healer and the trickster are often one and the same. The sacred clown tells the truth sideways. Zen masters answer deep questions with jokes. Sufis laugh with God, described as "sacred laughter."

Why?

Because truth delivered straight can feel like an attack. Truth wrapped in humor feels like an invitation.

Humor bypasses defenses. It sneaks insight past the bouncer. It opens the door just enough for wisdom to wander in barefoot.

THE COSMIC JOKE

If you're still trying to determine if God exists, humor may be one of the clearest signatures. Creation is extravagant. Life is improbable. Consciousness observing itself through 16 billion eyeballs is, frankly, a little absurd.

That absurdity is not nihilism, it's freedom.

Humor isn't the opposite of reverence. It's reverence without fear. It's what happens when awe meets humility, and they decide to be friends.

Laughter restores proportion. Instantly.

It reminds the body that fear is informative, not authoritative. That pain is real, but not absolute. That existence is strange, beautiful, and deeply unserious in the best possible way.

Laughter is the nervous system remembering that life is not a punishment.

It's a game.

And sometimes the most spiritual thing you can do, the most scientific thing you can do, the most healing thing you can do, is laugh at yourself before the universe does it for you.

Affirmation: *When life is fun, the game has been won.*

CHAPTER 15
Death Schmeth

Death is not the end. It is a transition into another world, where the ancestors receive us.
Malidoma Patrice Somé (1956–2021)

Let's talk about the elephant in the room. The invisible, lurking, shadowy, extremely reliable elephant known as Death.

You may know him from such classics as:

- "Why is this freckle shaped like Albania?"
- "Did I just pull a muscle, or is this *it*?"
- Or my personal favorite: Mortality panic at 3 a.m., followed by Googling 'How long do tortoises live?'

The fear of death is one of humanity's oldest neuroses, right up there with "What if I say something weird at the dinner party?", public speaking, and "Am I doing life wrong?"

Spoiler: We are *all* in this together, and everybody dies. That's kind of the point.

We are all going to die eventually. It's a mandatory, inevitable part of life.

Here's the thing: fearing death is completely normal. In fact, it's baked into your brain's survival software like a mandatory update. The amygdala doesn't particularly care for nuance. It's more like an overzealous car alarm that screams *"DANGER!"* whether you're being chased by a lion or accidentally ate dairy on a first date.

But what if I told you that the real problem isn't death itself, it's thinking about death the wrong way?

Because death, it turns out, might just be the ultimate teacher. A teacher with bad breath and questionable office hours, sure, but one who gives you the kind of homework that actually matters.

HOW WE KNOW ADULTS ARE SECRETLY JUST CHILDREN WITH ANXIETY

Have you ever noticed how kids aren't afraid of death? They play "dead" for fun. They bury worms with dignity. They dress up as skeletons and eat sugar until they vomit on Halloween.

But somewhere between our last juice box and our first job rejection, we started repressing the very thing that could make us feel most alive: the reality that this party won't last forever.

Instead of embracing mortality, we:

- Get Botox and pretend we're twenty-nine forever.
- Invest in cryogenics, like that's not horrifying.
- Spend thousands on supplements while ignoring our own emotions, bowel movements, and common sense.

We fear death because we forget how to live.

WHAT DEATH REALLY MEANS

In Buddhism, death is an invitation to wake up. In Christianity, it's a reunion. In Stoicism, it's a reminder to live with integrity. In childhood, it's a game of pretend. And in neuroscience, it's… a tricky, unobservable event that's hard to define, but probably involves a loss of electrical activity, preceded by a massive burst of DMT in your brain, and followed abruptly by a lot of paperwork.

When you really lean into the fear of death, it starts to transform. You begin to realize it's not death you're afraid of, it's *unlived life*. It's regret. It's never finishing that painting, or kissing that person, or forgiving your father, or wearing the outfit you secretly loved but thought was "too much."

The hilarious irony is that every single moment we spend fearing death is one less moment we spend living life. Remember that thing we're here to do?

DEATH CAN BE GOOD FOR YOU

Psychological research has shown that reflecting on mortality can lead to [213]:

Less materialism

Stronger relationships

Greater gratitude

And even increased fruit and vegetable consumption. (No joke. It's called the "scare-you-into-salad" effect.)

This phenomenon is called mortality salience. When you're reminded of your death in a non-terrifying way, you tend to live life more aligned with your values.

Meanwhile, ignoring death entirely because the topic makes us uncomfortable has been associated with anxiety, repression, chronic busyness, addictive behaviors, and unnecessary spending on anti-aging serums and stem cells [214, 215].

So death can actually *improve* your life. Not by happening sooner, but by reminding you to prioritize the right stuff *now*.

ANCIENT PRACTICES THAT TURN FEAR INTO FREEDOM

Across spiritual traditions, the fear of death is *the* doorway to awakening.

- Buddhist monks meditate in charnel grounds, contemplating their own decaying flesh until they find peace in impermanence.
- Sufi poets wrote love songs to death as the beloved who reunites us with the Divine.
- Judeo-Christian mystics spoke of death as a veil being lifted between this world and God's presence.

And you know what? They were onto something.

When we stop fighting impermanence, we start appreciating what we have while we have it. We begin to live in the only place life is actually happening: *right now.* Truthfully, according to the laws of entropy from our dear friend physics, nothing in this world lasts forever. If everything lasted forever, we would be bored out of our minds real quick.

IF YOU DIE BEFORE YOU DIE, YOU WON'T DIE WHEN YOU DIE

For millennia, Indigenous healers and Eastern mystics have shared a secret that science is only now beginning to understand: the path to immortality is through surrender, not survival.

In Indigenous traditions, from the Shipibo of the Amazon to the Lakota of North America, longevity was never defined by how many birthdays you celebrated. Instead, it was measured by how deeply you lived in alignment with nature, spirit, and community. To live a long life meant to live a life of balance, to walk gently, to listen, and to stay in rhythm with the Earth. Illness was seen not merely as a biological error, but as a disruption in one's spiritual or relational harmony.

In these cultures, elders are revered not for their productivity, but for their wisdom, because they've transcended the illusion of the self as separate. They've learned to die to their egos—to make peace with impermanence, and to live in humble reciprocity with the land and the unseen.

This echoes a profound teaching from the mystics of the East:

"If you die before you die, you won't die when you die."

This cryptic koan, found in Sufi poetry, Tibetan Buddhism, and echoed by Jesus in the Gnostic Gospels, is not about physical death. It's about ego death. The surrender of identity. The stilling of the inner noise that says, "I am separate."

To "die before you die" is to transcend fear while you're still alive. It's to detach from the ego's desperate clinging and step into the eternal self, the one that is not defined by body or name, but by presence, awareness, and unconditional love.

This is the heart of the yogi's path, the monk's path, the bodhisattva's vow: to awaken to truth, again and again, until self and other are no longer separate. In the Tibetan Book of the Dead, it's said that the one who has seen through the illusion of self while still embodied becomes free from the wheel of death. In other words, they live forever, not as a physical body, but as consciousness fully merged with Source, Divinity, God.

Neuroscience is beginning to validate these claims.

Long-term meditators show profound changes in brain structure and function. Tibetan monks and advanced yogis demonstrate increased cortical thickness in regions associated with attention and compassion, enhanced gamma wave coherence, and reduced age-related decline in memory and emotional regulation [216, 217].

Meditation slows telomere shortening, enhances vagal tone, and activates the prefrontal cortex, the seat of wisdom and choice [218, 219]. In short, those who practice dying daily through meditation tend to live longer, suffer less, and feel more alive.

Maybe that's the real secret. The monk lives forever not because he escapes death, but because he no longer fears it. The bodhisattva returns again and again, not because he must, but because he chooses to out of love.

True longevity isn't about postponing death. It's about making peace with it now, so that you can live fully, freely, and eternally in every breath.

WHY GROWN-UPS NEED MORE RECESS

Let's start with a controversial idea:

Maybe the secret to living a long and happy life is simply remembering how to play nicely, take naps, eat healthy snacks, and cherish every moment we have because they are fleeting.

I know what you're thinking. "That's ridiculous, Dr. Dave."

To which I reply: "Exactly. Now let's take it seriously."

Because somewhere between our last finger-painting session and our first existential crisis over taxes, we forgot that most of what keeps us healthy is movement, wonder, laughter, regular bowel movements, deep rest, unstructured time in nature, and genuine human connection. The same things that made us feel alive when we were five.

PLAY IS PREVENTIVE MEDICINE

Modern longevity science is fascinating. We have stem cells, mitochondrial boosters, metformin debates, and wearable trackers that tell you when to go to bed. But guess what?

Grandma didn't need a Fitbit to tell her that getting a good night's sleep and holding hands during church lowered her resting heart rate. She just *knew*.

And science agrees. People who play, who laugh, who dance awkwardly in kitchens, and who build community (even if just through a book club dedicated to wine and *not* books) tend to live longer, healthier lives.

WE'RE JUST TALL CHILDREN

Consider this: adults are really just children who've been asked to sit still longer. That's why we rebel with things like $12 matcha lattes, conspiracy theories, and silent retreats we can't afford.

We crave permission to stop pretending we're supposed to be emotionally constipated productivity robots.

Longevity, then, isn't about living forever. It's about not forgetting who we are while we're still here. It's about enjoying the fleeting nature of the impermanent while it lasts.

It's about dancing in your kitchen, getting sun on your face, hugging people like you mean it, and sometimes crying in the Trader Joe's parking lot because they're out of the plantain chips you were really looking forward to eating.

LONGEVITY IS AN INSIDE JOB

When you die, people won't remember your résumé. They'll remember your laugh. Your weird rituals. The time you held their hand. The way you made them feel seen.

You don't become immortal by avoiding death, injecting yourself with stem cells every week, or by transfusing yourself with your children's blood.

You become immortal by fully showing up for life.

Right here.

Right now.

The kids had it right.

If you eat good snacks, play every day, sleep when you're tired, cry when you're sad, hug freely, tell people the truth, and know that you are unconditionally loved just by being here now, you are most likely to live a very long time.

And even if, by some chance, you don't, you'll really enjoy the time you had.

DR. DAVE'S LONGEVITY TOOLKIT™: CHILDLIKE WONDER EDITION

So, how do we live longer *and* better?

Let's break it down:

1. Move like you're at recess

Exercise doesn't have to mean slogging on a treadmill while questioning your life choices. Think monkey bars. Think skipping. Think stretching and naked cartwheels (in designated zones).

Studies show that even moderate movement, like walking for fifteen minutes each day, gardening, or passionately rearranging your furniture at 3 a.m., lowers all-cause mortality and adds years to your life [220].

2. Sleep like it's storytime

Adults are chronically underslept, laden with responsibilities, and frequently overcaffeinated. If your five-year-old self needed 10–12 hours of sleep and a nap, maybe your forty-five-year-old self deserves a little more than 5 hours and an espresso IV drip. Quality sleep improves immune function, memory, emotional regulation, and even DNA repair.

Your inner child (and therefore you) was born to sleep for a third of your life on Earth. So, let your inner child win. Go to bed early. Wear cozy socks. Demand a bedtime story from your smart speaker, and most importantly, tell yourself that sleep is safe, fun, and something your body both wants and is really good at doing.

3. Take breaks

Breaks and recess as a kid were sacred times. Crackers, juice boxes, running around without a care in the world.

Breaks also have a nice way of giving us perspective on what we were doing before the break. It's a moment to pause and reflect, to gain insight, and maybe even to notice when to stay the course or take the road less traveled.

Some of the most transformative insights of all time have emerged not in moments of intense effort, but in states of rest, curiosity, or mental wandering. Archimedes (287–212 BCE) famously discovered the principle of buoyancy while relaxing in a bath, realizing that displacement occurred as he stepped into the water and exclaimed "Eureka!" Isaac Newton, during a quiet break under an apple tree, realized the concept of gravity. Friedrich August Kekulé (1829–1896) envisioned the ring structure of benzene in a daydream of a snake biting its tail. Dmitri Mendeleev (1834–1907) claimed that the complete organization of the elements of the periodic table came to him in a dream. Alexander Fleming discovered penicillin after returning from vacation and finding mold that inhibited bacterial growth. These moments suggest that when the mind relaxes, it often connects ideas more freely, allowing insights to surface beyond the constraints of focused work.

4. Breathe like you're blowing bubbles

Intentional, controlled breathing, especially slow, diaphragmatic breathing, improves vagal tone, lowers cortisol, and makes you feel safe, kind of like blowing bubbles under a tree when you were six [6, 8, 10, 12].

Now, purse your lips like when you're gently blowing a bubble to find out how big it can get before popping. Inhale by choice through your pursed lips until your lungs are as full as they can be. Then exhale slowly through your pursed lips until they're completely empty, like you're gently blowing that bubble so it doesn't pop. Then inhale the same way again, and when your lungs feel as full as they can be, try sighing like an exasperated toddler. That's called *emotional regulation*.

5. Laugh until you snort

Laughter strengthens immunity, reduces stress hormones, increases pain tolerance, and improves social bonding.

Laughing with others is especially potent. It tells your body: "I am safe. I belong. It's okay to be ridiculous."

And sometimes, snorting is just how the soul says *thank you*.

6. Connect like it's show-and-tell

Strong social relationships reduce mortality risk by up to 50% [221]. Regular (at least weekly) sexual activity that results in climax reduces all-cause mortality even more [222-224].

Every time you vulnerably share your weird dream or your third failed sourdough attempt, you are keeping yourself alive. Show-and-tell never stopped being medicine.

So, call your friend. Make the awkward invite. Hold hands in the park. Compliment a stranger's shoes. Curate for connection and intimacy as often as you can.

7. Believe in yourself AND something bigger

Now that you're getting an understanding of what you are capable of as a human being, there is no reason not to believe in yourself. You can manifest anything. Look at all that we have accomplished as a species thus far!

Notably, people who believe in something larger than themselves live longer and recover faster from many illnesses [225].

Whether you find God in the forest, in your neighbor's eyes, or in a perfectly symmetrical avocado, believing in something beyond yourself changes how your nervous system responds to life and death.

CHAPTER 16
All You Need Is Love

Love is the bridge between you and everything.
Rumi

Love.

It's the thing we crave the most and deny the hardest. It makes you cry at Pixar movies and text your ex when Mercury is in retrograde. It's also the only force in the universe that has the audacity to heal trauma, regulate your nervous system, and make you willingly share your fries.

Here's the best part that isn't taught very well: *you are love.*

I know, I know. That sounds like something written on a tea bag or in your aunt's Instagram bio, but I mean it scientifically, emotionally, and spiritually.

Let me explain.

WHY HUGS ARE BETTER THAN DRUGS

Love is not just an emotion. It's a full-body, biochemical symphony.

When you're in love, be that with a person, a dog, a tree, a song, or a perfect bite of something delicious, your brain lights up like a toddler seeing bubbles [226, 227].

You release:

- Dopamine (the "oooh, this is nice" chemical)
- Oxytocin (the "I feel safe and melty" hormone)
- Endorphins (the "heck yeah, let's cuddle forever" molecule)

- Serotonin (the meaning-making molecule)
- Vasopressin (the "we're building a cabin together" commitment molecule)
- Norepinephrine (the "butterflies in belly" molecule)

These are nature's originals. They regulate stress, reduce inflammation, increase trust, improve immune function, and even lower pain perception [228, 229].

We're not wired to *think* our way into healing. We're wired to *love* our way there.

Love exists in a positive feedback loop that is quite wonderful. Loving someone makes both people feel more love, which makes you want to show more love.

LOVE IS EMBODIED SAFETY

Love doesn't just live in your heart; it lives in your nervous system. It's your biological "green light." It says, "*You can rest now. You're safe. You're not under attack. You are enough just as you are.*"

Love is *co-regulation* [111]. It's not just a warm fuzzy feeling; it's your entire physiology shifting into a state of safety, healing, and possibility.

WHAT ABOUT THE MESSY KIND OF LOVE?

Oh yeah. That one. You know...jealousy, heartbreak, misread texts, unmet expectations, sex that felt spiritual until they ghosted you.

It's all part of it. Love isn't supposed to be neat. It's supposed to shake you up like a snow globe and make you remember that you have a heart.

Love teaches you where you still protect instead of trust. Where you hold back instead of open up. Where you self-abandon instead of speak your truth.

And every time you choose love again, especially after heartbreak or disappointment, your nervous system gets stronger and more resilient. Your capacity for connection grows. That's *hormesis* improving your constitution. That's neuroplasticity in action!

CHILDREN KNOW HOW TO LOVE. ADULTS JUST GET WEIRD ABOUT IT.

Children love freely, sloppily, and loudly. They don't wait three days to say "I missed you." They don't worry about seeming "too much." They don't read books called *Attached* to figure out why they want to hug their friends all the time.

They just love.

But somewhere along the way, we learned that love was conditional. That we had to *earn* it. That it could be *taken away*. That to love was to risk rejection, abandonment, or being labeled "too sensitive."

Social and emotional pain registers in the same parts of the brain as physical pain [230]. That's why heartbreak and rejection physically hurt. It's not in your imagination. It's your mind-body connection in action.

So we armored up. We learned to swipe, ghost, breadcrumb, orbit, and trauma bond. We confused love with validation, affection with approval, and safety with control.

Here's the truth:

Love isn't something you get. It's something you return to.

It's always been there. Under the armor, the shame, the spreadsheets, the adulting, and the loneliness.

Love is your default state. Everything else is a side effect of forgetting.

LOVE THE UNKNOWN

One of my favorite questions to ask patients when we start working together in order to expose an insidious lie we all tell ourselves is this:

"Is it possible that the way you were taught to see yourself and the world, and what you are capable of, isn't the full story?"

Everyone, when given enough time to ponder, responds, "Well, yes, it's certainly possible."

Once we accept the truth that there may be more to who we are than meets the eye, the door to non-judgmental self-discovery opens, and the "unknown" becomes much less scary. Remembering that *the meaning of life is to discover ourselves* is all we require to walk through this door and experience the tremendous joy of personal growth that is possible on the other side.

When we know that what we are discovering are bits and pieces of ourselves that yearn to be one with the whole, we can bravely enter without fear. To reassure you, scientifically speaking, it is literally impossible for the act of getting to know ourselves better to kill us or physically harm us permanently in any way.

It's actually quite the opposite. When the vulnerable parts of us are welcomed back in and feel safe enough to come out and play, they can be reintegrated back into the whole using the practices described here.

The result is the unlocking of potentially unlimited human potential. We really don't know what we're capable of yet as human beings, and that's an unknown I couldn't be more grateful to have the opportunity to discover.

HOW TO REMEMBER THAT YOU ARE LOVE

Here's your inner child's prescription for love (refills: infinite):

1. Touch More

Not creepily. Consensually, respectfully, and safely, but *more*. Hug like you mean it. High-five your barista. Hold each other's hands. Cuddle your pet like they just saved your life (because they do sometimes).

Touch evolved over hundreds of millions of years to be the single fastest way to regulate the nervous system and restore a sense of safety in the body. It releases oxytocin and serotonin to communicate that, "We're here. Together. This moment matters."

2. Say the Thing

Express gratitude to yourself and others. Say "Thank you." Tell people you love them. Tell them when you miss them. Tell them when they changed your life with that one weird compliment in 2007.

Most importantly, thank yourself for making it all this way. It wasn't easy. Don't wait for the perfect moment. It's already here.

3. Let People Love You

Stop pretending you're fine. Stop pushing help away. Let your friends carry your groceries. Let someone rub your back. Let the universe hold you.

Receiving love *is* an act of love.

4. Practice Loving Yourself Like You'd Love a Kid Who Looks Like You

Would you yell at a cute three-year-old for crying?

No?

Then stop doing it to yourself. Self-love isn't indulgence. It's repair. It's reconnection. It's radical re-parenting. It's telling your nervous system: *We're safe now. I've got you. You matter.*

5. Move Toward Love, Not Away From Fear

Every decision in life is made from one of two places: love or fear.

Love asks, "What's possible?"

Fear asks, "What could go wrong?"

Try choosing love more often, even if it makes you cry, look foolish, or dance offbeat. Actually, *especially* if it does. The power of this choice is yours and yours alone.

AMO, ERGO SUM—I LOVE, THEREFORE I AM

For centuries, Western thought has been quietly organized around a single sentence: *Cogito, ergo sum,* "I think, therefore I am." This was coined by Descartes, the same guy who aptly proposed that the pineal gland, which contains DMT, is the "seat of the soul" and who incorrectly concluded that the mind and body are separate.

In the seventeenth century, the Cogito emerged from a moment of radical doubt. If everything could be questioned (God, senses, body), one thing seemed undeniable: the existence of thought itself. It was a brilliant move for its time, anchoring identity in cognition and launching modern philosophy and science.

However, four centuries of neuroscience, psychology, and biology have shown us something that Descartes could not yet see: thinking is not primary. Thinking is downstream. Before we think, we feel. Before we reason, we attach. Before we form ideas about the world, we orient toward it through relationships.

Which brings us to a necessary and long-overdue twenty-first-century update to Descartes:

Amo, ergo sum: I love, therefore I am.

Love is not a poetic add-on to existence; it is an essential regulatory state. Attachment, connection, and care shape brain development, nervous system safety, immune function, lifespan, and even our thoughts. Human beings deprived of love and full of thoughts don't just suffer emotionally; they struggle to exist.

We don't come into being through thought alone.

We come into being through relationships.

Love isn't the opposite of reason.

It's the fertile soil in which reason grows.

Affirmation: *Amo, ergo sum - I love, therefore I am*

CHAPTER 17
Cause I Gotta' Have Faith

Faith is taking the first step even when you don't see the whole staircase.
Dr. Martin Luther King Jr. (1929–1968)

For as long as humans have gathered around fires and looked up at the stars, we've prayed, wondered, surrendered, and believed. Now, for the first time in history, neuroscience is beginning to map what these spiritual experiences do inside the brain, and the results are stunning.

Faith and spirituality are not mere psychological comforts or cultural relics. They are very real. They are biologically encoded tools for survival, healing, and transcendence. Case in point, people who believe in something greater than themselves live longer [225]. The structures of the human brain suggest that we were not only built to survive, but to relate to ourselves, to others, and to something greater than ourselves. When any part of that relationship is in jeopardy, dissonance results.

Let's begin with belief, as it has the most scientific evidence to support it. Modern research into the placebo and nocebo effects reveals something quietly revolutionary: belief itself is a biological force.

The *placebo effect* occurs when a positive expectation (belief that an intervention will succeed) produces real physiological improvement, even when the treatment itself is a sugar pill. The *nocebo effect* is its darker twin: negative expectation (believing an intervention won't succeed) can worsen symptoms or cause harm. This is why red pills always work better than blue pills, even if they're both made entirely of sugar [231, 232].

Taken together, they demonstrate that what we believe does not merely change how we interpret reality. It changes how the body functions, down to how likely we are to respond to a medication or a treatment. In many cases, belief has an impact on our physiology that is equal to or greater than that of pharmacology.

In clinical trials, placebo responses have been shown to alter pain perception, immune response, motor function, mood, and even measurable neurochemical activity [233]. Neuroimaging studies reveal that placebo analgesia activates endogenous opioid and dopamine pathways, the same systems targeted by pharmacologic painkillers. Belief, expectation, and meaning literally trigger the brain's internal pharmacy.

Just as striking, nocebo effects can induce nausea, fatigue, pain, anxiety, and worsened outcomes purely through expectation [234]. When patients are told to expect side effects, those effects appear at dramatically higher rates, even when no active drug is present. The nervous system, primed for threat, obliges.

This matters deeply for faith and prayer, and it provides scientific evidence for why it is so important to believe in yourself.

Prayer, intention, and belief are not magical overrides of biology; they are inputs into the nervous system's predictive machinery. The brain is constantly forecasting what will happen next. When belief signals safety, hope, or meaning, the autonomic nervous system shifts toward parasympathetic regulation [235]. Inflammation decreases, pain thresholds rise, emotional flexibility improves, and healing becomes more possible.

Crucially, placebo effects are strongest when belief is embodied, relational, and ritualized [236]. Trust in the caregiver, meaningful symbols, and repeated practices all contribute. Sound familiar? These are the same elements found in prayer, religious practices, and spiritual community across cultures and millennia. What science now confirms is that these practices work not because they bypass biology, but because they engage it exquisitely.

Belief does not mean denial of reality. Faith is not pretending everything is fine. It is choosing a relationship to uncertainty that does not collapse into fear. The placebo effect does not cure everything, and belief alone does not replace medicine. Belief powerfully shapes *how* the body responds to what we put into it, as well as its response to illness, stress, and suffering.

The lesson is humbling and hopeful: what we believe matters. What we tell ourselves matters. What we repeatedly rehearse in thought, prayer, or imagination becomes part of our energy and physiology.

HO'OPONOPONO

Ho'oponopono, an ancient Hawaiian prayer of reconciliation and forgiveness, is often distilled into four parts:

I'm sorry. Please forgive me. Thank you. I love you.

At first glance, it feels almost disarmingly simple, but beneath that simplicity lies a profound technology of consciousness. By repeating these phrases, whether directed toward others, yourself, or the unseen, you begin to clear the emotional and cognitive noise that obscures your connection to something deeper. This occurs through a four-step process similar to what we use in psychotherapy:

Before you begin, pause and recognize that an imbalance exists. Something feels off within you, between you and others, or between you and the natural world.

1. Next, take responsibility. Without blame or shame, acknowledge that harm can come from ignorance, distraction, or survival-driven behavior. Saying *I'm sorry* is not self-punishment; it is self-awareness.
2. Then, ask for forgiveness from nature, from others, from yourself. *Please forgive me.* This step opens the door to repair, even when you don't fully understand the impact.
3. Follow with gratitude. *Thank you.* Gratitude reinforces your connection to the systems that sustain you, reminding you that you are supported even as you learn.

4. Finally, return to love. *I love you.* This is the reorientation back to respect, care, and reciprocity with life itself.

Repeated sincerely, this becomes automated as a practice of living in harmony with the world around us.

THE HIERARCHY OF FAITH

Faith doesn't arrive fully formed. It grows. Slowly. Quietly. Often invisibly, like a seed underground doing something important while everyone above ground is busy arguing about whether seeds even work.

What we call *faith* is not a switch you flip. It's a process of accumulation, shaped by time, attention, repetition, and nervous system experience. And when you zoom out, you can see a very clear hierarchy. A ladder of knowing that moves from whisper to certainty, from curiosity to embodiment. This isn't philosophy for philosophers. This is how human brains learn what's real.

An inkling is the smallest unit of meaning. It's a hunch from our intuition. A gut feeling. A fleeting sense that something *might* be true. Neurologically, inklings are weak signals. Subthreshold activations that don't yet have enough evidence to demand action. Most inklings die young. They're ignored, dismissed, or drowned out by noise.

From a spiritual perspective, inklings may be much more important than we think.

DR. DAVE'S ESSENTIAL EQUATION #15:

Inkling × Time = Idea

When an inkling is given time, when attention lingers instead of fleeing, it becomes an idea. An idea has structure, language, and shape. The brain can now represent it, simulate it, and turn it over. This is where curiosity thrives. Ideas don't require commitment yet. They just ask, "What if?"

Stay with an idea long enough, and something changes.

DR. DAVE'S ESSENTIAL EQUATION #16:

Idea × Time = Hope

An idea, held over time and tested against experience, becomes hope. Hope is emotional. It's the nervous system beginning to lean forward instead of bracing back. Hope doesn't guarantee outcomes, it opens possibilities. This is why hope is so powerful in healing: it shifts physiology. Stress hormones decrease. Motivation increases. The future becomes less threatening.

Hope is still fragile, however. It wavers.

Given enough time, repetition, and lived reinforcement, hope becomes belief.

DR. DAVE'S ESSENTIAL EQUATION #17:

Hope × Time = Belief

Belief is no longer just emotional; it's predictive. The brain starts acting as if the thing is true. Behavior shifts. Choices align. Belief shapes perception, filtering what we notice and how we interpret events. This is why beliefs are so powerful, and so dangerous when they're wrong.

And finally, after belief survives contact with reality, after it's tested, challenged, failed, adapted, and reaffirmed, it crystallizes into knowing.

DR. DAVE'S ESSENTIAL EQUATION #18:

Belief × Time = Knowing

Knowing is embodied, quiet, and unshakable. It doesn't argue. It no longer needs proof because the nervous system has already imprinted it. Knowing lives in posture, tone of voice, timing, and trust. It's why someone who knows doesn't try to convince you. They simply live it.

This hierarchy matters because so much suffering comes from trying to skip steps on this journey. We demand belief without time and wonder why we still harbor disbelief. We demand certainty without experience, and we wonder why we keep feeling uncertain. The brain doesn't work that way, and neither does faith.

In this sense, faith is not blind. It is participatory. It is the nervous system saying, *"I am ready to heal. I am ready to take the wheel."* Faith is earned over time, with intentional attention, and by deepening our relationship with reality.

And when faith stems from knowing, it stops being an idea you hold.

It becomes something that holds you.

Psychologically, "faith" can be defined as the brain's capacity to hold uncertainty while maintaining a sense of coherence, safety, and purpose. It involves systems across the prefrontal cortex (abstract thinking and planning), the anterior cingulate cortex (emotional action and conflict resolution), the insula (interoception, introspection, and empathy), and the Default Mode Network (sense of self-identity) [236, 237]. When we activate these regions in concert, the result isn't blind belief. It's the neurobiology of inner alignment.

Now, let's time-travel back several thousand years for a moment.

There's a lesson we often miss in the Old Testament's creation story from the Judeo-Christian-Islamic tradition. One that speaks directly to the neuroscience of faith.

In the first book of Genesis, which literally means *creation,* we are told that God placed Adam and Eve in the Garden of Eden, a paradise of harmony, abundance, and divine connection, with but one rule: *do not eat from the Tree of Knowledge of Good and Evil.*

God didn't explain why in scientific terms. There were no slide decks or instructional videos. Just trust. Just faith in the invisible.

Then the serpent, a physical, visible creature, offered temptation: eat this fruit of the Tree of Knowledge, and your eyes will be opened.

We often frame this as "original sin", but perhaps that's not the main point we're supposed to be gleaning from this story. Could Eve have been framed? It doesn't take a psychiatrist to know that men are more impulsive and worse at following rules than women. Need I say more?

The deeper story appears to be one of original disconnection and deception.

In that moment of temptation by the serpent, we lost something far more profound than innocence. We lost faith. And we lost it because God, unseeable and unfathomable, required unquestioning inner trust. The serpent, on the other hand, was right there, physical and persuasive. So, in this single moment of grave error that we have now been talking about for over 5,000 years, we chose knowledge over faith. We abandoned divine knowing in favor of empirical knowing.

To top it off, with our newfound knowledge of shame, we tried to hide from God, denying what we had done. In doing so, we deceived ourselves and God. I like to refer to this as the "OT" or *original trauma*, the first internal fracture of self-trust that we as a species have not yet repaired.

And what did we gain? Data, information, responsibilities, and self-consciousness. The awareness of good and evil. The burden of discernment. The painful polarity of "right" and "wrong."

For the next several thousand years, we searched for meaning in the wilderness.

Perhaps God kicked us out to punish us, as it is often interpreted. Or perhaps *we walked out and lost the keys to the garden gate*, so intoxicated and distracted with unfiltered knowledge without context that we forgot where the keys were and how to feel for them. Like that time your buddy Bobby got so drunk at a music festival that he thought he lost his car keys for twenty-four hours, only to find them the next day in his pocket where he left them.

Despite our deceptive actions, the good book says that God left angels guarding the gate to the garden with a flaming sword so that we would not eat the fruit of the *Tree of Life* and gain immortality while we were in a "fallen" traumatized state of shame and deception. This is further evidence that God is compassionate, for if God did not care about our well-being, he or she would have absolutely let us eat the fruit from the Tree of Life, destined to live an immortal life of guilt, shame, and fear. That sounds a whole lot more like punishment to me.

The idea of God as compassionate, described on more than one occasion in the Old Testament, is extremely important because it allows us to fathom a path to redemption. A path back home to our garden paradise. If God is guarding the Tree of Life from us so that we cannot gain immortality while fallen, what happens if we rise to the occasion and heal ourselves?

If God is compassionate, he or she would afford us the opportunity to redeem ourselves, perhaps even to gain immortality as healed ascended human beings. Would the angel guards set down their flaming swords and let us back into the garden? Mystics in the Judeo-Christian-Islamic tradition say yes. Buddhism and most other religions I have studied, including ancient tribal cultures, all have a concept of redemption.

And despite our knowledge of this, over the last several thousand years, we built civilizations around what we could see: reason, law, proof, and empirical understanding. We fought constantly over things we believed in, but couldn't see. We developed science as a way of restoring order, explaining the world, and, perhaps unconsciously, trying to prove that God still exists to avoid mustering the courage that faith requires.

And now, astonishingly, we've done it!

We are the first generation in recorded history with scientific tools powerful enough to measure the physiological effects of belief, prayer, gratitude, and love. We can image the brain in near real time. We can trace the flow of consciousness and track the coherence between heart and mind. We now know that belief changes brain states, that prayer modulates immune function, that spirituality improves health outcomes, that DMT from our own brains facilitates access to reliable states of profound divine insight, and that presence itself is therapeutic.

In other words, we are using the very same knowledge we once traded for our innocence to return to a truth we once knew without needing to understand.

This is the great paradox: faith does not require knowledge. Faith lives in the body, in the felt sense of being held, guided, and loved. It is a deeper knowing, not based on empirical data, but on feeling, resonance, surrender, and awe.

The serpent promised knowledge, and what we got was complexity. Because too much knowledge without time or context to understand it is not wisdom, it's completely overwhelming. Wisdom requires time.

Now, standing here on the edge of a new epoch, we are starting to rediscover the garden not by abandoning science, but by evolving it. Science and spirit are no longer at odds. They are merging. And Indigenous and Eastern traditions knew it all along. Without the aid of technology.

We are finally learning that the keys to paradise were never lost. They were buried beneath fear, intellect, ego, and pride, and a whole lot of shame, but they have always been within us.

They are in our breath.

They are in our attention.

They are in every moment.

The neuroscience of faith doesn't deny God or spirituality. It reveals that intuition is real and that the architecture of the human brain is designed to perceive, connect with, and co-create the Divine in each of us as soon as we're ready to listen.

The sacred is not supernatural. It is the most natural thing in the world.

Now, after thousands of years of wandering, we are finally remembering how to feel it again.

With our bodies. With our breath.

With our science and with our souls.

CHAPTER 18
An Ancient User Manual for Society

Thou shalt keep thy religion to thyself.
George Carlin (1937–2008)

Most of us can't honestly say that we had zero instructions about how to live life because nearly everyone in the Western world has been exposed to the Bible and The Ten Commandments. Often with questionable levels of interpretation, of course.

At first glance, The Ten Commandments, another winner from the Old Testament, look like annoying rules.

At second glance, they look like religion.

At third glance, when you squint like a psychiatrist who has spent a career watching humans hurt themselves in remarkably predictable ways, they look like something else entirely: a compact operating system for social mammals with big brains, sensitive nervous systems, and a tendency to forget what keeps us alive.

Thousands of years before Christ, functional MRI machines, randomized controlled trials, and peer review, ancient cultures were running the same experiment we're still running today: What rules allow humans to live together without destroying one another, or themselves?

The Ten Commandments are not arbitrary moral edicts handed down to ruin anyone's fun. They are divine pattern recognition, distilled over generations, describing the behaviors that reliably destabilize individuals, families, and societies.

In modern language, the Commandments are about safety, internal safety, relational safety, and collective safety. They describe what happens when attention becomes fragmented, desire becomes uncontained, and power becomes unmoored from responsibility. Neuroscience now helps us see why these ancient insights work so well: each commandment maps cleanly onto known mechanisms of stress, reward, attachment, impulse control, and trust.

Think of them less as "thou shalt nots" and more as guardrails for consciousness. Or, if you prefer: a cheat code for playing the human game without rage-quitting halfway through.

WHY RULES APPEAR WHEN BRAINS GET BIG

As the human prefrontal cortex expanded, so did our capacity for imagination, planning, deception, and rationalization. That's a blessing and a liability. Bigger brains mean more ways to get what we want, and more ways to justify doing it at someone else's expense.

Anthropology and evolutionary psychology suggest that moral codes emerge precisely at this inflection point: when social groups grow large enough that trust must extend beyond immediate kin [238]. Rules stabilize cooperation. Cooperation reduces threat. Reduced threat allows creativity, culture, and meaning to flourish.

The Ten Commandments function as low-bandwidth, high-impact automations that protect against predictable failure modes of human behavior. Each one addresses a specific way we tend to destabilize ourselves when stress, fear, or unchecked desire takes the wheel.

Let's look at them not as religious artifacts, but as neuropsychological insights hiding in plain sight.

1. **"I am the LORD thy God, who brought thee out of the land of Egypt, out of the house of bondage."**

(Translation: God taking a moment for a formal reintroduction to humans with a reminder of the recent support that was provided.)

From a spiritual perspective, this commandment is about acceptance and faith. A compassionate reminder of God's presence and role in our lives.

From a psychological perspective, this commandment is about attention and attachment. Humans are meaning-making machines. We will worship *something*. If it's not a true, coherent set of values grounded in reality, it will be deceptive like money, status, power, beauty, productivity, or fear. Psychological flexibility, maintaining our steady grounding in truth while not getting too attached to our thoughts, is a key predictor of mental health [239].

2. **"You shall have no strange gods before Me. Thou shalt not make unto thee any graven image…"**

(Translation: Don't outsource your nervous system to idols.)

If we were taught that time is money, our brains crave efficiency and shortcuts. Symbols save energy, but mistaking the symbol for the thing itself is how meaning collapses into rigidity. Neuroscience shows that whatever consistently captures attention becomes reinforced through dopaminergic learning [240]. When external symbols become so ubiquitous that they replace internal values, behavior becomes compulsive, anxiety rises, and identity fragments.

Cognitively, this commandment protects against reification, treating abstractions as concrete truths. When symbols harden, curiosity dies. When curiosity dies, learning stops. When learning stops, we become stagnant.

This commandment is anti-addiction. It warns that when anything external becomes the primary regulator of safety and worth, the nervous system becomes brittle. Maps are useful, but confusing them with territory leads to suffering.

The source of healing always comes from within us, from our personal connection to the Divine, which becomes apparent through listening to our intuition. Everything outside of us is a tool. When we become dependent on our tools for healing, health breaks down.

3. "Thou shalt not take the name of the LORD thy God in vain."

(Translation: Words shape nervous systems. Use them carefully.)

Language is not neutral. Words carry emotional charge. Repeated careless or deceptive language erodes trust, boosts uncertainty, increases threat perception, and strengthens the illusion of separation.

When we speak ill of God, we speak ill of ourselves. Doing so reinforces a loop in our brains that falsely assumes that God is vengeful because our lives are challenging at times. If we assume that bad things happen to us because God is vengeful rather than compassionate, then we abdicate responsibility for our choices that may not be serving us, completely missing the growth opportunity being offered to us.

Studies in psycholinguistics show that language directly influences emotional regulation and interpersonal safety [241]. This commandment isn't about profanity; it's about the integrity of meaning. When words lose weight, relationships destabilize. Say what you mean. Mean what you say. Your nervous system, and everyone else's, will thank you.

4. "Remember the Sabbath day, to keep it holy."

(Translation: Rest is not optional.)

Chronic stress is toxic. Breaks are healing for the mind, body, and spirit. The Sabbath is a built-in intervention against burnout.

Modern medicine confirms what this commandment intuited: recovery is required for health. Sleep, rest, and rhythmic pauses restore prefrontal function, emotional regulation, and immune resilience [242].

A culture without rest becomes impulsive, short-sighted, cruel, and exhausted. This commandment is preventive medicine.

Even God rested on the seventh day.

5. "Honor thy father and thy mother."

(Translation: Respect the lineage that shaped you.)

Attachment research shows that early caregiving relationships shape stress responses for life [243]. Honoring parents does not mean excusing harm. It means acknowledging their influence on us and that we are part of them. Without our parents, we wouldn't have the gift of this life.

Psychological healing often begins when people recognize where their patterns came from, without becoming trapped in blame-and-shame spirals. This commandment promotes contextual understanding, reducing reactivity and increasing compassion.

6. "Thou shalt not kill."

(Translation: Violence destroys the system.)

Violence creates trauma. Trauma propagates trauma. Neuroscience shows that exposure to violence dysregulates stress systems and increases future aggression [41, 244].

This commandment is the clearest safety rule of all: killing destabilizes everything. Individual nervous systems, families, societies. It is the ultimate threat amplifier.

7. "Thou shalt not commit adultery."

(Translation: Betrayal breaks nervous systems.)

It's much faster to knock something down than to reconstruct it. Trust takes time and energy to build, but is devastatingly easy to destroy. Infidelity triggers attachment and abandonment trauma, activating threat circuitry similar to physical pain [245].

This commandment protects relational stability, the foundation of social safety. It's not about control. It's about predictability and trust, which allow nervous systems to relax.

8. "Thou shalt not steal."

(Translation: Scarcity thinking poisons communities.)

Stealing also erodes trust, heightening vigilance and reducing cooperation. Economic psychology shows that perceived unfairness heightens stress and reduces prosocial behavior [246].

This commandment protects collective trust. When people believe the system is safe, they participate. When they don't, everything degrades.

9. "Thou shalt not bear false witness against thy neighbor."

(Translation: Reality matters.)

Lying fractures shared reality. Chronic deception increases uncertainty, boosting cognitive load and stress while eroding social bonds [247].

Shared truth is the glue that holds groups together. Without it, paranoia replaces cooperation. This commandment is a prevention against collapse.

10. "Thou shalt not covet thy neighbor."

(Translation: Comparison is the thief of joy and safety.)

Coveting is not desire; it's a comparative obsession. Social comparison activates reward and threat circuits simultaneously, fueling dissatisfaction, jealousy, anxiety, and aggression [248].

This commandment targets the root of much of our suffering: the belief that someone else having something means you are unsafe. It's a cognitive error, and a painful one.

WHY THIS STILL WORKS

Taken together, The Ten Commandments reduce threat, stabilize trust, and preserve safe spaces in which meaning can be made. They are not about obedience. They are about alignment between biology, psychology, and community.

You don't have to believe they came from God to recognize that they are astonishingly well-tuned to human nervous systems. They describe what happens when desire outruns awareness and how to bring it back into balance.

These are not ancient rules for ancient people. They are a field guide for modern nervous systems trying to survive complexity without losing their humanity.

Seen this way, these Commandments are not constraints. They are freedom, encoded.

Follow them not out of fear, but out of understanding.

CHAPTER 19
Finding Your Way Home

We're all just walking each other home.
Ram Dass (1931–2019)

Congratulations! You've made it to the final level of this game called *Remembering How to Be Alive.*

This chapter is your treasure map. Your emergency rescue kit. Your laminated cheat sheet for when life feels like a chaotic episode of *Survivor: Late Capitalism*, and you're just trying to keep your inner child from melting down in the produce aisle.

So here it is: the easiest, simplest, most neurologically sound system for coming back home to yourself, your body, your breath, and your joy anytime, anywhere.

No incense required. Pajamas encouraged.

Let's start with a quick recap of Dr. Dave's Essential Equations™. Each of these equations represents a part of us that can be trained and fully automated with practice over time.

The only equation that differs from the others is Equation #8: the Distress Equation. I included this here because, while it is not a constructive skill that we would choose to train consciously, many of us were taught to practice distress and excel at it without realizing it [249]. It is very important to keep this equation in mind because transforming distress into eustress is the ticket to success.

Every time hardship comes, and we ask ourselves the right questions like "How can I grow from this challenge?", we're rewiring our brains to see stressful situations as growth opportunities automatically. The trick is to remember to do it whenever possible.

THE HIERARCHY OF WISDOM

1. *Attention x Time = Concentration*
2. *Listening x Time = Data*
3. *Data x Time = Information*
4. *Information x Time = Knowledge*
5. *Knowledge x Time = Wisdom*

THE HIERARCHY OF GRACE

6. *Play x Time = Joy*
7. *Eustress x Time = Ease*
8. *Distress x Time = Disease*
9. *Intention x Time = Manifestation*
10. *Practice x Time = Mastery*
11. *Curiosity x Time = Discovery*
12. *Gratitude x Time = Grace*
13. *Bravery x Time = Courage*
14. *Truth x Time = Righteousness*

THE HIERARCHY OF FAITH

15. *Inkling x Time = Idea*
16. *Idea x Time = Hope*
17. *Hope x Time = Belief*
18. *Belief x Time = Knowing*

As you probably noticed, "Time" appears in each of these equations because our time is the most important, most valuable asset we have as human beings. Technically speaking, this moment is the only time that we have with certainty. Every other future moment is uncertain. And because we have such limited time in this incredible life on Earth, if something is going to take some of that precious time, it better be worth it.

A skill improves with every repetition (rep) over time, like lifting weights in the gym. The more reps we do, the more entrained and automatic the skill becomes, and the tighter our neural networks grow together as the biological representation of that learning.

Let's slow things down for a moment.

From a linear perspective, there are only so many seconds in which we are awake to practice skills during a given day, so there's a finite amount of training and reps that can be accomplished.

However, when we take Einstein's theory of relativity into account, we know that our sense of time is also dependent on our perspective (position, motion, and gravity). As our speed changes (including movement of thoughts), our perspective of how quickly time passes changes proportionately.

The greater the percentage of our attention that is in the present moment (not in the past or the future), the more of us is here now, and the more of us is interacting with, and taking in, what's happening right now. Time appears to slow down and expand because we are taking in much more information from the present moment in less time. As such, the more present we are with something we are trying to learn, the faster we learn that thing because we can do more reps in a shorter amount of time.

If the past is already gone and the future hasn't happened yet, then everything exists only in the present. In this way, the present moment is filled with infinite possibilities for change, growth, and healing. These possibilities become realities simply by recognizing their existence and *choosing* to give them your attention.

Time dilation: When we slow down, like when breathing long, slow, deep breaths, our sense of time dilates (time appears to move more slowly). Commonly experienced in meditation, dreams, intimacy, and psychedelic states.

Time contraction: When we move quickly with jam-packed days and fast breathing, our sense of time contracts (time appears to move faster). Commonly experienced when rushing, doom scrolling, binge watching, attempting escape, and going through the motions.

Despite what chaos may be surrounding us at any given moment, noticing our breath is always our way back to controlling our perception of time.

This also shines a bright, beaming stadium spotlight on *patience*, the ability to wait peacefully, as an essential skill (because all of our other skills require effort to train). Patience is wonderfully elegant because it appears so tough much of the time, but we get better at it by literally doing nothing. Just calmly waiting for things to happen is all that is needed. Impulsively doing things (including thinking, scratching, shopping, scrolling, etc.) makes us more impatient and, therefore, impulsive. Rushing is the source of most of our mistakes.

Then the next question everyone asks me is, "Doc, I'm already so busy! How the heck do I get more time without setting aside a bunch of time to learn to do it?"

We take back our time moment by moment.

Right here.

Right now.

We must choose to take control of our attention and focus. The more we prioritize the practice of focusing our attention, the easier it becomes to focus on demand, and the more automatically the brain filters out distraction.

One of the best ways to take our time back is to learn to focus our attention on observing our thoughts, like clouds passing by, without engaging with them. We can practice this anytime, anywhere, while doing almost anything. Always remember that you are not your thoughts, but the observer of them. Your thoughts are like clouds passing overhead on a beautiful sunny day.

THE THOUGHT QUESTIONING TECHNIQUE

Here's a really easy way to start that yields both immediate and long-term gains quickly:

For a thought to be worthy of your time right in this moment, it must be both true and useful to you right now. This is one of the most powerful "secret weapons" of Cognitive Behavioral Therapy (CBT): thought questioning.

The practice of thought questioning presumes that not all thoughts are created equal. For example, not all thoughts we have are valuable to us in any given moment just because they decide to snag our attention. If we can agree that our time is our most valuable asset, then *any thought that is not both true and useful right now is not worthy of our time in this moment.* This means that we can observe the thought without engaging with it and come back to it later to reevaluate if it passes the test at a different time. Once we have reclaimed our attention from untrue and useless thoughts, we can: (1) Celebrate! and (2) Redirect our attention to something that is useful and true, such as taking a breath or expressing gratitude toward ourselves for taking back our time and attention.

The practice goes like this:

A negative intrusive thought, such as "I am a sad and/or unlovable person." Or "I have a bad memory" enters our awareness…

1. **Acknowledge** the thought:
    a. Such as saying in your head or out loud, "I see you, thought!"

2. **Question** the thought:
    a. As in, "Perhaps I can convince myself that this is true and that I do actually have a bad memory, but it is certainly not useful to think about right now because taking time to think about how bad my memory is decreases the amount of time I spend experiencing and learning what I'm trying to remember in the first place."

3. **Allow** the thought that fails the test to pass by and, eventually, vanish without engaging, analyzing, or judging it or yourself:
    a. If this thought is not useful to me right now, it is not worthy of my time right now, and I can come back to it later and reevaluate (put it through the test again). Do NOT engage with the

thought. Just watch. Be the observer of the thought, which is what we human beings are.

PRO TIP

When starting to integrate this practice, hold yourself accountable by blocking off 20–30 minutes each week for self-reflection. Review the wins and the losses of the week. What failed the thought questioning test this week can be reevaluated and retested as many times as we like during this time.

4. **Celebrate!**
    a. Express gratitude to yourself by thanking yourself for reclaiming your attention! Now you can focus on anything you like. I recommend starting with attending to your breath, anything else for which you can be grateful, or the original task at hand. You can also direct your attention to rewriting your story by saying something like this to yourself, "I have a good memory, and it will get even better with practice."
    b. I also nicknamed this the "gratitude interception" because just as darkness cannot exist in the light, fear cannot exist in gratitude. Gratitude can intercept our attention from untrue and useless thoughts, restoring it to our control at any moment, and can shine a bright light on our darkest moments. Practicing this technique strengthens both your gratitude and attention muscles (just like doing ab exercises in the gym strengthens your core).

Over time, your thoughts will generally fall into two camps:

1. **Useful and True**
    a. The thoughts that are generally constructive. Stick with these.
    b. Typically, under 15% of our thoughts, on average.

2. **Repeatedly Not Useful and/or Untrue**
    a. These thoughts are vampires. They can only enter our consciousness when we send them an invitation from our attention, and,

once allowed in, they suck us dry of all our energy if we don't let them go.

b. Typically, over 85% of our thoughts, on average.

You will also start to notice that certain thoughts are never useful and true to us. When we realize that a thought we've been having, quite possibly for decades, is never passing the test, it is likely a thought that was useful to us in the past, but is no longer serving us.

In this moment, we have recognized an opportunity to retire a thought from our awareness. I recommend using a visualization technique. There are many. My top favorite is *The Black Hole.* Another favorite is *The Garbage Disposal.* Once we have determined with repeated measures, beyond a reasonable doubt, that one of our thoughts is failing the test on a continuous basis, and that this thought is no longer true and useful to us at any time, we can retire it by visualizing the vampire thought being sucked into a black hole or being shredded up by a garbage disposal, in either case, never to be seen again.

THE BLACK HOLE TECHNIQUE

1. Close your eyes
2. Acknowledge the useless thought
3. Imagine a black hole
4. Watch the thought being sucked away into the black hole, imploding, and vanishing forever.

THE GARBAGE DISPOSAL TECHNIQUE

1. Close your eyes
2. Acknowledge the useless thought
3. Imagine turning on a garbage disposal
4. Watch the thought being sucked into the garbage disposal hole, getting ground up into little unrecognizable bits, and going down the drain, never to be seen again.

THE APOLLO TECHNOLOGY: A TOOL FOR REMEMBERING

Soothing touch is the original language of safety. Every single one of our bodies remembers the feeling of being in the womb and being rocked to sleep as an infant, even if we can't picture it. Cuddling and nursing babies is a behavior hardwired into our nervous systems, dating back to the first mammals that nursed their young over a hundred million years ago. Soothing touch activates the insula, triggering positive sensations that signal to the amygdala to dial down the fear response instantly.

Studying the neural pathways of soothing touch in the lab at the University of Pittsburgh taught me that we perceive it much as we do when one of our favorite songs comes on by surprise. Interestingly, both experiences activate the same regions in the emotional brain, conveying immediate safety, comfort, and in many cases, joy.

From this understanding, we developed Apollo Neuro—the first technology to effortlessly restore balance to the nervous system, boosting distress tolerance and resilience, by delivering low-frequency sound wave vibrations to the skin. Apollo's Vibes are soundtracks for your body: composed by translating the biological signatures of calm—breathing patterns drawn from decades of research into meditation, biofeedback, and soothing touch—into precise waveforms felt through the skin. Each Vibe is tuned to mirror the body's own natural signals of safety, so the nervous system recognizes them as a familiar cue from within. Vagus nerve activity improves, heart rate slows, HRV increases, and the body remembers that it is safe enough to just *be*.

Most recently, a clinical study conducted by Apollo Neuroscience and OURA Ring tracked over 900 people over 3 years and collected over 400,000 nights of data, making it one of the world's largest interventional sleep studies, enabled entirely by wearable technology [254]. This study demonstrated that wearing Apollo for at least 3 hours per night increases sleep by 46 minutes on average in as little as one night, while boosting REM sleep and preserving deep sleep architecture. On top of that, there was a 77% reduction in the odds of experiencing short sleep of under 6 hours. This amount of sleep improvement is comparable to the best prescription sleep drugs, without side effects, simply by improving safety and vagus nerve activity throughout the night with wearable technology.

This massive data set was used to train the SmartVibes AI that does the work for you, tuning Apollo specifically for your life. Now you can add one whole night of sleep back to your week simply by wearing Apollo to bed. More enthalpy without the effort. You're welcome!

What makes Apollo truly novel is that it doesn't just deliver vibrations on a fixed schedule—it listens. Apollo's SmartVibes AI, trained on hundreds of millions of data points from Oura Ring and Apple Health over five years, monitors your body in real time and responds dynamically—knowing when you're drifting toward wakefulness in the night and intervening with precisely timed Vibes to guide you back to deep, restorative sleep. If you have an Oura Ring, SmartVibes takes in your Oura data to customize Apollo vibration patterns that automatically improve your health biometrics without effort. In a world of technology engineered to pull you out of your body, SmartVibes works quietly within it keeping you present, grounded, and recovered at all times. Apollo vibrations train the body to access states of safety and presentness on its own.

In 2017, my wife Kathryn and I founded Apollo Neuroscience to bring this discovery to life—technology that works with the body rather than around it, accessible to everyone, that facilitates healing at scale. Seventeen clinical studies and over 2,000 research subjects later, the results are unambiguous: Apollo is the only technology proven to significantly reduce time to fall asleep, prevent middle-of-the-night wakeups, and boost HRV—effortlessly. In 2025 alone, our community gained nearly 144 million minutes of additional sleep. We had set out to give the world back 100 million minutes. The world needed more.

Technology can help us heal the world if we intend for it to do so. I have seen it with my own eyes.

FINDING YOUR WAY HOME IS AS EASY AS 6-5-4-3-2-1

The beauty of coming home to yourself is that, once you know what it feels like, coming back anytime is quite simple, and there is elegance in simplicity.

This is a map of territory I have charted so that you may always find your way home. As it turns out, there are many different paths you can take. Some of them are faster than others, but all roads lead to home.

6—THE SIX ELEMENTS OF CONTROL

These are the six things you *always* have access to that remind your body that you're in control. When life spins out, grab any one of these and hold on.

1. Breathe

Breathing by choice is your body's universal reset button. One conscious breath shifts your brain from threat mode to calm mode by turning up vagus nerve activity.

Try breathing slowly by choice. Just fill your lungs as much as you can, and then empty as much air as you can for a minute or two. Just notice the feeling of the air flowing in and out, and the feeling of your chest rising and falling with each breath. Every time you notice a thought, acknowledge it and return your attention to the feeling of your breath. When you start breathing, it's best not to count, so you can really focus on the feeling of the air.

PRO TIP

Pursing your lips when learning to breathe intentionally and breathing through your mouth (as if you're breathing through a straw or blowing a bubble) is the easiest way to start. No counting needed!

Once you're comfortable with this, you can practice 5-1-5-1 breathing and 4-7-8 breathing.

5-1-5-1 Breathing: inhale for 5 seconds, hold for 1, exhale for 5, hold for 1. Rinse and repeat for at least two minutes, filling your lungs slightly more and emptying them slightly more with each breath.

4-7-8 Breathing: inhale for 4 seconds, hold for 7 seconds, exhale for 8 seconds. Rinse and repeat for at least two minutes.

As you start to feel at ease with these techniques through pursed lips, try breathing through your nose as you do them to take the difficulty up a notch.

2. Touch

Safe, soothing touch instantly releases oxytocin (along with every other feel-good neurotransmitter you've ever taken a drug to get more of) and drops cortisol like it's hot.

Try a self-hug, a weighted blanket, a warm shower, Apollo, or hugging a friend, a dog, or a tree like your life depends on it (because it does).

PRO TIP

Soothing touch from a loved one is one of the simplest and most powerful healing techniques. Getting at least ten minutes of soothing touch each day will result in a massive improvement in mood, energy, distress tolerance, HRV, and overall nervous system regulation.

3. Move

Your body processes stress through movement: shaking, dancing, walking, feats of athleticism, and even interpretive floor flailing. Anything goes.

Try rolling your shoulders, stretching, dancing, walking, or wiggling like nobody's watching.

PRO TIP

As you move, just *notice* your body. *Notice* that your body is always here in the present moment doing its thing. Breathing for itself. Pumping blood for itself. *Notice* that it's been here all along, just waiting for you to *notice* it. *Notice* the simplicity in that truth, and allow yourself to have a good laugh at the absurdity.

4. Observe

What you notice, you can shift. Mindfulness activates the insula and quiets the fear circuits.

Try listening to the soundscape around you. What's the furthest sound you can hear? The quietest? Now you're present.

PRO TIP

Becoming a master observer comes down to practicing one key moment I call *The Return*. This is the moment when we choose to listen to something specific and start noticing other thoughts that pop into our awareness. Despair not! There is nothing wrong with you because this is happening. This is perfectly normal.

In this moment, your goal is to simply notice that your attention has wandered, and gently return it to what you originally chose to observe. Each time we complete this loop, we return a little faster. The faster the return, the stronger our attention 'muscle' becomes. This is very important for understanding meditation and mindfulness practices because we can practice them literally anytime, anywhere.

5. Nourish

When our survival is not in jeopardy, we can always take time to control what we eat and drink. At times, there is no better way to remind yourself that you're safe than putting something in your mouth. Food is a biochemical safety signal, and blood sugar stability is emotional stability.

Try eating something tasty, natural, and unprocessed. Maybe talk to your gut like it's your best friend (because it is). After you eat, notice how you feel. If you feel energized and elated, you're eating the right stuff. If you're feeling exhausted and down (or in pain), you're probably eating the wrong stuff.

PRO TIP

Drink more water than you think you need. Proper hydration is essential for maintaining high-level human functioning and preventing illness. The recommendation to drink eight cups of water each day is quite outdated. Since 2005, the National Academy of Medicine has recommended that the average healthy adult woman consume 91 ounces (11.5 cups) of water each day, and the average healthy adult man consume 125 ounces (15.5 cups) each day for optimal body function [250, 251]. Roughly 20% of this water comes from solid foods we eat. If you're exercising, pregnant, breastfeeding, or just sweating a lot, you'll need quite a bit more.

6. Rest

Your brain literally takes out the trash while you sleep. Dreaming is therapy with free special effects. Choosing to rest or sleep is a signal to your body that you're safe because the amygdala would not allow us to sleep if we were in real, immediate danger.

Try going to bed. No, really. Or just close your eyes for a few minutes and rest like a cat in a sunbeam, knowing that you're doing something nice for yourself. Your body will thank you.

You were born knowing how to sleep, and your body LOVES sleep. All we need to do is get out of the way and let it do its thing. It goes like this:

Remind yourself that you were born knowing how to sleep.

Breathe slow, deep, gentle breaths of gratitude for this knowing, as if you are already asleep.

PRO TIP

Breathing the way we do when we sleep helps the body feel like it's already there and activates safety circuitry in the brain.

5—THE FIVE SENSES

When in doubt, return to your senses. You can't panic and feel your feet at the same time.

1. **Sight**: Find one beautiful thing. Or three blue things. Or stare at the clouds like a philosopher-child.
2. **Smell**: Inhale something comforting. Lavender, coffee, fresh outside air, your own armpit (hey, whatever works). Just notice the aromas around you.
3. **Touch**: Pet your jeans. Rub your palms. Press your feet into the ground. Feel your edges.
4. **Sound**: Laugh, hum, sing, or name five things you can hear. It's impossible to ruminate when you hum, sing, or laugh.
5. **Taste**: Sip something warm. Chew slowly. Let a mint melt like it's sacred. Taste brings you back.

4—THE FOUR PILLARS OF SELF-TRUST

If our lives are like a house, the *Four Pillars of Self-Trust* are the foundation upon which your house is built. For the house to last our entire lives, it must have a strong foundation. The Shipibo people believe that simply by strengthening these four pillars through practice, we begin the healing process of learning to trust ourselves again on a foundation now stable enough to weather any storm.

Your inner child built this house. Let's make it a sanctuary.

1. Self-Gratitude

A simple "Thank you" to yourself for anything will do the trick.

"Thank you for making it to another day."

"Thank you for reclaiming my attention."

"Thank you for taking a breath."

Even "I'm proud of you for surviving that awkward lunch meeting" will work.

That's all it takes. The more often we notice good things, even seemingly small and mundane things within us for which we can find gratitude, the more grateful we feel, and the closer we are to grace. Grace is the goal state of living joyfully and peacefully in the present moment, without guilt, shame, or fear.

Affirmation: *There is no shame in being you.*

2. Self-Forgiveness

Jesus said to God mid-crucifixion, "Forgive them, for they know not what they do."

If Jesus can forgive the Romans for crucifying him (easily one of the most painful and unpleasant ways to go out) while it was happening, then we must be able to find it in our hearts to forgive ourselves.

Contrary to popular opinion, forgiveness is always for us, not for the other person. Forgiving ourselves is the practice of letting go of the resentment and regret we carry around much of the time that keeps us stuck in the past. The less you forgive, the more past baggage you carry with you, including guilt and shame, and those bags start to get mighty heavy faster than you think.

Yes, you messed up. There's nothing wrong with you. Welcome to humanity! Clean it up, learn the lessons, and carry on. The more we forgive, the lighter the load.

Affirmation: *Forgive them (including me!), for we know not what we do.*

3. Self-Compassion

Would you talk to a sad six-year-old or your best friend the way you talk to yourself? No? Then cut it out. Don't rush. Have patience as the process unfolds as it was meant to. Everything takes time, especially the behaviors we're trying to change. We didn't get here overnight. Accepting things as they are allows us to stop wasting our precious time wishing things were different and to start making them different right now.

Compassion is one of our most powerful allies in becoming a resilient, adaptable human being, and practicing it daily is the path to mastering our emotional regulation.

Affirmation: *Everything is as it should be right now (*because it couldn't possibly be any other way*).*

4. Self-Love

Not just the bubble-bath kind. This is the radical knowing that you are lovable and deserving of love even when you forget. Love is NOT conditional. It is always there for us, around us, and inside of us. Just by nature of being alive, you are loved. Simply noticing it invites it back into your life in full force and reminds you that you don't have to do anything special to deserve it. When we notice that we are loved and allow ourselves to feel love for ourselves without guilt or shame, we realize that we are quite content, without many other external needs.

PRO TIP

Start fortifying your foundation by simply writing down the *Four Pillars of Self-Trust* as the first thing you do when you wake up in the morning and the last thing you do before your head hits the pillow at night. This practice takes under 60 seconds and is infinitely better for your well-being than checking your text messages or doomscrolling.

Affirmation: *I am worthy of love.*

3—THE THREE MAXIMS OF THE TEMPLE OF APOLLO AT DELPHI

Way back in the day, Apollo was worshiped by the Greeks and Romans for giving the gifts of music, healing, and light to humanity. The ancient Greeks carved three deceptively simple instructions into the stone of the Temple of Apollo at Delphi. Consider them the original operating guidelines for your nervous system. They read:

1. Know Thyself.

A bold ask, considering most of us barely know what we want for lunch. Yet this maxim is the foundation of all healing: self-awareness. The Greeks understood that you can't change what you won't observe. Modern neuroscience agrees. Interoception and introspection, the awareness of internal signals, are the gateway to emotional regulation. In other words, noticing your breath, your heartbeat, your tension patterns, and your thoughts is literally how your insula strengthens, and your whole organism calms down. Knowing yourself isn't a personality test. It's embodied presence.

2. Nothing in Excess.

The nervous system loves moderation, making it one of the sexiest things on the planet to each other's bodies because moderation conveys strength through regulation and balance. Excess stress, stimulation, scrolling, responsibility, blue light, and consumption all push the body into threat mode. The Greeks warned us about overdoing it millennia before push notifications existed. They understood what we keep forgetting: balance is not a luxury; it's survival.

3. Certainty Brings Ruin.

This one is my personal favorite. The Greeks recognized that dogma, rigid certainty, and close-mindedness was a direct path to disaster. Neuroscience echoes this: psychological flexibility predicts resilience. Curiosity, humility, and the willingness to be wrong keep the brain adaptable. False certainty in uncertain situations is the amygdala in overdrive.

2—THE DIVINE UNION

This is the sacred tension of duality that makes you, you (Figure 5A). Whether you were born biologically male, female, or somewhere in between, both masculine and feminine, yin and yang, energies exist inside each and every one of us.

The strengths of your masculine side include logic, structure, action, focus, and ambition. When suppressed or overactive, it can come out as dominating, rigid, emotionally distant, and obsessed with control.

The strengths of your feminine side include intuition, feeling, receptivity, nurturing, and presence. When suppressed or overactive, it can come out as overly passive, manipulative, chaotic, and self-abandoning.

The masculine holds the container; the feminine fills it with life. The feminine senses the truth; the masculine speaks it. The masculine moves forward; the feminine makes sure we're aligned before we do.

We need both to live well.

We need both to be in balance to feel whole.

Healing begins when the inner masculine bows to the wisdom of the heart, and the inner feminine feels safe enough to dance.

1—LOVE

The singularity. The source of divinity. The reason you're here.

We are all made of the same stuff (stardust and 99.9% the same DNA), and we are therefore infinitely more similar than we are different, despite what our amygdala tells us when we're overwhelmed. Always acknowledging sameness first allows our differences to be enriching rather than scary. Focusing on what we have in common first signals to the amygdala that there is nothing to fear because what is around us is familiar and known to us.

Love is not only what we're all made of, but it's also the glue, the rhythm, the frequency of life, and it's always available to us with a simple shift of our attention.

My friend Nick Adkins, the founder of the Pinksocks gifting community, wisely said to me once in an interview on the science of love: "In every single moment, fear and love and everything in between exist. We get to choose what we pay attention to. We get to choose what we focus on and how we live."

This choice is the source of our power. Choosing love and kindness, approaching ourselves and the world from the perspective of love rather than fear, is an intentional choice that is ours alone to make. And we can make that choice at literally any moment and begin to recognize our full potential as human beings.

Every breath of air is a reminder that love wants to live through you.

Let it.

Amo, Ergo Sum—I Love, Therefore I Am

CONCLUSION
Welcome Home

Long ago, I was an atheist. As a curious Jewish kid growing up in the time just before the internet, I was bullied a lot in school. The teachers and my parents tried to help, but it didn't make the pain go away.

Despite the tremendous love I knew my parents had for me, it was a lonely time. A time where you start to wonder silly things like "What's the point?" and "Would anybody really miss me if I wasn't here?" It's easy to see why suicide rates in teens are higher than ever now that bullying has gone cyber. From studying holocaust history in school to the pangs of teenage loneliness, it was hard to imagine that there could possibly be a God at all if he or she would let these things happen to us.

In nightly moments of lonely despair, remembering the little education I had about God and the world from my parents, I prayed, because it made me feel anything other than alone. I wasn't sure if I believed in God yet, so I sheepishly said, "Dear God, if you're real, please send me my person, my partner, the one who will make sure I never feel alone again, and I will do everything I can to serve you and make the world a better place." And I prayed this prayer, over and over, nearly nightly, for many years.

Two decades later, while finishing medical school in my late twenties, I met Kathryn. Immediately, I knew there was something very special about her. We had countless unusual, uncanny similarities that I have never experienced with anyone else, which allowed us to get to know each other very quickly. Being together was an extremely safe place to easily *be* ourselves, nearly right away.

Kathryn was also the most intuitive person I had ever met. She was always listening and extremely in tune with her environment. She heard things I didn't hear. She saw things I glossed over. She felt things I had no idea were going on.

What really blew my logical, scientific mind away was that, without any empirical data, her intuition was always spot-on. As in, I can't remember a single time it was wrong, but I can remember many times where my scientific mind doubted her and made an error I later regretted. I quickly noticed that being around her was teaching me to tune into my own intuition because I now knew it was real.

Within several months of spending nearly all our non-work time together, gazing into her hazel-green eyes one morning, I realized, without any hesitation or doubt, that she was, in fact, the partner I had been praying for all those years. It was a feeling deep in my bones. My soul mate was literally the woman of my dreams, sitting right in front of me. Right at this very moment, a little voice chimed in the background of my thoughts with a helpful reminder: "Don't mess this one up, Dave!"

What I didn't quite realize the importance of at that time is that I received another exceptionally beautiful gift in that moment: knowing, without hesitation, that some sort of higher power exists and is listening to us because my prayers had been answered. It didn't come all at once; it came over time by practicing faith in something greater than myself through prayer, gratitude, and the techniques described in this guide. My quality of life improved exponentially, beyond my wildest dreams.

For starters, I no longer had to spend any time or effort questioning whether spirituality existed, because I now knew it, fully embodied in my life experience. Looking back, I can safely say that I would never have fathomed how much that specific software bug of doubt was wreaking havoc on my brain and my ability to function as a happy, healthy human being.

So, spirituality exists, and science can now prove it. No cap. The existence of DMT alone, the fact that we secrete it in our brains, and the universal effect it has of reminding us of our personal hotline to the

Divine is undeniable evidence of this, in and of itself. Some call it revelation, others call it stating the obvious. Whatever we choose to call it, it is a powerful reminder that we are all connected to something much bigger than us, something that includes us. Something that is somehow working with us toward our success. I had all the personal proof I needed. Now I just needed to figure out how to describe it scientifically for everyone else.

THE GOLDEN GATE IN YOUR HEAD

In the spring of 2017, Kathryn and I rented a room in a house perched high in the Berkeley Hills while attending Psychedelic Science, the world's largest conference discussing the latest developments in the field of psychedelic science and medicine. It was one of those rare California houses where the windows are so big you feel like you're inside the landscape, not just looking at it.

One evening, Dr. Ben Kelmendi, my psychiatrist colleague from Yale, came over to join my wife and me for tea, and the three of us found ourselves standing barefoot in the living room, gazing out over the most astonishing panoramic view of the entire San Francisco Bay.

Right in the center of the vista stood the Golden Gate Bridge, glowing in the soft light of dusk, like some kind of sacred punctuation mark between two worlds.

I turned to them and said, "Look at that! The left side of the bridge, San Francisco, is buzzing with noise, and buildings, and cars. It's dense, complex, and industrial. Full of motion and mind."

Then I pointed to the right, to the North Bay, where the land opened into soft rolling green hills. No honking horns. Fewer buildings. Just stillness, space, and beauty.

"It's like a metaphor for the brain," I remarked.

After a few hours of consideration, the crew agreed.

That moment, that view, became the clearest image I've ever found to describe what we're doing wrong and how to come home to what's right.

The left side of the bridge, like the left hemisphere of the brain, is busy, analytical, focused on parts, categories, timelines, logic, words, and control [252].

It's helpful when building bridges, but it's terrible at knowing you're standing on sacred ground.

The right side of the bridge, like the right hemisphere of the brain, is relational, whole, present, embodied, emotional, spatial, musical, and connected to everything, yet clinging to nothing [253].

It knows spirit without needing to name it.

When these hemispheres fall out of balance, as they have in modern life, we become split. We mistake the map for the territory. The text for the truth. We stop trusting our feelings. We begin to doubt the body. We lose connection to awe, and with it, our connection to the Divine source of all creation.

The result is self-deception, which leads to dissonance, disconnection, discomfort, and eventually, disease. What religious traditions have long called the Devil, and what neuroscience calls dysregulation.

In Latin, the words "evil" and "left" are from the same root: *sinister*. One way to interpret this is that eating the fruit from the Tree of Knowledge gave us knowledge of the left brain, the analytical part of our brain that questions, doubts, and judges everything. This is the part of our brains that pulls us out of the present. It's not actually "evil," it's just doubting and questioning everything, including divinity itself, and our connection to it. Over time, we mistake the illusion of separation for the whole story.

Presence, right brain-mediated, is trusting our intuition as our innate personal portal to the Divine. We can nurture our own internal source of divinity at any time by choosing to breathe, pray, or simply by listening to what the body has to say. When you know your prayers are being heard, it makes it a lot more fun to spend time praying. It also reminds us that we're never actually alone. We are always connected to something bigger.

AS ABOVE, SO BELOW

The ancient Hermetic principle *"As above, so below"* means that what is Divine in the heavens is also found in the Earth, in our flesh, our cells, our tears, and our DNA.

This is the part where we recognize the privilege of receiving the unexpected gift of a lifetime:

We are alive at the exact moment in history when science has finally proven, beyond all reasonable doubt, that God, spirituality, and divinity exist.

Not as a theory. Not as a metaphor. As a living, organizing, harmonizing, conscious intelligence that is accessible through our nervous systems, our breath, our attention, and our relationships.

Today, we bear witness to science revealing this spiritual truth:

Your *attention* shapes your brain.

Your *gratitude* alters your mood and immune function.

Your *prayers* regulate your nervous system.

Your *breath* speaks directly to your intuition.

Your *presence* entrains others' heart rhythms.

Your *consciousness* is entangled across space and time.

This isn't opinion anymore. It is now evidence-based scientific fact. It's happening in laboratories, peer-reviewed journals, clinics, biofeedback labs, and in those moments when you think fondly of someone and they surprise you by calling you shortly thereafter. And it's confirming what mystics and monks have always known:

The Divine is not just out there.

Access to the Divine is in each of us, simply by nature of being alive. In you. In me. In the spaces between.

And most miraculous of all?

You don't have to be a monk, mystic, priest, or scientist to access it.

All you have to do is breathe by choice. Be still. Feel. Listen.

Your feelings are the language of God.

Your body is the temple.

Your breath is the key.

Your gratitude and awe are the offering.

Your presence is the return.

THE TRUTH YOU CAN FEEL IN YOUR BONES

Let's take a breath together.

Inhale like you're smelling warm cookies. Exhale like you're sighing after finally taking off tight pants.

That breath?

That's the whole point.

It's the bridge between your mind, body, and spirit. Between fear and love. Between *doing* and *being*.

It's also your ticket home.

Because *home*, contrary to popular belief, is not a place on a map, or a person you're still texting, or a moment in the past before life got messy.

Home is *you*. Your body. This moment. This breath.

I felt this truth again, most recently, while standing outside Sagrada Família in Barcelona, a magnificent architectural and engineering masterpiece designed by Antoni Gaudí. Construction of this cathedral began in 1882 (long before calculators), and it has been under construction for nearly 150 years. It is nothing short of awe-inspiring.

What happened next wasn't a thought or an analysis. It was a visceral knowing.

The moment I stepped in front of that ornate sanctuary of sculpted light, built over multiple generations by an entire city, something humbling swept through me, like a wave of awe and reverence that started in my heart and rolled out to my skin. Chills. Full-body chills. A feeling I've never really had in or around a church before as a Jewish boy.

And when I felt those chills for a minute or so, I knew exactly what they were saying: *This cathedral was built for the glory of God. By tens of thousands of people whose faith was so unwaveringly strong that they spent nearly 150 years building it, not knowing for certain if its glory would ever be fully realized as they and Gaudí had imagined.*

What motivated this incredible collective effort of an entire community across generations was neither ego nor status, but inspiration. A textbook example of a human being (Gaudí) in intimate communion with the Divine. In collaboration with nature and his community. In service to something far bigger than self, yet fully inclusive of self.

It takes tremendous courage and audacity to build something unlike anything anyone has seen before. And you don't build something like that, something that carries so much risk if it fails, unless you *feel* spirit moving through you.

Just by taking it in, by standing still in its presence, I felt the truth of that union in my body. I didn't have to believe it. I *knew* it.

Later that night at 3:31 a.m., my one-year-old baby boy, Sammy, starts screaming at the top of his tiny lungs. He woke up because he was getting over a cold and was still stuffed up. I pick him up and hug him close to my chest in an attempt to rock him back to sleep. No dice. The screaming continues, and now it's right in my ear as I rock. Back and forth. Back and forth. He's not buying it.

I check into my body for a moment to see what's going on, and notice that my heart is racing and my lungs aren't too far behind. So I pause to take one slow, long, deep breath. Then another. Then another. All the while, gently rocking. As my breath slows, I notice my heart rate slowing as well. And I notice Sam starting to relax. His cries softening. His little head nuzzling into my chest as his breaths start to match mine. And then within just a few minutes of breathing long, slow, deep breaths, Sammy has returned to sound asleep status.

This isn't a one-off experience. This is co-regulation in action, and I use it often.

The next morning, I watch Sammy as his face lights up with pure delight when he discovers how to push a ball around the room and that spatulas come in all kinds of shapes and sizes. He is just being Sammy, enjoying the moment. Not a care in the world. A helpful reminder that the present moment is where all the magic happens. And we were all here once.

Now it's time to come back home.

The garden is here. It has always been here.

It's your body, humming with aliveness.

It's the smell of your lover's skin and crisp, fresh morning air.

It's the way your feet feel in the sand at the beach.

It's that moment of deep belly laughter that makes you snort and feel holy at the same time.

The return to the garden is not metaphorical. It's neurological.

It's the moment you feel safe enough to *be* again.

Safe enough for your inner child to come out and play.

Safe to realize that we have never been separate from holiness. We just got distracted and stopped listening.

But now... You remember.

You are not just a person. You are a portal. A living node in the Divine network. An embodied answer to the question, *"What would love look like if it had a body and the ability to observe itself?"*

You are the way back.

You are the gate.

You are the path.

Your breath is the first sacrament.

Your nervous system is your altar.

Your ability to feel, to play, to connect—that's the Divine in action.

You don't need to "find your purpose." *Being* you is all that is required. Your purpose is to discover yourself and what you are capable of in this lifetime.

Just to *be here now.*

To *be love.*

To *be alive.*

SO, NOW WHAT?

Now...live like you mean it.

Dance when it's awkward.

Nap like it's sacred.

Tell people you love them because you know the feeling is real.

Laugh until you forget your name and remember your soul.

Let your inner child run the show sometimes. Especially during brunch.

And when things get hard, and they will, come back to your map to remind you of the way:

- 6 Elements of Control
- 5 Senses
- 4 Pillars of Self-Trust
- 3 Maxims on the Temple of Apollo at Delphi
- 2 Parts of the Divine Union
- 1 Love

And finally…

Remember *The Forgotten Secret.*

That no matter how old you are in years, you are always a child at heart.

And children choose love by default.

So choose love!

Over and over.

Clumsily, joyfully, defiantly.

Choose it like it's your job.

Because it is.

In doing so, you are exercising free will and proving to yourself that you have a say in the outcome of your existence.

Walk confidently.

Speak truthfully.

Breathe deeply.

Love recklessly.

And live like someone who knows, not believes or hopes, but knows that they are one with the Divine.

Just by the nature of being born.

When you listen for it, you know it.

Welcome home.

You are the miracle you've been waiting for.

There is unfathomable joy awaiting you here.

And you deserve every last bit of it.

Simple Affirmations

1. *Be here now.*
2. *We have infinitely more in common than we have differences, just by nature of being alive.*
3. *Our greatest possible potential is unknown.*
4. *I am worthy of love.*
5. *Pain is inevitable. Suffering is avoidable.*
6. *The skin is the outermost layer of the soul.*
7. *Make space for the surprises the universe throws at us.*
8. *Slow is smooth and smooth is fast.*
9. *Perfect is the enemy of the good.*
10. *The ordinary is allowed to become extraordinary.*
11. *What can I learn from this challenge?*
12. *There is no rush.*
13. *Whenever you do something, try your best to do it right the first time or you will usually have to repeat it.*
14. *The temple was never made of stone. It's made of synapses, breath, and the silent space between.*
15. *We are not separate from the pattern.*
16. *The veil thins not by force, but by coherence.*
17. *I was born to sleep for one third of my life on earth just like every other human being.*
18. *We cannot fight for peace. Peace is the only way to invite more peace.*

19. *You don't have to do anything to be safe. You just have to stop pretending you're not.*
20. *When life is fun, the game has been won.*
21. *There is no shame in being you.*
22. *Forgive them (including me!), for we know not what we do.*
23. *Everything is as it should be right now (*because it couldn't possibly be any other way*).*
24. *Everything is falling into place.*
25. *If I am not for myself, who will be for me?*
26. *Amo, Ergo Sum: I Love, Therefore I am.*

References

BOOK 1

1. Morris, Desmond. *The Human Zoo*. New York: McGraw-Hill, 1969.
2. Berntson, Gary G., Karen S. Quigley, and Daniel L. Lozano. "Cardiovascular Psychophysiology." In *Handbook of Psychophysiology*, 4th ed., edited by John T. Cacioppo, Louis G. Tassinary, and Gary G. Berntson, 182–210. Cambridge: Cambridge University Press, 2017.
3. Widmaier, Eric P., Hershel Raff, and Kevin T. Strang. *Vander's Human Physiology: The Mechanisms of Body Function.* 15th ed. New York: McGraw-Hill Education, 2018.
4. Lehrer, Paul M., and Richard Gevirtz. "Heart Rate Variability Biofeedback: How and Why Does It Work?" *Frontiers in Psychology* 5 (July 21, 2014): 756. https://doi.org/10.3389/fpsyg.2014.00756
5. Rabin, David, and Greg Siegle. "S87. Toward Emotion Prosthetics: Emotion Regulation Through Wearable Vibroacoustic Stimulation." *Biological Psychiatry* 83 (2018): S380–S381. https://doi.org/10.1016/j.biopsych.2018.02.979
6. Hallihan, Cameron, and Greg J. Siegle. "Effect of Vibroacoustic Stimulation on Athletes Recovering from Exercise." *European Journal of Applied Physiology* 122, no. 11 (November 2022): 2427–35. https://doi.org/10.1007/s00421-022-05026-x
7. Hammaker, Krista, Haomin Hu, Maureen Laffoon, Leigh A. Freno, Robert Lafyatis, Yongseok Park, and Robyn T. Domsic. "Wearable in Systemic Sclerosis: A Pilot Study of the Apollo Wearable Demonstrates Improvement in Fatigue, Raynaud Phenomenon and Quality of Life in Patients with Systemic Sclerosis." *The Journal of Rheumatology* 52, no. 2 (February 1, 2025): 158–164. https://doi.org/10.3899/jrheum.2024-0551
8. McKennon, Sarah, Ruth Bindler, and Jennifer Miller. "Evaluating the Impact of Apollo Neuro™ Wearable on Wellbeing in Medical and Pharmacy Students: A Preliminary Prospective Randomized Controlled Study." *The American Journal of Medicine* 138 (2025): 1734–1741.e2. https://doi.org/10.1016/j.amjmed.2025.07.045

9. Apollo Neuroscience. "Apollo Neuroscience's 2025 Year in Review." Accessed March 19, 2026. https://apolloneuro.com/blogs/news/apollo-neurosciences-2025-year-in-review
10. Bromberg-Martin, Ethan S., Masayuki Matsumoto, and Okihide Hikosaka. "Dopamine in Motivational Control: Rewarding, Aversive, and Alerting." *Neuron* 68, no. 5 (December 9, 2010): 815–34. https://doi.org/10.1016/j.neuron.2010.11.022
11. Dresp-Langley, Birgitta. "From Reward to Anhedonia: Dopamine Function in the Global Mental Health Context." *Biomedicines* 11, no. 9 (September 6, 2023): 2469. https://doi.org/10.3390/biomedicines11092469
12. Skinner, B. F. "Two Types of Conditioned Reflex and a Pseudo Type." *Journal of General Psychology* 12 (1935): 66–77.
13. Skinner, B. F. *The Behavior of Organisms: An Experimental Analysis.* New York: Appleton-Century, 1938.
14. Social Media Addiction Trials Put Tech Companies on the Defensive." *New York Times*, January 27, 2026. https://www.nytimes.com/2026/01/27/technology/social-media-addiction-trials.html
15. Pellegrino, Alfonso, Alessandro Stasi, and Veera Bhatiasevi. "Research Trends in Social Media Addiction and Problematic Social Media Use: A Bibliometric Analysis." *Frontiers in Psychiatry* 13 (November 10, 2022): 1017506. https://doi.org/10.3389/fpsyt.2022.1017506
16. Manuali, Lorenzo. "Addictive Motivational Scaffolds and the Structure of Social Media." *Synthese* 206, no. 5 (November 2025): 224. https://doi.org/10.1007/s11229-025-05312-z
17. Kuss, Daria J., and Mark D. Griffiths. "Online Social Networking and Addiction: A Review of the Psychological Literature." *International Journal of Environmental Research and Public Health* 8, no. 9 (September 2011): 3528–52. https://doi.org/10.3390/ijerph8093528
18. Ratan, Zubair Ahmed, Anne-Maree Parrish, Sojib Bin Zaman, Mohammad Saud Alotaibi, and Hassan Hosseinzadeh. "Smartphone Addiction and Associated Health Outcomes in Adult Populations: A Systematic Review." *International Journal of Environmental Research and Public Health* 18, no. 22 (November 22, 2021): 12257. https://doi.org/10.3390/ijerph182212257.
19. Gold, Bizzie. *Your Brain Is a Filthy Liar.* Game Changer Publishing, 2025.
20. World Health Organization. "Burn-out an 'Occupational Phenomenon': International Classification of Diseases." May 28, 2019. https://www.who.int/news/item/28-05-2019-burn-out-an-occupational-phenomenon-international-classification-of-diseases
21. Padival, Mallika, Danielle Quinette, and J. Amiel Rosenkranz. "Effects of Repeated Stress on Excitatory Drive of Basal Amygdala Neurons In Vivo." *Neuropsychopharmacology* 38 (2013): 1748–1762. https://doi.org/10.1038/npp.2013.74

22. Kim, Eun Joo, Blake Pellman, and Jae Joon Kim. "Stress Effects on the Hippocampus: A Critical Review." *Learning & Memory* 22, no. 9 (2015): 411–416. https://doi.org/10.1101/lm.037291.114
23. Davis, W. Summer, Peter Anderson, and Sri Banerjee. "Cardiovascular Disease and All-Cause Mortality Among Individuals with Low Sexual Frequency." *Healthcare* 13, no. 5 (2025): 461. https://doi.org/10.3390/healthcare13050461
24. Sakurada, Kaori, Tsuneo Konta, Narumi Murakami, Naoko Kosugi, Takafumi Saito, Masafumi Watanabe, Kenichi Ishizawa, Yoshiyuki Ueno, and Takamasa Kayama. "Association between Lack of Sexual Interest and All-Cause Mortality in a Japanese General Population: The Yamagata Prospective Observational Study." *PLOS ONE* 17, no. 12 (2022): e0277967. https://doi.org/10.1371/journal.pone.0277967
25. Kontula, Osmo. *Between Sexual Desire and Reality: The Evolution of Sex in Finland.* Helsinki: The Family Federation of Finland, 2009. https://doi.org/10.13140/2.1.3286.3681
26. Kontula, Osmo. "The Evolution of Sex Education and Students' Sexual Knowledge in Finland in the 2000s." *Sex Education* 10, no. 4 (2010): 373–386. https://doi.org/10.1080/14681811.2010.515095
27. Bekhbat, Mandakh, Michael T. Treadway, and Jennifer C. Felger. "Inflammation as a Pathophysiologic Pathway to Anhedonia: Mechanisms and Therapeutic Implications." *Current Topics in Behavioral Neurosciences* 58 (2022): 397–419. https://doi.org/10.1007/7854_2021_294
28. Zwiep, Janna C., Femke Lamers, Christiaan H. Vinkers, Nic J. A. van der Wee, Brenda W. J. H. Penninx, Laura Nawijn, and Yvonne Milaneschi. "Inflammation, Metabolic Dysregulation, and Depression Profiles Related to Anhedonia and Atypical, Energy-Related Symptoms." *Brain, Behavior, and Immunity* 132 (2026): 106240. https://doi.org/10.1016/j.bbi.2025.106240
29. Wu, Congchong, Qingli Mu, Weijia Gao, and Shaojia Lu. "The Characteristics of Anhedonia in Depression: A Review from a Clinically Oriented Perspective." *Translational Psychiatry* 15, no. 1 (2025): 90. https://doi.org/10.1038/s41398-025-03310-w
30. Bornstein, Marc H., and Gianluca Esposito. "Coregulation: A Multilevel Approach via Biology and Behavior." *Children (Basel)* 10, no. 8 (2023): 1323. https://doi.org/10.3390/children10081323
31. Gilbert, Paul. "Affiliative and Prosocial Motives and Emotions in Mental Health." *Dialogues in Clinical Neuroscience* 17, no. 4 (2015): 381–389. https://doi.org/10.31887/DCNS.2015.17.4/pgilbert
32. Tomsia, M., J. Cieśla, J. Śmieszek, S. Florek, A. Macionga, K. Michalczyk, and D. Stygar. "Long-Term Space Missions' Effects on the Human Organism: What We Do Know and What Requires Further Research." *Frontiers in Physiology* 15 (2024): 1284644. https://doi.org/10.3389/fphys.2024.1284644

33. Guo, Zi, Guangming Zhou, and Wentau Hu. "Carcinogenesis Induced by Space Radiation: A Systematic Review." *Neoplasia* 32 (2022): 100828. https://doi.org/10.1016/j.neo.2022.100828
34. Arone, Alessia, Tiziana Ivaldi, Konstantin Loganovsky, Sergio Palermo, Eduardo Parra, Walter Flamini, and Donatella Marazziti. "The Burden of Space Exploration on the Mental Health of Astronauts: A Narrative Review." *Clinical Neuropsychiatry* 18, no. 5 (2021): 237–246. https://doi.org/10.36131/cnfioritieditore20210502
35. Peterson, Richard L. "The Neuroscience of Investing: fMRI of the Reward System." *Brain Research Bulletin* 67, no. 5 (2005): 391–397. https://doi.org/10.1016/j.brainresbull.2005.06.006
36. Pessiglione, Mathias, Liane Schmidt, Bogdan Draganski, Raffael Kalisch, Hakwan Lau, Ray J. Dolan, and Chris D. Frith. "How the Brain Translates Money into Force: A Neuroimaging Study of Subliminal Motivation." *Science* 316, no. 5826 (2007): 904–906. https://doi.org/10.1126/science.1140459
37. Breiter, Hans C., Randy L. Gollub, Robert M. Weisskoff, David N. Kennedy, Nikos Makris, Joshua D. Berke, Joel M. Goodman, Howard L. Kantor, David R. Gastfriend, John P. Riorden, Ramesh T. Mathew, Bruce R. Rosen, and Steven E. Hyman. "Acute Effects of Cocaine on Human Brain Activity and Emotion." *Neuron* 19, no. 3 (1997): 591–611. https://doi.org/10.1016/S0896-6273(00)80374-8
38. Kotlińska-Lemieszek, Agnieszka, and Zbigniew Żylicz. "Less Well-Known Consequences of the Long-Term Use of Opioid Analgesics: A Comprehensive Literature Review." *Drug Design, Development and Therapy* 16 (2022): 251–264. https://doi.org/10.2147/DDDT.S342409
39. Griffin, Charles E., III, Alan M. Kaye, Francisco R. Bueno, and Alan D. Kaye. "Benzodiazepine Pharmacology and Central Nervous System–Mediated Effects." *Ochsner Journal* 13, no. 2 (2013): 214–223. https://www.ncbi.nlm.nih.gov/pmc/articles/PMC3684331/
40. Gao, Yaqing, Binbin Su, Lei Ding, Danial Qureshi, Shenda Hong, Jie Wei, Chao Zeng, Guanghua Lei, and Junqing Xie. "Association of Regular Opioid Use With Incident Dementia and Neuroimaging Markers of Brain Health in Chronic Pain Patients: Analysis of UK Biobank." *American Journal of Geriatric Psychiatry* 32, no. 9 (2024): 1154–1165. https://doi.org/10.1016/j.jagp.2024.04.010
41. Legrand, Diego, Pierre Roberge, Alain Vanasse, Nathalie Carrier, and Claude Bocti. "Association between Benzodiazepines and Dementia: A Case-Control Study from Canadian Health Surveys and Medico-Administrative Databases." *Journal of the Neurological Sciences* 479 (2025): 123746. https://doi.org/10.1016/j.jns.2025.123746

42. Chong, Trevor T.-J., Erika Fortunato, and Mark A. Bellgrove. "Amphetamines Improve the Motivation to Invest Effort in Attention-Deficit/Hyperactivity Disorder." *Journal of Neuroscience* 36, no. 10 (2016): 2998–3007. https://doi.org/10.1523/JNEUROSCI.2967-15.2016
43. Shoptaw, Steven J., Uyen Kao, Keith Heinzerling, and Walter Ling. "Treatment for Amphetamine Withdrawal." *Cochrane Database of Systematic Reviews* 2009, no. 2 (2009): CD003021. https://doi.org/10.1002/14651858.CD003021.pub2
44. Griffiths, Roland R., Matthew W. Johnson, Michael A. Carducci, Annie Umbricht, William A. Richards, Brian D. Richards, Mary P. Cosimano, and Margaret A. Klinedinst. "Psilocybin Produces Substantial and Sustained Decreases in Depression and Anxiety in Patients with Life-Threatening Cancer: A Randomized Double-Blind Trial." *Journal of Psychopharmacology* 30, no. 12 (2016): 1181–1197. https://doi.org/10.1177/0269881116675513
45. Mithoefer, Michael C., Ann T. Mithoefer, Ananda B. Feduccia, et al. "3,4-Methylenedioxymethamphetamine (MDMA)-Assisted Psychotherapy for Post-Traumatic Stress Disorder in Military Veterans, Firefighters, and Police Officers: A Randomised, Double-Blind, Dose-Response, Phase 2 Clinical Trial." *The Lancet Psychiatry* 5, no. 6 (2018): 486–497. https://doi.org/10.1016/S2215-0366(18)30135-4
46. National Institute on Drug Abuse. "Overdose Death Rates." Accessed January 19, 2026. https://nida.nih.gov/research-topics/trends-statistics/overdose-death-rates
47. Substance Abuse and Mental Health Services Administration. "SAMHSA Releases Annual National Survey on Drug Use and Health." July 28, 2025. https://www.samhsa.gov/newsroom/press-announcements/20250728/samhsa-releases-annual-national-survey-on-drug-use-and-health
48. Drug Abuse Statistics. "Drug Abuse Statistics." Accessed January 19, 2026. https://drugabusestatistics.org/
49. RAND Corporation. *Estimating the Potential Demand for Psilocybin-Assisted Therapy in the United States.* Santa Monica, CA: RAND Corporation, 2024. https://www.rand.org/pubs/research_reports/RRA4334-1.html
50. Matzopoulos, Richard, Robert Morlock, Amy Morlock, Bernard Lerer, and Leonard Lerer. "Psychedelic Mushrooms in the USA: Knowledge, Patterns of Use, and Association with Health Outcomes." *American Journal of Drug and Alcohol Abuse* 49, no. 3 (2023): 266–277. https://doi.org/10.1080/00952990.2023.2180490
51. "Magic Mushroom Use by Young Adults Has Nearly Doubled in Three Years." *The Hill*, June 27, 2023. https://thehill.com/policy/healthcare/4054255-magic-mushroom-use-by-young-adults-has-nearly-doubled-in-three-years/

52. Centers for Disease Control and Prevention. "Accidental Injury." Accessed January 19, 2026. https://www.cdc.gov/nchs/fastats/accidental-injury.htm
53. Grof, Stanislav. *Realms of the Human Unconscious: Observations from LSD Research.* New York: Viking Press, 1975.
54. Olry, Régis, and Duane E. Haines. "Historical and Literary Roots of Münchhausen Syndromes: As Intriguing as the Syndromes Themselves." *Progress in Brain Research* 206 (2013): 123–141. https://doi.org/10.1016/B978-0-444-63364-4.00024-7
55. Savino, Adria C., and John S. Fordtran. "Factitious Disease: Clinical Lessons from Case Studies at Baylor University Medical Center." *Proceedings (Baylor University Medical Center)* 19, no. 3 (2006): 195–198. https://doi.org/10.1080/08998280.2006.11928168
56. Asher, Richard. "Munchausen's Syndrome." *The Lancet* 1, no. 6650 (1951): 339–341. https://doi.org/10.1016/S0140-6736(51)92313-6
57. Bass, Christopher, and Peter Halligan. "Factitious Disorders and Malingering: Challenges for Clinical Assessment and Management." *The Lancet* 383, no. 9926 (2014): 1422–1432. https://doi.org/10.1016/S0140-6736(13)62186-8
58. World Health Organization. "Anxiety Disorders." Accessed January 19, 2026. https://www.who.int/news-room/fact-sheets/detail/anxiety-disorders
59. Zhang, Ziwei, Xiaoxuan Chen, Shuilin Wu, Xin Chen, Xiaokun Wang, Chang Liu, Na Zeng, Yang Liu, Tiantian Huo, Xiaoxing Liu, Le Shi, Wei Yan, Kai Yuan, Shiqiu Meng, Ping Wu, Afzal Javed, Rowalt Alibudbud, Jie Shi, Yankun Sun, Lin Lu, and Yanping Bao. "Global, Regional and National Burden of Anxiety and Depression Disorders from 1990 to 2021, and Forecasts up to 2040." *Journal of Affective Disorders* 393, pt. A (2026): 120299. https://doi.org/10.1016/j.jad.2025.120299
60. Watson, Kurt B., Jennifer L. Wiltz, Khang Nhim, Robert B. Kaufmann, Christopher W. Thomas, and Kurt J. Greenlund. "Trends in Multiple Chronic Conditions Among US Adults, by Life Stage, Behavioral Risk Factor Surveillance System, 2013–2023." *Preventing Chronic Disease* 22 (2025): E15. https://doi.org/10.5888/pcd22.240539
61. Min, Jiwon, Katherine E. Hein, Austin R. Medlin, and Stephanie N. Mullins-Sweatt. "Prevalence Rate Trends of Borderline Personality Disorder Symptoms and Self-Injurious Behaviors in College Students from 2017 to 2021." *Psychiatry Research* 329 (2023): 115526. https://doi.org/10.1016/j.psychres.2023.115526
62. Fishbain, David A. "Secondary Gain Concept: Definition Problems and Its Abuse in Medical Practice." *APS Journal* 3, no. 4 (1994): 264–273. https://doi.org/10.1016/S1058-9139(05)80274-8

63. Porges, Stephen W. "Polyvagal Theory: A Science of Safety." *Frontiers in Integrative Neuroscience* 16 (2022): 871227. https://doi.org/10.3389/fnint.2022.871227
64. Dorahy, Martin J., Steven N. Gold, and John A. O'Neil, eds. *Dissociation and the Dissociative Disorders: Past, Present, Future.* 2nd ed. New York: Routledge, 2022. https://doi.org/10.4324/9781003057314
65. Yates, Gregory P., and Marc D. Feldman. "Factitious Disorder: A Systematic Review of 455 Cases in the Professional Literature." *General Hospital Psychiatry* 41 (2016): 20–28. https://doi.org/10.1016/j.genhosppsych.2016.05.002

BOOK 2

1. Fox, Michael D., Abraham Z. Snyder, Jessica L. Vincent, Maurizio Corbetta, David C. Van Essen, and Marcus E. Raichle. "The Human Brain Is Intrinsically Organized into Dynamic, Anticorrelated Functional Networks." *Proceedings of the National Academy of Sciences of the United States of America* 102, no. 27 (2005): 9673–9678. https://doi.org/10.1073/pnas.0504136102
2. Menon, Vinod. "20 Years of the Default Mode Network: A Review and Synthesis." *Neuron* 111, no. 16 (August 16, 2023): 2469–87. https://doi.org/10.1016/j.neuron.2023.04.023
3. Droit-Volet, Sylvie, Michaël Dambrun, and Florie Monier. "Awe and Time Perception." *Acta Psychologica* 245 (2024): 104232. https://doi.org/10.1016/j.actpsy.2024.104232
4. van Wassenhove, Virginie, Marc Wittmann, A. D. Craig, and Martin P. Paulus. "Psychological and Neural Mechanisms of Subjective Time Dilation." *Frontiers in Neuroscience* 5 (April 26, 2011): 56. https://doi.org/10.3389/fnins.2011.00056
5. Zander, Tobias, Michael Öllinger, and Kirsten G. Volz. "Intuition and Insight: Two Processes That Build on Each Other or Fundamentally Differ?" *Frontiers in Psychology* 7 (2016): 1395. https://doi.org/10.3389/fpsyg.2016.01395
6. Magnon, V., F. Dutheil, and G. T. Vallet. "Benefits from One Session of Deep and Slow Breathing on Vagal Tone and Anxiety in Young and Older Adults." *Scientific Reports* 11 (2021): 19267. https://doi.org/10.1038/s41598-021-98736-9
7. James, William. *The Principles of Psychology*. New York: Henry Holt and Company, 1918. https://www.gutenberg.org/files/57628/57628-h/57628-h.htm
8. Lehrer, Paul M., and Richard Gevirtz. "Heart Rate Variability Biofeedback: How and Why Does It Work?" *Frontiers in Psychology* 5 (July 21, 2014): 756. https://doi.org/10.3389/fpsyg.2014.00756
9. Calderone, A., D. Latella, F. Impellizzeri, P. de Pasquale, F. Famà, A. Quartarone, and R. S. Calabrò. "Neurobiological Changes Induced by

Mindfulness and Meditation: A Systematic Review." *Biomedicines* 12, no. 11 (November 15, 2024): 2613. https://doi.org/10.3390/biomedicines12112613

10. Ismail, A. M. A., N. S. S. A. El Gressy, M. D. Hegazy, O. S. M. Ahmed, and A. M. A. Elfahl. "Effects of Diaphragmatic Breathing Exercise on Sleeping Quality, Cortisol, Cardiovascular Autonomic Functions, Depression, and Fatigue: A Randomized-Controlled Trial in Women with Systemic Sclerosis." *Reumatologia* 63, no. 2 (April 30, 2025): 89–96. https://doi.org/10.5114/reum/200193
11. Sharp, P. B., B. P. Sutton, E. J. Paul, et al. "Mindfulness Training Induces Structural Connectome Changes in Insula Networks." *Scientific Reports* 8 (2018): 7929. https://doi.org/10.1038/s41598-018-26268-w
12. Lehrer, P., K. Kaur, A. Sharma, K. Shah, R. Huseby, J. Bhavsar, P. Sgobba, and Y. Zhang. "Heart Rate Variability Biofeedback Improves Emotional and Physical Health and Performance: A Systematic Review and Meta-Analysis." *Applied Psychophysiology and Biofeedback* 45, no. 3 (September 2020): 109–29. https://doi.org/10.1007/s10484-020-09466-z
13. Peters, Achim, Bruce S. McEwen, and Karl Friston. "Uncertainty and Stress: Why It Causes Diseases and How It Is Mastered by the Brain." *Progress in Neurobiology* 156 (2017): 164–88. https://doi.org/10.1016/j.pneurobio.2017.05.004
14. Berntson, Gary G., Karen S. Quigley, and Daniel L. Lozano. "Cardiovascular Psychophysiology." In *Handbook of Psychophysiology*, 4th ed., edited by John T. Cacioppo, Louis G. Tassinary, and Gary G. Berntson, 182–210. Cambridge: Cambridge University Press, 2017.
15. Widmaier, Eric P., Hershel Raff, and Kevin T. Strang. *Vander's Human Physiology: The Mechanisms of Body Function.* 15th ed. New York: McGraw-Hill Education, 2018.
16. Joyner, M. J., and D. P. Casey. "Regulation of Increased Blood Flow (Hyperemia) to Muscles During Exercise: A Hierarchy of Competing Physiological Needs." *Physiological Reviews* 95, no. 2 (April 2015): 549–601. https://doi.org/10.1152/physrev.00035.2013
17. Berdina, N. A., O. L. Kolenko, I. M. Kotz, A. P. Kuznetzov, I. M. Rodionov, A. P. Savtchenko, and V. I. Thorevsky. "Increase in Skeletal Muscle Performance during Emotional Stress in Man." *Circulation Research* 30, no. 6 (June 1972): 642–50. https://www.ahajournals.org/doi/epdf/10.1161/01.RES.30.6.642
18. Chaudhary, Rishabh, Ajay Prasad, Vipul Agarwal, Mujeeba Rehman, Anand Kumar, Arjun Singh Kaushik, Siddhi Srivastava, Sukriti Srivastava, and Vikas Mishra. "Chronic Stress Predisposes to the Aggravation of Inflammation in Autoimmune Diseases with Focus on Rheumatoid Arthritis and Psoriasis." *International Immunopharmacology* 125, pt. A (2023): 111046. https://doi.org/10.1016/j.intimp.2023.111046

19. Knezevic, E., K. Nenic, V. Milanovic, and N. N. Knezevic. "The Role of Cortisol in Chronic Stress, Neurodegenerative Diseases, and Psychological Disorders." *Cells* 12, no. 23 (November 29, 2023): 2726. https://doi.org/10.3390/cells12232726
20. Kandel, E. R. "The Molecular Biology of Memory Storage: A Dialogue between Genes and Synapses." *Science* 294, no. 5544 (November 2, 2001): 1030–38. https://doi.org/10.1126/science.1067020
21. Ruiz, Don Miguel. *The Four Agreements: A Practical Guide to Personal Freedom.* San Rafael, CA: Amber-Allen Publishing, 1997.
22. Siegel, Daniel J. *Aware: The Science and Practice of Presence.* New York: TarcherPerigee, 2018.
23. Chang, W., and J. G. Gu. "Effects on Tactile Transmission by Serotonin Transporter Inhibitors at Merkel Discs of Mouse Whisker Hair Follicles." *Molecular Pain* 16 (2020): 1744806920938237. https://doi.org/10.1177/1744806920938237
24. Dreisoerner, A., N. M. Junker, W. Schlotz, J. Heimrich, S. Bloemeke, B. Ditzen, and R. van Dick. "Self-Soothing Touch and Being Hugged Reduce Cortisol Responses to Stress: A Randomized Controlled Trial on Stress, Physical Touch, and Social Identity." *Comprehensive Psychoneuroendocrinology* 8 (October 8, 2021): 100091. https://doi.org/10.1016/j.cpnec.2021.100091
25. Eckstein, M., I. Mamaev, B. Ditzen, and U. Sailer. "Calming Effects of Touch in Human, Animal, and Robotic Interaction: Scientific State-of-the-Art and Technical Advances." *Frontiers in Psychiatry* 11 (November 4, 2020): 555058. https://doi.org/10.3389/fpsyt.2020.555058
26. Nummenmaa, Lauri, Lauri Tuominen, Robin Dunbar, Jussi Hirvonen, Sandra Manninen, Eveliina Arponen, Anna Machin, Riitta Hari, Iiro P. Jääskeläinen, and Mikko Sams. "Social Touch Modulates Endogenous μ-Opioid System Activity in Humans." *NeuroImage* 138 (2016): 242–47. https://doi.org/10.1016/j.neuroimage.2016.05.063
27. Jones, M. R., C. J. Haggarty, G. N. Petrie, et al. "Endocannabinoid Contributions to the Perception of Socially Relevant, Affective Touch in Humans." *Neuropsychopharmacology* 50 (2025): 849–55. https://doi.org/10.1038/s41386-025-02053-y
28. Abraira, V. E., and D. D. Ginty. "The Sensory Neurons of Touch." *Neuron* 79, no. 4 (August 21, 2013): 618–39. https://doi.org/10.1016/j.neuron.2013.07.051
29. McGlone, F., J. Wessberg, and H. Olausson. "Discriminative and Affective Touch: Sensing and Feeling." *Neuron* 82, no. 4 (May 21, 2014): 737–55. https://doi.org/10.1016/j.neuron.2014.05.001

30. Craig, A. D. "How Do You Feel? Interoception: The Sense of the Physiological Condition of the Body." *Nature Reviews Neuroscience* 3, no. 8 (August 2002): 655–66. https://doi.org/10.1038/nrn894
31. Craig, A. D. "How Do You Feel—Now? The Anterior Insula and Human Awareness." *Nature Reviews Neuroscience* 10, no. 1 (January 2009): 59–70. https://doi.org/10.1038/nrn2555
32. Strigo, I. A., and A. D. Craig. "Interoception, Homeostatic Emotions and Sympathovagal Balance." *Philosophical Transactions of the Royal Society B: Biological Sciences* 371, no. 1708 (2016): 20160010. https://doi.org/10.1098/rstb.2016.0010
33. Radke, Sina, Inge Volman, Idil Kokal, Karin Roelofs, Ellen R. A. de Bruijn, and Ivan Toni. "Oxytocin Reduces Amygdala Responses during Threat Approach." *Psychoneuroendocrinology* 79 (2017): 160–66. https://doi.org/10.1016/j.psyneuen.2017.02.028
34. Carozza, S., and V. Leong. "The Role of Affectionate Caregiver Touch in Early Neurodevelopment and Parent-Infant Interactional Synchrony." *Frontiers in Neuroscience* 14 (January 5, 2021): 613378. https://doi.org/10.3389/fnins.2020.613378
35. La Rosa, V. L., A. Geraci, A. Iacono, and E. Commodari. "Affective Touch in Preterm Infant Development: Neurobiological Mechanisms and Implications for Child-Caregiver Attachment and Neonatal Care." *Children* 11, no. 11 (November 20, 2024): 1407. https://doi.org/10.3390/children11111407
36. Golaya, S. "Touch-Hunger: An Unexplored Consequence of the COVID-19 Pandemic." *Indian Journal of Psychological Medicine* 43, no. 4 (July 2021): 362–63. https://doi.org/10.1177/02537176211014469
37. Kumka, M., and J. Bonar. "Fascia: A Morphological Description and Classification System Based on a Literature Review." *Journal of the Canadian Chiropractic Association* 56, no. 3 (September 2012): 179–91. https://www.ncbi.nlm.nih.gov/pmc/articles/PMC3430451/
38. Avila Gonzalez, Carla Alessandra, Mark Driscoll, Robert Schleip, Scott Wearing, Eric Jacobson, Tom Findley, and Werner Klingler. "Frontiers in Fascia Research." *Journal of Bodywork and Movement Therapies* 22, no. 4 (2018): 873–80. https://doi.org/10.1016/j.jbmt.2018.09.077
39. Bai, Y., J. Wang, J. P. Wu, J. X. Dai, O. Sha, D. Tai Wai Yew, L. Yuan, and Q. N. Liang. "Review of Evidence Suggesting That the Fascia Network Could Be the Anatomical Basis for Acupoints and Meridians in the Human Body." *Evidence-Based Complementary and Alternative Medicine* 2011 (2011): 260510. https://doi.org/10.1155/2011/260510

40. Kodama, Y., S. Masuda, T. Ohmori, A. Kanamaru, M. Tanaka, T. Sakaguchi, and M. Nakagawa. "Response to Mechanical Properties and Physiological Challenges of Fascia: Diagnosis and Rehabilitative Therapeutic Intervention for Myofascial System Disorders." *Bioengineering* 10, no. 4 (April 14, 2023): 474. https://doi.org/10.3390/bioengineering10040474
41. van der Kolk, Bessel. *The Body Keeps the Score: Brain, Mind, and Body in the Healing of Trauma*. New York: Viking, 2014.
42. Tozzi, Paolo. "Does Fascia Hold Memories?" *Journal of Bodywork and Movement Therapies* 18, no. 2 (2014): 259–65. https://doi.org/10.1016/j.jbmt.2013.11.010
43. Maurer, N., H. Nissel, M. Egerbacher, E. Gornik, P. Schuller, and H. Traxler. "Anatomical Evidence of Acupuncture Meridians in the Human Extracellular Matrix: Results from a Macroscopic and Microscopic Interdisciplinary Multicentre Study on Human Corpses." *Evidence-Based Complementary and Alternative Medicine* 2019 (March 21, 2019): 6976892. https://doi.org/10.1155/2019/6976892
44. Mehta, Piyush, Vishwas Dhapte, Shivajirao Kadam, and Vividha Dhapte. "Contemporary Acupressure Therapy: Adroit Cure for Painless Recovery of Therapeutic Ailments." *Journal of Traditional and Complementary Medicine* 7, no. 2 (2017): 251–63. https://doi.org/10.1016/j.jtcme.2016.06.004
45. National Center for Complementary and Integrative Health. "Acupuncture: Effectiveness and Safety." Accessed March 20, 2026. https://www.nccih.nih.gov/health/acupuncture-effectiveness-and-safety
46. He, L., R. Zhou, S. Hou, D. Huang, X. Zhao, M. Wang, M. Huang, T. Yin, H. Yin, and S. Yu. "Exploration of Key Brain Regions Involved in Acupuncture and Moxibustion Analgesia: An Imaging-Based Study." *Journal of Pain Research* 18 (April 15, 2025): 2051–67. https://doi.org/10.2147/JPR.S505312
47. Corniani, G., and H. P. Saal. "Tactile Innervation Densities across the Whole Body." *Journal of Neurophysiology* 124, no. 4 (October 1, 2020): 1229–40. https://doi.org/10.1152/jn.00313.2020
48. Penfield, Wilder, and Edwin Boldrey. "Somatic Motor and Sensory Representation in the Cerebral Cortex of Man as Studied by Electrical Stimulation." *Brain* 60, no. 4 (1937): 389–443. https://doi.org/10.1093/brain/60.4.389
49. Catani, M. "A Little Man of Some Importance." *Brain* 140, no. 11 (November 1, 2017): 3055–61. https://doi.org/10.1093/brain/awx270
50. Embong, N. H., Y. C. Soh, L. C. Ming, and T. W. Wong. "Revisiting Reflexology: Concept, Evidence, Current Practice, and Practitioner Training." *Journal of Traditional and Complementary Medicine* 5, no. 4 (2015): 197–206. https://doi.org/10.1016/j.jtcme.2015.08.008

51. Benjamin, M. "The Fascia of the Limbs and Back: A Review." *Journal of Anatomy* 214, no. 1 (January 2009): 1–18. https://doi.org/10.1111/j.1469--7580.2008.01011.x

52. Nakano, H., T. Kodama, T. Ueda, I. Mori, T. Tani, and S. Murata. "Effect of Hand and Foot Massage Therapy on Psychological Factors and EEG Activity in Elderly People Requiring Long-Term Care: A Randomized Cross-Over Study." *Brain Sciences* 9, no. 3 (March 4, 2019): 54. https://doi.org/10.3390/brainsci9030054

53. Wu, F., Y. Zhao, and H. Zhang. "Ocular Autonomic Nervous System: An Update from Anatomy to Physiological Functions." *Vision* 6, no. 1 (January 14, 2022): 6. https://doi.org/10.3390/vision6010006

54. Ghibaudo, V., M. Turrel, J. Granget, et al. "Pleasant Odors Specifically Promote a Soothing Autonomic Response and Brain–Body Coupling through Respiratory Modulation." *Scientific Reports* 15 (2025): 36417. https://doi.org/10.1038/s41598-025-20422-x

55. Chee, Zhong Jian, Chern Yi Marybeth Chang, Jean Yi Cheong, Fatin Hannah Binte Abdul Malek, Shahad Hussain, Marieke de Vries, and Alessio Bellato. "The Effects of Music and Auditory Stimulation on Autonomic Arousal, Cognition and Attention: A Systematic Review." *International Journal of Psychophysiology* 199 (2024): 112328. https://doi.org/10.1016/j.ijpsycho.2024.112328

56. Veldhuizen, Maria G., Danielle Douglas, Katja Aschenbrenner, Darren R. Gitelman, and Dana M. Small. "The Anterior Insular Cortex Represents Breaches of Taste Identity Expectation." *Journal of Neuroscience* 31, no. 41 (2011): 14735–44. https://doi.org/10.1523/JNEUROSCI.1502-11.2011

57. Cicero, N. G., M. Klimova, L. D. Lewis, and S. Ling. "Differential Cortical and Subcortical Visual Processing with Eyes Shut." *bioRxiv* (preprint, September 13, 2023). https://doi.org/10.1101/2023.09.11.557197

58. Dijkstra, N., and S. M. Fleming. "Subjective Signal Strength Distinguishes Reality from Imagination." *Nature Communications* 14, no. 1 (March 23, 2023): 1627. https://doi.org/10.1038/s41467-023-37322-1

59. Narby, Jeremy. *The Cosmic Serpent: DNA and the Origins of Knowledge.* New York: Tarcher/Putnam, 1998.

60. Rabin, David M., host. "The DNA of Consciousness: Visionary Plants, Indigenous Knowledge, and the Mind." *Your Brain Explained.* Podcast audio, Apple Podcasts. Published June 21, 2025. https://podcasts.apple.com/us/podcast/your-brain-explained/id1693658383?i=1000736779713

61. Narby, Jeremy. *Intelligence in Nature: An Inquiry into Knowledge.* New York: TarcherPerigee, 2005.

62. Brabec, Bernd. "'The Inkas' Song Emanates from My Tongue:' Learning and Performing Shipibo Curing Songs." In *La música y los pueblos indígenas*, edited by Juan Pablo Muñoz, 73–107. Montevideo: Centro de Documentación Musical, 2018.
63. Brabec de Mori, Bernd. "Sound—Trance—Healing: The Sound and Pattern Medicine of the Shipibo in the Amazon Lowlands of Peru." Research paper, University of Music and Performing Arts Graz, 2013.
64. Hume, Lynne. *Ancestral Power: The Dreaming, Consciousness and Aboriginal Australians*. Carlton South, VIC: Melbourne University Press, 2002.
65. Schneider, Tsim D. *The Archaeology of Refuse and Recourse: Coast Miwok Resilience and Indigenous Hinterlands in Northern California*. Tucson: University of Arizona Press, 2021.
66. Watson, J., and F. Crick. "Molecular Structure of Nucleic Acids: A Structure for Deoxyribose Nucleic Acid." *Nature* 171 (1953): 737–38. https://doi.org/10.1038/171737a0
67. Crick, Francis. *The Astonishing Hypothesis: The Scientific Search for the Soul*. New York: Scribner, 1994.
68. Taylor, M. J., N. Freemantle, J. R. Geddes, and Z. Bhagwagar. "Early Onset of Selective Serotonin Reuptake Inhibitor Antidepressant Action: Systematic Review and Meta-Analysis." *Archives of General Psychiatry* 63, no. 11 (November 2006): 1217–23. https://doi.org/10.1001/archpsyc.63.11.1217
69. Padala, P. R., K. P. Padala, A. S. Majagi, K. K. Garner, R. A. Dennis, and D. H. Sullivan. "Selective Serotonin Reuptake Inhibitors-Associated Apathy Syndrome: A Cross-Sectional Study." *Medicine* 99, no. 33 (August 14, 2020): e21497. https://doi.org/10.1097/MD.0000000000021497
70. Higgins, A., M. Nash, and A. M. Lynch. "Antidepressant-Associated Sexual Dysfunction: Impact, Effects, and Treatment." *Drug, Healthcare and Patient Safety* 2 (2010): 141–50. https://doi.org/10.2147/DHPS.S7634
71. Yamauchi, Miki, Takako Miyara, Tetsuya Matsushima, and Taiichiro Imanishi. "Desensitization of 5-HT2A Receptor Function by Chronic Administration of Selective Serotonin Reuptake Inhibitors." *Brain Research* 1067, no. 1 (2006): 164–69. https://doi.org/10.1016/j.brainres.2005.10.075
72. Rennwald, A., and M. P. Hengartner. "Post-Acute Withdrawal Syndrome (PAWS) after Stopping Antidepressants: A Systematic Review with Meta-Narrative Synthesis." *Epidemiology and Psychiatric Sciences* 34 (May 13, 2025): e29. https://doi.org/10.1017/S204579602500023X
73. Harvey, J. A. "Role of the Serotonin 5-HT(2A) Receptor in Learning." *Learning & Memory* 10, no. 5 (September–October 2003): 355–62. https://doi.org/10.1101/lm.60803

74. Preller, K. H., M. Herdener, T. Pokorny, A. Planzer, R. Kraehenmann, P. Stämpfli, M. E. Liechti, E. Seifritz, and F. X. Vollenweider. "The Fabric of Meaning and Subjective Effects in LSD-Induced States Depend on Serotonin 2A Receptor Activation." *Current Biology* 27, no. 3 (February 6, 2017): 451–57. https://doi.org/10.1016/j.cub.2016.12.030
75. Griffiths, R., W. Richards, M. Johnson, U. McCann, and R. Jesse. "Mystical-Type Experiences Occasioned by Psilocybin Mediate the Attribution of Personal Meaning and Spiritual Significance 14 Months Later." *Journal of Psychopharmacology* 22, no. 6 (August 2008): 621–32. https://doi.org/10.1177/0269881108094300
76. Kajonius, P. J., D. Sjöström, and E. Claesdotter-Knutsson. "Unveiling Psychedelics: One of the Most Meaningful Events in Life Associated with Improved Well-Being in Swedish Users." *Journal of Psychoactive Drugs* (2025): 1–7. https://doi.org/10.1080/02791072.2024.2444892
77. Wacker, D., S. Wang, J. D. McCorvy, R. M. Betz, A. J. Venkatakrishnan, A. Levit, K. Lansu, Z. L. Schools, T. Che, D. E. Nichols, B. K. Shoichet, R. O. Dror, and B. L. Roth. "Crystal Structure of an LSD-Bound Human Serotonin Receptor." *Cell* 168, no. 3 (January 26, 2017): 377–389.e12. https://doi.org/10.1016/j.cell.2016.12.033
78. Madsen, Martin Korsbak, Patrick MacDonald Fisher, Dea Siggaard Stenbæk, Sara Kristiansen, Daniel Burmester, Szabolcs Lehel, Tomas Páleníček, Martin Kuchař, Claus Svarer, Brice Ozenne, and Gitte M. Knudsen. "A Single Psilocybin Dose Is Associated with Long-Term Increased Mindfulness, Preceded by a Proportional Change in Neocortical 5-HT2A Receptor Binding." *European Neuropsychopharmacology* 33 (2020): 71–80. https://doi.org/10.1016/j.euroneuro.2020.02.001
79. Northoff, G., and D. J. Hayes. "Is Our Self Nothing but Reward?" *Biological Psychiatry* 69, no. 11 (June 1, 2011): 1019–25. https://doi.org/10.1016/j.biopsych.2010.12.014
80. Quednow, B. B., M. Kometer, M. A. Geyer, and F. X. Vollenweider. "Psilocybin-Induced Deficits in Automatic and Controlled Inhibition Are Attenuated by Ketanserin in Healthy Human Volunteers." *Neuropsychopharmacology* 37, no. 3 (February 2012): 630–40. https://doi.org/10.1038/npp.2011.228
81. Jenuwein, T., and C. D. Allis. "Translating the Histone Code." *Science* 293, no. 5532 (August 10, 2001): 1074–80. https://doi.org/10.1126/science.1063127
82. Yehuda, R. "Status of Glucocorticoid Alterations in Post-Traumatic Stress Disorder." *Annals of the New York Academy of Sciences* 1179 (October 2009): 56–69. https://doi.org/10.1111/j.1749-6632.2009.04979.x

83. Weaver, I. C. G., N. Cervoni, F. A. Champagne, et al. "Epigenetic Programming by Maternal Behavior." *Nature Neuroscience* 7 (2004): 847–54. https://doi.org/10.1038/nn1276
84. Klosin, Adam, et al. "Transgenerational Transmission of Environmental Information in *C. elegans*." *Science* 356 (2017): 320–23. https://doi.org/10.1126/science.aah6412
85. Yehuda, R., J. D. Flory, L. M. Bierer, C. Henn-Haase, A. Lehrner, F. Desarnaud, I. Makotkine, N. P. Daskalakis, C. R. Marmar, and M. J. Meaney. "Lower Methylation of Glucocorticoid Receptor Gene Promoter 1F in Peripheral Blood of Veterans with Posttraumatic Stress Disorder." *Biological Psychiatry* 77, no. 4 (February 15, 2015): 356–64. https://doi.org/10.1016/j.biopsych.2014.02.006
86. Yehuda, R., N. P. Daskalakis, L. M. Bierer, H. N. Bader, T. Klengel, F. Holsboer, and E. B. Binder. "Holocaust Exposure Induced Intergenerational Effects on FKBP5 Methylation." *Biological Psychiatry* 80, no. 5 (September 1, 2016): 372–80. https://doi.org/10.1016/j.biopsych.2015.08.005
87. Švorcová, J. "Transgenerational Epigenetic Inheritance of Traumatic Experience in Mammals." *Genes* 14, no. 1 (January 1, 2023): 120. https://doi.org/10.3390/genes14010120
88. Collinge, J., K. C. Sidle, J. Meads, J. Ironside, and A. F. Hill. "Molecular Analysis of Prion Strain Variation and the Aetiology of 'New Variant' CJD." *Nature* 383 (October 24, 1996): 685–90. https://doi.org/10.1038/383685a0
89. Prusiner, S. B. "Prions Are Novel Infectious Pathogens Causing Scrapie and Creutzfeldt–Jakob Disease." *BioEssays* 5 (1986): 281–86. https://doi.org/10.1002/bies.950050612
90. Lang, C. J. G., J. G. Heckmann, and B. Neundörfer. "Creutzfeldt–Jakob Disease via Dural and Corneal Transplants." *Journal of the Neurological Sciences* 160, no. 2 (1998): 128–39. https://doi.org/10.1016/S0022-510X(98)00226-3
91. Giles, K., A. L. Woerman, D. B. Berry, and S. B. Prusiner. "Bioassays and Inactivation of Prions." *Cold Spring Harbor Perspectives in Biology* 9, no. 8 (August 1, 2017): a023499. https://doi.org/10.1101/cshperspect.a023499
92. Prusiner, S. B. "Prions." *Proceedings of the National Academy of Sciences of the United States of America* 95, no. 23 (November 10, 1998): 13363–83. https://doi.org/10.1073/pnas.95.23.13363
93. Moreno-Gonzalez, I., and C. Soto. "Misfolded Protein Aggregates: Mechanisms, Structures and Potential for Disease Transmission." *Seminars in Cell & Developmental Biology* 22, no. 5 (July 2011): 482–87. https://doi.org/10.1016/j.semcdb.2011.04.002

94. Baez, S., F. Manes, D. Huepe, T. Torralva, N. Fiorentino, F. Richter, D. Huepe-Artigas, J. Ferrari, P. Montañes, P. Reyes, D. Matallana, N. S. Vigliecca, J. Decety, and A. Ibanez. "Primary Empathy Deficits in Frontotemporal Dementia." *Frontiers in Aging Neuroscience* 6 (October 10, 2014): 262. https://doi.org/10.3389/fnagi.2014.00262
95. Kim, E. J., M. Sidhu, S. E. Gaus, E. J. Huang, P. R. Hof, B. L. Miller, S. J. DeArmond, and W. W. Seeley. "Selective Frontoinsular von Economo Neuron and Fork Cell Loss in Early Behavioral Variant Frontotemporal Dementia." *Cerebral Cortex* 22, no. 2 (February 2012): 251–59. https://doi.org/10.1093/cercor/bhr004
96. Dijkstra, A. A., L. C. Lin, A. L. Nana, S. E. Gaus, and W. W. Seeley. "Von Economo Neurons and Fork Cells: A Neurochemical Signature Linked to Monoaminergic Function." *Cerebral Cortex* 28, no. 1 (January 1, 2018): 131–44. https://doi.org/10.1093/cercor/bhw358
97. Cauda, F., G. C. Geminiani, and A. Vercelli. "Evolutionary Appearance of von Economo's Neurons in the Mammalian Cerebral Cortex." *Frontiers in Human Neuroscience* 8 (March 14, 2014): 104. https://doi.org/10.3389/fnhum.2014.00104
98. Temple, S. "Division and Differentiation of Isolated CNS Blast Cells in Microculture." *Nature* 340 (1989): 471–73. https://doi.org/10.1038/340471a0
99. Sparrow, J. R., D. Hicks, and C. P. Hamel. "The Retinal Pigment Epithelium in Health and Disease." *Current Molecular Medicine* 10, no. 9 (2010): 802–823. https://doi.org/10.2174/156652410793937813
100. Leone, M., A. Magadum, and F. B. Engel. "Cardiomyocyte Proliferation in Cardiac Development and Regeneration: A Guide to Methodologies and Interpretations." *American Journal of Physiology—Heart and Circulatory Physiology* 309, no. 8 (2015): H1237–H1250. https://doi.org/10.1152/ajpheart.00559.2015
101. Zhang, S., J. Ren, R. Chai, S. Yuan, and Y. Hao. "Global Burden of Low Vision and Blindness Due to Age-Related Macular Degeneration from 1990 to 2021 and Projections for 2050." *BMC Public Health* 24, no. 1 (2024): 3510. https://doi.org/10.1186/s12889-024-21047-x
102. Liton, P. B., K. Boesze-Battaglia, M. E. Boulton, P. Boya, T. A. Ferguson, I. G. Ganley, A. Kauppinnen, G. W. Laurie, N. Mizushima, H. Morishita, R. Russo, J. Sadda, R. Shyam, D. Sinha, D. A. Thompson, and D. N. Zacks. "Autophagy in the Eye: From Physiology to Pathophysiology." *Autophagy Reports* 2, no. 1 (2023): 2178996. https://doi.org/10.1080/27694127.2023.2178996
103. Nieto-Torres, J. L., and M. Hansen. "Macroautophagy and Aging: The Impact of Cellular Recycling on Health and Longevity." *Molecular Aspects of Medicine* 82 (2021): 101020. https://doi.org/10.1016/j.mam.2021.101020

104. Di Scala, C., N. Yahi, S. Boutemeur, A. Flores, L. Rodriguez, H. Chahinian, and J. Fantini. "Common Molecular Mechanism of Amyloid Pore Formation by Alzheimer's ⊠-Amyloid Peptide and ⊠-Synuclein." *Scientific Reports* 6 (2016): 28781. https://doi.org/10.1038/srep28781
105. Brini, M., T. Calì, D. Ottolini, and E. Carafoli. "Neuronal Calcium Signaling: Function and Dysfunction." *Cellular and Molecular Life Sciences* 71, no. 15 (2014): 2787–2814. https://doi.org/10.1007/s00018-013-1550-7
106. Wang, Minghui, Hu Zhang, Jiling Liang, Jielun Huang, Tong Wu, and Ning Chen. "Calcium Signaling Hypothesis: A Non-Negligible Pathogenesis in Alzheimer's Disease." *Journal of Advanced Research* 77 (2025): 513–534. https://doi.org/10.1016/j.jare.2025.01.007
107. Garcia, Miguel A., W. James Nelson, and Natalie Chavez. "Cell–Cell Junctions Organize Structural and Signaling Networks." *Cold Spring Harbor Perspectives in Biology* 10, no. 4 (2018): a029181. https://doi.org/10.1101/cshperspect.a029181
108. Corbetta, M., and G. L. Shulman. "Control of Goal-Directed and Stimulus-Driven Attention in the Brain." *Nature Reviews Neuroscience* 3, no. 3 (2002): 201–215. https://doi.org/10.1038/nrn755
109. Gallwey, W. Timothy. *The Inner Game of Tennis.* New York: Random House, 1974.
110. Horvath, Jared Cooney. "Written Testimony on H.650." Vermont House Committee on Commerce and Economic Development, February 6, 2026. https://legislature.vermont.gov/Documents/2026/Workgroups/House%20Commerce/Bills/H.650/Witness%20Documents/H.650~Jared%20Cooney%20Horvath~Written%20Testimony~2-6-2026.pdf
111. Rilling, James K., David A. Gutman, Thorsten R. Zeh, Giuseppe Pagnoni, Gregory S. Berns, and Clinton D. Kilts. "A Neural Basis for Social Cooperation." *Neuron* 35, no. 2 (2002): 395–405. https://doi.org/10.1016/S0896-6273(02)00755-9
112. Lewis, Thomas, Fari Amini, and Richard Lannon. *A General Theory of Love.* New York: Random House, 2000.
113. Kirschner, Paul A., and Pedro De Bruyckere. "The Myths of the Digital Native and the Multitasker." Teaching and Teacher Education 67 (2017): 135–142. https://doi.org/10.1016/j.tate.2017.06.001
114. Qi, X. L., and C. Constantinidis. "Neural Changes after Training to Perform Cognitive Tasks." *Behavioural Brain Research* 241 (2013): 235–243. https://doi.org/10.1016/j.bbr.2012.12.017
115. Jamieson, J. P., M. K. Nock, and W. B. Mendes. "Mind over Matter: Reappraising Arousal Improves Cardiovascular and Cognitive Responses to

Stress." *Journal of Experimental Psychology: General* 141, no. 3 (2012): 417–422. https://doi.org/10.1037/a0025719

116. Muhtadie, L., K. Koslov, M. Akinola, and W. B. Mendes. "Vagal Flexibility: A Physiological Predictor of Social Sensitivity." *Journal of Personality and Social Psychology* 109, no. 1 (2015): 106–120. https://doi.org/10.1037/pspp0000016
117. Kloidt, J., and L. W. Barsalou. "Establishing a Comprehensive Hierarchical Construct of Eustress (CHE)." *Current Psychology* 43, no. 41 (2024): 32258–32273. https://doi.org/10.1007/s12144-024-06750-7
118. Kyriazis, M., L. Swas, and T. Orlova. "The Impact of Hormesis, Neuronal Stress Response, and Reproduction, upon Clinical Aging: A Narrative Review." *Journal of Clinical Medicine* 12, no. 16 (2023): 5433. https://doi.org/10.3390/jcm12165433
119. Bienertova-Vasku, J., P. Lenart, and M. Scheringer. "Eustress and Distress: Neither Good Nor Bad, but Rather the Same?" *BioEssays* 42 (2020): 1900238. https://doi.org/10.1002/bies.201900238
120. Hernández-Vicente, A., D. Hernando, A. Santos-Lozano, G. Rodríguez-Romo, G. Vicente-Rodríguez, E. Pueyo, R. Bailón, and N. Garatachea. "Heart Rate Variability and Exceptional Longevity." *Frontiers in Physiology* 11 (2020): 566399. https://doi.org/10.3389/fphys.2020.566399
121. Aliberti, S. M., F. De Caro, R. H. W. Funk, L. Schiavo, J. Gonnella, G. Boccia, and M. Capunzo. "Extreme Longevity: Analysis of the Direct or Indirect Influence of Environmental Factors on Old, Nonagenarians, and Centenarians in Cilento, Italy." *International Journal of Environmental Research and Public Health* 19, no. 3 (2022): 1589. https://doi.org/10.3390/ijerph19031589
122. Zulfiqar, U., D. A. Jurivich, W. Gao, and D. H. Singer. "Relation of High Heart Rate Variability to Healthy Longevity." *American Journal of Cardiology* 105, no. 8 (2010): 1181–1185. https://doi.org/10.1016/j.amjcard.2009.12.022
123. Tedeschi, R. G., B. A. Moore, and T. C. Greene. "Posttraumatic Growth as a Pathway to Wellness for Individuals and Organizations." *Behavioral Sciences* 15, no. 12 (2025): 1653. https://doi.org/10.3390/bs15121653
124. Rabin, David M. "Your Brain Explained." Podcast audio, episode, Published October 31, 2023. https://podcasts.apple.com/us/podcast/your-brain-explained/id1693658383?i=1000633190395
125. Tesla, Nikola. *Inventions, Researches, and Writings of Nikola Tesla.* Edited by Thomas Commerford Martin. New York: The Electrical Engineer, 1894.
126. Einstein, Albert. *The Collected Papers of Albert Einstein.* Princeton, NJ: Princeton University Press, 1987.
127. Ntoumanis, N., L. C. Healy, C. Sedikides, J. Duda, B. Stewart, A. Smith, and J. Bond. "When the Going Gets Tough: The 'Why' of Goal Striving Matters."

Journal of Personality 82, no. 3 (2014): 225–236. https://doi.org/10.1111/jopy.12047

128. Goats, Geoffrey C. "Appropriate Use of the Inverse Square Law." *Physiotherapy* 74, no. 1 (1988): 8. https://doi.org/10.1016/S0031-9406(10)63626-7
129. Pickles, James O. "Auditory Pathways: Anatomy and Physiology." Handbook of Clinical Neurology 129 (2015): 3–25. https://doi.org/10.1016/B978-0-444-62630-1.00001-9
130. Wallace, Wanda T. "Memory for Music: Effect of Melody on Recall of Text." Journal of Experimental Psychology: Learning, Memory, and Cognition 20, no. 6 (1994): 1471–1485. https://doi.org/10.1037/0278-7393.20.6.1471
131. Cohn-Sheehy, Benjamin I., Arielle Delarazan, Zachariah M. Reagh, et al. "The Hippocampus Constructs Narrative Memories Across Distant Events." Current Biology 31, no. 22 (2021): 4935–4945.e7. https://doi.org/10.1016/j.cub.2021.09.013
132. National Aeronautics and Space Administration (NASA). "Symphony of Stars: The Science of Stellar Sound Waves." Accessed April 22, 2026. https://science.nasa.gov/universe/exoplanets/symphony-of-stars-the-science-of-stellar-sound-waves/
133. Keeler, J. R., E. A. Roth, B. L. Neuser, J. M. Spitsbergen, D. J. Waters, and J.-M. Vianney. "The Neurochemistry and Social Flow of Singing: Bonding and Oxytocin." *Frontiers in Human Neuroscience* 9 (2015): 518. https://doi.org/10.3389/fnhum.2015.00518
134. Salimpoor, V., M. Benovoy, K. Larcher, A. Dagher, and R. J. Zatorre. "Anatomically Distinct Dopamine Release during Anticipation and Experience of Peak Emotion to Music." *Nature Neuroscience* 14 (2011): 257–262. https://doi.org/10.1038/nn.2726
135. Angkoontassaneeyarat, C., P. Detsurang, P. Vichiensanth, P. Chalermdamrichai, A. Wibulpolprasert, N. Athinartrattanapong, P. Phattharapornjaroen, N. Chiengchana, W. Kehasuwan, G. Huncharoen, K. Pothilert, P. Thipnangrong, S. Loungnarin, and C. Yuksen. "The Effect of Music Therapy on Treating Patients Pain and Anxiety in Emergency Department: A Randomized Controlled Trial." *International Journal of Emergency Medicine* 18, no. 1 (2025): 77. https://doi.org/10.1186/s12245-025-00878-4
136. Yue, W., X. Han, J. Luo, Z. Zeng, and M. Yang. "Effect of Music Therapy on Preterm Infants in Neonatal Intensive Care Unit: Systematic Review and Meta-Analysis of Randomized Controlled Trials." *Journal of Advanced Nursing* 77, no. 2 (2021): 635–652. https://doi.org/10.1111/jan.14630

137. Bennet, A., and D. Bennet. "The Human Knowledge System: Music and Brain Coherence." *VINE* 38, no. 3 (2008): 277–295. https://doi.org/10.1108/03055720810904817
138. Rabin, David, and Greg Siegle. "S87. Toward Emotion Prosthetics: Emotion Regulation Through Wearable Vibroacoustic Stimulation." *Biological Psychiatry* 83 (2018): S380–S381. https://doi.org/10.1016/j.biopsych.2018.02.979
139. Hallihan, Cameron, and Greg J. Siegle. "Effect of Vibroacoustic Stimulation on Athletes Recovering from Exercise." *European Journal of Applied Physiology* 122, no. 11 (November 2022): 2427–35. https://doi.org/10.1007/s00421-022-05026-x
140. Carbonaro, T. M., and M. B. Gatch. "Neuropharmacology of N,N-Dimethyltryptamine." *Brain Research Bulletin* 126, pt. 1 (2016): 74–88. https://doi.org/10.1016/j.brainresbull.2016.04.016
141. Gheban, B. A., I. A. Roşca, and M. Crişan. "The Morphological and Functional Characteristics of the Pineal Gland." *Medicine and Pharmacy Reports* 92, no. 3 (2019): 226–234. https://doi.org/10.15386/mpr-1235
142. Nichols, D. E. "N,N-Dimethyltryptamine and the Pineal Gland: Separating Fact from Myth." *Journal of Psychopharmacology* 32, no. 1 (2018): 30–36. https://doi.org/10.1177/0269881117736919
143. Timmermann, C., L. Roseman, S. Haridas, F. E. Rosas, L. Luan, H. Kettner, J. Martell, D. Erritzoe, E. Tagliazucchi, C. Pallavicini, M. Girn, A. Alamia, R. Leech, D. J. Nutt, and R. L. Carhart-Harris. "Human Brain Effects of DMT Assessed via EEG-fMRI." *Proceedings of the National Academy of Sciences of the United States of America* 120, no. 13 (2023): e2218949120. https://doi.org/10.1073/pnas.2218949120
144. Timmermann, C., H. Kettner, C. Letheby, F. E. Rosas, D. Erritzoe, R. Leech, D. J. Nutt, and R. L. Carhart-Harris. "Psychedelics Alter Metaphysical Beliefs." *Scientific Reports* 11 (2021): 22166. https://doi.org/10.1038/s41598-021-01209-2
145. Avakian, A. "Disintegration of Default Mode: Functional MRI Insights into N,N-Dimethyltryptamine (DMT), Consciousness, and Subcortical Connectivity." *Cureus* 17, no. 7 (2025): e88931. https://doi.org/10.7759/cureus.88931
146. Smith, R. L., H. Canton, R. J. Barrett, and E. Sanders-Bush. "Agonist Properties of N,N-Dimethyltryptamine at Serotonin 5-HT2A and 5-HT2C Receptors." *Pharmacology, Biochemistry and Behavior* 61, no. 3 (1998): 323–330. https://doi.org/10.1016/S0091-3057(98)00110-5
147. Strassman, R. J., and C. R. Qualls. "Dose-Response Study of N,N-Dimethyltryptamine in Humans. I. Neuroendocrine, Autonomic, and Cardiovascular Effects." *Archives of General Psychiatry* 51, no. 2 (1994): 85–97. https://doi.org/10.1001/archpsyc.1994.03950020009001

148. Strassman, R. J., C. R. Qualls, E. H. Uhlenhuth, and R. Kellner. "Dose-Response Study of N,N-Dimethyltryptamine in Humans. II. Subjective Effects and Preliminary Results of a New Rating Scale." *Archives of General Psychiatry* 51, no. 2 (1994): 98–108. https://doi.org/10.1001/archpsyc.1994.03950020022002
149. Strassman, R. J., C. R. Qualls, and L. M. Berg. "Differential Tolerance to Biological and Subjective Effects of Four Closely Spaced Doses of N,N-Dimethyltryptamine in Humans." *Biological Psychiatry* 39, no. 9 (1996): 784–795. https://doi.org/10.1016/0006-3223(95)00200-6
150. Strassman, Rick. *DMT: The Spirit Molecule: A Doctor's Revolutionary Research into the Biology of Near-Death and Mystical Experiences.* Rochester, VT: Park Street Press, 2001.
151. Mithoefer, M. C., M. T. Wagner, A. T. Mithoefer, L. Jerome, and R. Doblin. "The Safety and Efficacy of ±3,4-Methylenedioxymethamphetamine-Assisted Psychotherapy in Subjects with Chronic, Treatment-Resistant Posttraumatic Stress Disorder: The First Randomized Controlled Pilot Study." *Journal of Psychopharmacology* 25, no. 4 (2011): 439–452. https://doi.org/10.1177/0269881110378371
152. Oehen, P., R. Traber, V. Widmer, and U. Schnyder. "A Randomized, Controlled Pilot Study of MDMA (±3,4-Methylenedioxymethamphetamine)-Assisted Psychotherapy for Treatment of Resistant, Chronic Post-Traumatic Stress Disorder (PTSD)." *Journal of Psychopharmacology* 27, no. 1 (2013): 40–52. https://doi.org/10.1177/0269881112464827
153. Mithoefer, M. C., M. T. Wagner, A. T. Mithoefer, L. Jerome, and R. Doblin. "Durability of Improvement in Post-Traumatic Stress Disorder Symptoms and Absence of Harmful Effects or Drug Dependency after 3,4-Methylenedioxymethamphetamine-Assisted Psychotherapy: A Prospective Long-Term Follow-Up Study." *Journal of Psychopharmacology* 27, no. 1 (2013): 28–39. https://doi.org/10.1177/0269881112456611
154. Shulgin, Alexander, and Ann Shulgin. *TIHKAL: The Continuation.* Berkeley, CA: Transform Press, 1997.
155. Gasser, P., D. Holstein, Y. Michel, R. Doblin, B. Yazar-Klosinski, T. Passie, and R. Brenneisen. "Safety and Efficacy of Lysergic Acid Diethylamide-Assisted Psychotherapy for Anxiety Associated with Life-Threatening Diseases." *Journal of Nervous and Mental Disease* 202, no. 7 (2014): 513–520. https://doi.org/10.1097/NMD.0000000000000113
156. Grob, C. S., A. L. Danforth, G. S. Chopra, M. Hagerty, C. R. McKay, A. L. Halberstadt, and G. R. Greer. "Pilot Study of Psilocybin Treatment for Anxiety in Patients with Advanced-Stage Cancer." *Archives of General Psychiatry* 68, no. 1 (2011): 71–78. https://doi.org/10.1001/archgenpsychiatry.2010.116

157. Shulgin, Alexander, and Ann Shulgin. *PIHKAL: A Chemical Love Story.* Berkeley, CA: Transform Press, 1991.
158. Mithoefer, Michael C., Annie T. Mithoefer, and Rick Doblin. *MDMA-Assisted Psychotherapy Treatment Manual.* Version 7. Santa Cruz, CA: Multidisciplinary Association for Psychedelic Studies (MAPS), August 19, 2015. https://maps.org/research-archive/mdma/MDMA-Assisted-Psychotherapy-Treatment-Manual-Version7-19Aug15-FINAL.pdf
159. Mithoefer, M., A. Mithoefer, A. Feduccia, L. Jerome, M. Wagner, S. Wymer, A. Holland, S. Hamilton, B. Yazar-Klosinski, and R. Doblin. "3,4-Methylenedioxymethamphetamine (MDMA)-Assisted Psychotherapy for Post-Traumatic Stress Disorder in Military Veterans, Firefighters, and Police Officers: A Randomised, Double-Blind, Dose-Response, Phase 2 Clinical Trial." *The Lancet Psychiatry* 5 (2018): 486–497. https://doi.org/10.1016/S2215-0366(18)30135-4
160. Ot'alora G, M., J. Grigsby, B. Poulter, J. W. Van Derveer III, S. G. Giron, L. Jerome, A. A. Feduccia, S. Hamilton, B. Yazar-Klosinski, A. Emerson, M. C. Mithoefer, and R. Doblin. "3,4-Methylenedioxymethamphetamine-Assisted Psychotherapy for Treatment of Chronic Posttraumatic Stress Disorder: A Randomized Phase 2 Controlled Trial." *Journal of Psychopharmacology* 32, no. 12 (2018): 1295–1307. https://doi.org/10.1177/0269881118806297
161. Barone, W., J. Beck, M. Mitsunaga-Whitten, and P. Perl. "Perceived Benefits of MDMA-Assisted Psychotherapy beyond Symptom Reduction: Qualitative Follow-Up Study of a Clinical Trial for Individuals with Treatment-Resistant PTSD." *Journal of Psychoactive Drugs* 51, no. 2 (2019): 199–208. https://doi.org/10.1080/02791072.2019.1580805
162. Mitchell, J. M., G. Ot'alora M., B. van der Kolk, S. M. Mitchell, R. Bogenschutz, C. Lilienstein, A. M. Harrison, K. T. Kleiman, S. Mithoefer, M. C. Mithoefer, R. Doblin, and J. H. Walker. "MDMA-Assisted Therapy for Moderate to Severe PTSD: A Randomized, Placebo-Controlled Phase 3 Trial." *Nature Medicine* 29 (2023): 2473–2480. https://doi.org/10.1038/s41591-023-02565-4
163. Lewis, Gemma, Louise Marston, Larisa Duffy, Nick Freemantle, Simon Gilbody, Rachael Hunter, Tony Kendrick, David Kessler, Dee Mangin, Michael King, Paul Lanham, Michael Moore, Irwin Nazareth, Nicola Wiles, Faye Bacon, Molly Bird, Sally Brabyn, Alison Burns, Caroline S. Clarke, Anna Hunt, Jodi Pervin, and Glyn Lewis. "Maintenance or Discontinuation of Antidepressants in Primary Care." *New England Journal of Medicine* 385, no. 14 (2021): 1257–1267. https://doi.org/10.1056/NEJMoa2106356

164. Batelaan, N. M., R. C. Bosman, A. Muntingh, W. D. Scholten, K. M. Huijbregts, and A. J. L. M. van Balkom. "Risk of Relapse after Antidepressant Discontinuation in Anxiety Disorders, Obsessive-Compulsive Disorder, and Post-Traumatic Stress Disorder: Systematic Review and Meta-Analysis of Relapse Prevention Trials." *BMJ* 358 (2017): j3927. https://doi.org/10.1136/bmj.j3927
165. Gangadin, S. S., F. de Beer, B. Wijnen, M. Begemann, N. van Beveren, N. Boonstra, L. de Haan, M. Kikkert, S. Koops, J. van Os, W. Veling, S. Wiersma, HAMLETT-OPHELIA Consortium, and I. E. C. Sommer. "Risk of Relapse during Tapering of Antipsychotic Medication after a First Psychotic Episode: Association with D2 Receptor Affinity but Not with Tapering Speed." *World Psychiatry* 24, no. 2 (2025): 240–249. https://doi.org/10.1002/wps.21315
166. Hawkins, R. D., E. R. Kandel, and C. H. Bailey. "Molecular Mechanisms of Memory Storage in *Aplysia*." *Biological Bulletin* 210, no. 3 (2006): 174–191. https://doi.org/10.2307/4134556
167. VanElzakker, M. B., M. K. Dahlgren, F. C. Davis, S. Dubois, and L. M. Shin. "From Pavlov to PTSD: The Extinction of Conditioned Fear in Rodents, Humans, and Anxiety Disorders." *Neurobiology of Learning and Memory* 113 (2014): 3–18. https://doi.org/10.1016/j.nlm.2013.11.014
168. Barad, M., P. W. Gean, and B. Lutz. "The Role of the Amygdala in the Extinction of Conditioned Fear." *Biological Psychiatry* 60, no. 4 (2006): 322–328. https://doi.org/10.1016/j.biopsych.2006.05.029
169. Shi, Tianyao, Shufang Feng, Mingxiao Wei, and Wenxia Zhou. "Role of the Anterior Agranular Insular Cortex in the Modulation of Fear and Anxiety." *Brain Research Bulletin* 155 (2020): 174–183. https://doi.org/10.1016/j.brainresbull.2019.12.003
170. Carhart-Harris, R., K. Murphy, R. Leech, A. Erritzoe, T. Wall, D. J. Nutt, and S. J. Allen. "The Effects of Acutely Administered 3,4-Methylenedioxymethamphetamine on Spontaneous Brain Function in Healthy Volunteers Measured with Arterial Spin Labeling and Blood Oxygen Level–Dependent Resting State Functional Connectivity." *Biological Psychiatry* 78 (2015): 554–562. https://doi.org/10.1016/j.biopsych.2014.07.015
171. Gamma, A., A. Buck, T. Berthold, R. Liechti, M. Vollenweider, and F. X. Vollenweider. "3,4-Methylenedioxymethamphetamine (MDMA) Modulates Cortical and Limbic Brain Activity as Measured by [$H_2{}^{15}O$]-PET in Healthy Humans." *Neuropsychopharmacology* 23 (2000): 388–395. https://doi.org/10.1016/S0893-133X(00)00130-5

172. Feduccia, Allison A., and Michael C. Mithoefer. "MDMA-Assisted Psychotherapy for PTSD: Are Memory Reconsolidation and Fear Extinction Underlying Mechanisms?" *Progress in Neuro-Psychopharmacology and Biological Psychiatry* 84, pt. A (2018): 221–228. https://doi.org/10.1016/j.pnpbp.2018.03.003

173. Young, M., R. Andero, K. J. Ressler, and B. O. Rothbaum. "3,4-Methylenedioxymethamphetamine Facilitates Fear Extinction Learning." *Translational Psychiatry* 5 (2015): e634. https://doi.org/10.1038/tp.2015.138

174. Young, M. B., S. D. Norrholm, L. M. Khoury, K. J. Jovanovic, V. E. Rauch, and K. J. Ressler. "Inhibition of Serotonin Transporters Disrupts the Enhancement of Fear Memory Extinction by 3,4-Methylenedioxymethamphetamine (MDMA)." *Psychopharmacology* 234 (2017): 2883–2895. https://doi.org/10.1007/s00213-017-4684-8

175. Walpola, I., T. Nest, L. Roseman, M. Kaelen, R. Leech, D. J. Nutt, and R. L. Carhart-Harris. "Altered Insula Connectivity under MDMA." *Neuropsychopharmacology* 42 (2017): 2152–2162. https://doi.org/10.1038/npp.2017.35

176. Lewis, C. R., J. Tafur, S. Spencer, J. M. Green, C. Harrison, B. Kelmendi, D. M. Rabin, R. Yehuda, B. Yazar-Klosinski, and B. R. Cahn. "Pilot Study Suggests DNA Methylation of the Glucocorticoid Receptor Gene (NR3C1) Is Associated with MDMA-Assisted Therapy Treatment Response for Severe PTSD." *Frontiers in Psychiatry* 14 (2023): 959590. https://doi.org/10.3389/fpsyt.2023.959590

177. Hammaker, Krista, Haomin Hu, Maureen Laffoon, Leigh A. Freno, Robert Lafyatis, Yongseok Park, and Robyn T. Domsic. "Wearable in Systemic Sclerosis: A Pilot Study of the Apollo Wearable Demonstrates Improvement in Fatigue, Raynaud Phenomenon and Quality of Life in Patients with Systemic Sclerosis." *The Journal of Rheumatology* 52, no. 2 (February 1, 2025): 158–164. https://doi.org/10.3899/jrheum.2024-0551

178. McKennon, Sarah, Ruth Bindler, and Jennifer Miller. "Evaluating the Impact of Apollo Neuro™ Wearable on Wellbeing in Medical and Pharmacy Students: A Preliminary Prospective Randomized Controlled Study." *The American Journal of Medicine* 138 (2025): 1734–1741.e2. https://doi.org/10.1016/j.amjmed.2025.07.045

179. Apollo Neuroscience. "Apollo Psychedelic Harm Reduction Survey Study." Accessed April 22, 2026. https://apolloneuro.com/blogs/news/apollo-psychedelic-harm-reduction-survey-study

180. Cryan, J. F., and T. G. Dinan. "Mind-Altering Microorganisms: The Impact of the Gut Microbiota on Brain and Behaviour." *Nature Reviews Neuroscience* 13, no. 10 (2012): 701–712. https://doi.org/10.1038/nrn3346
181. Avram, M., L. Fortea, L. Wollner, J. J. R. Scheidegger, F. X. Vollenweider, and K. Preller. "Large-Scale Brain Connectivity Changes Following the Administration of Lysergic Acid Diethylamide, d-Amphetamine, and 3,4-Methylenedioxyamphetamine." *Molecular Psychiatry* 30 (2025): 1297–1307. https://doi.org/10.1038/s41380-024-02734-y
182. Carhart-Harris, Robin L., Robert Leech, David Erritzoe, Tim M. Williams, James M. Stone, John Evans, David J. Sharp, Amanda Feilding, Richard G. Wise, and David J. Nutt. "Functional Connectivity Measures After Psilocybin Inform a Novel Hypothesis of Early Psychosis." *Schizophrenia Bulletin* 39, no. 6 (2013): 1343–1351. https://doi.org/10.1093/schbul/sbs117
183. Nour, M. M., L. Evans, D. Nutt, and R. L. Carhart-Harris. "Ego-Dissolution and Psychedelics: Validation of the Ego-Dissolution Inventory (EDI)." *Frontiers in Human Neuroscience* 10 (2016): 269. https://doi.org/10.3389/fnhum.2016.00269
184. Ly, C., A. C. Greb, L. P. Cameron, J. M. Wong, E. V. Barragan, P. C. Wilson, K. F. Burbach, S. Soltanzadeh Zarandi, A. Sood, M. R. Paddy, W. C. Duim, M. Y. Dennis, A. K. McAllister, K. M. Ori-McKenney, J. A. Gray, and D. E. Olson. "Psychedelics Promote Structural and Functional Neural Plasticity." *Cell Reports* 23, no. 11 (2018): 3170–3182. https://doi.org/10.1016/j.celrep.2018.05.022
185. Calder, A. E., and G. Hasler. "Towards an Understanding of Psychedelic-Induced Neuroplasticity." *Neuropsychopharmacology* 48 (2023): 104–112. https://doi.org/10.1038/s41386-022-01389-z
186. Monroy, M., and D. Keltner. "Awe as a Pathway to Mental and Physical Health." *Perspectives on Psychological Science* 18, no. 2 (2023): 309–320. https://doi.org/10.1177/17456916221094856
187. Medori, R., P. Montagna, H. J. Tritschler, A. LeBlanc, P. Cortelli, P. Tinuper, E. Lugaresi, and P. Gambetti. "Fatal Familial Insomnia: A Second Kindred with Mutation of Prion Protein Gene at Codon 178." *Neurology* 42, no. 3, pt. 1 (1992): 669–670. https://doi.org/10.1212/wnl.42.3.669
188. Mason, G. M., S. Lokhandwala, T. Riggins, and R. M. C. Spencer. "Sleep and Human Cognitive Development." *Sleep Medicine Reviews* 57 (2021): 101472. https://doi.org/10.1016/j.smrv.2021.101472
189. Vandekerckhove, M., and Y. L. Wang. "Emotion, Emotion Regulation and Sleep: An Intimate Relationship." *AIMS Neuroscience* 5, no. 1 (2017): 1–17. https://doi.org/10.3934/Neuroscience.2018.1.1

190. Charest, J., and M. A. Grandner. "Sleep and Athletic Performance: Impacts on Physical Performance, Mental Performance, Injury Risk and Recovery, and Mental Health." *Sleep Medicine Clinics* 15, no. 1 (2020): 41–57. https://doi.org/10.1016/j.jsmc.2019.11.005

191. Liu, H., N. R. Barthélemy, V. Ovod, J. G. Bollinger, Y. He, S. L. Chahin, B. Androff, R. J. Bateman, and B. P. Lucey. "Acute Sleep Loss Decreases CSF-to-Blood Clearance of Alzheimer's Disease Biomarkers." *Alzheimer's & Dementia* 19, no. 7 (2023): 3055–3064. https://doi.org/10.1002/alz.12930

192. Jones, S. E., J. M. Lane, A. R. Wood, M. J. van Hees, J. Tyrrell, R. N. Beaumont, A. K. Jeffries, et al. "Genome-Wide Association Analyses of Chronotype in 697,828 Individuals Provides Insights into Circadian Rhythms." *Nature Communications* 10 (2019): 343. https://doi.org/10.1038/s41467-018-08259-7

193. Breus, Michael J. *The Power of When: Discover Your Chronotype—and the Best Time to Eat Lunch, Ask for a Raise, Have Sex, Write a Novel, Take Your Meds, and More.* New York: Little, Brown and Company, 2016.

194. Porges, Stephen W. "Polyvagal Theory: A Science of Safety." *Frontiers in Integrative Neuroscience* 16 (2022): 871227. https://doi.org/10.3389/fnint.2022.871227

195. Peper, Erik, I-Mei Lin, Richard Harvey, and Jacob Perez. "How Posture Affects Memory Recall and Mood." *Biofeedback* 45, no. 2 (2017): 36–41. https://doi.org/10.5298/1081-5937-45.2.01

196. Carney, D. R., A. J. Cuddy, and A. J. Yap. "Power Posing: Brief Nonverbal Displays Affect Neuroendocrine Levels and Risk Tolerance." *Psychological Science* 21, no. 10 (2010): 1363–1368. https://doi.org/10.1177/0956797610383437

197. Nair, S., M. Sagar, J. Sollers III, N. Consedine, and E. Broadbent. "Do Slumped and Upright Postures Affect Stress Responses? A Randomized Trial." *Health Psychology* 34, no. 6 (2015): 632–641. https://doi.org/10.1037/hea0000146

198. Strack, F., L. L. Martin, and S. Stepper. "Inhibiting and Facilitating Conditions of the Human Smile: A Nonobtrusive Test of the Facial Feedback Hypothesis." *Journal of Personality and Social Psychology* 54, no. 5 (1988): 768–777. https://doi.org/10.1037//0022-3514.54.5.768

199. Koncz, A., D. Egri, M. Yildirim, A. Lobko, E. Máté, J. W. McVige, and K. Schwartz. "Postural Responses in Trauma-Experienced Individuals." *Biomedicines* 12, no. 12 (2024): 2766. https://doi.org/10.3390/biomedicines12122766

200. Sapolsky, Robert M. *Why Zebras Don't Get Ulcers: The Acclaimed Guide to Stress, Stress-Related Diseases, and Coping.* New York: W. H. Freeman and Company, 1994.

201. Renninger, Lee Ann, T. Joel Wade, and Karl Grammer. "Getting That Female Glance: Patterns and Consequences of Male Nonverbal Behavior in Courtship Contexts." *Evolution and Human Behavior* 25, no. 6 (2004): 416–431. https://doi.org/10.1016/j.evolhumbehav.2004.08.006

202. Peper, Erik, Annette Booiman, I-Mei Lin, and Richard Harvey. "Increase Strength and Mood with Posture." *Beweegreden* 12 (2016): 14–17. https://doi.org/10.5298/1081-5937-44.2.04

203. Kandel, E. R., and J. H. Schwartz. "Molecular Biology of Learning: Modulation of Transmitter Release." *Science* 218, no. 4571 (1982): 433–443. https://doi.org/10.1126/science.6289442

204. Kandel, Eric R. *In Search of Memory: The Emergence of a New Science of Mind.* New York: W. W. Norton & Company, 2006.

205. Day, E. "Motivational Interviewing: A Guide for Medical Trainees." *BJPsych Bulletin* 41, no. 1 (2017): 62. https://doi.org/10.1192/pb.bp.115.052647

206. Polat, N. "The Body Talks: The Compassionate Inquiry Approach to Childhood Trauma." *Journal of Awareness* 10 (Özel Sayı) (2025): 61–69. https://doi.org/10.26809/joa.2891

207. Engen, H. G., and T. Singer. "Compassion-Based Emotion Regulation Up-Regulates Experienced Positive Affect and Associated Neural Networks." *Social Cognitive and Affective Neuroscience* 10, no. 9 (2015): 1291–1301. https://doi.org/10.1093/scan/nsv008

208. Diniz, G., L. Korkes, L. S. Tristão, R. Pelegrini, P. L. Bellodi, and W. M. Bernardo. "The Effects of Gratitude Interventions: A Systematic Review and Meta-Analysis." *Einstein (São Paulo)* 21 (2023): eRW0371. https://doi.org/10.31744/einstein_journal/2023RW0371

209. Mobbs, Dean, Michael D. Greicius, Eiman Abdel-Azim, Vinod Menon, and Allan L. Reiss. "Humor Modulates the Mesolimbic Reward Centers." *Neuron* 40, no. 5 (2003): 1041–1048. https://doi.org/10.1016/S0896-6273(03)00751-7

210. Stanford Lifestyle Medicine. "Laughter and Its Health Benefits." Accessed April 22, 2026. https://lifestylemedicine.stanford.edu/laughter-health-benefits/

211. Freud, Sigmund. *Jokes and Their Relation to the Unconscious.* Translated by James Strachey. Vol. 8 of *The Standard Edition of the Complete Psychological Works of Sigmund Freud.* London: Hogarth Press and the Institute of Psycho-Analysis, 1960.

212. Jung, C. G. *The Red Book: Liber Novus.* Edited by Sonu Shamdasani. Translated by Mark Kyburz, John Peck, and Sonu Shamdasani. New York: W. W. Norton & Company, 2009.

213. Sinclair, S. "Impact of Death and Dying on the Personal Lives and Practices of Palliative and Hospice Care Professionals." *Canadian Medical Association Journal* 183, no. 2 (2011): 180–187. https://doi.org/10.1503/cmaj.100511

214. Dursun, P., P. Alyagut, and I. Yılmaz. "Meaning in Life, Psychological Hardiness and Death Anxiety: Individuals with or without Generalized Anxiety Disorder (GAD)." *Current Psychology* 41, no. 6 (2022): 3299–3317. https://doi.org/10.1007/s12144-021-02695-3
215. Solomon, S., and S. Gupta. "The Denial of Death: A Three-Decade Long Case of Absent Grief." *Indian Journal of Psychological Medicine* 36, no. 1 (2014): 82–84. https://doi.org/10.4103/0253-7176.127261
216. Lazar, S. W., C. E. Kerr, R. H. Wasserman, J. R. Gray, D. N. Greve, M. T. Treadway, M. McGarvey, B. T. Quinn, J. A. Dusek, H. Benson, S. L. Rauch, C. I. Moore, and B. Fischl. "Meditation Experience Is Associated with Increased Cortical Thickness." *NeuroReport* 16, no. 17 (2005): 1893–1897. https://doi.org/10.1097/01.wnr.0000186598.66243.19
217. Lutz, A., L. L. Greischar, N. B. Rawlings, M. Ricard, and R. J. Davidson. "Long-Term Meditators Self-Induce High-Amplitude Gamma Synchrony during Mental Practice." *Proceedings of the National Academy of Sciences of the United States of America* 101, no. 46 (2004): 16369–16373. https://doi.org/10.1073/pnas.0407401101
218. Alda, M., M. Puebla-Guedea, B. Rodero, M. Demarzo, J. Montero-Marin, M. Roca, and J. Garcia-Campayo. "Zen Meditation, Length of Telomeres, and the Role of Experiential Avoidance and Compassion." *Mindfulness* 7 (2016): 651–659. https://doi.org/10.1007/s12671-016-0500-5
219. Sezer, Idil, and Matthew D. Sacchet. "Advanced and Long-Term Meditation and the Autonomic Nervous System: A Review and Synthesis." *Neuroscience & Biobehavioral Reviews* 173 (2025): 106141. https://doi.org/10.1016/j.neubiorev.2025.106141
220. Ungvari, Z., V. Fazekas-Pongor, A. Csiszar, and S. K. Kunutsor. "The Multifaceted Benefits of Walking for Healthy Aging: From Blue Zones to Molecular Mechanisms." *GeroScience* 45, no. 6 (2023): 3211–3239. https://doi.org/10.1007/s11357-023-00873-8
221. Holt-Lunstad, J., T. B. Smith, and J. B. Layton. "Social Relationships and Mortality Risk: A Meta-Analytic Review." *PLoS Medicine* 7, no. 7 (2010): e1000316. https://doi.org/10.1371/journal.pmed.1000316
222. Davis, W. S., P. Anderson, and S. Banerjee. "Cardiovascular Disease and All-Cause Mortality Among Individuals with Low Sexual Frequency." *Healthcare* 13, no. 5 (2025): 461. https://doi.org/10.3390/healthcare13050461
223. Curtis, Luke. "Sex Saves Lives." *European Journal of Preventive Cardiology* 29, no. 1 (2022): e38. https://doi.org/10.1093/eurjpc/zwaa102

224. Sakurada, Koji, Takamasa Konta, Noriko Murakami, Naoki Kosugi, Takashi Saito, Masafumi Watanabe, Kazuhiro Ishizawa, Yasuhiro Ueno, and Takashi Kayama. "Association between Lack of Sexual Interest and All-Cause Mortality in a Japanese General Population: The Yamagata Prospective Observational Study." *PLOS ONE* 17, no. 12 (2022): e0277967. https://doi.org/10.1371/journal.pone.0277967
225. Dominguez, L. J., N. Veronese, and M. Barbagallo. "The Link between Spirituality and Longevity." *Aging Clinical and Experimental Research* 36, no. 1 (2024): 32. https://doi.org/10.1007/s40520-023-02684-5
226. Seshadri, K. G. "The Neuroendocrinology of Love." *Indian Journal of Endocrinology and Metabolism* 20, no. 4 (2016): 558–563. https://doi.org/10.4103/2230-8210.183479
227. Babková, J., and G. Repiská. "The Molecular Basis of Love." *International Journal of Molecular Sciences* 26, no. 4 (2025): 1533. https://doi.org/10.3390/ijms26041533
228. Tamam, S., and A. H. Ahmad. "Love as a Modulator of Pain." *Malaysian Journal of Medical Sciences* 24, no. 3 (2017): 5–14. https://pmc.ncbi.nlm.nih.gov/articles/PMC5545613/
229. Younger, J., A. Aron, S. Parke, N. Chatterjee, and S. Mackey. "Viewing Pictures of a Romantic Partner Reduces Experimental Pain: Involvement of Neural Reward Systems." *PLOS ONE* 5, no. 10 (2010): e13309. https://doi.org/10.1371/journal.pone.0013309
230. Kross, E., M. G. Berman, W. Mischel, E. E. Smith, and T. D. Wager. "Social Rejection Shares Somatosensory Representations with Physical Pain." *Proceedings of the National Academy of Sciences of the United States of America* 108, no. 15 (2011): 6270–6275. https://doi.org/10.1073/pnas.1102693108
231. Jacobs, K. W., and F. M. Nordan. "Classification of Placebo Drugs: Effect of Color." *Perceptual and Motor Skills* 49, no. 2 (1979): 367–372. https://doi.org/10.2466/pms.1979.49.2.367
232. Meissner, Karin, and Klaus Linde. "Are Blue Pills Better Than Green? How Treatment Features Modulate Placebo Effects." In *International Review of Neurobiology*, vol. 139, edited by Luana Colloca, 357–378. Academic Press, 2018. https://doi.org/10.1016/bs.irn.2018.07.014
233. Vase, Lene, and Karolina Wartolowska. "Pain, Placebo, and Test of Treatment Efficacy: A Narrative Review." *British Journal of Anaesthesia* 123, no. 2 (2019): e254–e262. https://doi.org/10.1016/j.bja.2019.01.040
234. Colloca, L., and F. G. Miller. "The Nocebo Effect and Its Relevance for Clinical Practice." *Psychosomatic Medicine* 73, no. 7 (2011): 598–603. https://doi.org/10.1097/PSY.0b013e3182294a50

235. Finisguerra, Alessandra, Cristiano Crescentini, and Cosimo Urgesi. "Transcutaneous Vagus Nerve Stimulation Affects Implicit Spiritual Self-Representations." *Neuroscience* 412 (2019): 144–159. https://doi.org/10.1016/j.neuroscience.2019.05.059
236. McNamara, P., and J. Grafman. "Advances in Brain and Religion Studies: A Review and Synthesis of Recent Representative Studies." *Frontiers in Human Neuroscience* 18 (2024): 1495565. https://doi.org/10.3389/fnhum.2024.1495565
237. van Elk, Michiel, and André Aleman. "Brain Mechanisms in Religion and Spirituality: An Integrative Predictive Processing Framework." *Neuroscience & Biobehavioral Reviews* 73 (2017): 359–378. https://doi.org/10.1016/j.neubiorev.2016.12.031
238. Norenzayan, Ara, Azim F. Shariff, Will M. Gervais, Aiyana K. Willard, Rita A. McNamara, Edward Slingerland, and Joseph Henrich. "The Cultural Evolution of Prosocial Religions." *Behavioral and Brain Sciences* 39 (2016): e1. https://doi.org/10.1017/s0140525x14001356
239. Kashdan, Todd B., and Jonathan Rottenberg. "Psychological Flexibility as a Fundamental Aspect of Health." *Clinical Psychology Review* 30, no. 7 (2010): 865–878. https://doi.org/10.1016/j.cpr.2010.03.001
240. Volkow, Nora D., Roy A. Wise, and Ruben Baler. "The Dopamine Motive System: Implications for Drug and Food Addiction." *Nature Reviews Neuroscience* 18, no. 12 (2017): 741–752. https://doi.org/10.1038/nrn.2017.130
241. Lieberman, Matthew D., Naomi I. Eisenberger, Molly J. Crockett, Sandra M. Tom, Jennifer H. Pfeifer, and Baldwin M. Way. "Putting Feelings into Words: Affect Labeling Disrupts Amygdala Activity in Response to Affective Stimuli." *Psychological Science* 18, no. 5 (2007): 421–428. https://doi.org/10.1111/j.1467--9280.2007.01916.x
242. McEwen, Bruce S. "The Brain on Stress: Toward an Integrative Approach to Brain, Body, and Behavior." *Perspectives on Psychological Science* 8, no. 6 (2013): 673–675. https://doi.org/10.1177/1745691613506907
243. Bowlby, John. *A Secure Base: Parent-Child Attachment and Healthy Human Development*. New York: Basic Books, 1988.
244. Laricchiuta, Daniela, Anna Panuccio, Eleonora Picerni, Daniele Biondo, Benedetto Genovesi, and Laura Petrosini. "The Body Keeps the Score: The Neurobiological Profile of Traumatized Adolescents." *Neuroscience & Biobehavioral Reviews* 145 (2023): 105033. https://doi.org/10.1016/j.neubiorev.2023.105033
245. Eisenberger, Naomi I. "Broken Hearts and Broken Bones: A Neural Perspective on the Similarities Between Social and Physical Pain." *Current Directions in Psychological Science* 21, no. 1 (2012): 42–47. https://doi.org/10.1177/0963721411429455

246. Fehr, Ernst, and Simon Gächter. "Altruistic Punishment in Humans." *Nature* 415, no. 6868 (2002): 137–140. https://doi.org/10.1038/415137a

247. Sprigings, Sarah, Cameron J. V. Brown, and Leanne ten Brinke. "Deception Is Associated with Reduced Social Connection." *Communications Psychology* 1, no. 1 (2023): 19. https://doi.org/10.1038/s44271-023-00021-0

248. Fliessbach, Klaus, Bernd Weber, Peter Trautner, Thomas Dohmen, Ulrich Sunde, Christian E. Elger, and Armin Falk. "Social Comparison Affects Reward-Related Brain Activity in the Human Ventral Striatum." *Science* 318, no. 5854 (2007): 1305–1308. https://doi.org/10.1126/science.1145876

249. Shapiro, Shauna L., Linda E. Carlson, and Amishi P. Sawyer. *The Art and Science of Mindfulness*. 3rd ed. Washington, DC: American Psychological Association, 2025.

250. Institute of Medicine. *Dietary Reference Intakes for Water, Potassium, Sodium, Chloride, and Sulfate*. Washington, DC: The National Academies Press, 2005. https://doi.org/10.17226/10925

251. Popkin, Barry M., Kristen E. D'Anci, and Irwin H. Rosenberg. "Water, Hydration, and Health." *Nutrition Reviews* 68, no. 8 (2010): 439–458. https://doi.org/10.1111/j.1753-4887.2010.00304.x

252. Corballis, Michael C. "Left Brain, Right Brain: Facts and Fantasies." *PLoS Biology* 12, no. 1 (2014): e1001767. https://doi.org/10.1371/journal.pbio.1001767

253. McGilchrist, Iain. "Reciprocal Organization of the Cerebral Hemispheres." *Dialogues in Clinical Neuroscience* 12, no. 4 (2010): 503–515. https://doi.org/10.31887/DCNS.2010.12.4/imcgilchrist

254. Mandala, M., S. Krishnan, N. Weathington, Michael Breus, and David Rabin. "Association Between Duration of Transcutaneous Vibratory Stimulation Delivered by the Apollo Neuro Device and Extension of Total Sleep Time." *JMIR mHealth and uHealth* (forthcoming, 2026). https://doi.org/10.2196/79588

Glossary

Amphetamines
Stimulant medications often prescribed for attention disorders such as ADHD. They increase activity in certain brain chemicals, including dopamine and norepinephrine that promote sustained attention.

Amygdala
The brain's fear and contrast-detection center that responds to signs of threat in the environment, such as uncertainty.

Anterior Cingulate Cortex (ACC)
A region of the brain involved in emotional regulation, decision-making, attention, and resolving internal conflict.

Artificial Intelligence (AI)
Computer systems designed to perform tasks that typically require human intelligence, such as learning, reasoning, pattern recognition, and language processing.

Augmentation
The enhancement of human abilities through tools or technology.

Augmented Intelligence (Ai)
Leveraging artificial intelligence as a co-pilot or teammate that

intentionally amplifies human wisdom and capability rather than replacing human intelligence.

Autonomic Nervous System
Made up of the parasympathetic (rest-and-digest) and sympathetic (fight-or-fight) nervous systems that automatically control bodily functions such as heart rate, breathing, inflammation, digestion, immunity, reproduction, metabolism, sleep, and recovery.

Ayahuasca
A traditional Amazonian plant medicine brew, typically made from *Banisteriopsis caapi* and *Psychotria viridis*, used for millennia in ceremonial healing and spiritual practice. Ayahuasca is understood as a powerful psychedelic experience that can reveal deep emotional patterns, enhance self-awareness, and facilitate psychological and physiological healing of trauma. Its effects arise from the interaction of DMT and MAO inhibitors, producing altered states of perception, introspection, and meaning-making. Within a supportive context, ayahuasca is approached as a tool for insight, integration, and reconnection with self and nature.

Being Mode
A mental state characterized by presence, openness, and awareness rather than productivity or task completion.

Biofeedback
A technique developed in the 1960s that uses real-time physiological data (such as heart rate and breath rate) to help individuals learn to regulate bodily processes by breathing at 5-7 breaths per minute.

Chemical Comforts
The use of substances or behaviors to numb or distract from emotional discomfort rather than engaging directly with difficult feelings.

Circadian Rhythms
Natural, roughly 24-hour cycles in physiology and behavior that regulate sleep, hormone release, metabolism, and energy levels. Governed by internal biological clocks and influenced by light exposure, circadian rhythms help align the body with day-night cycles, supporting optimal functioning, recovery, and overall health.

Compassionate Inquiry
A therapeutic approach developed by Dr. Gabor Maté, MD that explores the root causes of emotional suffering through gentle, nonjudgmental questioning that focuses on patient safety.

Consensus Reality
The version of reality that most human beings in a given society or community generally agree upon.

Constitution
An individual's unique, dynamic baseline of biological, psychological, and environmental traits that shape how they experience and respond to the world. It includes factors such as genetics, nervous system sensitivity, learned patterns, developmental history, lifestyle, and current state of health.

Default Mode Network (DMN)
A network of brain regions representing the ego and active at rest. These parts of the brain talk to each other to keep us in the realm of what we know and functional day-to-day in society.

Diagnostic and Statistical Manual of Mental Disorders (DSM-5)
The primary manual used by clinicians to diagnose mental health conditions.

Discernment
The ability to judge carefully and distinguish what is true, accurate, or appropriate.

Distress
Stress that overwhelms coping capacity and disrupts health and/or performance.

Distributed Cognition
The idea that thinking is not confined to the brain alone but is shared across the body, environment, tools, and relationships. In this book, it reflects how intelligence emerges through interaction, not isolation.

Doing Mode
A goal-oriented mental state focused on productivity, achievement, and task completion.

Dopamine
A neurotransmitter involved in motivation, anticipation, reward, learning, and pleasure.

The Dopamine Economy
A cultural system built around exploiting the brain's reward circuitry to drive constant pursuit, validation-seeking, and consumption.

DMT (Dimethyltryptamine)
A naturally occurring psychedelic compound found in many plants and animals that produces intense, short-lived non-ordinary states of consciousness. DMT is produced in the human brain, specifically in the pineal gland along with melatonin, the hormone that regulates our circadian rhythms (sleep-wake cycles).

Ego
Our sense of personal identity that is responsible for keeping us alive and functional in consensus reality.

Emotional Intelligence (EQ)
The ability to recognize, understand, regulate, and effectively respond to one's own emotions and the emotions of others. It underlies empathy, social connection, resilience, and adaptive decision-making. In this framework, EQ reflects how skillfully we navigate internal states and relationships, especially under stress, shaping how we interpret experience and connect with others.

Empathy
The ability to understand and share another living thing's experience of the world, from their perspective.

Empathogen
A class of compounds, such as MDMA, that enhance feelings of emotional openness, empathy, and connection with others by increasing activity in social and affiliative neural circuits.

Empirical
Based on observation, measurement, or experimentation rather than theory alone.

Enthalpy
A measure of total energy within a system, often described as internal energy plus the energy required to maintain structure. In human terms, it can be thought of as the "cost" of maintaining our current state of being.

Entropy
A measure of disorder or randomness in a system. In the context of human life, entropy reflects the natural tendency toward chaos when energy, attention, and intention are not actively directed.

Equanimity
A state of mental and emotional stability in which one remains balanced and steady regardless of external circumstances. It is not the absence of feeling, but the ability to experience without being overwhelmed.

Escape Velocity
The minimum energy required to break free from a gravitational pull. Psychologically, it represents the threshold of effort needed to break out of habitual patterns, limiting beliefs, or dysfunctional states.

Epigenetics
The study of changes in gene expression that occur without altering the underlying DNA sequence, often influenced by environment and experience.

Eustress
Positive, adaptive stress that enhances performance and growth.

False Negative
A test result that incorrectly indicates a condition is absent when it is actually present.

False Positive
A test result that incorrectly indicates a condition is present when it is actually absent.

Growth Mindset
The belief that abilities, intelligence, and traits can be developed through effort, learning, and persistence. This mindset supports resilience, adaptability, and long-term transformation.

Harmony
A state of balance or coherent alignment between elements, whether in music, relationships, physiology, or society.

Healing

The process of restoring balance, function, and wholeness. The reestablishment of safety, connection, and adaptive flexibility within the nervous system. Results from one or more intense, meaningful, and challenging experiences over time where safety is established. Results in increased vagal tone and a more positive reference toward self and the world.

Heart Rate Variability (HRV)

The variation in time between heartbeats; a biomarker of autonomic nervous system flexibility, resilience, and vagus nerve activity.

Hippocampus

A seahorse-shaped structure in the brain's medial temporal lobe essential for forming, organizing, and retrieving memories. It also helps map spatial environments and contextualize experiences. The hippocampus plays a key role in learning, especially short-term memory.

Hormesis

A biological principle in which small, manageable doses of stress stimulate growth, adaptation, and resilience, while excessive stress becomes harmful.

Ibogaine

A naturally occurring psychoactive compound derived from the root bark of the African shrub *Tabernanthe iboga*, traditionally used as medicine and for coming-of-age ceremonies by the Bwiti people of Gabon. Ibogaine produces intense, long-lasting altered states of consciousness often described as introspective or dreamlike. Studies have shown to interrupt opioid addiction by reducing withdrawal symptoms and cravings, through effects on multiple neurotransmitter systems. Due to medical risks, including cardiac complications, ibogaine use requires careful screening and supervision.

The Immortality Hustle
The cultural pursuit of extreme longevity, driven primarily by fear of death rather than love of life.

Impulsivity
The tendency to act quickly without adequate reflection or forethought.

Inertia
The tendency of a system to resist change and remain in its current state. In human behavior, inertia explains why patterns persist even when they are no longer beneficial.

Insula
A region of the brain involved in emotion, empathy, introspection, and interoception.

Intelligence Quotient (IQ)
A measure of cognitive abilities such as reasoning, memory, problem-solving, and analytical thinking. It reflects how efficiently one can process information and learn new concepts. IQ represents cognitive capacity, providing the tools for understanding, while its real-world impact depends on how effectively it is guided and applied through emotional intelligence.

Interoception
The ability to sense internal body signals such as heartbeat, hunger, and muscle tension.

Introspection
The process of examining one's own thoughts, emotions, and internal experiences.

LSD (Lysergic Acid Diethylamide)
A semi-synthetic psychedelic compound derived from Ergot that alters perception, mood, and cognition. Effects generally last 10–12 hours.

MDMA (3,4-Methylenedioxymethamphetamine)
A psychoactive compound with empathogenic and psychedelic properties that enhances feelings of connection, safety, acceptance, and emotional openness. Effects generally last 4-6 hours.

Mescaline
A naturally occurring psychedelic compound found in certain cacti, including peyote and San Pedro. Effects generally last 14–18 hours.

Momentum
The force generated by movement over time. In behavioral terms, small consistent actions build momentum, making continued change easier and more self-sustaining.

Münchausen's Spectrum Disorder (MSD)
A proposed diagnosis for the next DSM update based on a reframing of factitious disorders as existing along a behavioral spectrum characterized by attention-seeking through accidentally automated subconscious illness narratives.

Neural Circuits
Networks of interconnected brain cells that work together to produce thoughts, emotions, and behaviors.

Neurobiology
The study of how the nervous system functions and influences behavior.

Neurocatalytic
A behavior or substance that increases neuroplasticity, expands awareness, or enhances perspective.

Neuroception

The nervous system's unconscious process of detecting safety or threat in the environment, shaping emotional and physiological responses without conscious awareness.

Neuroplasticity

The brain's ability to learn, reorganize, adapt, and form new neural connections from experience. Neuroplasticity also includes the birth of new neurons (neurogenesis) and the repair of damaged neurons (neuroregeneration).

Neurorigidity

A pattern of inflexible neural processing induced by neurostifling behaviors or substances that limits adaptability in thought and behavior. Continuing to engage in thoughts and behaviors that reinforce chronic stress and depressed or anxious thinking reflects a pattern of neurorigidity. Using neurostifling substances such as alcohol, benzodiazepines, and opioids also induce a state of neurorigidity.

Neurostifling

A property of an action or a substance that suppresses or represses curiosity, creativity, cognitive flexibility, awareness, perspective, or neuroplasticity. Sedatives and hypnotics including alcohol, benzodiazepines, and opioids are all neurostifling agents.

Non-Dual Consciousness

A state of awareness in which the perceived separation between self and other dissolves, leading to a direct experience of unity and/or interconnectedness.

Observer Mind

The capacity to witness thoughts, emotions, and sensations without becoming identified with them. It is the internal perspective that allows awareness without reactivity.

Original Trauma (OT)
A metaphor for humanity's first internal fracture of self-trust, symbolizing the shift from faith to self-conscious separation.

Pineal Gland
A small, pea-sized gland located deep in the center of the brain that helps regulate sleep and wake cycles by secreting the hormone melatonin. It also synthesizes DMT. The pineal gland responds to light and darkness, increasing melatonin production at night to promote sleep. In this framework, it acts as a biological timekeeper, synchronizing internal rhythms with the external environment.

Post-Traumatic Stress Disorder (PTSD)
A mental health condition that can develop after experiencing or witnessing one or more challenging events where safety is in question. Symptoms include hypervigilance, flashbacks, nightmares, negative changes to mood/cognition, and emotional numbness that last 6 months or more.

Psychedelic
A term meaning "mind-revealing," used to describe neurocatalytic substances, states, or experiences that expand awareness to that which was previously beneath our awareness. Psychedelic states enhance learning, perception, emotion, and sense of self. These experiences create opportunities to reduce rigid patterns of thinking and enhance neuroplasticity, allowing new perspectives to emerge. To access psychedelic states, no drugs are required.

Resonance
A deep emotional, physiological, and/or rhythmic alignment between beings, organ systems, or objects.

Sacred Biology
The idea that states like play, awe, and connection are both biologically and spiritually grounded processes.

Schadenfreude
Pleasure derived from another person's misfortune.

Secondary Gain
The indirect benefits a person may receive from a problem or illness, such as attention, avoidance of responsibility, or emotional validation, which can unconsciously reinforce the condition.

Serotonin
A neurotransmitter involved in meaning making, mood regulation, sleep, digestion, and emotional stability.

Social Media Addiction Disorder (SMAD)
A proposed behavioral addiction diagnosis for the next DSM update characterized by compulsive social media use, craving, withdrawal, and impaired self-control.

The Scientific Method
A systematic process of patient observation, hypothesis testing, experimentation, and revision used to understand reality.

Translational Neuroscience
The specialty of neuroscience that bridges the gap between research and the real world, accelerating the development of new treatments and preventative strategies for diseases.

Transcendence
A state of going beyond ordinary limits, often referring to elevated spiritual or psychological experience.

Trauma

Trauma is not the event itself, but the unresolved impact on the body. The response of the body to one or more intense, meaningful, and challenging experiences over time where safety is in question. Results in a decreased vagal tone, and a more negative reference toward self and the world, and a shift in perspective to one in which the individual sees themselves as the victim of circumstance (see victim mindset).

Vagal Tone

Vagal tone reflects the strength and responsiveness of the vagus nerve, which regulates rest, recovery, and resilience. Higher vagal tone supports better stress adaptability, emotional regulation, resilience, and heart rate variability (HRV), while low tone is linked to chronic stress and disease risk. It is trainable through practices that signal safety to the body, such as slow breathing, social connection, and meditation.

Vagus Nerve

Cranial Nerve X (ten) that innervates the entire body. The primary nerve of the parasympathetic nervous system governing rest, recovery, digestion, immunity, metabolism, heart rate, and empathy, to name a few.

Victim Mindset

A pattern of thinking in which one perceives themselves as powerless, attributing outcomes primarily to external forces, limiting growth and agency.

List of Figures

Register your book purchase to unlock the Simple Guide Vibe, the playlist, and lots more!
www.asimpleguidetobeingalive.com

Free Apollo Sessions iPhone App
www.TheHugVibe.com

My website
www.drdave.io

Follow me on Instagram
@drdavidrabin

Apollo Neuroscience
www.ApolloNeuro.com

The Board of Medicine
www.TheBoardofMedicine.org

The Psychedelic Report with Dr. Dave
www.thepsychedelicreport.com

Your Brain Explained with Dr. Dave
www.yourbrainexplained.co

www.ingramcontent.com/pod-product-compliance
Lightning Source LLC
LaVergne TN
LVHW102011210926
848483LV00015B/455/J
9781964421230